D1116272

A BIBLIOGRAPHY OF THE WRITINGS OF WYNDHAM LEWIS

BRADFORD MORROW
&
BERNARD LAFOURCADE

With
An Introduction
By
HUGH KENNER

BLACK SPARROW PRESS
SANTA BARBARA • 1978

A BIBLIOGRAPHY OF THE WRITINGS OF WYNDHAM LEWIS.

LIBRARY OF CONGRESS CATALOGING IN PUBLICATION DATA

Morrow, Bradford, 1951-
A bibliography of the writings of Wyndham Lewis.

Bibliography: p.
Includes index.
1. Lewis, Wyndham, 1882-1957—Bibliography.
I. Lafourcade, Bernard, joint author. II. Title.
Z8504.39.M67 [PR6023.E97] 016.828'9'1209
ISBN 0-87685-419-6 78-12757
ISBN 0-87685-420-X deluxe

CONTENTS

INTRODUCTION

by Hugh Kenner

Wyndham Lewis (1882–1957) had by the 1930's become—his own metaphor—a speaking skeleton in the closet of the British avant-garde. Things, said the skeleton, were not as they were normally represented. It was not true that contemporary painting was what Roger Fry said it was, nor that it had all been invented in Paris. It was not true—no—that Mrs. Woolf and Mr. Eliot commanded between them the impulse toward the literary modern. Up-to-date taste was far from up-to-date; it acclaimed little amusing mutations of the safe, reduced to nervous giggles by the thought of its own boldness. James Joyce, even, was insufficiently radical: was a charming word-musician whose panoplied devices hid a parlor tenor who sang again and again the simple-hearted substance of the thirteen poems in his *Pomes Penyeach.* History, Lewis perceived, is constantly being written, and not generally by historians: by journalists for instance, out of rumors going back perhaps five years. And the intent of a constant preoccupation with History is to enclose the present moment in its stream: to make whatever seems to be going on now (whatever someone wants to promote) seems the wholly reasonable outcome of an intelligible recent past, as much so as a puddle is the outcome of some mindless stream's pursuit of declivities. And it was out of a puddle, he thought, that loud-voiced frogs were proclaiming their conquest of the imagination's shining sea.

A stream, a descending stream, whether the "stream of consciousness," the Bergsonian flux or all-subsuming ever-rolling Time, was everybody's preferred metaphor. Conversely, *Time and Western Man* was the title (1927) of one of Lewis's most ambitious books: an assault from many directions on his contemporaries' delight in the thought that they and their doings were manifestations of onrolling inevitability. In Lewis's own version of history there had been a failure of nerve just when History had cracked open (1914–1918) and offered opportunities for a new civilization. To make History the dominant intellectual mode, the conferrer of authenticity and the gliding mirror in which today might see itself, had been a Victorian strategy. So if latterly "Victorian" had become a term of derogation for everything from which 20th century men yearned to be delivered, it made no sense to expect the Victorian demiurge, History, to deliver them.

Deliverance from the prison of the modish is performed by seemingly arbitrary mutations. El Greco, Cézanne, Leonardo, these were not men whose creating hands moved at the promptings of a Zeitgeist, and their hands all did what no hands had done before. The creative faculty, Lewis once memorably wrote, is "older than the fish": is primitive but never crude (crudity being pseudo-creation): is identical with the force that guided "the evolution of wings on the sides of a fish, the feathering of its fins; or the invention of a weapon within the body of a hymenopter to enable it to meet the terrible needs of its life." So is the rare intelligence that can grasp the import of such actions: that can instantly acclaim a mutation when it arrives: a Wyndham Lewis painting, for instance, a "Timon," a "Red Duet." That responding intelligence is not a genteel "taste" trained by mentors in "appreciation."

But—we come now to the principle of Lewis's more bewildering activities—the painter must live. He must be fed, normally by the sale of paintings, and paintings are bought by members of a social class among whom the incidence of critical intelligence is no more frequent than it is among Sunday painters. What a purchaser buys would normally leave him cold but for what he is told about it by dealers and critics, and what they tell him is that the picture he is considering is authenticated by art-history, which is what confers value. Art-history is guided by its custodians, and if you are a painter whom they elect for some reason to switch out of it, you starve. Thus Pre-Raphaelite paintings commanded enormous prices in the 1870's when art-history passed through them; were worthless in the 1930's when art-history was passing them by; are now enormously valuable again, the stream of art-history having once more been redirected.

So Wyndham Lewis, a painter first of all, was early persuaded that survival depended on playing the historians' game his own way. It was clear to him that however excellent his pictures all he could expect to sell was their place in some version of art-history. (Whistler had arrived at a similar perception, and set about "Making Enemies," which he called a Gentle Art.) Hence the energy Lewis devoted to devising revisionist versions of avant-garde history.

Inventing pasts for himself was an aspect of this, and biographical facts are consequently hard to be sure of. Most books of reference, and thousands of library cards, give his birth-date as 1884, a date he placed in circulation to substantiate rumors of precocity. (He was born in 1882, the same year as Joyce.) Where was he born? He would have preferred to have arrived from Mars, but gave out that the event had occurred, amid thunder and lightning, on a ship in Canadian waters, the father American, the mother English. (This is partly true; it may all be.) When he first put in an appearance in London, circa 1909, he affected a sombrero, a cape and long black hair, and was just back from Brittany, where they speak a language that might as well have been Martian. He let it be surmised that he had been sojourning there among fellow-extraplanetarians. Diligence might have tracked down a less glamorous past which included school days at Rugby, but Lewis had studiously eradicated every trace of his Rugby accent. Decades later he wrote a novel—*The Vulgar Streak*—about a man who has propelled himself into fashionable success after disciplining out of existence a working-class accent. The key to his success, it turns out, is passing counterfeit money, i.e. real pieces of paper equipped with a false history. (It took more skill to make them, probably, than to make the "real thing.")

And it is impossible to disentangle Lewis's first wholly idiosyncratic pictures, in the "Timon of Athens" portfolio of 1913, from the international avant-garde of those years, the cubism, the futurism. His works are by no means derivative: they crackle with a diagonal energy in notable contrast with cubism's horizontals, and could adumbrate human figures in spiky confrontation when Braque and Picasso were content to make stylish variations on the still-life (table-top, carafe, newspaper, guitar). Still, one would like to know what hints he may have derived from Munich and Paris, and his obfuscations of chronology and itinerary keeps us unsure.

His literary career is equally difficult to trace. There is no 20th century writer to the understanding of whom a detailed bibliography is more pertinent; nor is any fact registered by the bibliographers more Lewisian than the presence of his first novel as the last entry in the "A" section. It would not have done for readers of *Tarr* to suppose that that thunderclap from a clear sky had been preceded by prentice-work. Nor has it been clear until now that there are five versions of *Tarr,* not the two (1918, 1928) that Lewis was willing to acknowledge; in particular, that London and New York editions of the first version differ considerably (at variance with each other and with the serialized Egoist version which preceded them), and the 1952 reprint of the acknowledged revision of 1928 is itself further slightly revised. Time and again we find Lewis rescuing early work from oblivion for the sake of infusing it with his current complexities, then blandly claiming to be sponsoring merely a reissue. The systematic destruction of his own past may be described as an art-form Wyndham Lewis practised, of a piece with his habit of opening books with a fanfare behind which antecedents (of plot, in the novels; of precursors, in the polemics) are not easily ascertained.

His career, as he meant us to understand it, went something like this: before the 1914 war he had been at the center of Vorticism, a genuine avant-garde, the trumpet-blast of the new. History, in the shape of World War, had obliterated that. Still, *Tarr,* toward the end of the war, was a new kind of novel. After *Tarr,* though, having made his fictional point, he returned to painting, aware that the war had created the opportunites for a new civilization which no one but himself seemed to be noticing. The London milieu, in fact, wanted watching; he watched it, growled at it, whooped at it, in one-man periodicals (*The Tyro, The Enemy*), and toward the end of the 1920's commenced to anatomize it on a gargantuan scale, in polemic books (*The Art of Being Ruled, Time and Western Man, Paleface,* others) and in satiric fiction (*The Wild Body, The Apes of God, The Childermass*). In the 1930's fiction, painting and polemic went forward simultaneously. "I will go over my credentials," he wrote in 1937. "I am an artist—if that is a credential. I am a novelist, painter, sculptor, philosopher, draughtsman, critic, politician, journalist, essayist, pamphleteer, all rolled into one like one of those portmanteau-men of the Italian Renaissance." (Zest ran away with that sentence; there seems to be no evidence that he was ever a sculptor: that his Manichaean fingers ever touched clay or stone.) He was painting the best pictures of his life—the great portraits of 1938—when History once more cleared its throat with a rumble of cannon. After war years spent in North American exile he returned to England, went blind, and unable to paint turned to writing full-time. Two major works of imagination at least, *Self-Condemned* and *The Human Age,* preceded his death in 1957. His last words, addressed in hospital to an enquirer after the state of his bowels, are said to have been "Mind your own business."

Though this is as accurate a sketch as we carry in mind of the careers of most creative men, still it is simplified and mythologized by his life-long restless manipulations. The pre-war Vortex was considerably more a gathering of group energies than he liked to let on. The 1920's were a period of confusion, and the numerous books he published in the decade's last years seem mostly to have been fragments broken from a huge artifact called *The Man of the World* which he could neither shape nor stop adding to. There were to have been further parts to the 1928 *Childermass,* but it is difficult to believe that the sections he added in the 1950's—*Malign Fiesta, Monstre Gai*—bear much resemblance to what he envisaged then.

With a detailed account of his publications in their sequence now at last available, we may hope to start setting in order some understanding of what Wyndham Lewis did and portended. This will be no light task. The fact that his writings are listed makes them no easier to obtain, nor does having our attention drawn to variant texts absolve us from pondering what Lewis changed, and why—just at a certain time—he changed it. ("Can't you read?" was the only help he ever gave a typist who wanted to know why what had seemed a finished chapter of ms. had been wholly redrafted.) And the astonishingly long list of secondary sources cannot but bear, in a writer as alert to trends and self-images as Lewis, upon his sense of what people thought he was doing, and what he accordingly did next. He tended to attack whatever ideas might have been thought to most resemble his own, and a chess-match between Lewis and his critics—he making always the move that would prove them wrong—seems a conceivable model for the intricate ins and outs of his long polemic career.

Efforts to ignore him are to no avail. That energy, that order of combative intelligence, that unique slapshotting style will not go away; nor will the pictures. Like it or not, something that was not supposed to be happening was happening in England for some four decades: a one-man alternative avant-garde, by his own account the *real* one; certainly a tireless interactor with the avant-garde we think we know, our awareness of whom transforms what had looked like a seamless forward current into the staccato leaps of a chess-board's red-and-black duet. "Blocked. Renewal of contest," wrote Pound in a poem on the game of chess which he subtitled "Theme for a series of pictures." There is no better thematic statement for the role of his old Vorticist ally.

Baltimore, 1978.

PREFACE

by Bradford Morrow

This book was begun by Professor Lafourcade and myself, working separately, a number of years before it was suggested that we combine our notes in an effort to produce a bibliography of Wyndham Lewis's writings. By coincidence Lafourcade had compiled a list of periodical contributions and secondary sources while I had gathered bibliographic information about Lewis's own books and periodicals. Discovering our work to be effectively complementary, we spent the past two years reorganizing our materials for the present bibliography. All the work has been accomplished long-distance: Lafourcade writing from Carthage, Tunisia while I examined the Lewis archive at Cornell University in Ithaca, New York (a curious juxtaposition of place-names which would have, no doubt, amused our author).

Our indebtedness to checklists of Lewis's writings in John Gawsworth [Terence Ian Fytton Armstrong] *Apes, Japes and Hitlerism* (London: Unicorn Press, 1932) and Geoffrey Wagner *Wyndham Lewis A Portrait of the Artist as the Enemy* (New Haven: Yale University Press, 1957) will be obvious to all students of Lewis's work.

The bibliography is divided into seven sections, whose formal guidelines are briefly described below.

A. Books and Portfolios by Wyndham Lewis.

This section of the bibliography is devoted to English and American first editions of books by Wyndham Lewis, including three separately published portfolios reproducing art works by Lewis. Later editions or impressions published during Lewis's lifetime are described in detail when they include revisions or additions not present in the first edition. Reprints published during Lewis's lifetime are recorded briefly, while posthumous reprints are either wholly ignored or mentioned very briefly for the benefit of students who desire a textually accurate republication. All posthumous anthologies are described at length.

Entries are arranged chronologically, with various subsequent editions or impressions of a work appearing chronologically from the publication date of the first edition. Each entry follows relatively standard bibliographic practice, with most terminology correspondent to that set forth in Fredson Bowers, *Principles of Bibliographic Description* (Princeton: Princeton University Press, 1949). The methods of bibliographic description adopted in this section and in most of the rest of the bibliography owe much, as will be obvious to the reader, to the work of Donald Gallup. Each entry includes title page transcription; measurements of the leaves, collation, pagination and indication of the presence of endsheets; contents; binding and dustjacket information; and notes regarding the publication of the book.

The title page transcriptions are given in quasi-facsimile, with indications of rules, ornamental borders, publisher's devices, reproductions of designs by Lewis or special typographical layout given within brackets. Designs by Lewis which are reproduced in books, pamphlets and portfolios are designated throughout this bibliography by catalogue numbers assigned to Lewis's art works in Walter Michel, *Wyndham Lewis. Paintings and Drawings* (London: Thames and Hudson, 1971). Measurements of leaves are given in inches. Collational formulae used in this bibliography are standard, with unsigned gatherings designated by italicized, rather than roman, letters or numbers. While most of Lewis's books published in Great Britain are made up of signed gatherings, many American publications are unsigned. Pagination includes both unpaged and blank leaves, the indication of whether a page is numbered or not being clarified in the description of the book's contents. Endsheets are accounted for, when present.

Brief descriptions of the contents are given following page numbers. Inferred page numbers are enclosed within brackets, while blank pages are omitted altogether from the contents listing. Leaves of advertisements, often bound in at the end of a book, are also accounted for in the contents. In most cases the verso of the title page is described in quasi-facsimile form. Although a number of the books described have running-titles, head- or tail-pieces or press-marks, these have in all cases been ignored.

Bindings on the books are described in some detail, including cloth color and texture. Designation of various binding cloths follows the classification system used in Jacob Blanck, ed. *Bibliography of American Literature* (New Haven: Yale University Press, 1955). Whenever publisher's records or internal contents have established chronological priority among variant bindings, this is indicated in the description. Stamping on the binding is described in quasi-facsimile description, following a colon and terminated with a slash-mark and full stop. Descriptive information is occasionally given within brackets. Dustjackets, often designed and executed by Lewis himself, are described in some detail, indicating colors used in the printing. Most dustjackets issued with books published during Lewis's lifetime are reproduced (see pp. 118-174 and 213-220). An indication has been made whether the paper used in the book is wove or laid, and whenever the paper is watermarked, the watermark is described. In several cases paper bulk varies and this variation is indicated in inches, measurements being made midway along the top edge of the sheets (excluding the binding) after it has been clasped tightly enough to bring the leaves firmly together. Publisher's flyers or catalogues issued with the book (or before publication) are mentioned briefly, although due to the ephemeral nature of these items other examples not located by the compilers undoubtedly exist. Proof copies and trial bindings are also occasionally mentioned.

Publication information includes in most cases date of publication, number of copies printed and publication price of the book. For the most part these notes are derived from information supplied by the publishers, or from documents and letters preserved in the important Lewis archive housed at Cornell University, Ithaca, New York. In several instances the information has proved to be unobtainable because publisher's records have been destroyed, or publishers have preferred not to reveal it. Finally, because no definitive biography of Wyndham Lewis has yet been published, we have, whenever possible, supplied further information concerning the production of the books.

B. Books, Pamphlets and Exhibition Catalogues with Contributions by Wyndham Lewis.

Included in this section are published works with contributions by Lewis, including several books which contain reproductions of art work by Lewis executed either in collaboration with another author or specially for publication with a specific text. Anthologies and text-books which reprint written work previously published in book form are excluded, as are books, pamphlets and exhibition catalogues which contain reproductions of art works by Lewis which were not the result of direct collaboration with him. Bibliographic description of each entry is less exhaustive than in section A, but includes title page transcription, measurements, collation, pagination, binding and publication information. Lewis's contribution is indicated in the notes.

C. Periodicals and a Pamphlet edited by Wyndham Lewis.

This section describes in some detail Lewis's own journals—*Blast, The Tyro* and *The Enemy*—as well as *Satire & Fiction,* "Enemy Pamphlets No. 1." In every case, Lewis was both founder and editor, and in the cases of *The Enemy* and *Satire & Fiction* acted as publisher as well. All contributions, including both writings and art work, have been noted in the contents section of each entry, titles of articles, stories, and poems being listed between quotation marks. When titles for reproductions of art works have been included these are also listed between quotation marks, with an indication that the contribution is a graphic reproduction.

D. Contributions by Wyndham Lewis to Periodicals.

Chronologically arranged, this section attempts to list articles by Wyndham Lewis published in English language periodicals, including his own periodicals described in section C and also including reprint articles—of which there are a very few—published during Lewis's lifetime. Posthumous articles which contain substantial previously unpublished materials by Lewis are also included. We have endeavored to describe briefly the subject of these articles whenever possible, and have, for the benefit of students and scholars, indicated where reprints of the texts may be found.

Other Sections

Section E, "Translations into Foreign Languages of Books and Articles by Wyndham Lewis," briefly describes those publications which we have been able to locate. Incomplete information concerning several translations which we know to exist has prevented inclusion of some entries, while other materials have doubtless escaped cataloguing for a variety of reasons. We solicit any additions or corrections which would improve this (and any other) section of the bibliography.

Section F chronologically lists selected articles, books, pamphlets and contributions to books, containing criticism of Lewis's work, or biographical accounts of his life. The bibliographic format of these entries is necessarily brief. Standard biographical dictionaries, encyclopedias and general reference books have been purposely omitted, as well as numerous publications which print only passing references to Lewis. However, in some cases entries have been included for articles or essays to which Lewis made some direct, published response. As in Section D, we have briefly outlined the subject of the entries; when no description is given, it may be assumed that the material contains a number of general references to Lewis or his work.

Section G describes at some length several "ghost books" announced for publication, but not ultimately published.

Radio broadcasts made by the B. B. C. of *Tarr* and *The Human Age* with the assistance of Geoffrey Bridson in the 1950's, as well as any television appearances, unpublished speeches, tape or phonograph recordings, uncollected or unpublished letters and manuscripts (that is, all unprinted materials) we have excluded as being outside the scope of this bibliography which, as the title suggests, attempts to collect Lewis's published writings. The few exceptions we have allowed ourselves are described above and are included in the hope that they—along with the rest of the bibliography—will be useful to those interested in the work of Wyndham Lewis.

Santa Barbara, 1978

ACKNOWLEDGEMENTS

We are greatly indebted to a number of people who answered our many inquiries, allowed us to examine copies of books, manuscript materials and journals, and saved us from mistakes and omissions.

Mrs. Anne Wyndham Lewis has shown kindness on many occasions, and we are grateful for her permission to reproduce Lewis's artworks which are in her copyright.

We are especially grateful to Professors Edward P. Nolan (University of Colorado, Boulder) and Jean-Jacques Mayoux (Sorbonne, Paris) under whose thoughtful and intelligent guidance we were first introduced to Wyndham Lewis's writings. Dr. Donald D. Eddy, Director of the Department of Rare Books, Cornell University Libraries, not only originally proposed a collaboration between the authors, but has given encouragement and sound advice on many occasions. This bibliography might never have been finished were it not for his firm and generous assistance.

We are extremely grateful, furthermore, for the extensive help we have received from Mr. Edward Chaney (Warburg Institute), who read several sections of the book in manuscript and proof, and checked entries against copies of books and periodicals in the British Museum Library, London and Colindale. Mr. Chaney's diligence in running down information has helped make this a better book than it might otherwise have been: his friendship is highly valued.

Thanks are due also the Mr. C. J. Fox, who for many years gathered critical material and without whose generous help the list of secondary sources would have been sadly incomplete.

Mrs. Joan Winterkorn, assistant librarian in the Department of Rare Books at Cornell University, has given tireless and significant help throughout every stage of this project. Her knowledge of Lewis's books and manuscripts has directly resulted in the improvement of this bibliography.

It has been a privilege to examine copies of many of Lewis's rarest books in the private collections formed by Dr. James O'Roark (Santa Barbara, California) and Mr. Hugh Anson-Cartwright (Toronto, Canada). The hospitality and generosity they have repeatedly shown is truly appreciated.

We wish also to thank the following individuals who have helped in various ways: Jeffrey Bagley, Seamus Cooney, Professor Maria Teresa Delpiano, Donald Gallup, Mrs. Alison Howard, Dr. Tom Kinninmont, Archibald MacLeish, Edward Mendelson, Jeffrey Miller, Arthur Mizener, Alan Munton, Professor Arthur Naftalin, Omar Pound, Dr. Roger Raby and Prof. Dr. Klaus Reichert.

We thank the following booksellers for their generous assistance: Mrs. Louis Henry Cohn (House of Books, Ltd., New York); Peter B. Howard and Tom Goldwasser (Serendipity Books, Inc., Berkeley); James S. Jaffe (George S. MacManus Co., Philadelphia); Robert and Christine Liska (The Colophon Book Shop, LaGrange); William Pieper (Wm. Pieper, Rare Books, Whittier); Robert H. Ross (Robert H. Ross—Rare Books, Hanover); Anthony Rota (Bertram Rota Ltd., London); Richard Schwartz (Stage House II, Books and Prints, Boulder); Ralph Sipper and Larry Moskowitz (Joseph the Provider, Books, Santa Barbara); Eric and Joan Stevens (Eric and Joan Stevens, Books, London); J. Howard Woolmer (J. Howard Woolmer—Rare Books, Andes). The principal compiler especially wishes to thank Mr. Robert J. Barry, Jr. (C. A. Stonehill, Inc., New Haven), an important bookman who has greatly influenced him and has generated a continuing interest in the bibliographic examination of books.

We are very grateful for the assistance given us by the staff of librarians of Olin Library, Department of Rare Books, Cornell University, Ithaca, where the most extensive collection of Lewis books and papers is housed: Mary F. Daniels, John Loetterlee, Dr. James Tyler, Katherine R. Hall, Jane E. Woolston and the late Professor George Healey. Mr. G. Marvin Tatum (Reference Department) and Mr. Paul P. W. Cheng (Wason Collection of Oriental Books) also gave us assistance at Cornell. We wish to thank the following libraries and librarians as well: University of California at Berkeley; Bibliothèque Nationale, Paris (Jean Prinet, Conservateur en Chef); British Museum Libraries, London and Colindale; Lockwood Memorial Library, State University of New York at Buffalo (K. C. Gay, Curator of the Poetry Collection); Centre Nationale de la Recherche Scientifique, Paris; Nolin Library, University of Colorado at Boulder (Ellsworth Mason, Department of Rare Books); Library of Congress, Washington, D. C.; Bibliothèque Universitaire de Grenoble; Le Centre de Documentation et Recherches Bibliographiques de l'Universitè de Grenoble III; Houghton Library, Harvard University; Lilly Library, Indiana University (William R. Cagle, Director); New York Public Library; Bodleian Library, Oxford University; University of California at Santa Barbara; Tate Gallery Library; Humanities Research Center, University of Texas (F. Warren Roberts, Director); Bibliothèque Nationale, Tunis; Bibliothèque Universitaire de Tunis; Beinecke Rare Book and Manuscript Library, Yale University (Louis L. Martz and Donald Gallup).

We thank the following publishers who provided information about Lewis's books: George Allen & Unwin Ltd.; Associated Book Publishers Ltd. (Jan Hopcraft); Barnes & Noble Books (V. Ciringeon); University of California Press (William J. McClung and Barbara Zimmerman); Jonathan Cape Limited (Graham C. Greene); Cassell & Collier MacMillan Publishers Ltd. (Norman Lambert); Chatto and Windus Ltd. (Norah Smallwood); Coach House Press (Paul Collins); Crown Publishers, Inc. (Josephine Fagan); J. M. Dent & Sons Ltd. (John Sundell); Doubleday & Company Inc. (Joan Ward); Faber and Faber Ltd. (Peter du Sautoy); Gateway Editions, Ltd. (Henry Regnery); Gordon Press, Publishers; Robert Hale Limited (John Hale); Desmond Harmsworth Publishers (Desmond Harmsworth); Harper & Row Ltd. (Deborah Morrow); Haskell House Publishers Ltd.; A. M. Heath & Company Ltd. (Mark Hamilton); Hutchinson Publishing Group Limited (Gillian Dixon and L. Coverdale); Kenkyusha Limited Publishers (Yukiko Moriyasu); Alfred A. Knopf Inc. (Ashbel Green); MacDonald and Janes's Publishers Ltd. (Patricia James); McGraw-Hill Ryerson Limited (Marilyn Gray); Methuen & Co. Ltd.; The New American Library, Inc.; New Directions Publishing Corporation (Carla Packer); Russell & Russell Publishers (Mrs. E. Soschin); Thames & Hudson; Vision Press.

We wish also to thank Hugh Kenner who has patiently answered questions, suggested sources of information and who generously agreed to provide an introductory essay to this bibliography, drawing upon his remarkable knowledge of Lewis's work.

We are especially indebted to John Martin of Black Sparrow Press, whose own private collection of Lewis's books has always been available for examination, and whose knowledge of Lewis's books has saved us more than once from mistakes and omissions. He has solved a number of problems involved with the publication of this book with skill and success.

Finally we wish to thank Kathleen Morrow and Pierrette Lafourcade for their encouragement, understanding and help during the writing of this bibliography.

Bradford Morrow
Santa Barbara, 1978

Bernard Lafourcade
Grenoble, 1978

A NOTE ON ABBREVIATIONS

For the sake of clarity, abbreviations of titles of Lewis's books have not been used in this bibliography. However, abbreviations for the Department of Rare Books, Cornell University Library (NIC) and Lockwood Memorial Library, State University of New York at Buffalo (SUNY at Buffalo) have been adopted throughout. Walter Michel's *Wyndham Lewis. Paintings and Drawings* (London: Thames and Hudson, 1971, B33) is refered to as "Michel" along with catalogue numbers assigned by him to Lewis's art works. The reader is invited to refer to Michel's catalogue of paintings and drawings for further information about any given design by Lewis cited.

A NOTE ON THE PHOTOGRAPHS

The authors and publisher wish to extend their thanks to the following institutions and individuals who generously provided photographs of Lewis books in their possession: Hugh Anson-Cartwright (*Fifteen Drawings, Tarr* (Knopf, second American edition), *The Lion and the Fox, The Doom of Youth* (McBride, American edition), *The Apes of God* (McBride, American edition), *Enemy of the Stars, The Revenge for Love, Rude Assignment* and *The Writer and the Absolute*); Beinecke Rare Book and Manuscript Library, Yale University (*The Old Gang and the New Gang*); Donald Gallup (*The Wild Body*); Herbert F. Johnson Museum of Art, Cornell University (*Timon of Athens*); Lockwood Memorial Library, State University of New York at Buffalo (*The Jews Are They Human?* and *The Vulgar Streak*).

We are especially grateful to Ray Hartman, who arranged and photographed the balance of the books, from the collections of Dr. James O'Roark, John K. Martin and Bradford Morrow.

A. Books and Portfolios by Wyndham Lewis

A 1 TIMON OF ATHENS [1913]

First edition:

[*No title page or text, lettered on front cover of portfolio, designed by Lewis, Michel 91*] TIMON [*at angle*] ATHENS | TIMON | SHAKESPEARE | [*upside down*] TIMON | [*at angle*] WYNDHAM LEWIS

Leaves measure 15¼" x 10⅝". Collation: 16 leaves, 1 blank leaf. Loosely contained within portfolio, unpaged. Six color and ten black and white plates of designs by Lewis printed on two kinds of stock: heavy white coated paper and heavy cream wove paper. All versos blank.

Plates. [1] Michel 93, "Act I," coated paper, color; [2] Michel 94, "Act I," wove paper, black and white; [3] Michel 95, "Act III," wove paper, black and white; [4] Michel 96, "Act IV," wove paper, black and white; [5] Michel 97, "Act V," wove paper, black and white; [6] Michel 98, "Alcibiades," coated paper, color; [7] Michel 99, "Composition," coated paper, color (grey); [8] Michel 100, "The Creditors," coated paper, color; [9] Michel 101, "Figure," wove paper, black and white; [10] Michel 102, "Timon," coated paper, color (blue); [11] Michel 103, "Two Soldiers," wove paper, color (flesh and black); [12] Michel 104, "Two Soldiers," wove paper, black and white; [13] Michel 105, "Two Designs," wove paper, black and white; [14] Michel 106, "Two Designs," wove paper, black and white; [15] Michel 107, "Two Designs," wove paper, black and white; [16] Michel 108, "Two Designs," wove paper, black and white.

Portfolio measures 15½" x 11", heavy white textured card, designs by Lewis printed in black on front cover (Michel 91) and back cover (Michel 92), three folding flaps extending from top, fore and bottom edges of back cover, two dark brown or black (no priority) linen tape ties (10") at fore-edges of covers. Blank leaf of cream wove paper measures 14⅝" x 10¼". Prospectus distributed in November, 1913: . . A . . | [*one line printed in red*] Portfolio of Drawings | BY | WYNDHAM LEWIS. | 10/6 Net. 10/6 Net. | [*rule*] | THIS Series of Drawings, exhibited at the Grafton Galleries, | London, in the Second POST IMPRESSIONIST | Exhibition, were originally intended to accompany a Folio Edition | of Shakespeare's "TIMON OF ATHENS." In response to | a repeated demand, a limited number of Sets of the Drawings | have been put up separately in a portfolio for the benefit of | Collectors, and those who desire the Pictures for framing. The | Drawings have been reproduced with the utmost care and by | the most costly processes. | Price 10/6 Net. | [*rule*] | *Obtainable through all Booksellers or direct from* | [*one line printed in red*] Mr. MAX GOSCHEN, | Cromwell House, Surrey Street, Strand, London, W. C. |. 10½" x 8½". Single sheet (17" x 10½") folded once to make two unpaged leaves, printed in black and red on [1] only. Wove unwatermarked paper.

Notes. Published December 5, 1913 and sold at 10/6d.

Accepted for publication by Marjorie W. Tripp of Evelyn Benmar & Co. Ltd. in August, 1912. According to a letter from Tripp to Lewis dated August 19, 1912 (NIC) her partner, Evelyn Benmar, was initially reluctant to undertake the project ("First a curled lip and pinched nostril and 'My good girl that's mania not art!'"). However, the letter indicates that Benmar was ultimately "carried off his mental feet" by Tripp's insistence and the project was accepted. The publisher's original plans called for the "Timon" drawings to be included with the text of Shakespeare's tragedy in a single folio-sized volume, to be published as early as Autumn, 1912. From another letter, dated December 8, 1912, from Tripp to Lewis, it is apparent that the cost and problems involved with properly reproducing Lewis's designs resulted in the delay of publication. Proofs of the plates were submitted to Lewis in early December, with a request that he arrange the plates in their correct order. Lewis was evidently dissatisfied with the quality of the plates, however, and in response to his complaints Tripp (on behalf of Max Goschen, who had taken over Evelyn Benmar & Co. Ltd. in late Autumn, 1912) wrote Lewis, reminding him that Goschen was under no contractual obligation to publish the portfolio (December 17, 1912, NIC).

As indicated in the pre-publication leaflet distributed in early November, 1913, this series of Vorticist drawings, depicting various scenes from Shakespeare's *Timon of Athens* as well as unrelated abstract designs, was shown at the Second Post-Impressionist Exhibition, Grafton Galleries, October–December, 1912. Acknowledgement is made in the exhibition catalogue to "The Cube Publishing Co." for permission to display six of the Timon drawings. The six drawings exhibited were nos. "194-198" and "201" in the show. However, as they are neither titled nor reproduced in the catalogue it is impossible to determine which of the entire series of 16 drawings these were.

In order to satisfy "repeated demand[s]" a "limited number" were published by the Cube Press in December, 1913 and distributed by Max Goschen "for the benefit of Collectors" without inclusion of the proposed Shakespeare text. No titles for the designs included in the portfolio were printed on the plates: the titles assigned above are derived from Michel (see Michel, 91-108). *Timon of Athens* was the only publication of The Cube Press, which seems to have been a fictitious name chosen by Lewis himself under which the portfolio was published.

A2 THE IDEAL GIANT [1917]

First edition:

The Ideal Giant | The Code of a Herdsman | Cantelman's Spring-Mate | BY | P. WYNDHAM LEWIS | Privately printed for the London Office of | the Little Review, 5, Holland Place | Chambers, W. 8, where copies can be obtained | Printed by Shield and Spring, Lancelot Place, Brompton Road, London, S.W.

8½" x 5½". Collation: single unsigned gathering of 11 sheets folded to make 22 leaves. Pp. 44; wrappers (some copies).

[1] title; [3] THE IDEAL GIANT | [*design by Lewis, Michel 253*] | By WYNDHAM LEWIS; [5]-29 text of "The Ideal Giant"; 31-36 text of "The Code of a Herdsman"; 37-44 text of "Cantelman's Spring-Mate."

Bound in half light-blue V cloth folder with stiff white boards, stamped in light-blue on front cover: THE IDEAL GIANT | [*design by Lewis, Michel 253*] | By WYNDHAM LEWIS |. V cloth along spine unlettered. Single gathering of 22 leaves stapled to make inner printed pamphlet. Inner pamphlet measures 8¼" x 5½"; outer folder measures 9⅝" x 6¼". Inner pamphlet strung into folder by 3 silk threads which are sewn at top and bottom of cloth spine. Threads either two-strand or three-strand, and seen dyed light-green or white (status of these variants undetermined). Pastedowns inside folder are light green. All edges of inner pamphlets trimmed and unstained; wove unwatermarked paper. Lewis's copy, preserved at Cornell, has pink printed wrappers stapled to inner pamphlet, the printing in blue on front cover identical to the stamping on outer folder. It is possible that other copies exist with this printed inner-wrapper. A few copies were sent *gratis* to reviewers, prior to publication, without the outer half-cloth folder, bound instead in heavy yellow paper wrappers. These copies are stapled along spine, with front cover printed in black as on cover of regular issue.

Notes. Published November 8, 1917 in an edition of approximately 200 copies. Apparently distributed without charge.

The Ideal Giant, Lewis's first separately published literary effort, consists of "The Ideal Giant," "The Code of a Herdsman" and "Cantelman's Spring-Mate." "The Ideal Giant," originally titled " 'Miss Godd' and the Ideal Giant" (see Daniels, *Catalogue,* p. 19), was reprinted in *The Little Review* (D82) and *A Soldier of Humor* (A43). "The Code of a Herdsman" appeared earlier, in July 1917, as part of the *Imaginary Letters* series, in *The Little Review* (D71), and was incorporated in the story "The Crowd" in manuscript (NIC) as early as 1916 (see C2). "Cantelman's Spring-Mate" originally appeared in slightly different form in October 1917, in *The Little Review,* with the protagonist's name spelled "Cantleman." "Cantleman's Spring-Mate" was suppressed by United States postal authorities in the earlier periodical appearance (see D76 for details concerning Margaret Anderson's unsuccessful appeal). Revised version of the text, with standardized spelling "Cantleman" adopted, reprinted in *The Little Review Anthology* (B30), *Blasting and Bombardiering* (second edition only, A26), *A Soldier of Humor* (A43) and *Unlucky for Pringle* (A46). Also, French bilingual edition prints textual variants in D76, A2 and A26b.

The Code of a Herdsman later edited by Alan Munton and published separately (see A49).

A3a TARR 1918

First edition:

[*Broad and narrow double rule, closed at ends*] | TARR | Wyndham Lewis | [*narrow and broad double rule, closed at ends*] | [*publisher's device, Borzoi dog facing left, over single rule*] | New York Alfred A. Knopf 1918 | [*narrow and broad double rule, imperfectly closed*]

7½" x 5". Collation: *1-24*^{8}. Pp. 384; endsheets.

[3] half-title; [4] [*single rule frame within double rule frame, enclosing:*] SOME NEW BORZOI BOOKS | [*rule*] | [*list of 8 titles by various authors*]; [5] title; [6] COPYRIGHT, 1918, BY | WYNDHAM LEWIS | *Published June 1918* | PRINTED IN THE UNITED STATES OF AMERICA; [7] table of contents; 9-11 Preface; [13]-379 text.

Two variant bindings, priority as follows:

(1). Bound in cranberry-red V cloth, stamped in gold on front cover: [*broad and narrow double rule, closed at ends*] | TARR | Wyndham Lewis | [*narrow and broad double rule, closed at ends*] | . Stamped in gold on spine: [*broad and narrow double rule, closed at ends*] | TARR | [*narrow and broad double rule, closed at ends*] | *by* | Wyndham | Lewis | [*narrow and broad double rule, closed at ends*] | [*in blind relief, unstained, on rectangular gold blocked field:*] Alfred A Knopf | . Dustjacket (no example located but see John Gawsworth *Apes, Japes and Hitlerism* (London, 1932) p. 85A for note on presence of dustjacket on a copy examined, though no mention is made concerning its physical appearance). Top edge trimmed and stained red; other edges trimmed and unstained. Endsheets white machine-finished paper; wove unwatermarked paper. Boards measure 7⅞".

(2.) Dark blue B patterned boards, printed in orange as (1) except that "Alfred A Knopf" is printed in orange at foot of spine, not in blind relief. Sheets measure 7⅜" x 4⅞" (same sheets as (1), trimmed by binder); boards measure 7$^{9}/_{16}$". All edges untrimmed and unstained. Endsheets as (1).

Notes. Published June 27, 1918 and sold at $1.75.

Contract agreement between Knopf and Lewis for publication of *Tarr* dated September 18, 1917 (DS, Knopf termination of American rights, 1951, NIC). *Tarr,* Lewis's first published novel, was serially printed by Harriet Shaw Weaver in *The Egoist* from April 1916 to November 1917 in nineteen instalments (see D54, D55, D56, D57, D58, D59, D60, D61, D62, D63, D64, D65, D66, D68, D70, D72, D73, D75 and D77). Harriet Weaver, who co-edited *The Egoist* with Dora Marsden, had paid Lewis £50 for serialization rights of the novel, although from a letter to Lewis dated January 11, 1916 it would appear that her agreement to publish *Tarr* was not the result of her uncritical approval of its contents: ". . . I have read Part I of your novel carefully. You are right, I do not like it—but I should like to print it, which, as you say, is what you care about" (NIC).

The text of the Knopf edition differs considerably from the earlier serialized version. The draft used for this edition was apparently completed by November 1915 in London, and revised from time to time until Lewis left it in Ezra Pound's hands before Lewis (by then a subaltern in a Siege Battery) was transferred to France, for active military duty at the front. The text had been considerably abbreviated in many sections by Lewis himself (see Rose, *Letters,* p. 77), and most probably by Pound, who had urged Miss Weaver to publish *Tarr* in the first place, and who was in possession of the manuscript during this period. Fundamental differences between the Knopf and *The Egoist* (serial) editions can be readily seen by refering to the notes provided with each separate "D" entry for *Tarr.*

Pound, acting as Lewis's literary agent, sent the manuscript of *Tarr* to Knopf on August 20, 1917. Pound informed Lewis of this fact in a letter dated August 25, 1917, stating that the text dispatched was "more or less" correct, and indicating that Helen Saunders (a Vorticist artist and friend of Lewis) corrected foreign language spellings (see D.D. Paige, ed., *The Letters of Ezra Pound* (New York,

1950) 172, *passim).* In a letter from Pound to John Quinn, posted several days before (August 21, 1917), Pound mentions that the New York publishers B. W. Huebsch had approached Miss Weaver at *The Egoist* about American publication rights for *Tarr.* Apparently, at Quinn's insistence Knopf was to be given first refusal of the novel.

The final version of the American text contains quite a number of minor errors (prompting Lewis to refer to it as "the bad American *Tarr*" in a letter to Alick Schepeler, undated, but circa November 1918, NIC). A number of these misprints are given below to aid identification of this printing:

[p.] 60, [line] *26*	"mammels" for "mammals"
63, *21*	"Gefuhld" for "Gefuhl"
69, *14*	"ca!" for "ça!"
87, *14*	"fecond" for "fecund"
103, *17*	"crick" for "click"
108, *23*	"isches" for "dishes"
112, *9-10*	"schaufspiel- | erin" for "schauspiel- | erin"
135, *26*	"Wass wunchen sie" for "Was wünschen Sie"
138, 7	"sense'" for "senses'"
157, *13*	"then" for "than"
196, *12*	"negligeable" for "negligible"
308, *2*	"farcial" for "farcical"
317, *36*	"in to" for "into"
329, *19*	"excuperating" for [?]
338, 7	"*me;*" for "*me*";"
359, *31*	"your" for "you"

All of the above are corrected in the first English edition (A3b) with the following exceptions: passages including "mammels," "then" and "excuperating" entirely omitted; "crick" and "*with me*;" uncorrected; "sense' " and "isches" altered for different readings. For further differences see notes for A3b.

Composition dates for *Tarr* are difficult to determine, but certainly the novel was begun as early as 1909, upon Lewis's return from Paris (where he lived mostly from 1902-1909). Evidently Lewis wrote the pot-boiler, *Mrs. Dukes' Million,* generally refered to as his first novel, in order to help support himself while he completed work on *Tarr* (see Rose, *Letters,* no. 42). His efforts to get *Mrs. Dukes' Million* published were, however, unsuccessful (see A51). Most of the writing of *Tarr* was done in 1914-1915, as is evident in his letters to Augustus John, Captain Guy Baker and others during this period. The novel was offered to John Lane, who had published *Blast* (see C1 and C2), but Lane considered the book "too strong." Lewis also approached his friend and important art-patron, Guy Baker, proposing that the novel be brought out by a small publisher, with printing expenses to be paid by

Baker and reimbursed by sales. This suggestion was also abandoned.

Lewis entirely rewrote *Tarr* for the "revised edition" published by Chatto and Windus in 1928 (see A3d).

A3b *First English edition:*

TARR | BY | P. WYNDHAM LEWIS | LONDON | THE EGOIST LTD. | 23 ADELPHI TERRACE HOUSE, W.C. | 1918

7" x 4⅜". Collation: a^4, b^2, A-U^8. Pp. xxi, 320; endsheets.

[i] half-title; [iii] title; [iv] PRINTED AT | THE COMPLETE PRESS | WEST NORWOOD, S.E.; [v] two quotations in French from Montaigne; vii table of contents; ix-xii Prologue [*under text,* p. xii: "P. WYNDHAM LEWIS | 1915"]; 1-318 text; 319-[320] Epilogue [*imprint at foot of* p. [320]: "PRINTED AT THE COMPLETE PRESS, WEST NORWOOD, LONDON"].

Bound in orange-brown B cloth, single rule border blind-stamped around edges of front cover, stamped in gold on spine: TARR | [*short rule*] | P. WYNDHAM | LEWIS | THE EGOIST LTD. |. Issued in white coated paper dustjacket, printed in black. All edges trimmed and unstained. Wove unwatermarked paper. Three flyers issued by The Egoist Ltd. giving extracts from reviews of *Tarr* have been examined (some were laid into copies of *The Caliph's Design,* A4):
(a). [2] pp. on single leaf (8½" x 5½") as follows: [1] EXTRACTS FROM PRESS NOTICES | OF | TARR | By P. WYNDHAM LEWIS | [*rule*] | [*publisher's address*] | Price 6s. net: by post, 6s. 4d. | [*rule*] | [*8 review extracts*]; [2] 15 review extracts.
(b). [4] pp. on single sheet (6⅛" x 4⅛") folded once to make two leaves, as follows: [1] same as (a), but with review extracts only; [2-4] review extracts.
(c). [4] pp. on single sheet (9⅜" x 7⅜") folded once to make two leaves, as follows: [1] advertisement for "The Poets' Translation Series"; [2-3] same as (a), pp. [1]-[2]; [4] order form for "The Poets' Translation Series."
All are printed in black on white wove paper.

Notes. Published July 18, 1918 in an edition of 1000 copies, and sold at 6s.

Tarr had been serialized in *The Egoist* (see D54), and Harriet Shaw Weaver determined to publish a complete version of the text in book form in Winter, 1918. According to publisher's records, 729 copies were sold and 87 were distributed without charge to reviewers and friends of the publisher and author. By March 26, 1924, Miss Weaver reported to Lewis that approximately 200 copies remaining unsold were being kept in storage at her residence. The final number of copies left unsold, which were probably returned to Lewis himself, was about 165. Production costs of £167 against sales profits of £145 left the publishers with a £22 loss on the publication. Interestingly, however, *Tarr* afforded The Egoist Ltd. its largest single *gross* sales, outgrossing Eliot's *Prufrock,* Pound's *Quia Pauper Amavi,* H. D.'s *Hymen* and others, but production costs exceeded this figure.

Textual differences between this and the Knopf edition are numerous, and are for the most part minor. Notable differences include the alteration of the "Preface" in the Knopf edition to make a "Prologue" (ix-xii) and "Epilogue" (319-[320]) in the Egoist edition (the "Prologue" includes four entire paragraphs (pp. x-xii) not present in the Knopf "Preface"; the "Epilogue" is taken from pp. 10-11 of the "Preface" ("The artists of this country . . . | . . . logical and deliberate grimace") of the Knopf edition. Part I, entitled "Overture" in the Knopf edition, has been retitled "Bertha" (1-64). Eccentric punctuation present in the Knopf edition, especially Lewis's use of the double hyphen or dash mark (" =") between sentences, is not present in the Egoist edition. The first half of Part I, Chap. 1 in the Egoist edition is substantially different than the corresponding passage in the Knopf edition. Part II, Chap. 1 in the Egoist edition has a three-page passage (pp. 69-71) which is greatly expanded from the Knopf edition. Part III, Chap. 1 of the Egoist edition wholly omits a seven-page section present in the Knopf edition (pp. 150-157). Although the first half of Part IV, Chap. 7 is identical in both editions, Chap. 8 of the Knopf edition begins with the second half of Chap. 7 of the Egoist edition (from p. 177, paragraph 2 to end of chapter). The subsequent four chapters of Part IV are accordingly renumbered so that Chap. 8 (Egoist) is Chap. 9 (Knopf), Chap. 9 (Egoist) is Chap. 10 (Knopf), Chap. 10 (Egoist) is Chap. 11 (Knopf) and Chap. 11 (Egoist) is Chap. 12 (Knopf). The text of thse renumbered chapters, and the rest of the novel, is essentially the same in both editions, with occasional rewording and reparagraphing. It should also be noted that misprints not present in the American edition are introduced in the Egoist text (for example Kreisler's name is misspelled in line 1, p. 120 of the Egoist edition—an error not present in the Knopf edition).

A3c *Second American edition:*

[*Broad and narrow double rule, closed at ends*] | TARR | Wyndham Lewis | [*narrow and broad double rule, closed at ends*] | [*publisher's device, Borzoi dog facing left within oval frame, which encloses field of parallel horizontal lines*] | New York Alfred A · Knopf 1926 | [*narrow over broad double rule, closed at ends*]

7½" x 5". Collation: *1-22*^{8}. Pp. x, 342; endsheets.

[i] half-title; [ii] *Some* BORZOI *novels* | [*list of 5 titles by various authors*]; [iii] title; [iv] COPYRIGHT, 1918, BY WYNDHAM LEWIS | MANUFACTURED IN THE UNITED STATES OF AMERICA; v-vii Preface; ix table of contents; [1]-341 text; [342] A NOTE ON THE TYPE IN | WHICH THIS BOOK IS SET | [*note on "Old Style No. 1" type*] | [*publisher's device, as on title*] | SET UP, ELECTROTYPED AND PRINTED | BY THE VAIL-BALLOU PRESS, INC., | BINGHAMTON, N. Y. · ESPARTO | PAPER MANUFACTURED IN | SCOTLAND AND FURNISHED | BY W. F. ETHERINGTON & | CO., NEW YORK · BOUND | BY H. WOLFF ESTATE, | NEW YORK.

Bound in bright red V cloth, stamped in gold on front cover: [*broad and narrow double rule, closed at ends*] | TARR | Wyndham Lewis | [*narrow and broad double rule, closed at ends*] |. Stamped in gold on spine: [*broad and narrow double rule, closed at ends*] | TARR | [*narrow and broad double rule, closed at ends*] | *by* | Wyndham | Lewis | [*narrow and broad double rule, closed at ends*] | Alfred A Knopf |. Publisher's device blind-stamped within rectangular compartment, at bottom right of back cover: BORZOI | [*Borzoi dog facing left*] | BOOKS |. Issued in bright orange dustjacket, printed in black. Top edge trimmed and stained green (also yellow); fore-edge partially uncut and unopened; bottom edge rough-trimmed. Decorative endsheets, with publisher's device as on back cover in white against rectangular fields printed alternately in pink and green. Wove unwatermarked paper.

Notes. Published July 12, 1926 and sold at $2.50.

The type was entirely reset for this edition, introducing only modest ornamental typographical changes (such as rules above and below running headlines and ornamental initial letters at chapter openings). Textually this edition closely follows the 1918 Knopf edition, reprinting—anachronistically—the original Preface, as well as the earlier misprints.

A3d *First revised edition:*

TARR | *By* | WYNDHAM LEWIS | [*device of phoenix rising from flames*] | [*rule*] | CHATTO AND WINDUS | LONDON

6¾" x 4⅜". Collation: π^{4}, A-U^{8}, X^{4}. Pp. [viii], 328; endsheets. Some copies have [4] pp. of publisher's advertisements mounted between X^{3}/X^{4}.

[i] half-title; [ii] *THE PHOENIX LIBRARY* | [*list of 28 titles by various authors*] | [*star*] | 97 & 99 St. Martin's Lane | London, W.C.2; [iii] title; [iv] First published 1918 | First issued (revised edition) in the Phoenix Library | 1928 | Printed in

Great Britain : all rights reserved; [v] Preface; [vii] table of contents; [viii] two quotations in French from Montaigne; [1]-326 text; [327] Printed in Great Britain | by T. and A. CONSTABLE LTD. | at the University Press | Edinburgh

Bound in orange smooth V cloth, with double-rule frame blind-stamped around edges of front and back covers, publisher's device of phoenix rising from flames blind-stamped at center on front cover, and stamped in gold on spine: [*ornamental rule of linked diamonds with ring at both ends*] | TARR | [*star*] | WYNDHAM | LEWIS | [*ornamental rule, as above*] | [*flower ornament with two leaves and scroll stem, repeated three times*] | CHATTO | AND | WINDUS | [*decorative rule, as above*] |. Issued in maroon dustjacket, decorated with white leaf and flower ornaments and phoenixes rising from flames, lettering in white and black against white fields. Title list on back and front flaps for "Phoenix Library" series. All edges trimmed and unstained. Wove unwatermarked paper. A small number of copies bound in leather were distributed at slightly higher price.

Notes. Published December 5, 1928 in an edition of 5250 copies, and sold at 3s. 6d.

Contract between Lewis and Chatto to republish a revised, "cheap" edition was signed on May 29, 1928. Lewis proposed that the novel be published in a more expensive "Library" format, to be followed by an inexpensive trade edition. Lewis's editor, Charles Prentice, disagreed however, asserting that the novel had already been published in a "7/6" format (refering to the Egoist Ltd. edition, see A3b). In a letter dated May 5, 1928 Prentice ended this disagreement with a statement that a "Library" edition "would only prevent and delay the book's chances in a cheaper form" (NIC).

This edition prints a totally revised text of the novel, and adds a new preface which Lewis wrote in late October, 1928. Most of Lewis's numerous revisions were made directly in a copy of the 1918 Knopf edition (A3a), which is now preserved in the Lockwood Library (SUNY at Buffalo). A specimen page from this revised copy is reproduced in facsimile in an advertisement for the first revised edition, in *The Enemy, No. 3* (p. *xviii).* The same specimen is also reproduced in *Lewisletter No. 7*, p. 29 (F1916). Lewis delivered the new preface to Prentice in early November, 1928.

Lewis received an advance of £150 for this revised edition, which proved to be Chatto's most commercially successful publication of any work by Lewis. At least 1900 copies sold by May, 1929. Reprinted by Chatto & Windus in 1935 in an edition of 3000 copies, and sold at 3s. 6d. Of this reprint, 1460 copies were rebound with cancel titles and published in the Pelham Library series in July, 1941 (see A3e).

A3e *Pelham Library reissue of first revised edition:*

TARR | *By* | WYNDHAM LEWIS | PELHAM LIBRARY | CHATTO & WINDUS | LONDON: 1941

6⅝" x 4¼". Collation, pagination and contents same as A3d, except titlepage ([iii]-[iv]) is a cancel and [iv] is altered to give corrected series name and date of publication.

Bound in blue V cloth, stamped in white on spine. Issued in white dustjacket printed in blue and black. Top edge trimmed and stained blue; fore- and bottom edges trimmed. Wove unwatermarked paper.

Notes. Published July, 1941 in an edition of 1460 copies, and sold at 4s.

The sheets used for this reissue of *Tarr* are taken from the 3000 sets reprinted by Chatto and Windus in 1935, bound up with a cancel title. Text identical to A3d.

A3f *Second (revised) edition:*

TARR | BY | WYNDHAM | LEWIS | METHUEN : LONDON

7¼" x 4¾". Collation: π^4, $1\text{-}11^{16}$. Pp. viii, 352; endsheets.

[i] half-title; [iii] title; [iv] *Originally published in 1918* | *Second edition, rewritten 1928* | *First published by Methuen & Co., Ltd. 1951* | [*publisher's device*] | [*catalogue registration*] | PRINTED IN GREAT BRITAIN; v table of contents; vii two quotations in French from Montaigne; 1-352 text, imprint at foot of p. 352: *"Printed by Jarrold and Sons Ltd., Norwich"*

Bound in light grey V cloth, two turquoise rectangular fields stamped at head and foot of spine upon which is printed in red: [*at head of spine:*] TARR | BY | WYNDHAM | LEWIS | [*at foot of spine:*] METHUEN |. Issued in light blue dustjacket, with decorative designs on front cover and spine in orange, yellow and blue, and lettering printed in orange (back cover only) and blue. Jacket design by Lewis (Michel 1125A) with Mrs. Lewis's help. White machine-finished endsheets; wove unwatermarked paper. Uniform in size and general appearance with *Rotting Hill* (A36a).

Notes. Published June 7, 1951 in an edition of 3000 copies, and sold at 9s. 6d.

This edition was set up from a corrected copy of the 1928 Phoenix edition of *Tarr* (A3d) now located at NIC, and differs textually from the first revised edition as follows: Phoenix preface (dated November, 1928) is deleted (Lewis intended to rewrite the original preface but never did so; the printer's copy (NIC) bears note in his hand on p. {v}, "To be rewritten"); "advantages.—He" (Phoenix edition, 21) altered to "advantages. He" (Methuen edition, 22); "funeral" (Phoenix edition, 67) altered to "funerary" (Methuen edition, 71). Otherwise the present edition reprints accurately the first revised edition.

Geoffrey Grigson's pamphlet *A Master of Our Time* was published by Methuen simultaneously with *Tarr* in order to promote sales of the novel (see F803).

This was the last edition of *Tarr* published during Lewis's lifetime.

Two English language foreign editions of *Tarr* were published (texts not edited or reviewed by Lewis).

First German English language edition:

Tarr. Leipzig: Bernard Tauchnitz, 1931. Pp. 344. Bound in white paper wrappers, printed in black. Published Autumn, 1931, and sold at 2 DM. Contract signed March, 1931; Lewis received 1000 DM. for publishing rights. Text omits preface, prologue and epilogue, and essentially follows 1928 Phoenix edition (A3d). Volume 4989 in the "Collection of British and American Authors" series.

First Japanese English language edition:

Tarr. Tokyo: Kenkyusha Limited Publishers, 1935. Pp. xxxi, 461. Hardbound. Published November 25, 1935. Text edited by Prof. Rintaro Fukuhara, with notes in Japanese at end of volume.

Penguin edition (not published):

In June 1948 Penguin Books, Ltd. had made with Lewis all arrangements precedent to the actual signing of a contract for paperback publication of *Tarr.* The novel was to be issued in an edition of not fewer than 50,000 copies, to be sold at 2s. Mr. A.S.B. Glover, Penguin's representative who negotiated with Lewis royalty agreements and two clauses in the drafted contract, abruptly terminated proceedings in a letter to Lewis dated July 27, 1948 (NIC), apparently just prior to the conclusion of a formal agreement. The letter from Glover states that a "general conference" among the editorial and sales staff of Penguin Books about future publishing plans resulted in the decision to "hold our hand" with regard to various titles under consideration. Glover proceeds to inform Lewis that *Tarr* unfortunately falls into this category, and asks Lewis if he "will not mind if [Lewis and Penguin Books] let the question of a contract lie fallow" temporarily. The project was eventually abandoned altogether.

B.B.C. broadcast:

Tarr was adapted by Lewis's friend Geoffrey Bridson, with Lewis's assistance, for an abbreviated dramatic radio broadcast, the production of which was aired by the B.B.C. in two 2½ hour segments, on July 18 and 20, 1956. Music for the program was composed by Walter Goehr.

Reprinted by Jupiter Books (London: Calder and Boyars, 1969) at 10/6. The price was later changed to 75p. Also reprinted by Jubilee Books, published September 10, 1970 in an edition of 250 copies, at $4.50 (cloth) and $1.95 (paper).

A4 THE CALIPH'S DESIGN 1919

First edition:

The Caliph's Design | *Architects! Where is your Vortex?* | *BY* | *WYNDHAM LEWIS* | LONDON : THE EGOIST LTD. | 23 Adelphi Terrace House, 2 Robert Street, W.C.2 | 1919

8¼" x 5¼". Collation: A-D^8, E^4. Pp. 72; endsheets.

[1] title; [2] *By the same writer:* | TARR | (The Egoist, Ltd. 6/- net).; [3] table of contents; 5-8 Preface; [9]-[71] text, imprint at bottom of p. [71]: "Printed at the Pelican Press, 2 Carmelite Street, E.C."; [72] publisher's advertisements, within single rule frame.

Bound in mottled blue and white paper boards, white label printed in black on front cover: [*within rectangular single rule frame:*] *THE CALIPH'S DESIGN* | *Architects! Where is your Vortex?* | *BY* | *WYNDHAM LEWIS* | *Price 3/- net* |. All edges trimmed and unstained. Plain spine, issued without wrappers. Wove unwatermarked paper. Publisher's order prospectus, single leaf, pale brown wove paper, printed in black on both sides: [1] THE EGOIST Ltd., | will publish on October 15th, 1919, | "Architects! | Where is your Vortex?" | By WYNDHAM LEWIS. | [*description and price*]; [2] order form. This flyer, issued separately, was distributed without charge several months prior to publication.

Notes. Published October 31, 1919 in an edition of 1000 copies, and sold at 3s.

By March 26, 1924 the publisher, Harriet Shaw Weaver, was able to report to Lewis that of the total edition of 1000 copies, 707 had been sold at the retail price, 84 had been sold at a somewhat reduced cost, 121 had been distributed to reviewers and friends of the author and publisher. The remaining copies were kept in storage at Miss Weaver's London flat. Whether these copies were sold or destroyed is unknown.

Revised version published in *Wyndham Lewis the Artist* (A29), pp. 217-319. This later version reprinted in *Wyndham Lewis on Art* (A45).

A5 FIFTEEN DRAWINGS [1920]

First edition:

WYNDHAM LEWIS | Fifteen Drawings | [design by Lewis, Michel 331, printed on coated paper and mounted] | The Ovid Press

16" x 11". 15 unnumbered, loose mounting-cards upon which are mounted 15 leaves of plates; contained within portfolio (portfolio boards measure 17" x 12"). Mounting-cards are heavy, grey, textured paper printed at bottom beneath plate in black: [*plate title in English over French, see below*] From the WYNDHAM LEWIS [*beneath:*] PORTFOLIO [*device*] THE OVID PRESS |. Plates printed in various colors, as given below, on heavy cream, coated paper. Portfolio folder is white imitation vellum paper over stiff boards, printed in black on front cover (as transcribed above) and printed in black on back around three sides of device designed by Edward Wadsworth, as follows: [*running down left of device:*] 43 BELSIZE-[*running along bottom of device:*]-PARK GARDENS-[*running up right of device:*]-LONDON N.W.3 |. No title page or text. Front cover opens from left to right. Wing flaps at top, fore and bottom edges of front cover. Inside of portfolio lined with white coated paper. Inside front cover bears limitation notice, handwritten in ink by John Rodker: 250 copies | This is No [*number written*] | [*initialled in most copies:*] J. R. |. One copy examined (no. 23) in a private collection, has variant plate mounted on front cover (Michel 339). It is probable that other copies exist which bear different plates on the cover.

[1] Blue Nudes | Nus Bleus |.Michel 120, blue, 7" x 8½"; [2] Group | Groupe |. Michel 331, light blood red, 9⅛" x 12¼"; [3] Post Jazz |. Michel 150, black and grey, 12¼" x 9⅛"; [4] British Museum Reading Room | Salle de lecture |. Michel 209, black, 4⅝" x 9¾"; [5] Timon of Athens I | Drawings for | Dessin Pour |. Michel 359, black, 10½" x 9"; [6] Timon of Athens II | Drawing for | Dessin Pour |. Michel 174, black, 6½" x 4½"; [7] Ezra Pound Esq. |. Michel 345, black, 12¾" x 10¼"; [8] Nude I | Nû I |. Michel 339, green, black and red, 8⅞" x 9½"; [9] Nude II | Nû II |. Michel 340, red, brownish red and black, 7" x 9½"; [10] Nude III | Nû III |. Michel 341, greenish tan and black, 13⅜" x 7½"; [11] Nude IV | Nû IV |. Michel 342, tan and black, 13¼" x 7⅞"; [12] The Pole Jump | Le Saut à la Perche |. Michel 344, black and grey, 9¾" x 13¼"; [13] Head I | Tête I |. Michel 332, black, 11⅜" x 10⅜"; [14] Head II | Tête II |. Michel 333, black, 11⅞" x 11"; [15] Seraglio | Sérail |. Michel 84, yellow, 12¼" x 9".

Notes. Published January, 1920 in an edition of 250 copies, and sold at £2 2s. (later £2 net).

This portfolio is Lewis's second "non-literary" publication, preceded by *Timon of*

Athens (A1). It is unaccompanied by text and reproduces selected drawings by Lewis which are not bound by any obvious thematic unity like the earlier Timon portfolio and *Thirty Personalities and a Self-Portrait* (Lewis's only other portfolio, see A19). Represented are drawings by Lewis executed between 1912 ("Seraglio," Michel 84) and 1919 ("Drawing for Timon of Athens I," Michel 359).

Will Ransom has asserted in *Private Presses and Their Books* (New York: R. R. Bowker Company, 1929), p. 374, that "250 copies were announced, but actually not more than 50 were issued." Although the scarcity of this portfolio would tend to verify this statement, if we may assume that the limitation notices were numbered sequentially—and not randomly—considerably more than 50 copies were published, as a number of copies examined bear high limitation numbers.

A6a THE ART OF BEING RULED 1926

First edition:

THE ART | OF BEING RULED | *BY* | WYNDHAM LEWIS | LONDON | CHATTO AND WINDUS | 1926

8⅝" x 5½". Collation: a^6, A-Z^8, 2A-$2D^8$, $2E^2$ (a^3 is missigned "a2"). Pp. xii, 436; endsheets.

[i] half-title; [ii] and they make | A doctrinal and witty hieroglyphic | Of a blessed kingdom. | *Chapman: from 'Charles Duke of Byron.';* [iii] title; [iv] PRINTED IN GREAT BRITAIN | BY T. AND A. CONSTABLE LTD. | AT THE UNIVERSITY PRESS | EDINBURGH | ALL | RIGHTS RESERVED; [v]-x table of contents; xi-xii Introduction; [1]-434 text; [435] quotation in English from Parmenides ("*Fragment viii. 61.*"); [436] EXTRACTS FROM PRESS NOTICES | OF 'TARR' AND OTHER WORKS BY | WYNDHAM LEWIS | [*single star*] | [*three paragraphs quoting T. S. Eliot from* The Egoist, *Rebecca West from* The Nation, *J. W. N. Sullivan from* The Times].

Two variant bindings, priority as follows:
(1). Bound in bluish-grey V cloth, with single rule border blind-stamped around edges of upper and lower covers, and stamped in gold on spine: [*rule*] | [*double rule*] | THE ART | OF | BEING RULED | [*star*] | WYNDHAM | LEWIS | CHATTO & WINDUS | [*double rule*] | [*rule*] |. Issued in tan dustjacket, rules, star and lettering printed in orange. Top edge trimmed and stained blue; fore-edge trimmed; bottom edge untrimmed. Laid unwatermarked paper.
(2). Intense blue smooth V cloth, omitting blind-stamped single rule borders, otherwise same as (1).

Notes. Published March 11, 1926 in an edition of 1500 copies, and sold at 18s.

This was the first of eight Lewis titles published by Chatto and Windus with the painstaking assistance of Charles Prentice, an editor with Chatto, between the years 1926-1932 (the last was *The Doom of Youth* (A15b), withdrawn shortly after publication under threat of libel suits). Prentice, who directed Chatto's affairs with Lewis, accepted *The Art of Being Ruled* for publication on October 7, 1925. Final typescript was completed and delivered by the end of November 1925, and was yent to the printers in early December. An unidentified "little drawing" of a "figure" which Lewis made on a sheet of the manuscript was to have been redrafted and printed as centerpiece on the title page. Prentice returned the sketch to Lewis on December 9, asking that it be redrawn and "reduced to a height of 2¾" to properly fit the page (TLS, Prentice to Lewis, December 9, 1925, NIC). Receipt of the new draft is acknowledged in a letter to Lewis from Prentice, dated December 23, 1925 (NIC). Apparently, Lewis was asked to make further revisions. The manuscript went to the printers on February 1, 1926, and in a letter of the same date Prentice made final mention of the drawing, lamenting the fact that he had not received the final draft, and that therefore the title page would have to "be bare."

Only 323 copies had been sold by May 23, 1926, according to a letter from Prentice to Lewis (NIC). In another letter to Lewis dated October 8, 1926 (NIC) it is apparent that sales continued to be slow. Prentice blamed poor sales on the Printers' and Binders' Strike "which have depressed the book trade badly."

Part VII, Chap. 7 reprints with revisions Section 3 of an article published earlier in *The Calendar of Modern Letters,* "Science, Puritanism and the Feminine" (see D124). *The Art of Being Ruled* constituted part of Lewis's enormous "The Man of The World" manuscript, written during a period of semi-retirement in 1921-1926.

Reprinted by Haskell House (New York, 1972) in series #80 at $14.95.

A6b *First American edition:*

THE ART | OF BEING RULED | *BY* | WYNDHAM LEWIS | [*publisher's device*] | NEW YORK AND LONDON | HARPER & BROTHERS PUBLISHERS | 1926

8⅛" x 5½". Collation: *1-29*^{8}. Pp. xii, 452; endsheets.

[i] half-title; [ii] and they make | A doctrinal and witty hieroglyphic | Of a blessed kingdom. | *Chapman: from 'Charles Duke of Byron.'*; [iii] title; [iv] THE ART OF BEING RULED | [*fine rule*] | Copyright, 1926, by | WYNDHAM LEWIS | Printed in the U. S. A. | [*fine rule*] | *First Edition* | G-A; v-ix table of contents;

xi-xii Introduction; 1-450 text; [451] *'I wish to communicate this view | of the world to you exactly as it | manifests itself: and so no human | opinion will ever be able to get | the better of you.' | Fragment viii.* 61. | *Parmenides.*

Bound in reddish brown T cloth, stamped in gold on spine: [*fine rule*] | [*fine double-rule*] | THE ART | OF | BEING RULED | [*star*] | WYNDHAM | LEWIS | HARPERS | [*fine double-rule*] | [*fine rule*] |. Issued in red and blue flecked cream dustjacket, ruled and lettered in maroon (file copy with dustjacket in Harper Library, New York). Top and bottom edges trimmed; fore-edge uncut; all edges unstained. Wove unwatermarked paper.

Notes. Published September 3, 1926 in an edition of 1500 copies, and sold at $4.00.

Accepted for publication by Eugene F. Saxton of Harper & Brothers on February 26, 1926. Contract agreement signed on August 20, 1926, the delay occuring because of confusion over Lewis's initial agreement to grant Alfred A. Knopf first option on any books following *Tarr,* an option which had not been extended by Lewis in the case of *The Art of Being Ruled.* It was Lewis's claim that Knopf had failed to exercise the option on *The Caliph's Design,* and had thereby waived further rights to first refusal of any of Lewis's books. By April 15, Saxton was able to report to Harper's London representative that the "Wyndham Lewis affair has been straightened out with Knopf" (TL, Eugene F. Saxton to Cass Canfield, April 15, 1926 (Harper)). Lewis received £50 advance for the book.

On December 22, 1929, 550 sets of unsold sheets were destroyed, and the title was declared out of print.

A7a THE LION AND THE FOX 1927

First edition:

THE | LION AND THE FOX | THE RÔLE OF THE HERO IN | THE PLAYS OF SHAKESPEARE | BY | WYNDHAM LEWIS | [*leaf ornament*] | LONDON | GRANT RICHARDS LTD. | ST MARTIN'S STREET | 1927

8½" x 5½". Collation: A^8, B-U^8, X^4. Pp. 328; endsheets.

[1] half-title; [3] title; [4] Printed in Great Britain | by The Riverside Press Limited | Edinburgh; [5] quotations in Italian, French and English from Machiavelli, Voltaire and Nash, respectively; 7-9 table of contents; 11-24 Introduction; [25]-326 text; [327-328] extracts from press notices of *Tarr* and other works.

Four variants, priority as follows:
(1). Bound in smooth grey-blue V cloth, bevelled boards, stamped in gold on front cover: THE LION AND THE FOX | By | WYNDHAM LEWIS |. Stamped in gold on spine: THE LION | AND | THE FOX | · | WYNDHAM | LEWIS | GRANT | RICHARDS |. Issued in cream laid paper dustjacket, ornamental rules printed in dark blue, lettering printed in dark blue. Top edge trimmed and gilt; fore-edge slightly trimmed; bottom edge mostly untrimmed. Laid unwatermarked paper; wove paper endsheets.
(2). Same as (1), but spine omits the word "GRANT."
(3). Same as (2), but printed on wove unwatermarked paper.
(4). Bound in navy blue rough BD cloth, lettered on spine as (2) but with slightly larger type. Top edge trimmed and stained blue; other edges same as (1). Printed on wove unwatermarked paper from same type as (1) and (2). Issued in dustjacket identical to (1).

Notes. Published in early January, 1927 in an edition of 1076 copies, and sold at 16s.

Richards' copyright on *The Lion and the Fox* is dated May 6, 1925. Publication of *The Lion and the Fox* was to have occurred before Chistmas, 1926 but was delayed at the printers (TLS, Prentice to Lewis, November 26, 1926, NIC).

One copy examined (Agnes Bedford—Anson-Cartwright) contains the following corrections in Lewis's hand:

[p.] 11, [line] *4*	the (for *the)*
48, *21*	Galilei (for Galileo)
52, *2*	Galilei (for Galileo)
59, *4*	*commédia* (for *commedia)*
68, *6*	cleverer, (for cleverer.)
72, *5*	Henry (for Henri)
80, *14*	*lly* (for *le y)*
91, *19*	*citta* (for città)
98, *26*	Brothers Karamazov (for *Brothers Karamazov)*
103, *33*	as man (for as a man)
114, *10*	contemporiares (for contemporaries)
132, *15*	*commédia* (for *commedia)*
132, *34*	Henry (for Henri)
216, *13*	interpretated (for interpreted)
315, *9*	traces (for trace)

When Richards' successors sold the rights for this title to Methuen in June, 1951, 50 unsold copies from the original stock were passed over into Methuen's hands, and sold by them. The entire first printing of *The Lion and the Fox* was not finally sold out until the end of 1954.

Originally a part of Lewis's massive philosophical-sociological-fictive work "The Man of the World," written during his five-year period of concentrated study and writing (1921-1926). Part V, Chap. 4 ("Othello as the Typical Colossus") appeared earlier as Section 6 in Lewis's essay "The Foxes' Case," published October, 1925 in *The Calendar of Modern Letters* (D124). Also included in "The Foxes' Case" (Section 7) is "The Transformed Shaman," reprinted with revisions as Part VI, Chap. 4 ("Falstaff") in *The Lion and the Fox.*

A7b *First American edition:*

THE | LION AND THE FOX | THE RÔLE OF THE HERO IN | THE PLAYS OF SHAKESPEARE | BY | WYNDHAM LEWIS | [*publisher's device*] | HARPER & BROTHERS PUBLISHERS | NEW YORK AND LONDON

8½" x 5½". Collation: A^8, B-U^8, X^4. Pp. 328; endsheets.

[1] half-title; [3] title; [4] Printed in Great Britain | by The Riverside Press Limited | Edinburgh; [5] quotations from Machiavelli, Voltaire and Nash; 7-9 table of contents; 1-24 Introduction; [25]-326 text; [327-328] extracts from press notices.

Bound in three-quarter smooth blue V cloth with decorative pink, yellow, blue and white marbled paper boards, light green label on spine printed in blue: [*triple rule, center rule composed of short vertical hatch-marks*] | THE | LION AND | THE FOX | [*short rule*] | WYNDHAM | LEWIS | [*triple rule, as above*] | [*between small tilted triangles*] HARPERS |. Top edge stained orange; other edges mostly trimmed. Laid unwatermarked paper.

Notes. Published March 18, 1927 in an edition of 1000 copies, and sold at $4.00.

Sheets for American edition imported from England on February 3, 1927 from Richards, and bound up in the United States.

A7c *Second edition:*

THE LION | AND | THE FOX | The rôle of the hero in | the plays of Shakespeare | WYNDHAM LEWIS | METHUEN & CO LTD | 11 New Fetter Lane, London EC4

8¾" x 5¾". Collation: A^8, B-U^8, X^4. Pp. 328; endsheets

[1] half-title; [2] *BY THE SAME AUTHOR* | [*list of six titles*]; [3] title; [4] Originally published by Grant Richards Ltd, 1927 | First published by Methuen & Co. Ltd, 1951 | Printed in Great Britain by John Dickens & Co Ltd, Northampton; [5] quotations in Italian, French and English from Machiavelli, Voltaire and Nash; 7-9 table of contents; 11-24 Introduction; [25]-326 text.

Bound in navy blue smooth V textured boards, lettering stamped in gold on spine on two rectangular fields at top and bottom: [*at head of spine*] THE | LION AND | THE FOX | [*star*] | Wyndham | Lewis | [*at foot of spine*] Methuen |. Issued in white dustjacket, red on spine and front cover, lettering printed in black and white, with design by Lewis in black on front (not in Michel). Later state of the dustjacket omits this design. All edges trimmed and unstained. Wove unwatermarked paper.

Notes. Published June, 1951 and sold at 30s.

Photographic reprint of the first edition (A7a). Rights acquired by Methuen in Spring, 1951. The remaining stock of 50 copies of Grant Richards' first edition was taken over by Methuen in late May, 1951. Reprinted June 9, 1955 and sold at 21s., with imprint on verso of title altered to read: "James Burn & Co. Ltd, London and Esher." Reprinted again in July, 1966 (University Paperback series) and in 1977.

A8a TIME AND WESTERN MAN 1927

First edition:

TIME AND | WESTERN MAN | *BY* | WYNDHAM LEWIS | [*design by Lewis, Michel 640*] | CHATTO AND WINDUS | LONDON | 1927

8¾" x 5½". Collation: π^4, A-Z^8, 2A-$2G^8$, $2H^4$. 1 leaf, pp. vi, 488; endsheets.

[i] half-title; [ii] *By Wyndham Lewis* | THE ART OF BEING RULED | THE LION AND THE FOX | THE WILD BODY; [iii] title; [iv] PRINTED IN GREAT BRITAIN | BY T. AND A. CONSTABLE LTD. | AT THE UNIVERSITY PRESS | EDINBURGH | ALL | RIGHTS RESERVED; v-vi table of contents; [1]-481 text; 482-487 Index; [488] advertisements for three titles by Lewis.

Two variants, priority as follows:

(1). Light red V cloth, printed on heavier paper. Usual paper bulk: 1 7/16".

(2). Smooth darker red V cloth, printed on thinner paper. Usual paper bulk: 1 5/16".

Both variant bindings have double rule border blindstamped around edges of front and back covers, and stamped in gold on spine: [*rule*] | [*double rule*] | TIME AND | WESTERN MAN | [*star*] | WYNDHAM | LEWIS | CHATTO & WINDUS | [*double rule*] | [*rule*] |. Issued in cream dustjacket, lettering printed in black, rules and star in red. Top edge stained red; bottom edge untrimmed. Laid unwatermarked paper. Some copies have tissue leaf mounted between [ii] and [iii] (no priority).

Notes. Published September 29, 1927 in an edition of 2000 copies, and sold at 21s.

Accepted by Charles Prentice of Chatto and Windus on April 26, 1927 for publication. Contract between Lewis and Chatto drawn up in May 1927 and signed on May 21, stipulating that Lewis was to receive an advance of £100. Of the 2000 copies, which were printed by T. and A. Constable in Edinburgh in Summer 1927, 74 copies were distributed without charge to reviewers and as author's complimentary copies. 225 copies were sold by advance order. 401 copies were initially bound (which may constitute the number in binding (1) described above), while 1300 sets of sheets were left in quires. By March, 1933, 1236 copies had been sold.

Time and Western Man, perhaps Lewis's single most important philosophical work, was written during his period of intense study and work, 1921-1926, as part of the manuscript of "The Man of the World." Portions of the book were originally printed in *The Calendar of Modern Letters* ("Creatures of Habit and Creatures of Change," Part II) D128 and in *The Enemy, No. 1* ("The Revolutionary Simpleton," most of Parts I and II) D132. These were revised for the first edition in book form.

Published by The Beacon Press, Boston, in paperback in 1957 and sold at $1.50. Thomas A. Bledsoe, editor at Beacon Press, wrote Lewis on December 31, 1956 inviting him to write a new preface for the book, which Lewis agreed to do in a letter dated January 7, 1957 (NIC). This project was unfortunately left uncompleted at the time of Lewis's death in March, 1957.

A8b *First American edition:*

TIME AND WESTERN MAN | *by* | WYNDHAM LEWIS | [*design by Lewis, Michel 640*] | *New York* | HARCOURT, BRACE AND COMPANY

8⅝" x 5½". Collation: *1-30*^{8}, *31*^{4}. Pp. xvi, 472; endsheets.

[i] half-title; [ii] *By Wyndham Lewis* | [*list of five titles*]; [iii] title; [iv] COPYRIGHT, 1928, BY | HARCOURT, BRACE AND COMPANY, INC. | PRINTED IN THE U.S.A.; v-vi table of contents; vii-xv Preface; [1]-463 text; 464-469 Index; [470-472] advertisements.

Bound in dark blood red T cloth, with double rule frame blind-stamped around edges of front cover and square publisher's device blind-stamped at center of front cover, stamped in gold on spine: TIME AND | WESTERN MAN | [*star*] | WYNDHAM | LEWIS | HARCOURT, BRACE | AND COMPANY |. Issued in cream laid paper dustjacket, watermarked "Rittenhouse Laid," design by Lewis printed in black (Michel 640) on front, lettering printed in red on spine and front cover, and in black on flaps and back cover. Top edge trimmed and unstained; fore-edge uncut; bottom edge partially trimmed. Wove unwatermarked paper.

Notes. Published on January 19, 1928 in an edition of 1500 copies, and sold at $5.00.

This edition adds a new "Preface" (pp. vii-xv) and deletes the "Preface to Book I" in the English edition (pp. 3-18); save for minor alterations and corrections, it closely reprints English edition. Sales were slower than anticipated (864 copies sold by May 2, 1928) and although Montgomery Belgion of Harcourt, Brace had expressed interest in publishing *The Childermass* and *The Apes of God* (which is in fact listed as being "in preparation" on p. [ii] of this edition) *The Wild Body* (A9b) was in fact the only further book by Lewis published by Harcourt, Brace and Company. Yale possesses an advance review copy, which is stamped on front endsheet and filled in with ink stating that date of publication was February 2, 1928 and cost was "probably $5." The publisher's records state date of publication as given above.

A9a THE WILD BODY 1927

Limited, signed edition:

THE | WILD BODY | [*rule*] | A SOLDIER OF HUMOUR | AND OTHER STORIES | [*rule*] | *By* | WYNDHAM LEWIS | [*star*] | LONDON | CHATTO & WINDUS | 1927

7½" x 5". Collation: π^4, A-S^8, T^4. Pp. viii, 296; endsheets.

[i] *Of this Special Edition of* | THE WILD BODY | *seventy-nine copies have been* | *printed. There are also six* | *complimentary copies.* | *This is No.* [*number written in ink*] | [*signature of author in ink*]; [iii] title; [iv] PRINTED IN GREAT BRITAIN | ALL RIGHTS RESERVED; v-vi Foreword, dated "*July* 6, 1927." (p. vi); vii table of contents; [1] list of nine stories; 3-250 text; [251] list of two stories; 253-[295] text; [296] Printed in Great Britain | by T. and A. CONSTABLE LTD. | at the University Press | Edinburgh

Bound in half cranberry smooth V cloth, with red, green and yellow decorative marbled-boards, stamped in gold on spine: THE | WILD BODY | [*star*] | WYNDHAM | LEWIS |. Issued in inner glassine wrapper and outer buff dustjacket, rules printed in red, lettering printed in black. Top edge trimmed and gilt; fore- and bottom edges uncut. Wove paper, watermarked "BASINGWERK PARCHMENT—". Folder of advertisements for "BOOKS BY | WYNDHAM | LEWIS" (6⅜" x 3¾") laid in.

Notes. Published on November 24, 1927 in an edition of 85 copies, and sold at 15s.

Contract for publication of this collection of stories signed on July 7, 1927. Corrected proofs sent off to printers by October 11, 1927. This limited edition, printed on higher quality paper, was printed before the regular edition: "The prelims are pulled as for the Special Edition, which is being done first" (ALS, Prentice to Lewis, October 28, 1927, NIC). The limitation page was signed and numbered on November 4-5, 1927. Prentice was able to report to Lewis on November 28, that the entire edition of 79 copies for sale had been sold out. Lewis received 20% royalty for the book.

Collection of stories including a number of previously published stories which Lewis revised for this edition: "Beau Séjour" originally published May, 1909 in *The English Review* as "The Pole" (D1); "Bestre" originally a part of "Some Innkeepers and Bestre," published June, 1909 in *The English Review* (D2); "The Cornac and his Wife" published in August, 1909 under the title "Les Saltimbanques" in *The English Review* (D3); "Franciscan Adventures" published in September, 1910 in *The Tramp,* under the title "Le Père François (A Full-Length Portrait of a Tramp)" (D7); "Brotcotnaz" published earlier as "Brobdingnag" in *The New Age,* January 5, 1911 (D9); "Inferior Religions" published in *The Little Review,* September, 1917, under the same title (D74); "A Soldier of Humour" published originally in two parts in December, 1917 and January, 1918, *The Little Review* (D78 and D79); "Sigismund" published in Winter, 1920, *Art and Letters* (D94). A second revised version of "Bestre" was also published in *The Tyro, No. 2,* March, 1922 which is textually similar to the final version published in this edition.

A9b *First trade edition:*

THE | WILD BODY | [*rule*] | A SOLDIER OF HUMOUR | AND OTHER STORIES | [*rule*] | *By* | WYNDHAM LEWIS | [*star*] | LONDON | CHATTO & WINDUS | 1927

7½" x 5". Collation: π^4, A-S^8, T^4, U^2 (last two conjugate leaves mounted and unsigned). Pp. viii, 300; endsheets.

[i] half-title; [ii] *By Wyndham Lewis* | [*three titles*]; [iii] title; [iv] PRINTED IN GREAT BRITAIN | ALL RIGHTS RESERVED; v-vi Foreword; vii table of contents; [1] list of nine stories; 3-250 text; [251] list of two stories; 253-[295] text; [296] Printed in Great Britain | by T. and A. CONSTABLE LTD. | at the University Press | Edinburgh; [297-300] publisher's advertisements.

Two variant bindings, priority as follows:
(1). Bound in orange V cloth, double rule border blind-stamped around edges of upper and lower covers, stamped in gold on spine: [*triple wavy rule*] | THE | WILD BODY | [*star*] | WYNDHAM | LEWIS | CHATTO AND | WINDUS | [*triple wavy rule*] |. Issued in heavy paper cream dustjacket with rules, star and frame printed in red, and lettering printed in black. Advertisement on front inner-flap in black: *Mr. Wyndham Lewis's new novel,* | THE APES OF GOD, *will be* | *published early in 1928* |. Top edge trimmed and stained orange; fore-edge trimmed; bottom edge untrimmed. Unwatermarked laid paper.
(2). Red V cloth, stamped in black as (1). Otherwise same as (1).

Notes. Published November 24, 1927, simultaneously with the limited, signed edition, in an edition of 2500 copies, and sold at 7s. 6d.

Sales were initially good and within four days after publication Prentice informed Lewis that 812 copies had already been sold and that it was not too early to begin considering an order for the second impression. However, by May 18, 1928 Prentice reported that only 1100 copies had been sold, leaving £80 of Lewis's £150 advance still unearned (2460 copies had been sold by March 31, 1933).

A second impression of 1150 copies was in fact issued in May, 1932, and sold at 3s. 6d. The text and binding are identical to the first impression, but this later impression was issued in a Centaur Library series dustjacket, designed by Edward Bawden (white dustjacket printed in black with design of centaurs printed in green and yellow).

Reprint published by Haskell House, New York, series #80, 1970, at $14.95.

A9c. *First American edition:*

THE | WILD BODY | [*rule*] | A SOLDIER OF HUMOUR | AND OTHER STORIES | [*rule*] | By | WYNDHAM LEWIS | [*publisher's device*] | New York | HARCOURT, BRACE AND COMPANY

7½" x 5¼". Collation: *1-18*^{8}, *19*^{10}. Pp. viii, 300; endsheets.

[i] half-title; [ii] *By Wyndham Lewis* | [*list of five titles, last title* "(in preparation)"];

[iii] title; [iv] COPYRIGHT, 1928, BY | HARCOURT, BRACE AND COMPANY, INC. | PRINTED IN THE U.S.A. BY | QUINN & BODEN COMPANY, INC. | RAHWAY, N.J.; v-vi Foreword; [vii] table of contents; [1] list of nine stories; 3-251 text; [253] list of two stories; 255-298 text.

Bound in red V cloth, stamped on spine in gold: [*triple wavy rule*] | THE | WILD BODY | [*star*] | WYNDHAM | LEWIS | HARCOURT, BRACE | AND COMPANY | [*triple wavy rule*] |. Issued in buff dustjacket, ruled compartment on front cover and rules at head and foot of spine in dark red, lettering printed in black. Top edge trimmed and unstained; fore-edge uncut; bottom edge slightly trimmed. Laid unwatermarked paper; wove unwatermarked endsheets.

Notes. Published February 9, 1928 in an edition of 1500 copies, and sold at $2.50. Declared out of print in August, 1929.

A10a THE CHILDERMASS. SECTION I. 1928

Limited, signed edition:

THE | CHILDERMASS | BY | WYNDHAM | LEWIS | *SECTION I* | 1928 | [*row of solid triangles*] | CHATTO AND WINDUS | LONDON

8¼" x 5⅜". Collation: π^4, A-U^8, X^2. Pp. [viii], 324; endsheets.

[i] half-title; [iii] limitation page, *Of this Special Edition of* | THE CHILDERMASS: SECTION I | *there have been printed* 225 *copies* | *for sale, and* 6 *for private* | *distribution.* | NO. [*number written in ink*] | [*author's signature in ink*]; [v] title; [vi] PRINTED IN GREAT BRITAIN | BY T. AND A. CONSTABLE LTD. | AT THE UNIVERSITY PRESS | EDINBURGH | ALL | RIGHTS RESERVED; [vii] THE | CHILDERMASS | SCENE: | OUTSIDE HEAVEN | Section 1; [1]-322 text.

Bound in smooth yellow V cloth, stamped in gold on spine: [*thick rule over narrow rule*] | [*row of inverted solid triangles*] | THE | CHILDER | ~MASS | I | WYNDHAM | LEWIS | [*row of solid triangles*] | [*narrow rule over thick rule*] |. Issued in white dustjacket, lettering printed in orange (on front inner flap: NOTE | *The Childermass* will be published in three | Sections. It is hoped that the Second and | Third Sections will be ready in the autumn | of 1928. There are two Editions:—The | Special Edition limited to 225 numbered | sets signed by the Author, each set con- | sisting of the three volumes, price 3 guineas | net per set. The ordinary edition, price | 8s. 6d. per volume.). Top edge trimmed and gilt;

fore-edge uncut; bottom edge untrimmed. Heavy wove paper, watermarked "BASINGWERK PARCHMENT—." Presentation copies numbered "226-231."

Notes. Published on June 21, 1928 in an edition of 231 copies, and sold at £1.

Contract to publish three separate volumes under the general title *The Childermass* was completed on February 3, 1928, Chatto undertaking to publish and Lewis to write a "total Work [of] . . . at least 180,000 words" (TDS, February 3, 1928, NIC). The projected three-volume work was to have been published in its entirety in 1928, the two subsequent sections to have been concurrently published in Autumn. A composite one-volume edition of the whole work was supposed to have been published within two years after the appearance of the third section.

Lewis delivered the typescript to Chatto and Windus on March 4, 1928, and it was sent to the printers on March 5. An advance of £200 was made for *The Childermass. Section I.* Because Lewis failed to produce the second and third sections of the work a breach of contract suit was lodged by Chatto and Windus against Lewis on November 8, 1932 in attempt to recover money advanced against the future delivery of the manuscript. The contract was transfered to Methuen on June 26, 1951 and the complete trilogy was not finally published until November, 1955 when Methuen published *Monstre Gai* and *Malign Fiesta* in a single volume. *The Childermass. Section I.* together with *Monstre Gai* and *Malign Fiesta* constitute collectively Lewis's longest single fictive work and are together titled *The Human Age.* A fourth and final volume, tentatively entitled *The Trial of Man,* was left unwritten at Lewis's death.

D. G. Bridson, a producer at the B.B.C., approached Lewis on April 17, 1951 with the proposal that *The Childermass* be adapted for radio and broadcast by the B.B.C. Bridson, long an admirer of Lewis's work, found Lewis receptive to this idea, and assisted Lewis in the preparation of a dramatic script of the novel. Walter Goehr composed the score for the final production which was broadcast on the Third Programme, June 18, 1951 with the actor Donald Wolfit as the Bailiff. Because the broadcast was received with such approval, the B.B.C. commissioned Lewis to write the as yet unfinished two-volume sequel to *The Childermass,* which had been announced some twenty-three years earlier by Chatto and Windus. The sole condition of their sponsorship was that the second and third volumes of the completed trilogy be similarly adapted for radio production and broadcast before publication of the novels. The entire trilogy was eventually broadcast under Bridson's direction, introduced by T. S. Eliot, on May 24, 26 and 28, 1955. Eliot had read much of *Monstre Gai* and *Malign Fiesta* in manuscript, and had published "A Note on *Monstre Gai*" in *The Hudson Review,* VII, no. 4 (Winter [1954/]1955) [522]-526. See A40.

Passage from *The Childermass* reprinted in *A Chatto & Windus Miscellany* (London: Chatto & Windus, 1928), 44-53, published November 8, 1928 in an edition of 3500 copies, at 2s. 6d. A very poorly edited version of the text was reprinted with *Malign Fiesta* and *Monstre Gai* under general title *The Human Age* (London: Calder and Boyars, 1965-1966), 3 vols., 6/6 per volume (later 65p.). This edition published as a Jupiter paperback has an essay by Hugh Kenner in [III] discussing the projected fourth volume *The Trial of Man,* printing part of Lewis's "rejected synopsis." Also published by Dufour Editions (Chester Springs, Pennsylvania, 1965-1966), 3 vols., paperbacks.

A10b *First trade edition:*

THE | CHILDERMASS | BY | WYNDHAM | LEWIS | *SECTION I* | 1928 | [*row of solid triangles*] | CHATTO AND WINDUS | LONDON

8¼" x 5¼". Collation and pagination same as Special Edition.

[iii] half-title; [iv] NOTE | THE CHILDERMASS will be published | in 3 Sections. Sections II and III will | appear in the autumn of 1928. | Other books by Wyndham Lewis are: | [*list of five titles*] | [*star*]; [v] title; [vi] PRINTED IN GREAT BRITAIN | BY T. AND A. CONSTABLE LTD. | AT THE UNIVERSITY PRESS | EDINBURGH | ALL | RIGHTS RESERVED; [vii] THE | CHILDERMASS | SCENE: | OUTSIDE HEAVEN | Section 1; [1]-322 text.

Bound in bright yellow V cloth, decoratively bordered on upper and lower boards with row of solid triangles within thick rule stamped in red, and stamped in red on spine: [*thick rule over slightly less thick rule*] | [*row of solid, inverted triangles*] | THE | CHILDER | ~MASS | I | WYNDHAM | LEWIS | CHATTO & WINDUS | [*row of solid triangles*] | [*rule over slightly thicker rule*] |. Issued in white dustjacket, ornamented in red with rules and rows of triangles similar to spine decoration, lettering printed in black. Top edge trimmed and stained yellow; fore-edge trimmed; bottom edge partially trimmed. Laid unwatermarked paper. Flat spine.

Notes. Published June 21, 1928, simultaneously with the limited, signed edition, in an edition of 2500 copies, and sold at 8s. 6d.

In 1931 500 sets of sheets were destroyed by the publishers, and 500 further sets were destroyed in 1946, at which time the title was declared out of print.

A10c *First American edition:*

THE | CHILDERMASS | BY | WYNDHAM | LEWIS | PART I | 1928 | *New York* : COVICI-FRIEDE : *Publishers*

9⅜" x 6⅛". Collation: *1-19*^{8}, *20*^{12}. Pp. [vi], 322; endsheets.

[i] half-title; [ii] NOTE | THE CHILDERMASS will be published | in two Parts. Part II will appear | in the Spring of 1929. | Other books by Wyndham Lewis are: | [*five titles listed*]; [iii] title; [iv] COPYRIGHT, 1928, BY COVICI, FRIEDE INC. | PRINTED IN THE UNITED STATES; [v] THE | CHILDERMASS | SCENE: | Part I; [1]-322 text.

Bound in black FL cloth, stamped in red on front cover: THE | CHILDERMASS | [*rule*] | WYNDHAM LEWIS |. Stamped in red on spine: [*double rule*] | THE | CHILDER- | MASS | [*short rule*] | Wyndham | Lewis | [*Y-shaped ornament*] | PART | ONE | [*rule with inverted Y-shaped extension centered above*] | Covici | - | Friede | [*rule with Y-shaped extension below*] |. Issued in light tan dustjacket, with decorative rule in red across top and bottom, and lettering printed in black. Top edge trimmed and stained red; fore-edge partially trimmed; bottom edge mostly trimmed. Wove unwatermarked paper.

Variant binding: Another copy, bound in red CM cloth, stamped in black on front cover and spine as above, issued in the same dustjacket and with edges trimmed and stained as above, has been examined (NIC). This may be a rejected trial binding.

Notes. Published September 3, 1928 and sold at $1.75 (price later raised to $3.00). Probably 1500 copies.

A10d *First illustrated (second English) edition:*

WYNDHAM LEWIS | [*double rule, thin and very fine*] | The Human Age | BOOK ONE | CHILDERMASS | [*short double rule, as above*] | *Illustrations by Michael Ayrton* | [*publisher's device*] | METHUEN & CO. LTD | 36 ESSEX STREET, LONDON W.C.2

8½" x 5⅜". Collation: *A*^{8}, B-Z^{8}, AA^{8}, BB^{4}, CC^{8}. Pp. [vi], 402; endsheets.

[iii] half-title; [iv] THE HUMAN AGE | Book One | · | CHILDERMASS | [*star*] | Book Two | · | MONSTRE GAI | Book Three | · | MALIGN FIESTA | [*star*] | Book Four | · | THE TRIAL OF MAN; [v] title; [vi] *First published in 1928* | *This edition published in 1956* | [*catalogue registration*] | PRINTED AND BOUND IN

GREAT BRITAIN | BY BUTLER AND TANNER LTD, FROME AND LONDON; [1] BOOK ONE | [*double rule, thin and very fine*] | Childermass; [3] *Scene* | OUTSIDE HEAVEN; 5-401 text.

Plates. Illustrations by Michael Ayrton printed in black and white are on pp. [13], [133] and [218], all reverse sides blank.

Bound in smooth grey-blue V cloth, brick-red fields blocked across top and bottom of front cover, line design by Michael Ayrton in brick red towards lower right, stamped in gold over upper field: The Human Age | Book 1 | Childermass |. Stamped in gold over brick-red fields blocked at head and foot of spine: [*at head*] THE | HUMAN AGE | I | Wyndham Lewis | [*at foot*] METHUEN |. Issued in decorative dustjacket designed by Michael Ayrton, white paper lettered in black and white, with design printed in red and black. All edges trimmed and unstained. Machine finished wove paper, unwatermarked.

Notes. Published November 22, 1956 in an edition of 3191 copies, and sold at 25s.

This edition is uniform with *The Human Age, Book Two: Monstre Gai, Book Three: Malign Fiesta* (A38) published the year before and prints a slightly revised version of first edition (1928). Michael Ayrton, who illustrated this edition at Lewis's request, sent Lewis his preliminary design for the dustjacket on July 24, 1956. Because Lewis was totally blind, Ayrton's letter of this date (NIC) fully describes the dustjacket, indicating that the figure on the front cover is the Bailiff, with his "booth" running up the spine. Lewis's approval of the dustjacket was given about August 2, 1956 and the book went to press later that month. This edition out of print on January 18, 1967.

A11 PALEFACE 1929

First edition:

PALEFACE | THE PHILOSOPHY OF THE | 'MELTING-POT' | *By* | WYNDHAM | LEWIS | LONDON | CHATTO & WINDUS | 1929

8" x 5". Collation: a^6, A-T^8 (a^3 signed "a^2"). Pp. xii, 304; endsheets.

[i] half-title; [ii] *By Wyndham Lewis* | [*list of eight titles*]; [iii] title; [iv] PRINTED IN GREAT BRITAIN | BY T. AND A. CONSTABLE LTD. | AT THE UNIVERSITY PRESS | EDINBURGH | ALL | RIGHTS RESERVED; v-vi Preface; vii-xi table of contents; [1]-286 text; [287]-300 Appendix; 301-[304] Index.

Bound in smooth half white V cloth, with smooth black V cloth boards, and stamped in black on spine: [*thick zigzag double rule*] | PALE- | FACE | [*diamond ornament*] | WYNDHAM | LEWIS | CHATTO & WINDUS | [*thick zigzag double rule*] |. Issued in white dustjacket, spine designed by Lewis printed in black, front panel designed by unidentified commercial artist and reworked by Lewis printed in green, yellow, brown and pink with lettering in black. Top edge trimmed and unstained; fore-edge trimmed; bottom edge untrimmed. Laid unwatermarked paper.
Publisher's prospectus issued in advance of publication:
PALEFACE | 'The Philosophy of the Melting-Pot' | By Wyndham Lewis | Large Cr. 8vo. 7s. 6d. net | [*star*] | [*review extracts*]. 6" x 4¼". Single leaf folded once to make [4] pp., as follows: [1] title, as above; [2-3] review extracts; [4] review extracts over advertisement with publisher's address. Laid white paper, printed in black.
Yale possesses a copy variantly bound in half black V cloth, white V cloth boards, stamped as trade binding on spine in gold instead of black.

Notes. Published May 9, 1929 in an edition of 2000 copies, and sold at 7s. 6d.

Accepted by Charles Prentice of Chatto and Windus for publication, on October 3, 1927, and printed in March, 1929. This is a revised and considerably expanded version of the lengthy essay "Paleface" in *The Enemy, No. 2* (C6), written during Lewis's visit to the United States in Summer, 1927. Although *Paleface* was offered to a least one American publisher (Viking Press), it was never published in the United States during Lewis's lifetime. Lewis received an advance of £100 from Chatto and Windus. By March, 1933 publisher's records show that 1550 copies had been sold (NIC).

After publication of *Paleface,* Lewis's Arthur Press sent out an advertisement flyer for *Paleface* and *The Apes of God:* [*The following six lines printed at left of design by Lewis, Michel 631:*] THE ARTHUR PRESS | *113 . a . Westbourne Grove . London . W 12.* | *Extracts from some notices of* | PALEFACE | *by* WYNDHAM LEWIS | *(published by Chatto & Windus . 1929).* | [*review extracts*]. 8½" x 6¾". Single sheet folded once to make [4] pp., as follows: [1] title, as above; [2-4] extracts from reviews of *Paleface,* and announcement of forthcoming publication of *The Apes of God* at bottom of [4]. Cream wove unwatermarked paper, printed in black.

Excerpts reprinted in *Wyndham Lewis An Anthology* (A44), including Part I, Section 16 (excerpt); Part II, Introduction; Conclusion. Reprinted by Haskell House (New York, 1969) at $14.95 and by Scholarly Press (St. Clair Shores, Michigan, 1971). Also published by Gordon Press, New York, in May, 1972 at $44.95.

A12a THE APES OF GOD 1930

Limited, signed edition:

THE | APES OF GOD | BY | WYNDHAM LEWIS | [*design by Lewis, Michel 681*] | LONDON | THE ARTHUR PRESS | 1930

9¾" x 7". Collation: a^2, b^8, C-Z^8, AA-RR^8, SS^1 (C2-Z2, AA2-RR2 signed). Pp. [iv], 626; endsheets.

[i] title; [iii] THIS EDITION IS LIMITED TO SEVEN HUNDRED | AND FIFTY SIGNED AND NUMBERED COPIES, FOR | SUBSCRIPTION ONLY, AT £3.3.0 PER COPY, OF | WHICH THIS IS NO [*number written in ink over ⅝" rule of dots, with author's signature beneath*]; [iv] Other books by WYNDHAM LEWIS are | as follows: | [*list of nine titles, with erroneous publication dates for* The Ideal Giant *and* The Caliph's Design]; [1-2] table of contents, at foot of [2]: *"The designs in this book are by Wyndham Lewis."*; [3] internal half-title; [5]-625 text; [626] [*design by Lewis, Michel 696*] | PRINTED IN GREAT BRITAIN BY THE WHITEFRIARS PRESS, LTD., | LONDON AND TONBRIDGE.

Bound in light tan BD cloth, stamped in bluish turquoise on spine: THE | APES | OF | GOD | [*short rule*] | WYNDHAM | LEWIS |. Issued in white dustjacket, designed by Lewis, printed in orange and black on front cover (Michel 679), and in black on spine (Michel 680), lettering printed in black. All edges trimmed and unstained. Wove paper, watermarked: "BASINGWERK PARCHMENT—." Vignette illustrations by Lewis printed in black on the following pages: [i] Michel 681; [5] Michel 682; [25] Michel 683; [57] Michel 684; [111] Michel 685; [131] Michel 686; [141] Michel 687; [175] Michel 688; [193] Michel 689; [219] Michel 690; [235] Michel 691; [317] Michel 692; [325] Michel 693; [347] Michel 694; [605] Michel 695; [626] Michel 696. All but pp. [i] and [626] are on divisional half-titles of the Prologue and the thirteen parts of the novel.

A number of prospectuses were published by Lewis's Arthur Press in order to generate interest in the novel, and to answer criticism:
(a). THE APES OF GOD | A NOVEL. By WYNDHAM LEWIS | [*design by Lewis, Michel 678*] | [*over rule:*] THE ARTHUR PRESS. [*rule ends*] 113a Westbourne Grove · London W· ·2
8½" x 6½". Single leaf folded to make [4] pp., as follows: [1] title, as above; [2-3] synopsis of the novel and publication information, written by Lewis; [4] order form. Printed in black on laid paper, watermarked "[*crown*] | Glascow Laid." Title page of this prospectus reproduced in Michel (678). Published Summer, 1930.
(b). BUY THE APES OF GOD [*novel title over rule*] AND | SEE FOR YOURSELF WHAT | ALL THIS IS ABOUT! | [*text and self-portrait by Lewis, Michel 703*].

16½" x 7½". Broadside printed in red and black on one side only. Published Fall, 1930 by the Arthur Press to promote interest in *The Apes of God,* this satirical broadside prints Lewis's fictitious quotations of "Chorus of Apes of God (Off Stage)" and "Extracts from some notices of The Apes of God" such as: " *'This is a gross and tedious book.'*–The Simian Sentinel."

(c). A STOP-PRESS EXPLOSION | from another quarter! | [*text*] | AN "AGONY" SURPRISE | FOR CHELSEA. | [*rule*] | ONE ARTIST AND ANOTHER ARTIST'S PAINTINGS. | [*rule*] | "FOR SALE." | [*text*].

10" x 7½". Single leaf printed on both sides, [2] pp. Lewis's response to an advertisement in *The Times,* September 3, 1930 run by the painter Richard Wyndham offering two of Lewis's paintings at ridiculously low prices: "Percy Wyndham Lewis.—Two paintings for sale, 9 ft. by 7 ft. and 6 ft. by 4 ft., £20 and £15: inspection.—Captain Wyndham, Bedford Gardens." Wyndham, who had apparently felt that he was the object of satire in *The Apes of God,* probably placed the advertisement by way of revenge on Lewis. See F345.

Two circular letters were also sent out by The Arthur Press and are briefly described below:

(d). [*Round robin, undated, sent to critics and writers eliciting opinions about* The Apes of God.]

Single leaf sent along with a complimentary copy of *The Apes of God* in June-August, 1930. Text reprinted in *Satire & Fiction* (C8) p. 22 and Rose, *Letters* (A42) pp. 191-192. Probably 30-40 copies only.

(e). [*Circular letter, undated, sent to potential advertisers for a popular edition of* The Apes of God, *soliciting advertisement subscriptions.*]

Single leaf sent to various booksellers and companies promoting subscriptions for advertisements in an announced "cheap edition" of *The Apes of God,* to be published "shortly . . . at 7/6d." The letter states that this unique edition will be "the *first novel* since the age of Dickens to carry advertisements." Rates given are £5 for a full-page, £2.10.0 for a half-page. Sent out by The Arthur Press about October-September, 1930. This edition was never published. Reprinted in Rose, *Letters* (A42) pp. 196-197.

Notes. Published June 3, 1930 in an edition of 750 copies, and sold at £3.3.0 (the price was reduced by March 1931 to £3 to hasten sale of remaining copies, see advertisement on back of dustjacket, *The Diabolical Principle and the Dithyrambic Spectator,* A12).

Charles Prentice of Chatto and Windus read portions of the typescript of *The Apes of God* as early as April 11, 1926, and expressed interest periodically for years in publishing the manuscript, as Lewis continued to work on the book: " . . . we would very much like, as I have often told you, to have the pleasure and privilege of being the publishers of *The Apes of God*" (TLS, Prentice to Lewis, September 29,

1930, NIC). Although Chatto and Windus proposed two possible schemes for reaching agreement to publish the novel—either in a two-volume limited, signed edition of 1250 copies to be sold at £2.2.0 per set, or a single volume limited, signed edition of 950 copies to be sold at 25s. per copy—neither the proposed formats, nor Prentice's advance offers were acceptable to Lewis, who determined to publish it himself. In a letter dated August 12, 1929 from Lewis to Prentice, the author announces his decision to publish a "private edition" himself, since "the discrepancy between my view as regards my book and those of your firm is of such a nature that there is no possibility at all of our accomodating them" (NIC).

Lewis's publishing house, The Arthur Press, had already published the three numbers of *The Enemy* (see C5 for further information about The Arthur Press). The success of The Arthur Press edition of *The Apes of God* is evident in an unpublished and apparently unposted letter from Lewis to Prentice dated September, 1930 (NIC), in which Lewis claims that he has made already from his own edition of *The Apes* more than Chatto and Windus offered for the book, with many copies still to sell. He further states that Chatto's final offer for the novel was so much "out of all proportion to the dimensions of the work . . . the position it must occupy among my books and in my life" that, in view of the success of Lewis's limited edition, he has decided that *The Apes* is "a closed book" between them "as a business matter." Prentice and Lewis were consequently unable to agree upon terms for publication of a less expensive trade edition of the work, which was finally published by Nash and Grayson the following year.

The dedicatees, Sir Nicholas and Lady Audrey Waterhouse, whose names appear in the preliminaries of most subsequent editions of *The Apes of God,* apparently gave Lewis the financial assistance needed to bring out the novel in this limited edition (see Rose, *Letters* (A42) pp. 216-217).

Originally a part of the "five hundred thousand word book, *The Man of the World*" (so-called in a letter to Ezra Pound, April 29, 1925, Yale), *The Apes of God* was written intermitently from 1922-1930. Two passages were published in earlier draft form in *The Criterion,* with the help of T.S. Eliot. These are "Mr. Zagreus and the Split-Man," *The Criterion,* II, no. 6 (February 1924) which corresponds to Part XI of *The Apes of God* (see D113) and "The Apes of God," *The Criterion,* II, no. 7 (April 1924) which corresponds to Part III of the novel (see D116). Although other fragments were sent to Eliot at *The Criterion* these were not published at Lewis's insistence (see letter #139 to Eliot in Rose, *Letters* (A42) p. 149).

A12b *First trade edition:*

THE | APES OF GOD | BY | WYNDHAM LEWIS | [*design by Lewis, Michel 681*] | NASH & GRAYSON | CURZON STREET | MAYFAIR LONDON

8½" x 5¼". Collation: *a*², b⁸, C-Z⁸, AA-RR⁸, S². Pp. [iv], 628; endsheets.

[i] half-title; [ii] Some Appreciations which appeared on the | Publication of the Original Limited Edition at | Three Guineas. | [*five paragraphs, the first a publisher's blurb, and four extracts from reviews by Richard Aldington, Roy Campbell, Dr. Meyrick Booth and J. D. Beresford*]; [iii] title; [1] dedication; [2] Other books by WYNDHAM LEWIS are | as follows: | [*list of nine titles, with erroneous publication dates for* The Ideal Giant *and* The Caliph's Design]; [3-4] table of contents, at foot of [4]: *"The designs in this book are by Wyndham Lewis."*; [5]-625 text; [626] [*design by Lewis, Michel 696*] | PRINTED IN GREAT BRITAIN BY | LOWE AND BRYDONE (PRINTERS) LTD., LONDON.

Bound in greyish buff BD cloth, stamped in blue on front cover: THE | APES *of* GOD | WYNDHAM LEWIS |. Stamped in blue on spine: THE | APES OF | GOD | WYNDHAM | LEWIS | NASH & | GRAYSON |. Issued in white dustjacket, designed by Lewis, printed in black and orange on front cover (Michel 679) and in black on spine (Michel 680), lettering printed in black. Vignette designs by Lewis same as limited, signed edition (A12a). Top edge trimmed and stained blue; other edges trimmed and unstained. Wove unwatermarked paper.

Notes. Published early November, 1931 in an edition of 1900 copies, and sold at 10s. 6d.

Contract with Nash and Grayson for first "Cheap" edition dated April 30, 1931; Lewis received an advance of £150 in April, 1931. First printing of this edition out of print about March 4, 1932.

A second printing was published on March 11, 1932, same as first printing with the following exceptions:

1.) Publisher's imprint on title page altered to read "GRAYSON & GRAYSON."

2.) Verso of title page altered to read *"First Cheap Edition* | *Published November 1931* | *Second Impression . . . March 1932* |.

3.) Bound in lighter tan BD cloth, lettering identical but stamped in black rather than blue (publisher's name at foot of spine reading "NASH & | GRAYSON"). Top edge unstained.

An unknown number of copies of the first issue sheets were bound specially for The Times Book Club in dull royal blue V cloth, stamped on spine in gold: THE APES | OF GOD | W. LEWIS | NASH & GRAYSON |. On rear pastedown is a small label reading: The [*ornament*] Times | Book Club | 42 Wigmore Street | London W1 |. Copies were distributed to members in August, 1932.

A third printing was published in July, 1934, same as second printing with verso of title page expanded to read *"First Cheap Edition* | *Published November* 1931 | *Second Impression . . . March* 1932 | *Third Impression . . . July* 1934 |. Out of print by December 31, 1937.

A12c *First American edition:*

THE | APES OF GOD | BY | WYNDHAM LEWIS | [*design by Lewis, Michel 681*] | NEW YORK MCMXXXII | ROBERT M. McBRIDE & COMPANY

7⅞" x 5½". Collation: *1-20*^{16}, *21*^{12}. Pp. [iv], 628; endsheets.

[i] half-title; [iii] title; [iv] COPYRIGHT, 1932 | BY WYNDHAM LEWIS | *First published, February, 1932* | ALL RIGHTS RESERVED | THE APES OF GOD | [*rule*] | PRINTED IN THE UNITED STATES OF AMERICA; [1-2] table of contents, at foot of [2]: *"The designs in this book are by Wyndham Lewis."*; [3] internal half-title; [5]-625 text; [626] [*design by Lewis, Michel 696*].

Bound in grey V cloth, broad red rule running down left margin of front cover, stamped in red on front cover: THE | APES | OF | GOD | WYNDHAM | LEWIS |. Stamped in red on spine: THE | APES | OF | GOD | [*rule*] | WYNDHAM | LEWIS | McBRIDE |. Issued in brown dustjacket, lettering printed in green and red, ruled in red, and with five designs by Lewis from the book in green on front cover. Top edge trimmed and stained red; fore-edge untrimmed; bottom edge uncut. Vignette illustrations by Lewis printed in black on the following pages: [iii] Michel 681; [5] Michel 682; [25] Michel 683; [57] Michel 684; [111] Michel 685; [131] Michel 686; [141] Michel 687; [175] Michel 688; [193] Michel 689; [219] Michel 690; [235] Michel 691; [317] Michel 692; [325] Michel 693; [347] Michel 694; [605] Michel 695; [626] Michel 696. All but pp. [iii] and [626] are on divisional half-titles, printed in black. Wove unwatermarked paper; grey endsheets.

Notes. Published February 24, 1932 and sold at $3.00

Photographically reprints A12a, with title page altered. Montgomery Belgion of Harcourt, Brace and Co. expressed interest in publishing the American edition of the novel as early as October, 1927. Belgion even submitted a proposed pre-publication advertisement for the novel to Lewis on October 19, 1927 (TLS, Belgion to Lewis, NIC). Lewis was favorably disposed to letting Harcourt, Brace publish the book and in a letter to Belgion dated December 6, 1927 (NIC) asked an advance of £1000 for the rights. Belgion declined to offer this much, and the project was abandoned. McBride offered to publish *The Apes of God* in July, 1931, and their offer was accepted by Lewis sometime in August, 1931.

A12d *Twenty-fifth Anniversary edition:*

THE | APES OF GOD | BY | WYNDHAM LEWIS | [*design by Lewis, Michel 681*] | LONDON | ARCO PUBLISHERS LIMITED

9¾" x 7¼". Collation: π^2, A^8, B-Z^8, AA-PP^8, QQ^4. Pp. [x], 626; endsheets.

[i] half-title; [iii] THIS EDITION IS LIMITED TO ONE THOUSAND | SIGNED AND NUMBERED COPIES, FOR SUBSCRIPTION | ONLY, AT £3.3.0 PER COPY, OF WHICH THIS IS | NO [*number written in ink on dotted line*] | [*author's signature in ink*]; [iv] *THIS EDITION 1955*; [v-vi] table of contents; [vii] title; [viii] This edition first published | in 1955 by | ARCO PUBLISHERS LIMITED | 10 Fitzroy Street | LONDON W.1 | [*publisher's device*] | Copyright Wyndham Lewis | Printed in Great Britain by D. R. Hillman & Sons Ltd., Frome; [ix-x, 1-3] Introduction to the Twenty-Fifth Anniversary Edition; [5]-625 text; [626] [*design by Lewis, Michel 696*] | Printed in Great Britain by | D. R. HILLMAN & SONS LIMITED | Frome Somerset.

Two variant bindings, priority as follows:
(1). Bound in light pearl brown BD cloth, stamped in black and red on spine: [*in black*] THE APES | OF GOD | by | WYNDHAM | LEWIS | [*design of ape clutching book stamped in red, designed by Michael Ayrton, repeated from same design on spine of dustjacket*] | [*publisher's device of arc on waves, within circle, stamped in black*] |. Issued in white pictorial dustjacket, designed by Michael Ayrton, printed in red and black. All edges trimmed and unstained. Wove unwatermarked paper. Plates same as A12a.
(2). Same as (1), except bound in light yellowish khaki V cloth, stamped as above on spine in yellow.

Notes. Published February 11, 1955 in an edition of 1000 copies, and sold at £3.3.0.

Photographically reprints A12a with the addition of a new "Introduction" by Lewis especially for this publication. Arco Publishers Limited approached Methuen on December 22, 1953 stating interest in reprinting the novel on its twenty-fifth anniversary. Bernard Hanison, after receiving Methuen's approval, contacted Lewis in a letter dated December 29, 1953 (NIC) offering to publish *The Apes of*

God, indicating that Methuen had no plans to reissue the title. Draft agreement sent to Lewis on March 5, 1954 (NIC). The final contract was signed and Lewis advanced £175 about mid-March.

Lewis wrote the new "Introduction" for this edition in April and delivered the manuscript by May 10, 1954. The limitation sheets (sig. π^2) were sent by Hanison to Lewis on May 11, 1954 and signed by him in his flat at Kensington Gardens Studio. Lewis asked Michael Ayrton to design a new dustjacket for the book in late December, 1953, and Ayrton agreed on January 3, 1954. Ayrton finished work on the design in May, 1954. The dedication to Sir Nicholas and Lady Waterhouse was dropped in this edition.

A13 HITLER 1931

First edition:

HITLER | BY | WYNDHAM LEWIS | CHATTO & WINDUS, LONDON | 1931

8" x 5". Collation: a^6, A-M^8, N^6 (a2 signed). 1 leaf, pp. x, 204; endsheets. 8 leaves of plates mounted, not included in collation or pagination.

[i] half-title; [ii] *By Wyndham Lewis* | [*list of nine titles*]; [iii] title; [iv] PRINTED IN GREAT BRITAIN | BY T. AND A. CONSTABLE LTD. | AT THE UNIVERSITY PRESS | EDINBURGH | ALL RIGHTS RESERVED; [v] quotation in German from Fichte; vii-viii table of contents; ix list of illustrations; [1]-202 text; [203] Printed in Great Britain | by T. and A. CONSTABLE LTD. | at the University Press | Edinburgh

Plates. Photographs printed on coated paper, mounted facing the following pages: [iii], 8 (Simplicissumus cartoon), 24, 52, 90, 104, 174, 194. All credits printed in small italic, within parentheses (Simplicissumus cartoon credit within brackets), captions in roman. All plates printed on one side only.

Two bindings noted (no priority determined, though the first binding is much more common than the second):
(1). Bound in tan BD cloth (interlacing orange threads), with black swastika (1 7/16") stamped on front cover, and spine stamped in red and black: [*thick black rule over red rule over waving red rule*] | [*in black*] HITLER | [*reversed swastika*] | WYNDHAM | LEWIS | [*red waving rule over red rule*] | [*in red*] AND | CHATTO WINDUS | [*thick black rule*] |. Issued in white dustjacket designed by Lewis, lettered and decorated with swastika designs in black and grey. Top edge trimmed and stained yellow; fore-edge trimmed; bottom edge untrimmed. Unwatermarked laid paper.

(2). Same as (1) except cloth is grey with interlacing tan threads (copy at Lilly Library, Indiana University).

Notes. Published March 26, 1931 in an edition of 2000 copies, and sold for 6s.

On January 12, 1931 Charles Prentice of Chatto and Windus agreed to publish *Hitler,* and offered an advance of £100. The book was printed in February, 1931. Although it was offered to at least one American publisher (William Morrow), *Hitler* was never published in the United States during Lewis's lifetime. 1367 copies sold by March, 1933.

Serially published in *Time and Tide* from January 17 to February 14, 1931 as follows: "Hitlerism—Man and Doctrine: The Weimar Republic and the Dritte Reich" (D154) corresponds to Part I, Chap. 1; "Hitlerism—Man and Doctrine: Berlin Im Licht!" (D155) corresponds to Part I, Chap. 2; "Hitlerism—Man and Doctrine: The Oneness of 'Hitlerism' and of Hitler" (D156) corresponds to Part II, Chaps. 1 and 2; "Hitlerism—Man and Doctrine: The Doctrine of the Blutsgefuhl" (D157) corresponds to Part V, Chaps. 1 and 2; "Hitlerism—Man and Doctrine: Creditcrankery Rampant" (D159) corresponds to Part VI, Chap. 4. All of these earlier articles revised and reorganized for book publication. Other passages published for the first time in this edition.

Reprinted by Gordon Press in June, 1972, at $64.95. Also incorporated in *Hitler, the Germans and the Jews* published by Gordon Press in 1973.

A14 THE DIABOLICAL PRINCIPLE AND THE DITHYRAMBIC SPECTATOR 1931

First edition:

THE | DIABOLICAL PRINCIPLE | *AND* | THE DITHYRAMBIC | SPECTATOR | *By* | WYNDHAM LEWIS | [*design by Lewis, Michel 652*] | LONDON | CHATTO AND WINDUS | 1931

7½" x 4¾". Collation: π^8, A-P^8, Q^2 (sig. Q mounted). 1 blank leaf, pp. xiv, 244; endsheets.

[i] half-title; [iii] *By Wyndham Lewis* | [*list of nine titles*]; [iii] title; [iv] PRINTED IN GREAT BRITAIN | BY T. AND A. CONSTABLE LTD. | AT THE UNIVERSITY PRESS | EDINBURGH | ALL | RIGHTS RESERVED; v-x Preface; xi-xiv table of contents; [1] divisional fly-title, THE DIABOLICAL PRINCIPLE | [*quotation in English from Lao-tze*]; 3-156 text; 157 note for *The Dithyrambic Spectator*; 159 divisional fly-title, THE DITHYRAMBIC SPECTATOR | AN ESSAY ON THE ORIGINS AND | SURVIVALS OF ART;

161-238 text; 239-242 Index; [243] Printed in Great Britain | by T. and A CONSTABLE LTD. | at the University Press | Edinburgh

Two variant bindings, priority as follows:
(1). Smooth cranberry V cloth, stamped in gold on spine: THE | DIABOLICAL | PRINCIPLE | *AND* | THE DITHYRAMBIC | SPECTATOR | [*star*] | WYNDHAM | LEWIS | CHATTO & WINDUS |. Issued in bright yellow dustjacket designed by Lewis (incorporating Michel 652), decorations and rules in red, lettering printed in black. Top edge trimmed and stained yellow; fore-edge trimmed; bottom edge untrimmed. Laid unwatermarked paper.
(2). Orange-cranberry V cloth, stamped in black on spine, same as (1). Issued in same dustjacket with erroneous note at bottom of back panel, stating that *Hitler* is "*IN PREPARATION*" and will be ready "*Immediately.*" Top edge trimmed and unstained; other edges as (1).

Notes. Published April 30, 1931 in an edition of 2000 copies, and sold at 7s. 6d.

Accepted on December 6, 1928 by Charles Prentice for publication with Chatto and Windus. Sent to the printers in January, 1931, Lewis receiving £100 advance for the book. *The Dithyrambic Spectator,* originally entitled "The Perfect Action," was written as early as 1924 and was originally supposed to form an Appendix to *Time and Western Man,* but at the suggestion of Charles Prentice in a letter dated April 26, 1927 (NIC) the essay was excluded from that book in order to save space. "The Perfect Action" was to be published by T.S. Eliot in *The Criterion* in January, 1925, but when Eliot requested that the essay be published in parts (since *The Criterion* was unable to print the essay—some 20,000 words—in unabridged form) Lewis refused. Although *The Criterion* announced that the polemical essay would be published in an upcoming issue, Lewis wrote Eliot on January 30, 1925 stating that "The Perfect Action" had been sold to *The Calendar of Modern Letters* (see Rose, *Letters* (A42) pp. 147-149). The essay was, however, ultimately published in two parts in *The Calendar* after it was retitled by Lewis: "The Dithyrambic Spectator: An Essay on the Origins and Survivals of Art. Introduction" (D121) and "The Dithyrambic Spectator: An Essay on the Origins and Survivals of Art. Part II" (D122), April and May, 1925. With the exceptions of Section II, Chap. 9 and "Note for Dithyrambic Spectator," *The Diabolical Principle* was included in its entirety in *The Enemy, No. 3* (see C7). All earlier published passages were revised by Lewis for first book publication.

First published in United States by Haskell House as part of their series #80, 1971, at $12.95. Partially reprinted in *Enemy Salvoes, Wyndham Lewis An Anthology of his Prose* and *Wyndham Lewis on Art.*

A15a THE DOOM OF YOUTH 1932

First edition:

[*Double rule*] | THE | DOOM | OF | YOUTH | WYNDHAM LEWIS | NEW YORK MCMXXXII | ROBERT M. McBRIDE & COMPANY

8 1/16" x 5⅜". Collation: a^8, b^8, A^8, B-Q^8, R^7 (*a* and *A* unsigned; R2 signed). Initial blank leaf not included in collation; pp. xxxii, 270; endsheets.

[i] half-title; [iii] title; [iv] COPYRIGHT, 1932 | By WYNDHAM LEWIS | *First Published, March, 1932* | THE DOOM OF YOUTH | [*rule*] | PRINTED IN THE UNITED STATES OF AMERICA; [v] two quotations in English from Trotsky and Fourier; vii-xii Foreword; xiii-xx Introduction; xxi-xxix table of contents; [xxxi] internal half-title; [1]-266 text.

Bound in light grey-blue V cloth, blind lettered within three gold rectangular frames on front cover: THE DOOM | OF YOUTH | WYNDHAM LEWIS |. Blind lettered within gold field on spine: THE | DOOM | [*within another gold field*] OF | YOUTH | [*within another gold field*] LEWIS | [*lettering stamped in gold*] M^c^Bride |. Issued in bright yellow dustjacket printed in red on front cover and spine, and in blue on panels. Top edge trimmed and stained yellow; fore-edge uncut; bottom edge trimmed. Wove unwatermarked paper.

Notes. Published March 30, 1932 and sold at $2.50.

Passages serially published in *Time and Tide* prior to the publication of this edition: "Youth Politics. Foreword: The Everymans" (D163) corresponds to the Foreword; "Youth-Politics. The Age Complex" (D164) corresponds to the Introduction and parts of Chap. V; "Youth-Politics. Youth-Politics Upon the Super-Tax Plane" (D166) corresponds to Part I, Chap. 4; "Youth Politics. There is *Nothing* Big Business can't Ration" (D167) corresponds to Part I, Chap. 1 and passages in Chap. 2; "Youth-Politics. The *Class-War* of Parents and Children" (D168) corresponds to Part I, Chap. 12; "Youth-Politics. Government by Inferiority Complex" (D169) corresponds to Part V, Chap. 1; "Youth-Politics. How Youth-Politics will Abolish Youth" (D170) corresponds to Part V, Chap. 1. All of these earlier published passages are revised by Lewis for this edition. For further information see A15b, note.

Reprinted by Haskell House, as part of their series #80, 1973, at $14.95.

A15b *First English edition:*

DOOM OF YOUTH | *BY* | WYNDHAM LEWIS | LONDON | CHATTO & WINDUS | 1932

8¾" x 5½". Collation: $*^8$, b^8, A-Q^8, R^6 (*1 not included in paging). 1 signed leaf, pp. xxx, 268; endsheets.

[i] half-title; [ii] *By Wyndham Lewis* | [*list of ten titles*]; [iii] title; [iv] PRINTED IN GREAT BRITAIN | ALL RIGHTS RESERVED; [v] quotations from Trotsky and Fournier; vii-xii Foreword; xiii-xx Introduction; xxi-xxix table of contents; 1-266 text; [267] Printed in Great Britain | by T. and A. CONSTABLE LTD. | at the University Press | Edinburgh

Bound in smooth tan V cloth, stamped in black on spine: [*ornamental rule of joined expanding crosses*] | DOOM | OF | YOUTH | [*short rule*] | WYNDHAM | LEWIS | [*ornamental rule, as above*] | CHATTO & WINDUS |. Issued in light cream dustjacket, rules printed in black, lettering in black. Top and fore-edges trimmed and unstained; bottom edge uncut. Unwatermarked laid paper.

Notes. Published June 30, 1932 in an edition of 1518 copies (550 copies extant after March, 1934), and sold at 10s. 6d. Withdrawn.

Accepted for publication March 23, 1931; contract signed April 1, 1931 with projected publication date in early September, 1931. Lewis completed the manuscript and delivered it to Chatto and Windus by April, 1931. Printing of the final sheets was delayed until May, 1932 primarily because Lewis, who was working on *Filibusters in Barbary* in Morocco, was delinquent in returning corrected proofs, which Charles Prentice had sent him in Summer, 1931. Lewis received an advance of £150.

Several weeks after publication of the book, on July 27, 1932, Charles Prentice informed Lewis that Chatto and Windus had "received a letter from Alec Waugh's solicitors demanding the instant withdrawal of *Doom of Youth,* in default of which a writ of libel will be immediately served" (NIC). An affidavit dated August 9, 1932 filed by Rubinstein, Nash & Co. on behalf of Alec Waugh against Lewis and his publishers, cited the following passages in *Doom of Youth* as being libellous: p. 109, paragraph 1; p. 113, paragraph 1; p. 113, paragraph 3 ("Mr. Cardew is as crazy about small boys as is Mr. Waugh himself . . ."); p. 114. The affidavit stated that "The innuendoes of which I complain are (1) that the passages suggest that I [Alec Waugh] am obsessed with literary work of an obscene nature and in particular of a homo-sexual and/or sexually perverted nature, and that I myself am a sexual pervert and (2) that as an author I compose and can compose nothing but books about schoolboys" (NIC). Earlier, on July 20, Chatto and Windus had received another letter from Gisborne & Co. on behalf of Godfrey Winn, demanding that *Doom of Youth* "immediately . . . be withdrawn from circulation and all copies already out . . . be called in" (NIC), claiming that the chapter entitled "Winn and Waugh" (pp. 98-108) constituted a libel upon Winn, calculated to damage his reputation as a writer and "as an individual." Chatto and Windus's attorneys, Walker Martineau & Co. contacted Barnes and Butler, Lewis's legal representatives, about July 22, 1932 advising them that Lewis's allusion to Winn as a "hack" (p. 105) and a "salaried revolutionary agent" (p. 106) were indeed libellous. Futhermore, in a letter from H. D. Barnes to Lewis dated July 22 (NIC), Lewis's lawyer reported that Walker Martineau & Co. considered the tone of the entire chapter essentially slanderous insofar as it tended to hold Winn up to unwarranted ridicule. As a consequence of these legal pressures, Chatto and Windus decided to recall and suppress the book, rejecting Lewis's protests that the text was not libellous. By August 30, 1932 a total of 549 copies had been sold. 138 unsold copies were returned to the publishers by booksellers, and in March, 1934 the remaining stock of 250 bound copies and 718 copies still in quires was stripped and pulped, a single office copy having been retained by Chatto and Windus. A printed statement of claim for damages was filed by Waugh's lawyers on October 28, 1932 with the High Court of Justice, citing the passages given above as libellous, and adding passages from pp. xxv, 112 and 206.

The matter was settled by May, 1933 with the agreement that *Doom of Youth* would not again be published to include any portion of Chapter 7, that Waugh be indemnified from all expenses in connection with the suit and that he accepted Lewis's assurance that it had not been his intention to make "personal reflections" upon him. Lewis, upset with his publisher's compliance with demands made by Waugh's attorneys, did not publish any other titles with Chatto and Windus.

A16a FILIBUSTERS IN BARBARY [1932]

First edition:

FILIBUSTERS IN BARBARY | [RECORD OF A VISIT TO THE SOUS] | BY | WYNDHAM LEWIS | GRAYSON | CURZON STREET | MAYFAIR LONDON

8½" x 5¼". Collation: A^8, B-R^8. Pp. x, 262; endsheets.

[i] half-title; [ii] *By the same Author* | APES OF GOD [*Third Edition*]; [iii] title; [iv] *First Published by* | *Grayson & Grayson Ltd.* | 1932 | *Printed in Great Britain* | *by the Kemp Hall Press, Ltd.* | *in the City of Oxford;* [v] table of contents; [vii]-ix Foreword; [1]-[258] text.

Bound in yellowish tan V cloth, stamped on front cover, all lettering in green: FILIBUSTERS | [*red double rule*] | IN BARBARY | [*design of setting sun, clouds, palm trees and horizon in green and red*] | WYNDHAM | [*red double rule*] | LEWIS |. Stamped on spine, lettering in green: FILIBUSTERS | [*red double rule*] | IN | [*red double rule*] | BARBARY | BY | WYNDHAM | [*red double rule*] | LEWIS | [*design of clouds behind palm trees, in green*] | GRAYSON |. Issued in heavy tan dustjacket, lettered in green, and with designs as on binding printed in green and red, price in green on spine above design. Top edge trimmed and stained green; other edges trimmed. Laid unwatermarked paper.

Notes. Published early June, 1932 in an edition of 1500 copies, and sold at 12s. 6d. Withdrawn.

Contract between Lewis and Grayson & Grayson for *Filibusters in Barbary* dated October 9, 1931, Lewis receiving an advance of £150. Over a year after publication of the book of travel sketches based on Lewis's visit to Morocco in 1931-1932, Soames, Edwards & Jones, representing their client Major T.C. Macfie, contacted Grayson & Grayson about libellous passages in *Filibusters in Barbary*. In a letter dated December 21, 1933, Macfie complained through his attorneys that *Filibusters* contained "false and malicious matter of the most serious character [about Macfie]" (NIC). This letter cites the following passages as constituting a libel upon his character: p. 122, lines 25-32 beginning with "It is not of course the British Consular authorities who are responsible . . ."; pp. 123-124, lines 9-35 and 1-13; p. 125, lines 31-35 beginning " . . . and I wondered what order of risks . . ."; p. 153, lines 30-35 ending with p. 154, line 1. In a note of the proceedings conducted against Lewis, his publisher and the printers, Kemp Hall Press Ltd., by Macfie's lawyers, on February 23, 1934 the plaintiff's charges are more clearly established. The hearing which took place was presided over by Mr. Justice Acton, who heard testimony claiming that Macfie was libelled by passages in *Filibusters* "which are capable of being understood to refer to [Macfie] . . . [accusing him] of defying the French Authorities [in Morocco] and . . . engaging in contraband traffic and smuggling of arms." Lewis protested that he had not intentionally refered to Macfie anywhere in the text of the book. However Grayson & Grayson agreed to withdraw the book from circulation and pay Macfie compensatory fees.

Originally published serially by *Everyman* from October 29, 1931 to January 7, 1932: "High Table: The Packet to Africa" (D171) corresponds to Book I, I, Chap. 3; "Turning Darks into Whites" (D173) corresponds to Book I, I, Chap. 7; "Islamic Sensations" (D174) corresponds to Book I, I, Chap. 8; "Petrol-Tin Town" (D176) corresponds to Book I, I, Chap. 12; "The Mouth of the Sahara" (D177) corresponds to Book I, II, Chap. 1. "The Blue Sultan," published in *The Graphic* for November 7, 1931, corresponds to Book II, Chaps. 11 and 14.

Reprinted by Haskell House, as part of their series #80 (Wyndham Lewis Series), 1973, at $16.95.

A16b *First American edition:*

FILIBUSTERS | IN BARBARY | BY | WYNDHAM LEWIS | [*rule*] | NATIONAL TRAVEL CLUB | NEW YORK MCMXXXII

8⅝" x 5½". Collation: *1-20*^{8}, *21*^{4}. Pp. 312; endsheets, and eight mounted plates. Pp. [1-12] numbered [i]-xii.

[i] half-title; [ii] BOOKS BY MR. LEWIS | [*rule*] | [*list of ten titles*]; [iii] title; [iv] COPYRIGHT, 1932 | BY WYNDHAM LEWIS | *Published for National Travel Club, June, 1932* | FILIBUSTERS IN BARBARY | [*rule*] | PRINTED IN THE UNITED STATES OF AMERICA; v-vi table of contents; vii-viii table of plates; ix-xii Foreword; [13]-308 text; [309] map.

Bound in black V cloth, thick and thin double rule blind-stamped around border of upper board, with medallion blocked in gold on center of front cover depicting ship over two globes under initials "N.T.C."; stamped in gold on spine: [*decorative rule, long horizontal rectangle and two short vertical rectangles, repeated*] | FILIBUSTERS | IN | BARBARY | WYNDHAM | LEWIS | [*circular medallion, with ship, clouds and waves*] | N·T·C· | [*decorative rule, same as above*] |. Issued in white dustjacket with decorative design in blue, yellow, red, green, violet and brown on front and spine, of Moroccan street scene; lettering and zigzag rules in black. Back cover and inner flap blank, no price on front flap. Top edge trimmed and stained red; fore-edge untrimmed; bottom edge slightly trimmed. Tan endsheets. Wove unwatermarked paper.

Plates. Plates of photographs, brown and white half-tone, mounted, on machine-finished paper, facing the following pages: p. 3, The French have not attempted to change the native | cities of Morocco. Most of the thoroughfares remain | as they have been for centuries.; 48, The roadway to Marrakech is lined with thousands of palm trees which are laden with | golden clusters in the fruit season.; 49, *(Above)* The old gateways of Marrakech are impres- | sive reminders of the city's heroic past. | *(Below)* Story tellers and fortune tellers are always | popular with the feminine audience.; 64, The Berber women of the mountain tribes are more vigorous and independent than their | Arab sisters. They come to market with their faces uncovered.; 65, In the market places of Moroccan cities, magicians and story tellers welcome | all who care to gather about them; 112, [*beneath two photographs*] Fez lies within a valley encircled by massive gray-green mountains. It is still | surrounded by massive ramparts surmounted by square towers and broken by | magnificent gateways.; 113, Fez, "The Sacred City," is famous for its mosques and medersas. It was founded in 808 by | Edres II.; 128, The Moroccan wife's ambition is summed up in the first question she asks a | foreign woman, "Have you any children?"; 129, Patterns of light and shadow are formed by the trellis-covered streets typical of so many | Moroccan cities.; 192, The immense and desolate empire of the Touaregs | stretches from the Hoggar to Mauretania and the | Rio de Oro.; 193, In the sheltered patio of the Arab house, the women | may enjoy privacy amid flowers and luxuriant foliage.; 208, The Fiddians of the mountainous regions along the north coast of Morocco have maintained | a fierce independence for centuries.; 209, Tetuan is one of the principal cities of the Riff. It was founded in 1492 by Andalusian Moors.; 272, Superbly mounted and commanded by a French officer, the Sultan's Black Lancers is one of | the finest military units in Morocco.; 273, The Moroccan population often greets a visiting celebrity with elaborate figurines held | aloft on poles.

Notes. Published June 27, 1932 in an edition of 1000 copies, and sold at $2.50 (as part of a set along with Isaac Don Levine, *Red Smoke,* advertised in *Travel* magazine, see D183).

A16c *Second American edition (first separate American trade edition):*

FILIBUSTERS | IN BARBARY | BY | WYNDHAM LEWIS | [*publisher's device*] | [*expanding rule*] | ROBERT M. MCBRIDE & COMPANY | NEW YORK MCMXXXII

Bound from same sheets as the National Travel Club Edition, with the verso of the title page altered to read: COPYRIGHT, 1932 | BY WYNDHAM LEWIS | *First Published, September, 1932* | FILIBUSTERS IN BARBARY | [*rule*] | PRINTED IN THE UNITED STATES OF AMERICA |. Bound in rough tan V cloth, lettering stamped in gold at angles across front cover, between zigzag rules stamped in red: FILIBUSTERS | IN BARBARY |. Lettering stamped in gold on spine: [*red zigzag rule*] | FILIBUSTERS | IN | BARBARY | [*short red zigzag rule*] | WYNDHAM | LEWIS | [*red zigzag rule*] | McBRIDE |. Top edge stained red; all edges trimmed. Issued in dustjacket identical to National Travel Club edition, with "N.T.C." at foot of spine altered to read "McBRIDE," advertisements printed in black on back cover and back flap, and with price printed at top of front flap. Endsheets tan. Wove unwatermarked paper.

Notes. Published in September, 1932 and sold at $3.50.

A17 ENEMY OF THE STARS 1932

First edition:

ENEMY OF THE | STARS | BY | WYNDHAM LEWIS | [*design by Lewis, Michel 748*] | DESMOND HARMSWORTH | LONDON | 1932

11⅛" x 8½". Collation: A-I^4. Pp. [vii], 65; endsheets.

[iii] half-title; [v] title; [vi] *Enemy of the Stars* by Wyndham Lewis was first published in | book form in MCMXXXII by Desmond Harmsworth Ltd. at | 44 Great Russell Street W.C. 1 and was made and printed in | Great Britain by The Westminster Press; [vii] table of contents; [1] divisional fly-title, THE PLAY | [*design by Lewis, Michel 749*]; 3-47 text (design by Lewis, Michel 750, on 47); [49] divisional fly-title, PHYSICS OF THE | NOT-SELF | [*design by Lewis, Michel 751*]; 51-59 text; [61] NOTE | *This version of* Enemy of the Stars *differs in detail from* | *that to be found in* Blast No. 1. *There were several versions–* | *the author has restored passages removed from, or not used in,* | *the* Blast *version, and has added new ones. In other respects it* | *is substantially the same.;* [62] [*printer's device*] | The Westminster Press | 411a Harrow Road | London, W.9

Three variant bindings, priority as follows:

(1). Half red smooth V cloth, stamped in gold running *down* spine: ENEMY OF THE STARS—WYNDHAM LEWIS |. Cream paper boards printed in black on front cover: ENEMY OF THE STARS | [*design by Lewis, Michel 747*] | WYNDHAM LEWIS |. Boards measure 11 5/16" x 8¾". Issued in light cream dustjacket with design by Lewis (not in Michel, but expanded version of Michel 748) printed in pink, yellow and grey; lettering printed in black, title and author's name running up jacket spine. Advertisement for apparent "ghost"—*A Tip from the Augean Stable*–on back inner flap: Further New Books by | WYNDHAM LEWIS | THE OLD GANG & THE NEW GANG | Or "THE GREAT BLANK OF THE MISSING GENERATION" | Crown 8vo. 50pp. 3/6 | Ready Shortly | A TIP FROM THE AUGEAN STABLE | Portrait jacket by the Author | Crown 8vo. 50pp. 3/6 | Ready Shortly | WYNDHAM LEWIS | A discursive exposition | By *Hugh Gordon Porteus* | Early Autumn | DESMOND HARMSWORTH | 44 GREAT RUSSELL STREET, W. C. 1 | JANUS [*printer's device*] PRESS |. Top and fore-edges trimmed and unstained; bottom edge mostly trimmed. Wove unwatermarked paper.

(2). Same as (1), but lettering stamped in gold running *up* spine.

(3). Red V cloth, stamped in black on front cover: ENEMY OF THE STARS | WYNDHAM LEWIS |. Stamped in black running down spine: ENEMY OF THE

STARS—WYNDHAM LEWIS |. Boards measure 11 5/16" x 8 11/16". Issued in same dustjacket and with edges and paper identical to binding (1).

The text is found in two states, affecting various signatures as indicated below, and is almost invariably found mixed and bound up in any of the variant bindings. It may be noted, however, that the first state of the text as given herebelow is more commonly found bound up in the pictorial bindings (1) and (2):

	FIRST STATE	SECOND STATE
p. 41, l. *1*	indelicate	ndelicate
55, *34*	ἀρετς (slightly above baseline)	ἀρετς (slightly below baseline)
28, *1*	th␣e 2 mm.	th␣e 3mm.
30, 28	sickly␣silhouette 2 mm.	sickly␣silhouette 3mm.
32, *26*	chew (justified properly against outer margin of type page)	chew (indented 1mm. from outer margin of type page)

Notes. Published about May 31, 1932 and sold at 10s. 6d.

Following the withdrawal of *The Doom of Youth* (Chatto and Windus) and *Filibusters in Barbary* (Grayson & Grayson), Lewis had ended his association with these publishers and turned to a smaller publishing house which was managed by an old acquaintance, Mrs. Winifred Henderson, and Desmond Harmsworth. Lewis and Harmsworth contracted to bring out a revised edition of *Enemy of the Stars* about March 23, 1932. The book was printed and proofread from late April to mid-May, 1932, with Lewis making sufficiently numerous corrections and additions in the text at proof stage that the publication schedule was somewhat delayed. These delays may have contributed to the fact that one of the titles by Lewis announced on the rear flap of the dustjacket, *A Tip from the Augean Stable,* was abandoned (see G2).

The Janus Press device at the bottom of the back flap of the dustjacket is by Lewis (this is confirmed by a TLS from John Sithorpe to Lewis, May 13, 1932, NIC).

Enemy of the Stars was originally published in *Blast, No. 1* (C1), and the text was considerably revised for this first book publication, adding dramatic dialogues. *Physics of the Not-Self* was published in an earlier version in *The Chapbook* (see D125) and was partially reprinted in the present version in Tomlin, *Wyndham Lewis An Anthology*. *Blast* version of *Enemy of the Stars* reprinted in *A Soldier of Humor* (A43).

See also B16.

A18 SNOOTY BARONET [1932]

First edition:

SNOOTY BARONET | by | WYNDHAM LEWIS | AUTHOR OF "TARR," "THE WILD BODY," | "THE APES OF GOD," ETC. | [*publisher's device*] | CASSELL | and Company, Ltd. | London, Toronto, Melbourne | and Sydney

7¼" x 4¾". Collation: A^8, B-U^8. Pp. viii, 312; endsheets.

[iii] half-title; [v] title; [vi] *First published, 1932* | PRINTED IN GREAT BRITAIN BY BUTLER AND TANNER LTD., | FROME AND LONDON | [*catalogue registration*]; vii table of contents; 1-[309] text.

Two variant bindings, priority as follows:
(1). Brownish pink V cloth, single rule frame blind-stamped around edges of front cover, stamped in gold on spine: *SNOOTY* | *BARONET* | [*thick rule*] | *Wyndham* | *Lewis* | *CASSELL* |. Issued in blue dustjacket, printed in black. All edges trimmed and unstained. Laid unwatermarked paper.
(2). Brown V cloth, stamped in black on spine as above. Otherwise same as (1).

Notes. Published September 15, 1932 in an edition of 2791 copies, and sold at 7s. 6d.

Manuscript completed in January, 1932 and submitted to Desmond Flower of Cassell & Company in late February. This is the first of three books published for Lewis by Cassell, the contract for three titles having been drawn up and signed in April, 1932. Lewis received £300 advance for the novel. Printed in Summer, 1932. On January 24, 1938 Cassell received a demand from Gordon Dadds & Co., representing Rupert Grayson (who published *Apes of God* and *Filibusters in Barbary)* that *Snooty Baronet* be withdrawn from publication. The allegation behind this request was that the novel presented, in the character of Humph, an "unjustified and unwarranted attack upon [Grayson's] character" (TL [copy], Dadds to Cassell, January 24, 1938, NIC).

An uncorrected proof copy, printed on heavy coated paper and bound in plain chocolate wrappers is in the collection of Hugh Anson-Cartwright.

Reprinted by Haskell House, as part of their series #80, 1971, at $14.95. See F1715, for Grayson's recollections of the "Humph" suit.

A19 THIRTY PERSONALITIES AND A SELF-PORTRAIT [1932]

First edition:

THIRTY PERSONALITIES | AND A | SELF-PORTRAIT | *by* | WYNDHAM LEWIS | DESMOND HARMSWORTH | LONDON

14⅞" x 10¾". Collation: 65 leaves, unattached and unsigned. Pp. 6, 11. [62].

[1] title; [2] THIRTY PERSONALITIES AND A SELF-PORTRAIT | BY WYNDHAM LEWIS WAS FIRST PUBLISHED | IN MCMXXXII BY DESMOND HARMSWORTH | LTD., AT 44 GREAT RUSSELL STREET, W.C.I, | AND WAS MADE AND PRINTED IN GREAT | BRITAIN AT THE CHISWICK PRESS, NEW | SOUTHGATE, N.11 | *This edition is limited to two hundred* | *sets signed and numbered by the Artist.* | *This is No.* [*number written in grey ink*] | [*Lewis's signature*]; 3-5 introduction; [62 leaves] title leaves and plates.

Plates. Portfolio contains 31 plates, each preceded by loose title leaf of lightweight tissue paper on which the subject's name is printed in black at center. Versos of both title leaves and plates blank. Plates printed on heavy unwatermarked wove paper. Contents are as follows:
[1] THE HON. ANTHONY ASQUITH; [2] plate, Michel 733; [3] IVOR BACK, ESQ.; [4] plate, Michel 734; [5] MISS STELLA BENSON; [6] plate, Michel 735; [7] DR. MEYRICK BOOTH; [8] plate, Michel 737; [9] G. K. CHESTERTON, ESQ.; [10] plate, Michel 738; [11] MARCHIONESS OF CHOLMONDELEY; [12] plate, Michel 739; [13] C. B. COCHRAN, ESQ.; [14] plate, Michel 740; [15] NOEL COWARD, ESQ.; [16] plate, Michel 741; [17] REVD. M. C. D'ARCY, S.J.; [18] plate, Michel 743; [19] THOMAS EARP, ESQ.; [20] plate, Michel 746; [21] MISS EDITH EVANS; [22] plate, Michel 752; [23] MRS. DESMOND FLOWER; [24] plate, Michel 754; [25] NEWMAN FLOWER, ESQ.; [26] plate, Michel 755; [27] DESMOND HARMSWORTH, ESQ.; [28] plate, Michel 756; [29] MRS. DESMOND HARMSWORTH; [30] plate, Michel 757; [31] AUGUSTUS JOHN, ESQ.; [32] plate, Michel 769; [33] HENRY JOHN, ESQ.; [34] plate, Michel 770; [35] JAMES JOYCE, ESQ.; [36] plate, Michel 396; [37] CONSTANT LAMBERT, ESQ.; [38] plate, Michel 772; [39] DAVID LOW, ESQ.; [40] plate, Michel 773; [41] DUNCAN MACDONALD, ESQ.; [42] plate, Michel 774; [43] MISS NAOMI MITCHISON; [44] plate, Michel 718; [45] MISS MARIE NEY; [46] plate, Michel 775; [47] WING COMMANDER ORLEBAR; [48] plate, Michel 776; [49] J. B. PRIESTLEY, ESQ.; [50] plate, Michel 777; [51] VISCOUNTESS RHONDDA; [52] plate,

Michel 778; [53] VISCOUNT ROTHERMERE; [54] plate, Michel 779; [55] IVOR STEWART-LIBERTY, ESQ.; [56] plate, Michel 783; [57] A. J. A. SYMONS, ESQ.; [58] plate, Michel 785; [59] MISS REBECCA WEST; [60] plate, Michel 786; [61] SELF-PORTRAIT; [62] plate, Michel 781.

Leaves loosely contained in half white BD cloth portfolio, with black coated paper boards. Cream laid paper pastedowns inside portfolio; three folding wing flaps of white BD cloth with grey and white mottled marbled paper inner facing; white linen ties; white label (3½" x 5") printed in black on front cover: WYNDHAM LEWIS | THIRTY PERSONALITIES | AND A | SELF-PORTRAIT |. Boards measure 15 3/16" x 11¼". Ties measure 10".

Notes. Published early September, 1932 in an edition of approximately 200 copies, and sold at £2.2s.

As Lewis points out in his introduction to the series of portraits, all but two of the drawings were executed in 1932 (the two exceptions are "Naomi Mitchison," Michel 718 which was completed in 1931 and "Drawing of James Joyce," Michel 396 which dates from 1920). Although Lewis claims in his "Preface" to the *Thirty Personalities* exhibition catalogue (Lefevre Galleries, October, see B17) that the drawings were done during the months of July and August, 1932, in a letter to Harmsworth dated June 15, 1932 he asserts that only 20 of the 30 drawings are done (see Rose, *Letters* (A42) no. 198). In this letter Lewis asks Harmsworth, who was traveling in Paris, to secure James Joyce's permission to reproduce Lewis's early drawing of him. Harmsworth replied to Lewis on June 26, 1932 with the news that Joyce had agreed to be included with the other "personalities."

Thirty Personalities and a Self-Portrait was the last of three portfolios of Lewis's art published during his lifetime. Lewis discussed the possibility of publishing another portfolio of portrait drawings featuring "personalities in New York" with Florence Codman, of Arrow Editions in March, 1940. However the project was abandoned because Codman worried that there would not be enough "people well enough informed to buy it," and that therefore commercially the venture would be too risky (see TLS, Florence Codman to Lewis, March 12, 1940, NIC).

A20 THE OLD GANG AND THE NEW GANG 1933

First edition:

THE OLD GANG AND | THE NEW GANG | BY | WYNDHAM LEWIS | DESMOND HARMSWORTH | 44 Great Russell Street | London | 1933

7½" x 4⅞". Collation: A-B^{8}, D^{8}, C^{8} [sic]. Pp. 64; endsheets.

[1] half-title; [3] title; [4] Printed in England at | The Westminster Press | 411a Harrow Road | W.9; 5-6 Foreword; [7]-62 text; [64] [*printer's device*] | The Westminster Press | 411a Harrow Road | London, W.9

Two variant bindings, no priority (binding (2) much rarer than (1) however):
(1). Bound in grey and black pepper-colored BF cloth, in a zigzag pattern, stamped in black running down spine: THE OLD GANG & THE NEW GANG WYNDHAM LEWIS |. Issued in grey dustjacket printed in red (advertisement for *A Tip from the Augean Stable* on back inner flap, never published, see G2). Top edge trimmed and unstained; other edges partially trimmed. Heavy laid unwatermarked paper.
(2). Bound in red V cloth, stamped in black as above. Otherwise same as (1).

Notes. Published January, 1933 in an edition of 1000 copies, and sold at 3s. 6d.
Subsequent to the withdrawal of the English edition of *The Doom of Youth* (A15b) in late Summer, 1932, Lewis published this short treatise concerning the emergence of the new school of political dictators rising to replace the "old gang" of capitalist politicians. The theme reviewed in *The Old Gang and the New Gang* reiterates the argument presented originally in Chap. 8 of *The Doom of Youth,* "The Old and the New Capitalism" ([33]-39).
Reprinted by Haskell House, series #80, 1972, at $7.95.

A21a ONE-WAY SONG [1933]

Limited, signed edition:

BY WYNDHAM LEWIS | [*within partially framing design by Lewis, Michel* 795] ENGINE FIGHT-TALK | THE SONG OF THE MILITANT ROMANCE | IF SO THE MAN YOU | ARE | ONE-WAY SONG | ENVOI | [*beneath framing design*] LONDON | FABER AND FABER LIMITED | 24 RUSSELL SQUARE

8¾" x 6". Collation: *A*^{8}, B-G^{8}, H^{10}. Pp. 132; endsheets.

[1] *This Edition printed on English hand-made paper is* | *Limited to forty signed and numbered copies* | *This is number* [*number and signature in ink, in Lewis's hand*]; [3] ONE-WAY SONG; [5] title; [6] FIRST PUBLISHED IN NOVEMBER MCMXXXIII | BY FABER AND FABER LIMITED | 24 RUSSELL SQUARE LONDON W. C. 1 | PRINTED IN GREAT BRITAIN BY | R. MACLEHOSE

AND COMPANY LIMITED | THE UNIVERSITY PRESS GLASGOW | ALL RIGHTS RESERVED; 7 table of contents; [9]-132 text.

Bound in white vellum, stamped in gold on front cover: ONE-WAY SONG | WYNDHAM LEWIS |. Stamped in gold running down spine: ONE-WAY SONG *by* WYNDHAM LEWIS F&F |. Fore-edges of boards fold over to cover paper fore-edges. Headband at crown; top edge trimmed and gilt; fore-edge uncut; bottom edge trimmed. Wove unwatermarked hand-made paper, untrimmed edges deckled. Issued in plain tissue jacket.
Publisher's prospectus issued in advance of publication:
ONE-WAY | SONG | [*design by Lewis, Michel* 795] | WYNDHAM LEWIS |. 8¾" x 5¾". Single sheet folded once to make [4] pp. as follows: [1] title, as above; [2-3] text, extracts from reviews; [4] advertisements and order form. Wove unwatermarked cream paper, printed in black.

Plates. Besides the title page design, Lewis designed the vignettes reproduced on the four divisional half-titles: [9] Michel 797; [19] Michel 798; [31] Michel 799; 83, Michel 800. "Envoi" has no divisional half-title (see Michel 804, for Lewis's design for "Envoi" which was not used).

Notes. Published November 2, 1933 in an edition of 40 copies, and sold at 31s. 6d.

Originally entitled *The Song of the Front,* this book of satirical poetry was to be published by Cassell & Co. in December, 1932 but Lewis failed to deliver the manuscript by the end of September, as the production schedule stipulated, and Cassell waived rights. In a letter to Desmond Harmsworth dated June 15, 1932 Lewis indicates that he is working on the poem and that at Harmsworth's request he will show it to him when the piece is finished (see Rose, *Letters* (A42) p. 210). The final version of the poem as published in the first edition contains the following five sections: *Engine Fight-Talk–The Song of the Militant Romance–If So the Man You Are–One-Way Song–Envoi.* Canto 20 of "If So the Man You Are" (p. 55) consists only of a facsimile reproduction of a telegram sent from Lewis to Faber with a message reading "Delete that canto enemy." Lewis received an advance of £150. This edition went out of print on May 11, 1943. A few copies were issued with the words "Out of series" written in ink above Lewis's signature on the limitation page.

A second edition of *One-Way Song* was published by Methuen on February 25, 1960 at 15s., containing a foreword by T. S. Eliot (7-10). Although Eliot indicates in his foreword that the text of the second edition is identical to the text of the first edition, the canto mentioned above consisting of a telegram is omitted without explanation, and subsequent cantos are renumbered accordingly. Furthermore, lines 9-12 of canto 18 in "If So the Man You Are" are deleted, with surrounding lines altered to grammatically accomodate the change. Lines 21-22 of the same canto are also omitted, with an alteration in line 23 made silently to cover the alteration. From canto 25 of "If So the Man You Are" (which is numbered "24" in the second edition), lines 20-22 are also deleted, without alterations in adjacent lines, inexpertly leaving one of the rhymed couplets (the form in which the entire poem is written) halved and incomplete. The reason for these deletions seems to be centered around Lewis's theme in the passages in question: Lewis's *Hitler* and its controversial reception. Who was responsible for these silent alterations in the text is undetermined. The text of the second edition contains, also, a number of printer's errors, many of which are listed in Tom Kinninmont, "A Note on One-Way Song," *Lewisletter, No. 3* (F1821) 7.

"The Song of the Militant Romance" was broadcast by the B.B.C. Third Programme on January 14, 1949. According to a letter from B.B.C. representative E.M. Layton to Lewis dated February 10, 1949, the context of the reading of Lewis's poem was to "illustrate" arguments set forth by Julian Symons in his broadcast talk "The Romantic Reaction in Modern Poetry."

A21b *First trade edition:*

BY WYNDHAM LEWIS | [*within partially framing design by Lewis, Michel* 795] ENGINE FIGHT-TALK | THE SONG OF | THE MILITANT ROMANCE | IF SO THE MAN YOU | ARE | ONE-WAY SONG | ENVOI | [*beneath framing design*] LONDON | FABER AND FABER LIMITED | 24 RUSSELL SQUARE

8 11/16" x 5½". Collation: A^8, B-G^8, H^{10}. Pp. 132; endsheets.

[3] half-title; [5] title; [6] FIRST PUBLISHED IN NOVEMBER MCMXXXIII | BY FABER AND FABER LIMITED | 24 RUSSELL SQUARE LONDON W. C. 1 | PRINTED IN GREAT BRITAIN BY | R. MACLEHOSE AND COMPANY LIMITED | THE UNIVERSITY PRESS GLASCOW | ALL RIGHTS RESERVED; 7 table of contents; [9]-132 text.

Bound in light tan V cloth, stamped in blue on front cover: ONE-WAY SONG | WYNDHAM LEWIS |. Stamped in blue running down spine: ONE-WAY SONG *by* WYNDHAM LEWIS F&F |. Issued in white dustjacket, with design by Lewis (Michel 795) printed in blue on front cover, and lettering printed in black. Top edge trimmed and stained blue; fore-edge uncut; bottom edge slightly trimmed. Unwatermarked wove paper.

Notes. Published November 2, 1933 and sold at 7s. 6d.

Textually identical to A21a. The Sir William Rothenstein-Cornell copy has the following corrections in Lewis's hand:

p. 35, line *6*	"by" corrected "my"
54, *8*	"every" corrected "very"
99, *1*	"it's" corrected "it is"
123, *14*	"clatter" corrected "chatter"

This edition went out of print March 26, 1943.

A22 MEN WITHOUT ART [1934]

First edition:

[*Double rule, thick over fine*] | MEN WITHOUT ART | [*double rule, fine over broad*] | *By* | WYNDHAM LEWIS | [*publisher's device*] | CASSELL & COMPANY LIMITED | London, Toronto, Melbourne | and Sydney

8½" x 5¼". Collation: *A*^{8}, B-T^{8}. Pp. 304; endsheets.

[1] half-title; [3] title; [4] *First published* 1934 | PRINTED IN GREAT BRITAIN | BY THE EDINBURGH PRESS, EDINBURGH | [*registration code*]; 5 table of contents; 7-14 Introduction; [15]-292 text; [293]-[304] Appendix.

Bound in dark green V cloth, stamped in gold on spine: [*rule*] | MEN | WITHOUT | ART | [*star*] | WYNDHAM | LEWIS | CASSELL | [*rule*] |. Issued in brick-red dustjacket, printed in black. Top edge stained green; all edges trimmed. Laid unwatermarked paper; endsheets wove cream paper. Some copies issued with publisher's advertisement for *The English Novel, Twenty Essays by Contemporary Novelists,* edited by Derek Verschoyle laid in.

Notes. Published October 4, 1934 in an edition of 1500 copies, and sold at 10s. 6d.

Lewis received £150 advance on royalties for this collection of essays and criticism. Sections of *Men Without Art* were previously published in *Satire & Fiction* (D152, "The Taxi-Cab-Driver Test"), *Time and Tide* (D184, "Fénelon and his Valet"; D185, "The Artist and the New Gothic"; D186, "Flaubert as a Marxist"), *Life and Letters* (D200, "The Dumb Ox: a Study of Ernest Hemingway"—see also D203 for reprint preceding book publication; D202, "A Moralist with a Corn Cob: A Study of William Faulkner"), *The New Statesman and Nation* (D201, "In Praise of Outsiders"—considerably rewritten for inclusion in II, Chap. 2), *The Bookman* (D206, "Art in a Machine Age"; D214, " 'Classical Revival' in England"), *Current History* (D207, "The Propagandist in Fiction") and *The London Mercury* (D215, "Studies in the Art of Laughter"). In a letter dated July 19, 1934 from Lewis to Desmond Flower, director of Cassell, he regrets that the title of the book cannot be changed from *Men Without Art* to *Literary Barrens* (see Rose, *Letters* (A42) no. 211). Apparently production of the book was too far advanced to allow for this alteration.

Lewis received notice from Cassell that *Men Without Art* and *The Revenge for Love* had been officially declared out of print by the publishers, and wrote Flower on September 9, 1946 asking whether they intended to reprint the books (NIC). Lewis mentions in this letter that extensive revisions would be required before either book could be republished, and suggests that a new contract be drawn up. In Flower's response, dated September 17, 1946, he declines to reprint *The Revenge for Love* and proposes to bring out *Men Without Art* in a "cheap edition" after Lewis has made necessary revisions to the text to bring it up to date (NIC). Flower offers, furthermore, to make payment of an advance on publication equal to the amount of royalty earned on subscription sales. Lewis's indignant response to Flower, dated October 12, 1946, essentially terminated his business relations with Cassell. In this letter (NIC) Lewis states that a revised edition of *Men Without Art* with a new preface would have excellent chances of selling well, but not in a "cheap" edition, and that since Cassell evidently had no serious intentions regarding the book he believes the only "decent" thing to do is revert rights to him, so that he can have the book properly republished.

First American edition photographically reprinting A22, published by Russell & Russell, February, 1964 in an edition of 817 copies, sold at $7.50. Reprinted in 1966, 420 copies at $9.50, and in 1969, 400 copies at $9.50. First two printings bound in light brown V cloth, issued in plain brown dustjacket printed in black on front only; third printing bound in green V cloth. Excerpts reprinted in *A Soldier of Humor* (A43), *Enemy Salvoes* (A48) and Roger Sale, ed. *Discussions of the Novel* (Boston: D. C. Heath and Company, [1960]), pp. [88]-90 ("The Taxi-Cab Driver Test for 'Fiction' ").

A23 LEFT WINGS OVER EUROPE [1936]

First edition:

LEFT WINGS | OVER | EUROPE: | or, | How to Make a War | About Nothing | *by* | WYNDHAM LEWIS | [*publisher's device*] | JONATHAN CAPE | THIRTY BEDFORD SQUARE | LONDON

7⅞" x 5¼". Collation: A^8, B-X^8. Pp. 336; endsheets.

[1] half-title; [2] By the same author | [*list of nineteen titles; sixth title reads:* "THE ROARING QUEAN | (in preparation)"]; [3] title; [4] FIRST PUBLISHED 1936

| JONATHAN CAPE LTD. 30 BEDFORD SQUARE, LONDON | AND 91 WELLINGTON STREET WEST, TORONTO | PRINTED IN GREAT BRITAIN IN THE CITY OF OXFORD | AT THE ALDEN PRESS | BOUND BY A.W. BAIN & CO. LTD. | PAPER MADE BY JOHN DICKINSON & CO. LTD.; 5-9 table of contents; 11-21 Foreword; [29]-333 text.

Bound in bright red V cloth, stamped in black on front cover: LEFT WINGS OVER EUROPE |. Stamped in black on spine: LEFT WINGS | OVER | EUROPE | WYNDHAM | LEWIS | [*publisher's device at foot*] |. Issued in dustjacket black on spine and front cover, white on other faces; lettering in red, white and black. Top edge trimmed and stained red; fore-edge trimmed; bottom edge untrimmed. Wove unwatermarked paper.

Notes. Published June, 1936 in an edition of 1500 copies, and sold at 7s. 6d.

Original title for the book was *Bourgeois-Bolshevism and World War,* which Lewis was still using as late as April, 1936 (see Rose, *Letters* (A42) p. 237). Advance subscription orders for over 500 copies were received by the publisher by late May, 1936; 1378 copies sold by August 27, 1936. A second printing was made in late August, 1936, and is identical to the first edition, with the spelling of Lewis's novel *The Roaring Queen* altered on p. [2] from "QUEAN" to read "QUEEN" and publication information on p. [4] revised.

Reprinted by Gordon Press in June, 1972, at $60.00. Concepts outlined in Part I, Chap. 1 reiterated in an article published in *The English Review* for July, 1936 (D241), "The Big Soft 'Centre.' "

A24 COUNT YOUR DEAD: THEY ARE ALIVE! [1937]

First edition:

COUNT YOUR DEAD: | THEY ARE ALIVE! | *or* | A NEW WAR IN THE MAKING | *by* | WYNDHAM LEWIS | [*design by Lewis, Michel 884*] | LOVAT DICKSON LIMITED | PUBLISHERS | LONDON

7¾" x 5¼". Collation: A^8, B-Z^8. Pp. viii, 360; endsheets.

[i] half-title; [ii] *BY THE SAME AUTHOR* | [*list of twenty titles*]; [iii] title; [iv] FIRST PUBLISHED 1937 | [*publisher's device*] | LOVAT DICKSON LIMITED 38 BEDFORD STREET LONDON | AND ST MARTIN'S HOUSE BOND STREET TORONTO | SET AND PRINTED IN GREAT BRITAIN BY | LATIMER TREND & COMPANY LIMITED MOUNT PLEASANT

PLYMOUTH | PAPER SUPPLIED BY SPALDING & HODGE LIMITED | BOUND BY G. & J. KITCAT LIMITED | SET IN MONOTYPE BASKERVILLE; v-vii table of contents; 1-9 Foreword; [11]-358 text; [360] publisher's advertisements.

Bound in light yellow V cloth, rectangular rule frame designed by Lewis (Michel 885, similar to Michel 884) stamped in blue on front cover, and stamped in blue on spine: COUNT | YOUR DEAD | -THEY ARE | ALIVE! | WYNDHAM | LEWIS | [*publisher's device*] | LOVAT DICKSON |. Issued in white dustjacket, printed in black, and with design by Lewis in black on spine (Michel 885) and front cover (Michel 884). Top edge trimmed and stained blue; other edges trimmed. Wove unwatermarked paper.
Publisher's prospectus issued in advance of publication:
[*Design by Lewis, Michel 884, at left*] A NEW VENTURE | IN AUTHORSHIP | [*text about the book*]
8" x 5¼". Single leaf folded to make 4 pp. as follows: [1] title, as above; 2-3 text advertising the book; [4] text over order form. White wove paper, printed in black.

Notes. Published April 26, 1937 in an edition of approximately 1500 copies, and sold at 7s. 6d.

Although a letter from Lewis to Lovat Dickson (undated, but about March, 1937, see Rose, *Letters* (A42) p. 244) reveals that one of the publisher's libel lawyers who had read *Count Your Dead* considered passages refering to Lloyd George "presumably another invention or distortion of the author's," and potentially libellous, publication was not delayed and no actions were brought against the book.

First American edition published June, 1972 by Gordon Press at $50.00. Excerpts reprinted in *The American Review* (D244).

A25a THE REVENGE FOR LOVE [1937]

First edition:

THE REVENGE | FOR LOVE | By | WYNDHAM LEWIS | [*publisher's device*] | CASSELL | AND COMPANY, LIMITED | LONDON, TORONTO, MELBOURNE | AND SYDNEY

7⅜" x 5¼". Collation: A^8, B-I^8, J^8, K-U^8, V-W^8, X-Z^8, $2A^8$. Pp. [viii], 424; endsheets.

[iii] half-title; [iv] *BY THE SAME AUTHOR* | [*rule*] | [*list of twenty titles*]; [v] title; [vi] First published 1937 | Printed in Great Britain by | Greycaine Limited, Watford, Herts. | F.337; [vii] table of contents; [1]-422 text.

Bound in pink V cloth, stamped in gold on spine: *THE* | *REVENGE* | *FOR LOVE* | [*thick rule*] | *Wyndham* | *Lewis* | *CASSELL* |. Issued in blue dustjacket, printed in black, rules in black, uniform with *Men Without Art* and *Snooty Baronet*. All edges trimmed and unstained. Wove unwatermarked paper. Some copies have blue paper label printed in black giving adjusted price of "6′-/NET," which is tipped on to spine of dustjacket over printed price of "8′6 / NET."

Notes. Published May, 1937 in an edition of 2389 copies, and sold at 8s. 6d. (later reduced to 6s. net).

Originally entitled *False Bottoms,* and later changed at the request of the publisher, *The Revenge for Love* was largely written by Lewis in 1934-1935 between long periods of illness and concern with producing articles and pieces of journalism to support himself. The manuscript was completed in Autumn, 1935 and was submitted to Desmond Flower of Cassell in early November, 1935. Lewis was contractually committed to publish one more book with Cassell (who had already brought out *Men Without Art* and *Snooty Baronet*). In a note from Flower to Lewis dated November 12, 1935 he states that his initial reaction to the novel is most favorable and that he is "enjoying" reading it. However, publication was considerably delayed due to Cassell's recurrent demands that various alterations be made in the text of the novel to preclude libel suits. Lewis sent Flower a formal complaint on May 6, 1936 (NIC), asserting that delays caused by the censor's department of Boots Lending Library and Cassell have forced him to decide that he must "immediately . . . terminate [his] contract" with Cassell. Flower's response, dated May 8, 1936, indicates that Boots' report on the book was extremely unfavorable, and that further "radical" alterations would have to be made before the book could have a fair chance of selling. Flower also mentions in this letter (NIC) that he is "reluctantly compelled" to agree with Lewis's suggestion that the contract be ended. Newman Flower, co-director of Cassells, wrote Lewis on May 25, 1936, stating that although the author has been "very kind" in taking out certain libellous passages from the novel, it still seems "unsuited" and "wrong" for Cassells. On July 22, 1936 he wrote Lewis once more, suggesting that Jonathan Cape (who had just published *Left Wings Over Europe*) take the novel.

Finally Cassell agreed to publish *The Revenge for Love.* Lewis spent mid-November, 1936 through March, 1937 correcting galleys and page proofs of the novel, with Arthur Hayward overseeing the production on behalf of Cassell. In an interesting letter (November, 1936) to Desmond Flower, Lewis states that as he was correcting proofs he realized that "this book that is thus about to be contemptuously flung upon the market is probably the best complete work of fiction I have written; & you may agree that [it is just possible?] that in the future it will be considered one of the best books in English to appear during the current 12 months" (see Rose, *Letters* (A42), no. 230: phrase within brackets omitted from Rose's text though present in the original fragment, NIC). As late as February 23, 1937 Lewis was still being asked to alter potentially libellous passages (TLS, Hayward to Lewis, NIC).

On August 24, 1938 500 copies were reprinted from the same type and bound as above edition, with paper label pasted on spine of dustjacket giving new price of 6s. Out of print August 11, 1942. Paper edition published by Penguin at 60p., 1972.

A25b *Second English edition:*

The Revenge for Love | WYNDHAM LEWIS | [*publisher's device*] | METHUEN & CO. LTD., LONDON | *36 Essex Street, Strand, W.C.2*

7¼" x 4¾". Collation: *1*^{8}, 2-24^8. Pp. [vi], 378; endsheets.

[i] half-title; [ii] *By the same author* | [*list of three titles*]; [iii] title; [iv] *Originally published in 1937* | *First published by Methuen & Co. Ltd. in 1952* | [*catalogue number*] | PRINTED IN GREAT BRITAIN; [v] table of contents; 1-[377] text; [378] PRINTED BY | JARROLD AND SONS LTD. | NORWICH

Bound in light grey V cloth, stamped in gold upon two red rectangular fields at head and foot of spine: [*at head:*] THE | REVENGE | FOR | LOVE | [*star*] | Wyndham | Lewis | [*at foot:*] Methuen |. Issued in light blue dustjacket, decorative design in blue and pale salmon, lettering printed in blue, designed by Charles Handley-Read. All edges trimmed and unstained. Wove unwatermarked paper.

Notes. Published June 19, 1952 in an edition of 3000 copies, and sold at 15s.

Lewis wrote the dustjacket blurb in September, 1951. This edition reprints A25a.

A25c *First American edition:*

THE REVENGE | *FOR LOVE* | [*rule*] | WYNDHAM LEWIS | [*publisher's device*] | HENRY REGNERY COMPANY | CHICAGO, 1952

8¼" x 5⅜". Collation: *1-11*^{16}. Pp. [vi], 346; endsheets.

[i] half-title [ii] *By the same author* | ROTTING HILL | [*rule*]; [iii] title; [iv] Copyright 1952 | HENRY REGNERY COMPANY | Chicago 4, Illinois | Manufactured in the United States of America; [v] table of contents; [1] internal half-title; [3]-341 text.

Bound in smooth blue V cloth, stamped in gold running down spine: LEWIS | [*double rule running across spine*] | *THE REVENGE FOR LOVE* | [*double rule, as above*] | REGNERY |. Issued in white coated paper dustjacket, with decorative design printed on front cover and spine in blue, green and yellow, lettering in black, white and blue. All edges trimmed and unstained. Wove unwatermarked paper.

Notes. Published in October, 1952 in an edition of 5000 copies, and sold at $3.50.

A26 BLASTING AND BOMBARDIERING 1937

First edition:

BLASTING | *&* | *BOMBARDIERING* | [*ornamental flourish*] | *Wyndham* | *Lewis* | *London* | *Eyre & Spottiswoode* | *1937*

8½" x 5½". Collation: π^4, 1-19^8, *20*^{4}. Pp. 312; endsheets. 20 plates not included in collation or pagination.

[i] half-title; [ii] *Mr. Wyndham Lewis has also written* | [*list of 21 titles in six sections*]; [iii] title; [iv] FIRST PRINTED - 1937 | PRINTED IN GREAT BRITAIN FOR | EYRE AND SPOTTISWOODE (PUBLISHERS) LTD.; [v]-vi table of contents; [vii] list of illustrations; 1-308 text; 309-312 Index.

Two variant bindings, priority as follows:

(1). Orange V cloth, stamped in black on spine: BLASTING | AND | BOMBARDIERING | WYNDHAM | LEWIS | Eyre and | Spottiswoode |. Issued in light cream dustjacket decorated in yellow and black, and lettered in black. Top edge trimmed and stained yellow; other edges trimmed and unstained. Laid unwatermarked paper; cream wove endsheets.

(2). Bound in orange V cloth over slightly limp boards, stamped in black on spine as (1). All edges trimmed and unstained. Otherwise same as (1).

Plates. Wove, unwatermarked paper, leaves mounted facing pages as given below, all plates printed in black: [iii], Michel 725; 32, two photographs of Lewis, "The Bombardier" and "The Battery Officer"; 91, photograph of Lewis, "The Author of *Tarr*"; 94, Michel 786; 188, two photographs of Lewis's parents, "The Mother and Father of the Author"; 198, Michel 769; (four plates printed on 4 leaves sewn in middle of Sig. 14, first two plates on rectos of leaves, last two plates on versos of third and fourth leaves) Michel 643, 614, 483, 459; 224, Michel 854; 228, Michel 743; 230, Michel 776; 238, Michel 524; 272, Michel 396; 280, Michel 412; 284, Michel 947; 305, photograph of Lewis, "Mr. Wyndham Lewis"; 306, Michel 891.

Notes. Published October, 1937 in an edition of 2000 copies, and sold at 15s.

Blasting and Bombardiering is the first of two primarily autobiographical books, followed by *Rude Assignment: A Narrative of My Career Up-to-Date* (A35), which is not, however, textually sequential. *Blasting and Bombardiering* covers the period from 1914-1926, as stated on the dustjacket. Of the 2000 copies printed, 40 were distributed to reviewers without charge; 1007 copies bound up initially in binding (1) in 1937; copies bound in 1938 (400 sets of sheets) and 1941 (100 sets of sheets) in binding (2); 879 copies sold by December 6, 1937. William Morrow and Co. had contracted with Lewis to publish the book in the United States (contract dated February 6, 1937, copy in NIC) but declined to publish it, declaring that the book was unmarketable in America.

Second edition published by Methuen in October, 1970 (hardbound priced £2.10; paperbound edition priced £1.25). which includes a new Preface by [Mrs.] Anne Wyndham Lewis ([vii]), "The King of the Trenches" (171-183, previously unpublished), "Cantleman's Spring-Mate" (304-311), "The War Baby" (312-336) as well as numerous alterations, deletions and additions to the text by Mrs. Lewis. This edition eliminates the index present in the first edition, and reproduces the same illustrations in a different sequence. On July 10, 1967 the University of California Press published the first American edition using the same sheets as the Methuen edition, with the title page and dustjacket altered to give their imprint. Approximately 1500 copies published at $7.50. Excerpts reprinted in *A Soldier of Humor* (A43) and *Wyndham Lewis An Anthology* (A44).

A27 THE MYSTERIOUS MR BULL 1938

First edition:

The Mysterious Mr Bull | [*swelled rule*] | *BY* | WYNDHAM LEWIS | [*publisher's device*] | LONDON | ROBERT HALE LIMITED | 102 GREAT RUSSELL STREET W.C.1 | MCMXXXVIII

7⅝" x 4⅞". Collation: A^8, B-S^8. Pp. 288; endsheets.

[3] half-title; [4] *By the same author* | [*list of twenty-three titles*]; [5] title; 7-8 table of contents; 9-21 Foreword; [23]-287 text; [288] PRINTED IN GREAT BRITAIN | BY WESTERN PRINTING SERVICES LTD., BRISTOL

Two variant bindings, priority as follows:
(1). Pink V cloth, spine stamped in gold: [*in grey blocked field framed with gold rule border*] THE | MYSTERIOUS | MR BULL | *Wyndham* | *Lewis* | [*at foot, not in blocked field*] Robert Hale |. Issued in pinkish cream dustjacket, front cover and spine pink, with decorative designs in light blue and black, lettering in black. All edges trimmed; top edge stained blue. Wove unwatermarked paper.
(2). Blue V cloth, stamped in gold on spine: [*within single rule rectangular frame*] THE | MYSTERIOUS | MR BULL | Wyndham | Lewis | [*at foot, not within frame*] Robert Hale |. All edges trimmed and unstained, otherwise same as (1).

Notes. Published November 7, 1938, and sold at 7s. 6d. Number of copies printed unknown (publisher's records destroyed).

A28 THE JEWS ARE THEY HUMAN? [1939]

First edition:

The Jews | ARE THEY HUMAN? | *BY* | WYNDHAM LEWIS | [*double rule, thin over thick*] | LONDON | *George Allen & Unwin Ltd* | MUSEUM STREET

7¼" x 4¾". Collation: A^8, B-G^8. Pp. 112; endsheets.

[1] half-title; [2] *of similar interest* | THE SHORTEST WAY WITH | THE JEWS | *by* | PETER HARLOW; [3] title; [4] FIRST PUBLISHED IN 1939 | *All Rights Reserved* | *Made and Printed in Great Britain by C. Tinling & Co., Ltd.,* | *Liverpool, London, and Prescot.;* [5] table of contents; 7-14 Foreword; 15-111 text.

Bound in red V cloth, and stamped in black on front cover: *The Jews* | ARE THEY | HUMAN | ? | [*triple rule*] | . Stamped in black on spine: WYNDHAM | LEWIS | [*triple rule*] | *The* | *Jews* | ARE | THEY | HUMAN | ? | [*triple rule*] | GEORGE | ALLEN & | UNWIN | . Issued in pale salmon scarlet dustjacket, lettering and rules printed in black. All edges trimmed and unstained. Wove unwatermarked paper.

Notes. Published March 21, 1939 in an edition of 1750 copies, and sold at 3s. 6d.

This discussion of anti-Semitism was reprinted by Gordon Press, New York, in June, 1972 at $45.00; also incorporated in *Hitler, the Germans and the Jews* published by Gordon Press.

A29 WYNDHAM LEWIS THE ARTIST, FROM 'BLAST' TO BURLINGTON HOUSE [1939]

First edition:

WYNDHAM LEWIS | THE ARTIST | FROM 'BLAST' TO BURLINGTON HOUSE | By | Wyndham Lewis | LAIDLAW [*triple rule*] & LAIDLAW

9" x 6¼". Collation: *A*[8], B-Z[8], 2A[6] (12 leaves mounted not included in collation, see plates below). Pp. 380; endsheets.

[1] half-title; [3] title; [4] First published 1939 | LAIDLAW & LAIDLAW LTD. | 32 Alfred Place, London W.C. 1 | Made in Great Britain | Printed by Sherratt & Hughes, at the St. Ann's Press | Timperley, Cheshire | Set in Caslon [*sic*] Old Face; 5 Preface; 7 table of contents; 9 list of illustrations; [11]-[380] text.

Bound in green V cloth, stamped in gold on spine: WYNDHAM | LEWIS | THE ARTIST | FROM | 'BLAST' | TO | BURLINGTON | HOUSE | WYNDHAM | LEWIS | LAIDLAW | . Issued in light brown dustjacket, with color plate reproduction of Lewis's portrait of T.S. Eliot (Michel P80) printed on coated paper, mounted on front, and design in black on spine (Michel 942); lettering printed in black. *First issue* has top edge trimmed and stained green, *second issue* has top edge unstained; both issues have fore-edge uncut and bottom edge partially trimmed.
Prospectus issued in advance of publication:
WYNDHAM LEWIS | THE ARTIST | FROM 'BLAST' TO BURLINGTON HOUSE | By | Wyndham Lewis | A BOOK FOR ARTISTS AND THOSE | INTERESTED IN THE ARTS | [*within double rule compartment:*] With Three Reproductions in Colour, | Six in Half Tone, and Numerous Line | Blocks |

PRICE 15/-NET | [*below compartment, above triple rule:*] LAIDLAW [*beneath triple rule:*] & LAIDLAW

9¼" x 6¼". Single leaf folded once to make [4] pp. as follows: [1] title, as above; [2] table of contents and list of illustrations; [3] publisher's blurb, review extracts; [4] publisher's advertisements, order form. Issued with color reproduction of Lewis's portrait of T.S. Eliot (Michel P80) printed on single leaf of coated paper, laid in. Prospectus printed in black on coated paper.

Plates. Printed on coated paper, mounted and stabbed, in black and white unless otherwise noted, facing the following pages: [3], Michel P80 (color reproduction); 48, Michel 809; 80, Michel P72 (color); 112, Michel 476; 144, Michel 627; 176, Michel 780; 224, Michel P61 (color); 240, Michel 634 (printed on uncoated wove paper); 352, Michel 847. All versos blank. Vignette designs by Lewis on 186, 232 (same design as on spine), 237 and 267.

Notes. Published May, 1939 and sold at 15s.

Contract between Lewis and Laidlaw & Laidlaw signed January 6, 1939. Although Lewis agreed in March, 1939 to write another book for Laidlaw & Laidlaw, and accepted an advance of £40 against the projected receipt of the manuscript in July, 1939, this is in fact the only title he published with this firm.

Reprints slightly revised versions of the following previously published texts: "Vorteces and Notes" *(Blast, No. 1,* D24, with additional notes in this version and the deletion of "The Melodrama of Modernity"), "A Review of Contemporary Art" and "The Art of the Great Race" *(Blast, No. 2,* D41 and D42, the first article omitting an introductory note and the second adding one), "The Caliph's Design" (A4), "Essay on the Objective of Plastic Art in Life" *(The Tyro, No. 2,* D107) and a number of letters concerning the rejection of the Eliot portrait by the Royal Academy.

Reprinted by Haskell House, as part of series #80, 1971, at $17.95. Excerpts reprinted in *A Soldier of Humor* (A43) and *Wyndham Lewis on Art* (A45).

A30 THE HITLER CULT [1939]

First edition:

The hitler Cult | BY WYNDHAM LEWIS | DENT · LONDON

7⅝" x 5". Collation: A^6, B-R^8, S^6. Pp. x, 270; endsheets.

[i] half-title; [iii] title; [iv] *All rights reserved* | *Made in Great Britain* | *at The Temple Press Letchworth* | *for* | *J. M. Dent & Sons Ltd.* | *Aldine House Bedford St. London* |

First Published 1939; v-vi table of contents; vii-x Foreword; [1]-255 text; [257]-267 Index; [269] printer's device.

Bound in black V cloth, stamped in silver on spine: The | hitler | Cult | WYNDHAM | LEWIS | [*blind-stamped*] DENT |. Issued in yellow dustjacket, printed in black and red. Top edge trimmed and stained red; other edges trimmed. Wove unwatermarked paper.

Notes. Published December 7, 1939 in an edition of 2500 copies (1750 copies extant after July, 1949), and sold for 7s. 6d.

Sales were initially brisk, 665 copies having been sold in England and 209 in Canada and the United States by December 31, 1939. However, a total of only 1750 copies were sold by July 22, 1949 at which time the publishers declared the title out of print and destroyed the remaining copies. In a letter to Lewis from his friend Iris Barry, dated November 29, 1939 (NIC) it is apparent that Random House had considered publishing the book in the United States, but had declined. Barry reports that the manuscript "isn't lost after all" and that she will try to get the book serialized, but that Lewis should not count on success since she is not "in with the literary pundits or powers-that-be" in the New York publishing world. *The Hitler Cult* did not appear under an American imprint until Gordon Press published a reprint in June, 1972 at $63.95. Also incorporated in their edition of *Hitler, the Germans and the Jews.*

A31 AMERICA, I PRESUME [1940]

First edition:

[*Title within frame, thick and fine double rule*] America, | I Presume | [*swelled rule*] | *By Wyndham Lewis* | [*rule*] | HOWELL, SOSKIN & CO. · *Publishers*

7⅜" x 4⅞". Collation: *1-19*^{8}. Pp. [vi], 298; endsheets.

[i] half-title; [iii] title; [iv] *Copyright, 1940, by Wyndham Lewis* | ALL RIGHTS RESERVED | MANUFACTURED ENTIRELY IN THE UNITED STATES | AMERICAN BOOK—STRATFORD PRESS, INC., NEW YORK; [v] table of contents; [1] internal half-title; 3-298 text.

Bound in red V cloth, stamped in blue on front cover: America, | I presume |. Stamped in blue on spine: WYNDHAM | LEWIS | [*ornament*] | America, | I Presume | [*ornament*] | HOWELL, | SOSKIN |. Issued in white dustjacket, light blue on front and spine; decorated with black fields, white rules, and light blue triangular ornamental rules; lettered in pink, black and white. All edges trimmed and unstained. Wove unwatermarked paper.

Notes. Published August 12, 1940 and sold at $2.50.

Reprinted by Haskell House, New York, in 1972, at $14.95. Excerpts reprinted in *Wyndham Lewis An Anthology* (A44).

A32 ANGLOSAXONY: A LEAGUE THAT WORKS [1941]

First edition:

ANGLOSAXONY: | A League that Works | BY | WYNDHAM LEWIS | Author of *Time and Western Man, The Lion and the Fox,* | *The Revenge for Love,* etc. | [*publisher's device*] | THE RYERSON PRESS ~TORONTO

7½" x 5⅛". Collation: 1-5^8. Pp. [iv], 76.

[i] title; [ii] COPYRIGHT, CANADA, 1941, BY | THE RYERSON PRESS, TORONTO | All rights reserved. No part of this | book may be reproduced in any | form, by mimeograph or any other | means (except by reviewers for the | public press), without permission | in writing from the publishers. | PRINTED AND BOUND IN CANADA | BY THE RYERSON PRESS, TORONTO; [iii] table of contents; 1-75 text.

Bound in bright yellow paper wrappers, measuring same as sheets, printed in black on front cover: ANGLOSAXONY: | *A League that Works* | WYNDHAM LEWIS |. Printed in black running down spine: ANGLOSAXONY: *A League that Works* ~ WYNDHAM LEWIS |. Review extracts in black on back. Wove unwatermarked paper. Sewn; spine flat. Some copies have printed business slip for American distributors, Bruce Humphries, Inc., Publishers, laid in (NYPL, SUNY at Buffalo).

Notes. Published June 30, 1941 in an edition of 1500 copies, and sold at 75¢.

Only 284 copies were sold by the end of 1941, and 26 further copies were sold by February 28, 1944. No record of further sales nor information on the disposition of the remaining 1190 copies exists, according to the publishers. In most copies distributed in the United States the distributors, Bruce Humphries, Inc. Publishers, had a printed slip mounted over "[*publisher's device*] | THE RYERSON PRESS~TORONTO" on the titlepage, printed in black, which reads: "BRUCE HUMPHRIES, INC. PUBLISHERS | [*publisher's device*] | BOSTON, U.S.A. |."

A33a THE VULGAR STREAK [1941]

First edition, first impression:

THE | VULGAR STREAK | *By* | WYNDHAM LEWIS | Robert Hale Limited | 102 Great Russell Street | London WC 1

7¼" x 4¾". Collation: A^6, $B\text{-}P^8$, Q^6. Pp. 248; endsheets.

[1] half-title; [2] By the same author | [*rule*] | [*list of twenty-four titles*]; [3] title; [4] *First published in Great Britain,* 1941 | PRINTED IN GREAT BRITAIN | BY WESTERN PRINTING SERVICES LTD., BRISTOL; 5-6 table of contents; [7]-247 text.

Bound in light blue V cloth, stamped in silver on spine: THE | VULGAR | STREAK | [*star*] | WYNDHAM | LEWIS | ROBERT | HALE |. Issued in salmon-pink dustjacket, printed in blue and black. All edges trimmed and unstained. Wove unwatermarked paper.

Notes. Published December 8, 1941 and sold at 8s. Number of copies printed unknown (publisher's records destroyed during World War II).

First impression has unbattered "e" on p. 5, line *21* in "circle." The manuscript of *The Vulgar Streak*–originally titled *Men at Bay*–was received by Robert Hale on June 12, 1941 and was set up by the printers from late June through early August, 1941. Lewis, who was living in Toronto, Canada during the war, was sent the first proofs for correction on August 8, 1941. The scarcity of this book is mainly due to two reasons: because of the wartime paper shortage in England (repeatedly mentioned by Hale in his correspondence with Lewis during this period) the printing was probably very small, and apparently a part of the unsold stock was destroyed by bombing (see Kenner, *Wyndham Lewis,* p. 163). The validity of the second story mentioned here has been questioned on several occasions, but in light of the fact that Hale's offices were indeed blitzed during the war, destroying the firm's publishing records, and that it was reprinted within one month, it seems plausible that stock in storage might have been affected as well.

Lewis began writing this novel in England in 1939 and completed work on it during his stay in Long Island, New York during the Summer of 1940. Reprinted by Jubilee Books, New York in 1973.

A33b *First edition, second impression:*

[*Titlepage transcription, measurements, collation, pagination, contents, binding and dustjacket same as* A33a.]

Notes. Printed in late January, 1942, and sold at 8s.

Second impression identifiable by battered "e" in "circle" on p. 5, line *21*, and verso of titlepage reads: "*Reprinted January 1942*."

A34a AMERICA AND COSMIC MAN [1948]

First edition:

WYNDHAM LEWIS | [*large centered dot*] | AMERICA | AND | COSMIC | MAN | NICHOLSON & WATSON LTD. | *LONDON* [*fine rule*] *BRUSSELS*

7 5/16" x 4¾". Collation: A^8, B-N^8, O^{12} (N^1 signed "N*"). Pp. 232; endsheets.

[1] half-title; [2] *Author of* | [*list of eleven titles*]; [3] title; [4] FIRST PUBLISHED IN 1948 BY | NICHOLSON & WATSON, | 26 MANCHESTER SQUARE, W.1 | *Set by* | *Cole & Co. (Westminster) Ltd., London, S.W.1* | *Printed and Bound by* | *Love & Malcomson Ltd., Redhill, Surrey;* [5]-6 table of contents; 7-231 text.

Two states of the binding have been noted, the earliest of which was submitted to Lewis on July 1, 1948 (three trial copies) and was disdainfully criticized as being "hideous" (TLS, Lewis to Roberts, July 2, 1948, NIC). Consequently a second binding was immediately ordered and distributed shortly after publication.
(1). Bound in green V cloth, stamped in red on spine: AMERICA | & | COSMIC | MAN | · | Wyndham | Lewis | NICHOLSON | and | WATSON |. Top of letters in headline to bottom of letters in baseline measures 6¼". Issued in white dustjacket, light blue on spine and front, lettering printed in black, swirling line design printed in white on spine and front cover, photograph of Lewis on back. All edges trimmed and unstained. Wove unwatermarked paper; sheets measure 7 5/16" x 4¾". Boards measure 7½" x 4¾". Rejected by the author.
(2). Bound in light blue V cloth, stamped in black on spine as above, but distance from top of letters in headline to bottom of letters in baseline measures 6⅜". Sheets measure 7½" x 4¾". Boards measure 7¾" x 4⅝".

Notes. Published in early July, 1948 in an edition of 2000 copies, and sold at 10s. 6d.

Contract dated January 26, 1948, stipulating that Lewis was to receive £500 advance. Title was originally intended for publication in May or June, 1946, but was considerably delayed as a result of production difficulties and recurrent disagreements as to terms. 42 review copies distributed in June, 1948.

This second study concerning America (see also A29) was the ultimate product of Lewis's lectures at Assumption College in 1943. Lewis was planning *America and Cosmic Man* as early as summer, 1942 and began writing the final manuscript in 1945. An essay entitled "The Cosmic Uniform of Peace," previously published in *The Sewanee Review* (D271) is incorporated with revisions in Chaps. 21, 22, 23 and 26 of *America and Cosmic Man.*

Reprinted by Kennikat Press (Port Washington, New York), 1969.

A34b *First American edition:*

AMERICA | *and Cosmic Man* | [*rule*] | BY WYNDHAM LEWIS | DOUBLEDAY & COMPANY, INC., GARDEN CITY, N. Y., 1949

8" x 5¾". Collation: *1-8*^{16}. Pp. [iv], 252; endsheets.

[1] half-title; [3] BY WYNDHAM LEWIS | [*list of six titles*]; [5] title; [6] The extracts from *The Republic,* by Charles Beard, are reprinted by per- | mission of the Viking Press, Inc. | The extracts from *American Commonwealth,* by Rt. Hon. Viscount Bryce, | are copyright 1893 by Macmillan and Co., 1910 & 1914 by The Mac- | millan Company; 1921 by Rt. Hon. Viscount Bryce. | The extracts from *Grammar of Politics,* by Harold Laski, are reprinted by | permission of Yale University Press. | The extract from Dorothy Thompson's column of July 19, 1945, is re- | printed by permission of Miss Thompson and the Bell Syndicate, Inc. | FIRST PUBLISHED, 1949, IN THE UNITED STATES | COPYRIGHT, 1948, BY WYNDHAM LEWIS | ALL RIGHTS RESERVED | PRINTED IN THE UNITED STATES | AT THE COUNTRY LIFE PRESS, GARDEN CITY, N. Y. | FIRST EDITION; [7]-8 table of contents; [9] internal half-title; 11-247 text.

Bound in smooth black V cloth, stamped in gold running down spine: AMERICA [*over rule which extends beyond last word*] *and Cosmic Man* [*under same rule as above which terminates above final letter of last word*] WYNDHAM LEWIS · DOUBLEDAY |. Issued in white dustjacket, spine and front black; lettering printed in yellow, white, light-blue and black, with decorative borders and designs printed in light-blue and grey. Top edge trimmed and unstained; fore-edge untrimmed; bottom edge partially trimmed. Cream machine-finished endsheets; wove unwatermarked paper.

Notes. Published June 9, 1949 in an edition of 3000 copies (1442 copies extant after December 1), and sold at $2.75.

Title out of print on December 1, 1949, total sales having amounted to 1442 copies; the publishers have indicated that the remaining copies were apparently destroyed. Lewis's friend and agent, Felix Giovanelli, submitted *America and Cosmic Man* to Doubleday in September, 1948, and the book was accepted by the publishers in late September. Contract signed October 6, 1948. Lewis received an advance of $750.00. Textually similar to the English edition with minor alterations which were proposed by John Sargent of Doubleday (obvious clarifying changes such as "In England . . .", p. 207, paragraph 1, in American edition for "On this side of the Atlantic . . .", p. 185, paragraph 3, of the English edition) and the omission of the first two paragraphs of Chapter VIII (p. 46 in English edition) and the Postscript "Rotarian Cæsar" (pp. 225-231 in English edition).

Excerpts reprinted in *Personality, Work, Community: An Introduction to Social Science* (Chicago: Lippincott, [1950]), 3 vols., edited by Arthur Naftalin, Benjamin N. Nelson, Mulford Q. Sibley, Donald C. Calhoun and Andreas G. Papandreou. Reprinted in single volume edition, 1953.

A35 RUDE ASSIGNMENT [1950]

First edition:

RUDE ASSIGNMENT | *A narrative of my* | *career up-to-date* | by | WYNDHAM LEWIS | *Illustrated with works by the Author* | HUTCHINSON & CO. (Publishers) LTD | *London New York Melbourne Sydney Cape Town*

9" x 6". Collation: A^8, B-O^8, P^4. Pp. 232; endsheets. Unsigned, unpaged signature of 8 leaves bound in between O8 and P1, containing plates; four leaves mounted, containing plates.

[1] half-title; [2] BY THE SAME AUTHOR | [*list of twenty-three titles*] | etc.; [3] title; [4] *Printed in Great Britain by* | *William Brendon & Son, Ltd.* | *The Mayflower Press (late of Plymouth)* | *at Bushey Mill Lane* | *Watford, Herts*; 5-6 table of contents; 7 list of illustrations; 9-222 text; 223 bibliography; 225-231 index.

Bound in red V cloth, stamped in gold on spine: RUDE ASSIGNMENT | [*short rule*] | *A* | *Narrative* | *of My* | *Career* | *Up-to-date* | [*short rule*] | WYNDHAM | LEWIS | HUTCHINSON | . Issued in grey coated paper dustjacket, with design by Lewis (Michel 1125) in black on front, lettering in black and red. All edges trimmed and unstained. Wove unwatermarked paper. Second printing in similar binding, but color of V cloth is slightly darker red (see note below).

Plates. Four leaves mounted, facing the following pages, and not included in paging or collation: [3], frontispiece photograph of Lewis, 1928, printed on verso; 64, David Low cartoon on recto, drawing of Lewis by Augustus John, 1903, on verso; 112, photograph of Lewis on recto, photograph of Lewis in uniform, 1916, on verso; 160, photograph of Lewis with Jacques Maritain, 1942, on recto, drawing of Mrs. Lewis by Lewis (Michel 875), on verso. Unpaged signature bound in between O8 and P1 contains plates as follows: Michel 633—Michel 649—Michel 634—Michel 780 (reproduced as "Mr. Sealyham at Rest")—Michel P85—Michel 417—Michel P86—Michel 786—Michel 971—Michel 847 (reproduced as "Sunset-Atlas")—Michel P61—Michel 614 (reproduced as "Hero's Dream")—Michel 637—Michel 433 (reproduced as "Study for Painting (Seated Lady)")—Michel 467—Michel P49. All plates printed in monochrome black and white, printed on glossy machine-finished paper.

Notes. Published November 23, 1950 in an edition of 2500 copies, and sold at 21s.

Accepted for publication July 17, 1946. Contract agreement dated July 17, 1946 and signed August 10, 1946 (using original title, later changed, *Story of a Career).* 75 review copies distributed in September-November, 1946; a total of 1096 copies were subscribed up to the date of publication and on the strength of pre-publication orders, a second printing of 1000 copies was ordered on December 22, 1950 and published in early January, 1951. Second printing bound in darker red V cloth, stamped in similar manner on spine using slightly different type, issued in same dustjacket. The titlepage was reset with verso altered to read: *First Published November* 1950 | *Reprinted January* 1951 |.

Rude Assignment is the second of Lewis's two autobiographical books, preceded by *Blasting and Bombardiering* (A26). Reprints "Puritans of the Steppes" in Part III, Chap. 27, originally published in *The Listener* (D278) and broadcast on March 16, 1947, 8:00-8:20, B.B.C. Third Programme with the title "A Crisis of Thought." Excerpts reprinted in *Enemy Salvoes* (A48).

A36a ROTTING HILL [1951]

First edition:

ROTTING HILL | *by* | WYNDHAM LEWIS | [*publisher's device*] | METHUEN & CO. LTD., LONDON | *36 Essex Street, Strand, W.C.2*

7¼" x 4¾". Collation: *A*^{8}, B-U^8. Pp. xii, 308; endsheets.

[i] half-title; [ii] *By the same author* | TARR; [iii] title; [iv] *First published in 1951* | [*catalogue number*] | PRINTED IN GREAT BRITAIN; [v] table of contents; [vii]-xii Foreword; [1]-307 text; [308] PRINTED IN GREAT BRITAIN BY | WYMAN AND SONS LTD., | LONDON, FAKENHAM AND READING

Bound in light blue V cloth, lettering stamped in yellow on blue rectangular fields at head and foot of spine: [*at head of spine:*] ROTTING | HILL | [*star*] | Wyndham | Lewis | [*at foot of spine:*] Methuen |. Issued in light grey-blue dustjacket printed in darker blue, designed by Charles Handley-Read. All edges trimmed and unstained. Wove unwatermarked paper. Binding uniform with *Tarr* (A3e).

Notes. Published November 29, 1951 in an edition of 3600 copies, and sold at 14s.

Accepted for publication by J. Alan White on behalf of Methuen, on December 15, 1949. In the original ordering of the stories "The Bishop's Fool" was placed between "My Disciple" and "Parents and Horses." The other stories were arranged in the same sequence which was finally adopted, with "The Rot Camp" added as an *envoi* to the collection just before the book reached proof stage. Stories included in this collection are: *The Bishop's Fool–My Fellow Traveller to Oxford–The Rot–The Room Without a Telephone–Time the Tiger–Mr. Patricks' Toy Shop–The Talking Shop–My Disciple–Parents and Horses–Envoi: The Rot Camp.* Cornell possesses two proof copies, the earlier of which bears extensive revisions: (1). first proof copy, bound in tan wrappers, dated June 22, 1951, has Foreword and "Parents and Horses" heavily corrected in Lewis's hand; (2). second proof copy, bound in pink wrappers, dated August 29, 1951, has five minor corrections in Lewis's hand.

Single story previously published: "The Rot: a Narrative" (D296, *Wales;* reprinted in *The American Mercury,* D339 and in *The Sewanee Review,* D309). Stories reprinted in *A Soldier of Humor* and *Unlucky for Pringle.*

A36b *First American edition:*

ROTTING HILL | By | Wyndham Lewis | [*publisher's device*] | Henry Regnery Company | Chicago, 1952

8⅛" x 5⅜". Collation: *1*-*9*^{16}. Two blank leaves, pp. xiv, 270; endsheets.

[i] half-title; [iii] title; [iv] Copyright 1952 | Henry Regnery Company | Chicago 4, Illinois | Manufactured in the United States of America | by American Book—Stratford Press, Inc., New York; [v]-x Foreword; [xi] table of contents; [xiii] internal half-title; [1]-265 text.

Bound in smooth dark blue V cloth, stamped in gold on spine: Lewis | [*running downwards*] ROTTING HILL | [*running across bottom*] Regnery |. Issued in white dustjacket, spine and front cover lime green, with black, white and lime green decorative design of street scene on front, crossed umbrella and shovel in black and white on spine, lettering in white and black, Douglas Glass photograph of Lewis on back. All edges trimmed and unstained. Wove unwatermarked paper.

Notes. Published on April 9, 1952 in an edition of 5000 copies, and sold at $3.00.

A37 THE WRITER AND THE ABSOLUTE [1952]

First edition:

THE WRITER | AND THE ABSOLUTE | *by* | WYNDHAM LEWIS | [*publisher's device*] | METHUEN & CO., LTD., LONDON | *36 Essex Street, Strand, W.C.2*

8½" x 5½". Collation: 1^8, $2\text{-}13^8$. Pp. vi, 202; endsheets.

[i] half-title; [ii] *By the same Author* | [*list of four titles*]; [iii] title; [iv] *First published in 1952* | [*catalogue registration*] | PRINTED IN GREAT BRITAIN; v-vi table of contents; [1]-198 text; 199-202 index.

Bound in light blue V cloth, stamped in gold over two rectangular fields of red at head and foot of spine: [*at top of spine*] THE | WRITER | AND THE | ABSOLUTE | [*star*] | Wyndham | Lewis | [*at bottom of spine*] Methuen |. Issued in light bluish grey dustjacket designed by Charles Handley-Read, lettered and decorated in light blue. All edges trimmed and unstained. Wove unwatermarked paper. Binding uniform with *Tarr* (A3e).

Notes. Published June 26, 1952 in an edition of 2000 copies, and sold at 21s.

Contract for *The Writer and the Absolute* (originally titled *The Artist and the Absolute)* dated November 27, 1950. Dustjacket blurb written by Lewis in October, 1951. Lewis began work on *The Writer and the Absolute* as early as February, 1948. Excerpts reprinted in *A Soldier of Humor* (A43) and *Enemy Salvoes* (A48).

A38a SELF CONDEMNED [1954]

First edition:

WYNDHAM LEWIS | SELF | CONDEMNED | [*rule*] | METHUEN & CO. LTD. LONDON

7¼" x 4¾". Collation: A^{*16}, $2\text{-}13^{16}$ (A^{*5} signed "A*"). Pp. vi, 410; endsheets.

[i] half-title; [ii] *By the same author* | [*star*] | [*list of five titles*]; [iii] title; [iv] *First published in 1954* | [*publisher's device*] | [*catalogue number*] | PRINTED IN GREAT BRITAIN; v-vi table of contents; [1]-407 text; [408] Printed in Great Britain by | Butler & Tanner Ltd., | Frome and London

Bound in light tan smooth V cloth, stamped in gold over two brown rectangular fields at top and bottom of spine: [*at top*] SELF | CONDEMNED | [*star*] | Wyndham | Lewis | [*at bottom*] Methuen |. Issued in white dustjacket with design by Michael Ayrton on front and spine in black, grey, yellow and red; lettering printed in red, black and white. All edges trimmed and unstained. Wove unwatermarked paper.

Notes. Published April 22, 1954 in an edition of 3000 copies, and sold at 15s.

A second printing of 2000 copies was published in June, 1954, and sold at the same price, with the verso of the title page altered, reading "Reprinted 1954." Third impression of 2000 copies was published in February, 1955, with verso of title page altered to read "Reprinted 1954 and 1955" in second line. Declared out of print on August 10, 1960. Based on Lewis's experiences in Toronto during his self-exile from Europe during World War II, this novel was begun as early as 1946 under its original title, *Chateau Rex* (see Mary Daniels, *Catalogue,* p. [18] for facsimile reproduction of corrected typescript of Lewis's "Synopsis of novel, 1946" which became *Self Condemned*). In a letter to D.G. Bridson dated October 19, 1951, written in London, Lewis mentions that he is finishing work on the novel.

Parts of *Self Condemned* were broadcast in Spanish as "Book of the Week" by the Latin American Service of the B.B.C. in May, 1954 (TLS, B. H. Alexander to Lewis, April 27, 1954, NIC).

A38b *First American edition:*

WYNDHAM LEWIS | SELF | CONDEMNED | [*rule*] | HENRY REGNERY COMPANY | CHICAGO, 1955

Measurements and collation same as English edition. Contents same as English edition, with two exceptions: [iv] revised to read "*All rights reserved* | *Henry Regnery Company, Chicago, Illinois* | Printed and Bound in Great Britain by Butler & Tanner Ltd., Frome and London"; printer's imprint on p. [408] of English edition deleted in American edition.

Bound in light tan V cloth similar to English edition, stamped in gold on two brown rectangular fields at top and bottom of spine: [*at top*] SELF | CONDEMNED | [*star*] | Wyndham | Lewis | [*at bottom*] Regnery |. Issued in white coated paper dustjacket, light green halftone photograph of sculpted head on front cover, lettering printed in green. All edges trimmed and unstained. Wove unwatermarked paper.

Notes. Published on May 9, 1955 in an edition of 3000 copies, and sold at $4.00.
Reprinted by Henry Regnery, Gateway Editions, 1965, at $1.95, adding an introduction by Hugh Kenner.

A39a THE DEMON OF PROGRESS IN THE ARTS [1954]

First edition:

The | *Demon of Progress* | *in the Arts* | *by* | WYNDHAM LEWIS | [*publisher's device*] | METHUEN & CO. LTD LONDON | *36 Essex Street, Strand, WC2*

7¾" x 5¼". Collation: *1*^{8}, 2-5^8, 6^4, 7^8 (unsigned gathering of single sheet folded once to make two leaves, coated paper, sewn between 4^4 and 4^5; unsigned gathering of single sheet folded twice to make four leaves, coated paper, sewn between signatures 4 and 5, not included in collation or paging, see below). Pp. vi, 98; endsheets.

[i] half-title; [ii] *By the same Author* | [*star*] | [*list of five titles*]; [iii] title; [iv] *First published in 1954* | 1.1 | CATALOGUE NO. 5710/U | PRINTED AND BOUND IN GREAT BRITAIN BY | BUTLER AND TANNER LTD., FROME AND LONDON; v-vi table of contents, list of illustrations on vi; [1]-10 Introduction; [11]-92 text; [93]-97 Postscript.

Bound in smooth black V cloth, stamped in gold running down spine: *The Demon of Progress in the Arts*–WYNDHAM LEWIS |. Issued in yellow dustjacket, ornamental rules printed in red and black, lettering printed in red and black. All edges trimmed and unstained. Cream endsheets. Laid paper, watermarked: [*crown design*] | Abbey Hills | Greenfield |.

Plates. "Explanatory Note on the Plates" printed on recto and verso of first unsigned leaf, following p. 50. Plate in black and grey, of design by Bombelli on recto of leaf *2;* design by Engel-Pak in black and grey, on verso of leaf *2.* Recto of leaf *1* of unsigned gathering after Sig. 4 prints black and white halftone plate of portrait of Sir William Walton, by Michael Ayrton; leaf *2,* recto, "Man in a Chair" by Francis Bacon; leaf *3,* recto, "Portrait of a Young Woman" by Robert Colquhoun; leaf *4,* recto, "The Gamblers" by John Minton. All versos of unsigned gathering after Sig. 4 are blank.

Notes. Published on November 18, 1954 in an edition of 1500 copies, and sold at 12s. 6d.

Second printing identical to first printing with verso of title altered to indicate date of first and second printings. Selections from *The Demon of Progress in the Arts,* translated into French, were quoted in the B.B.C. French Service review of the book, broadcast January 13, 1955 (TLS, B.H. Alexander to Lewis, January 12, 1955, NIC).

A39b *First American edition:*

The | *Demon of Progress* | *in the Arts* | *by* | WYNDHAM LEWIS | Henry Regnery Company | *Chicago, Illinois, 1955*

8¼" x 5½". Collation: $1\text{-}3^{16}$, 4^{8}. Pp. vi, 98 (4 unpaged leaves included in collation, plates and text); endsheets.

[i] half-title; [ii] *By the same Author* | [*star*] | [*list of three titles*]; [iii] title; [iv] ALL RIGHTS RESERVED. FIRST PUBLISHED IN THE UNITED STATES | IN 1955. MANUFACTURED IN THE UNITED STATES OF AMERICA.; v-vi table of contents, list of illustrations on p. vi; [1]-10 Introduction; [11]-92 text; [93]-97 Postscript.

Bound in light blue V boards, stamped in gold running down spine: WYNDHAM LEWIS—*The Demon of Progress in the Arts* |. Issued in coated paper dustjacket, yellowish tan on front and spine, white on other sides, ornamental rules and lettering printed in black. All edges trimmed and unstained. Wove unwatermarked paper.

Plates. "Explanatory Note on the Plates" printed on recto and verso of 2^{13}; 2^{14} recto, design by Bombelli; 2^{14} verso, design by Engel-Pak; 3^{3} recto, "Sir William Walton" by Michael Ayrton; 3^{3} verso, "Man in a Chair" by Francis Bacon; 3^{4} recto, "Portrait of a Young Woman" by Robert Colquhoun; 3^{4} verso, "The Gamblers" by John Minton. All plates black and white halftone, printed on same paper as text.

Notes. Published October 10, 1955 in an edition of 5000 copies, and sold at $3.00.

Due to a printer's error the divisional half-title to the Conclusion, p. [89], reads "POSTSCRIPT" and the divisional half-title to the Postscript, p. [93], reads "Part V | CONCLUSION."

A40 THE HUMAN AGE [1955]

First edition:

WYNDHAM LEWIS | [*double rule, thick over thin*] | The Human Age | BOOK TWO | MONSTRE GAI | BOOK THREE | MALIGN FIESTA | [*brief double rule, thick over thin*] | *Illustrations by Michael Ayrton* | [*publisher's device*] | METHUEN & CO. LTD | 36 ESSEX STREET, LONDON W.C.2

8 7/16" x 5⅜". Collation: A^{16}, B-R^{16}, S^{14}. Pp. [vi], 566; endsheets.

[i] half-title; [ii] THE HUMAN AGE | Book One · THE CHILDERMASS | [*star*] | Book Two . [*note: dot on baseline*] MONSTRE GAI | Book Three · MALIGN FIESTA | [*star*] | Book Four · THE TRIAL OF MAN; [iii] title; [iv] *First published in 1955* | [*catalogue registration*] | PRINTED AND BOUND IN GREAT BRITAIN BY | BUTLER AND TANNER LTD., FROME AND LONDON; [v] divisional half-title, BOOK TWO | [*double rule, thick over thin*] | Monstre Gai; [1] table of contents; 3-304 text (of *Monstre Gai*); [305] divisional half-title, BOOK THREE | [*double rule, thick over thin*] | Malign Fiesta; 307 table of contents; 309-566 text (of *Malign Fiesta*).

Bound in smooth white V cloth with broad black rules running around front, spine and back cover at top and (somewhat narrower) at bottom, line design of two heads stamped in black on front, and stamped in gold over black band at top of front cover: The Human Age | Book 2 Monstre Gai | Book 3 Malign Fiesta |. Stamped in gold over black band at top of spine: THE | HUMAN AGE | II | Wyndham Lewis |. Stamped in gold over black band at bottom of spine: METHUEN |. Issued with white dustjacket which has elaborate pictorial design by Michael Ayrton on front, spine and back printed in black, white and red. All edges trimmed and unstained. Smooth finished wove, unwatermarked paper.

Illustrations. Black and white illustrations by Michael Ayrton on pp. [15], [151], [273], [313], [397] and [563]. All versos blank.

Notes. Published October 27, 1955 in an edition of 4750 copies, and sold at 30s.

Monstre Gai and *Malign Fiesta,* first published in book form in this volume, constitute the second and third parts of Lewis's *The Human Age,* begun in 1928 with the publication of the first part, *The Childermass* (A10). A fourth volume tentatively titled *The Trial of Man* was left unfinished at Lewis's death.

Following the successful broadcast of a dramatized version of *The Childermass* on the B.B.C. Third Programme, June 18, 1951 (see A10a, notes), the B.B.C. commissioned Lewis to complete his unfinished trilogy, begun in 1928, on the condition that when they were finished similar broadcast dramatizations would precede book publication. As a result of this sponsorship—largely the work of B.B.C. producer D.G. Bridson—Lewis was able to write *Monstre Gai* and *Malign Fiesta.* With Bridson's assistance, the manuscripts of the novels were duly adapted for radio production, and the entire trilogy was broadcast on May 24, 26 and 28, 1955. T.S. Eliot, who had read much of the manuscripts of the novels as they were being written, and had made suggestions and comments to Lewis about the texts, discussed *Monstre Gai* and *Malign Fiesta* during the Third Programme on May 25, 1955 (9:30-9:50 PM).

A press release for the radio adaptation of *The Human Age* was published by the B.B.C. prior to the broadcast:

[*Beneath broken triple rule, printed in blue:*] from | the BBC PRESS SERVICE [*broken triple rule*] | [*printed from typewritten text, in black:*] BBC COMMISSIONS NEW WORK BY WYNDHAM LEWIS [*underscored*] | Third Programme—May 24, 26 and 28 [*underscored*] | [*text*].

10" x 8¼". Single leaf printed on both sides, as follows: [1] title, as above; [2] [*text*] | WITH COMPLIMENTS FROM THE BBC, LONDON, W.1 | [*initials and date*] |. Announces broadcast of radio adaptation, giving cast members and mentioning that the May 24 broadcast of *The Childermass* was first broadcast in Summer, 1951. Also announces that Graham Hough will read prefatory comments during the May 23, 1955 Third Programme, and that T.S. Eliot will discuss the trilogy on May 25, 1955 Third Programme. This press release, printed on wove unwatermarked paper in blue and black, was sent out on May 2, 1955.

For reprints see A10a, *notes.*

A41 THE RED PRIEST [1956]

First edition:

The Red Priest | by | WYNDHAM LEWIS | METHUEN AND CO. LTD. | 36 ESSEX STREET, LONDON, W.C.I

7¼" x 4¾". Collation: A^8, B-T^8. Pp. vi, 298; endsheets.

[i] half-title; [ii] *by the same author* | [*star*] | [*five titles*] | [*star*] | [*two titles*]; [iii] title; [iv] *First published in 1956* | [*publisher's device*] | [*catalogue number*] | PRINTED IN GREAT BRITAIN BY | THE CAMELOT PRESS LTD., LONDON AND SOUTHAMPTON; v-vi table of contents; 1-298 text.

Bound in maroon V cloth, stamped in gold on two black rectangular fields at top and bottom of spine: [*at top*] THE RED | PRIEST | [*star*] | Wyndham | Lewis | [*at bottom*] Methuen | . Issued in white dustjacket, with design of Father Augustine Card in red and black by Michael Ayrton, lettering in black, red and white. All edges trimmed and unstained. Wove unwatermarked paper.

Notes. Published August 30, 1956 in an edition of 5700 copies, and sold at 15s.

The Red Priest was the last book by Lewis to be published before his death in March, 1957 (a novel tentatively entitled *Twentieth Century Palette* was begun by Lewis after he finished work on *The Red Priest,* but was left unrevised and partially incomplete at his death). Michael Ayrton, who was working in Amalfi, was sent a proof copy of the novel in early April, 1956, and Lewis requested that he design the dustjacket for the book. Ayrton agreed to undertake the project, in a letter to Lewis dated April 26, 1956 (NIC). Geoffrey Bridson, who had assisted Lewis with his adaptation of *The Human Age* for the B.B.C. (see A10a and A40, notes), considered the possibility of adapting *The Red Priest* for radio dramatization but told Lewis in a letter dated March 6, 1956 (NIC) that the form of the novel precluded successful adaptation, since it is over-episodic for radio and the scenes would not lend themselves to effective dramatization. Therefore this idea was abandoned. Not published in the United States.

A42a THE LETTERS OF WYNDHAM LEWIS [1963]

First edition:

THE LETTERS OF | WYNDHAM LEWIS | [*short double rule, thick over fine*] | EDITED BY | W. K. ROSE | METHUEN & CO LTD | 36 Essex Street London WC2

8½" x 5½". Collation: A^{16}, B-S^{16}, T^{18} (*A* 5-S5 signed A*-S*; T2 signed "T*"; T6 signed "T**"). Pp. xxxii, 580; endsheets. 13 leaves of plates mounted: color frontispiece and 16 monochrome plates on remaining 12 leaves. Plates not included in collation or paging.

[i] half-title; [3] title; [iv] *First published* 1963 | *Text* ©1962 *Mrs Wyndham Lewis* | *Editorial Matter* ©1962 *W. K. Rose* | *Printed in Great Britain by* | *Western Printing*

Services Ltd, Bristol | [*catalogue registration*]; v-xiv table of contents; xv list of illustrations; xvii-xxiv Preface; xxv-xxvii Notes on Editing; xxix-xxxi Acknowledgements; 1-567 text; 568-580 Index.

Bound in red V cloth, stamped in gold on spine: The | Letters of | Wyndham | Lewis | [*thick rule*] | EDITED BY | Professor | W. K. Rose | METHUEN |. Issued in white dustjacket, blocked on spine and front cover in black and red, lettering in white, red and black. Top edge trimmed and stained yellow; other edges trimmed and unstained. Wove unwatermarked paper; plates printed on coated paper. Frontispiece printed in four color halftone, other plates monochrome black and white.

Notes. Published April 4, 1963 in an edition of 3000 copies, and sold at 63s.

Proof copies bound in brown wrappers printed on spine and front cover in black give projected publication date as January, 1962. Prof. Rose's *Preface* as printed in the proof copies differs considerably from the text finally published in March, 1963. Publication of Lewis's letters was delayed primarily because of numerous alterations and deletions which were made in the text prior to publication.

Reprints letters previously published in various periodicals: "Epstein and his Critics, or Nietzsche and his Friends" (D12), "Mr. Arthur Rose's Offer" (D13), "Futurism" (D17, D18 and D19), "Mr. Clive Bell and 'Wilcoxism' " (D93), "The Hypocrite in the Drawing-Room" (D133), "Mr. Wyndham Lewis Replies to his Critics" (D158), "Arnold Bennett as Critic: Mr. Wyndham Lewis Replies" (D181), "One Way Song" (D195), "The Criticism of Mr. Wyndham Lewis" (D222), "Mr. Lewis and Mr. Murry" (D226), "[Letter to the editor.]" (D227), "Mr. Lewis and Mr. Murry" (D228), "The Academy and Modern Art. Is Burlington House Too Advanced?" (D249), "The Rejected Portrait. Policy of the Royal Academy. Art and Nature" (D251), "The Rejected Portrait" (D252), "The Rejected Portrait" (D253), "Abstract Art Turns Over" (D263), "Satire in the Twenties" (D279), "Standards of Art Criticism" (D287), "Standards in Art Criticism" (D288), "Standards in Art Criticism" (D289), "Standards in Art Criticism" (D290), "Henry Moore's 'Head of a Child' " (D326), "Nature and Art" (D330), "Nature and Art" (D331), "Nature and Art" (D333) and "Wyndham Lewis and the Archangel Michael" (D352). Also reprinted are "[*Round robin, undated, sent to critics and writers eliciting opinions about* The Apes of God]" (A12a, prospectus (d).) and "[*Circular letter, undated, sent to potential advertisers for a popular edition of* The Apes of God, *soliciting advertisement subscriptions*]" (A12a, prospectus (e).). Most of these reprinted letters are either abbreviated or give slightly different readings than previously published versions, since the editor of *The Letters,* W.K. Rose, worked directly from originals, copies and even drafts of the letters themselves rather than from printed texts of the letters.

A42b *First American edition:*

THE LETTERS OF | WYNDHAM LEWIS | [*short double rule, thick over fine*] | EDITED BY | W. K. ROSE | NEW DIRECTIONS | Norfolk · Connecticut

8" x 5⅜". Collation: A-I^{16}, K^{8}, L-T^{16} (sig. K not included in pagination). Pp. xxviii, 580. Frontispiece plate mounted facing title; A5 signed "A*". Endsheets.

[i] half-title; [iii] title; [iv] Text ©1963 by Mrs Wyndham Lewis. Editorial Matter | ©1963 by W. K. Rose. First published in 1963. | Library of Congress Catalog Card Number: 61-10121 | THIS BOOK WAS MANUFACTURED IN THE UNITED | STATES OF AMERICA, EXCLUDING ONLY THE FOLLOW- | ING ILLUSTRATIONS, WHICH WERE PRINTED IN ENG- | LAND: FRONTISPIECE AND ALL ILLUSTRATIONS BE- | TWEEN PAGES 292 AND 293. | New Directions Books are published by James Laughlin at | Norfolk, Connecticut, New York office: 333 Sixth Avenue, 14.; v-xiv table of contents; xv list of illustrations; xvii-xxiv Preface; xxv-xxvi Notes on Editing; xxvii-[xxviii] Acknowledgements; 1-567 text; 568-580 Index.

Bound in turquoise blue V cloth, stamped in gold on spine: The | Letters | of | Wyndham | Lewis | edited by | W.K. Rose | New | Directions |. Issued in simulated wood-grain dustjacket, lettering and design by Lewis (Michel 26) printed in black. All edges trimmed and unstained. Blue false headband and tailband. Laid unwatermarked paper. Plates printed on coated paper.

Notes. Published on March 25, 1964 in an edition of 1000 copies, and sold at $8.50.

Sheets imported from Methuen in January, 1964.

A43 A SOLDIER OF HUMOR AND SELECTED WRITINGS [1966]

First edition:

WYNDHAM LEWIS | A SOLDIER OF HUMOR | *And Selected Writings* | Edited, with an Introduction, by | RAYMOND ROSENTHAL | [*publisher's device*] | A SIGNET CLASSIC | PUBLISHED BY THE NEW AMERICAN LIBRARY, NEW YORK AND TORONTO | THE ENGLISH LIBRARY LIMITED, LONDON

7" x 4⅛". Pp. 464.

[1] half-title (with drawing of Lewis); [3] title; [4] [*three line description of Signet Classic series*] | INTRODUCTION COPYRIGHT 1966 BY RAYMOND ROSENTHAL | All rights reserved | *First Printing, October, 1966* | [*twenty-four lines giving catalogue registration, acknowledgements, copyright notices, Signet trademark information and publisher's address*] | PRINTED IN THE UNITED STATES OF AMERICA; [5-7] table of contents; 9-18 Introduction, by Raymond Rosenthal (with a note on the text); 19-459 text; 460-461 Selected Bibliography.

Perfect bound in heavy paper wrappers, printed in black, purple, pink, brown and blue, with design on front cover. All edges trimmed and stained. Spine glued and signatures unsewn. Wove unwatermarked paper.

Notes. Published October, 1966 in an edition of 54000 copies and sold at 95¢.

Contains "A Soldier of Humor," "The Death of the Ankou" and "Inferior Religions" (pp. 22-73, from *The Wild Body)*; "The Enemy of the Stars" (pp. 74-105, from *Blast, No. 1)*; "Cantleman's Spring Mate" (pp. 106-112, from *The Little Review,* D76); "The Ideal Giant" (pp. 113-129, from *The Little Review,* D82); "The Bishop's Fool" and "My Disciple" (pp. 130-199, from *Rotting Hill)*; "Bombardiering," "The Romance of War," "Howitzers," "A Day of Attack," "Passchendaele" and "The 'O.Pip' on the Ridge" (pp. 201-235, from *Blasting and Bombardiering)*; "The Bull Sounds," "The Politician's Apathy," "Machinery and Lions," "The Artist Older than the Fish," "The Physiognomy of Our Time," "Our Æsthetes and Plank-Art" and "The Bawdy Critic" (pp. 237-253, from *The Caliph's Design)*; "The Objective of Art in Our Time" (pp. 254-270); "Ernest Hemingway: The 'Dumb Ox' " (pp. 272-294, from *Men Without Art)*; "Jean-Paul Sartre: 'Plunged Back into Time,' " "Malraux and Escape through Action," "A Derelict Author in Search of a Public" and "Twentieth Century Nihilism" (pp. 295-352, from *The Writer and the Absolute)*; "Freedom of Speech at Its Zenith," "How One

Begins," "Early Life and Shakespeare," "First Published Work," "The Puritans of the Steppes," "The Schicksal—The German in my Fiction," "A Renaissance Prophet of Action" and "Advice to the Inmates of the Power House" (pp. 355-424, from *Rude Assignment)*; "Tlemcen" and "Film Filibusters" (pp. 427-441, from *Filibusters in Barbary)*; and "The Clubman Cæsar" and "Cosmic Society and Cosmic Man" (pp. 442-459, from *America and Cosmic Man)*.

A44 WYNDHAM LEWIS AN ANTHOLOGY OF HIS PROSE [1969]

First edition:

[*Ornamental ruled pattern, forming a maze*] | [*rule*] | WYNDHAM LEWIS | *An Anthology of his Prose* | *Edited with an Introduction by* | *E.W.F. TOMLIN* | METHUEN & CO LTD | 11 NEW FETTER LANE LONDON EC4

9 3/16" x 6". Collation: A^8, B-Z^8, AA^8, BB^4, CC^8. Pp. x, 398; endsheets.

[i] half-title; [ii] books by Wyndham Lewis | [*list of eight titles*]; [iii] title; [iv] *First published in 1969* | *This anthology ©1969 by Mrs Wyndham Lewis* | *Introduction ©1969 by E.W.F. Tomlin* | *Printed in Great Britain by* | *Butler & Tanner Ltd, Frome and London* | *Other books by E.W.F. Tomlin* | [*list of five titles*]; v table of contents; vi Acknowledgements; vii Note; ix quotation from *The Art of Being Ruled* beneath ornamental maze design and rule; 1-20 Introduction; [21]-397 text.

Bound in black cloth patterned boards, spine stamped in white: [*ornamental maze design over two lines running down spine:*] WYNDHAM LEWIS | [*beside this line:*] AN ANTHOLOGY OF HIS PROSE | [*ornamental maze design*] | METHUEN |. Issued in white coated paper dustjacket, with portrait drawing of Lewis by Michael Ayrton in black on front; front, back and spine chocolate brown, with lettering and rules printed in black, white and mustard orange. All edges trimmed and unstained. Laid unwatermarked paper; wove paper endsheets.

Notes. Published March 27, 1969 in an edition of 3000 copies, and sold at L4.

Contains selected excerpts from *Paleface* (pp. 24-81), *The Art of Being Ruled* (pp. 84-233), *The Doom of Youth* (pp. 235-252), *The Enemy of the Stars* (pp. 253-258), *The Caliph's Design* (pp. 262-266), *Men Without Art* (pp. 268-295), *The Diabolical Principle and the Dithyrambic Spectator* (pp. 297-311), *Blasting and Bombardiering* (pp. 322-329), *Rude Assignment* (pp. 331-349), *Filibusters in Barbary* (pp. 354-369), *America and Cosmic Man* (pp. 374-385) and *America, I Presume* (pp. 385-390).

Contains, also, the complete texts of Lewis's preface to Dr. Henry Somerville, *Madness in Shakespearian Tragedy* (pp. 312-317) and "The Sea-Mists of the Winter" (pp. 393-397).

"The Sea-Mists of the Winter" first published in book form in this edition (see D337).

A45 WYNDHAM LEWIS ON ART [1969]

First edition:

WYNDHAM LEWIS | ON ART | *Collected writings 1913-1956* | EDITED AND INTRODUCED BY | WALTER MICHEL and C.J. FOX | [*publisher's device*] | THAMES AND HUDSON · LONDON

8¼" x 6". Collation: A-P^{16} (A1 unsigned; A5-P5 signed "A2-P2"). Pp. 480; endsheets.

[1] half-title; [3] title; [4] ©1969 Mrs Wyndham Lewis and Thames and Hudson Ltd | *All Rights Reserved. No part of this publication may* | *be reproduced, stored in a retrieval system, or* | *transmitted, in any form or by any means, electronic,* | *mechanical, photocopying, recording or otherwise,* | *without the prior permission of the Publishers.* | *Printed in Great Britain by R. & R. Clark, Ltd., Edinburgh;* [5]-7 table of contents; [8]-9 acknowledgements; [11]-24 Introduction; [25]-98 text; [99]-103 Introduction; [104]-225 text; [227]-231 Introduction; [232]-361 text; [363]-366 Introduction; [367]-[459] text; [460]-473 Notes; [474]-475 Select Bibliography; [477]-480 index.

Bound in dark tan V cloth, stamped in gold over black rectangular field on spine: [*double rule, thick over thin, above black field*] | WYNDHAM | LEWIS | ON ART | [*rule*] | MICHEL | & FOX | [*double rule, thin over thick, below black field*] | THAMES | AND | HUDSON |. Publisher's device stamped in gold at center of front cover. Issued in white coated paper dustjacket; front, spine and back tan printed in black, white, blue and ochre, with painting by Lewis (Michel P25) reproduced on front. All edges trimmed and unstained. Laid unwatermarked paper; wove endsheets. False white head and tail bands.

Notes. Published September 22, 1969 and sold at £3.15. Number of copies printed not disclosed.

Contains first book printings of "Long Live the Vortex!" (pp. [25]-26, C1), "Manifesto" (pp. [27]-31, C1), "Frederick Spencer Gore" (pp. [54]-55, C1), "Room III. The Cubist Room" (pp. [56]-57, B2), "[*Introductory note to:*] A Review of Contemporary Art" (pp. [58]-59, the rest of the article printed in *Wyndham Lewis the Artist,* A29), "The London Group" (pp. [85]-89, C2), "History of the Largest Independent Society in England" (pp. [90]-94, C2), "Life has no Taste" (p. [95], C2), "Vorticist Exhibition" (pp. [96]-98, B6), "Guns" (pp. [104]-106, B8), "The Men Who Will Paint Hell" (pp. [107]-108, D84), "What Art Now?" (pp. [113]-116, D86), "Prevalent Design" (pp. [117]-128, D87, D88, D89 and D90), "Group X" (pp. [184]-186, B10), "Tyros and Portraits" (pp. [187]-190, B11), "The Coming Academy" (pp. [191]-192, D103), "The Objects of this Paper" (pp. [193]-194, C3), "The Children of the New Epoch" (pp. [195]-196, C3), "Roger Fry's Role as Continental Mediator" (pp. [197]-199, C3), "Essay on the Objective of Plastic Art in our Time" (pp. [200]-215, C4), "The Credentials of the Painter" (pp. [216]-225, D105 and D110), "Art Chronicle" (pp. [232]-234, D119), "A World Art and Tradition" (pp. [255]-259, D143), "The Kasbahs of the Atlas" (pp. [260]-265, D193), "What it Feels like to be an Enemy" (pp. [266]-267, D182), "Plain Home-Builder: Where is your Vorticist" (pp. [276]-285, D221), "Power-Feeling and Machine-Age Art" (pp. [286]-290, D219), "Foreword to Catalogue" (pp. [301]-302, B22), "Picasso" (pp. [346]-357, D261), "After Abstract Art" (pp. [358]-361, D264), "Religious Expression in Contemporary Art" (pp. [367]-380, previously unpublished), "The 1949 Retrospective Exhibition" (pp. [449]-450, B27), "The 1956 Retrospective at the Tate Gallery" (pp. [451]-453, B31), "The Vorticists" (pp. [454]-458, D349) and "L'Arlesienne" (p. [459], previously unpublished). Also, contains excerpts from Lewis's "Round the London Galleries," reviews published in *The Listener* (pp. [393]-448, D272, D276, D277, D281, D282, D284, D285, D286, D293, D298, D299, D301, D304, D305, D306, D308, D310, D311, D314, D315, D316, D317, D318, D321, D322, D324, D325, D328 and D334).

Reprints "Vortices and Notes" (pp. [32]-53, A29), "The Art of the Great Race" (pp. [78]-84, A29), "Harold Gilman" (pp. [109]-112, B9), "The Caliph's Design" (pp. [129]-183, reprints revised version published in A29, originally published A4), "The Dithyrambic Spectator" (pp. [235]-244, A14), "Pure Poetry and Pure Magic" (pp. [245]-247, A8), "The Values of the Doctrine Behind 'Subjective' Art" (pp. [248]-254, A11), "Art in a Machine Age" (pp. [268]-275, A22), "Beginnings" (pp. [291]-296, B18), "Art and Patronage" (pp. [297]-300, B20), "Super-Nature Versus Super-Real" (pp. [303]-333, A29), "The Skeleton in the Cupboard Speaks" (pp. [334]-345, A29) and "Towards an Earth Culture" (pp. [381]-392, B25).

First American edition published by Funk & Wagnalls, December, 1969, at $10.00. Title page altered to read: WYNDHAM LEWIS | ON ART | *Collected writings 1913-1956* | WITH INTRODUCTIONS AND NOTES BY | WALTER MICHEL and C. J. FOX | FUNK & WAGNALLS | NEW YORK |. Verso of title altered to read: Copyright ©1969 by Mrs Anne Wyndham Lewis | Copyright ©1969 by Walter Michel and C. J. Fox | All Rights Reserved | Library of Congress Catalog Card Number: 77-87140 | Published by Funk & Wagnalls, *A Division of* Reader's Digest Books, Inc. | Printed in Great Britain by R. & R. Clark, Ltd., Edinburgh | . Sheets, binding and dustjacket identical to English edition with publisher's name and price altered.

A46 UNLUCKY FOR PRINGLE: UNPUBLISHED AND OTHER STORIES [1973]

First edition:

UNLUCKY FOR PRINGLE: | UNPUBLISHED AND | OTHER STORIES | By | WYNDHAM LEWIS | Edited and Introduced by | C. J. FOX and ROBERT T. CHAPMAN | VISION

8½" x 5⅜". Collation: A^{16}, B-G^{16}. Pp. 224; endsheets.

[1] half-title; [3] title; [4] Vision Press Limited | 157 Knightsbridge | London SW1X 7PA | [*catalogue registration*] | ©1973 Vision Press | All rights reserved | Printed in Great Britain by | Clarke, Doble & Brendon Ltd | Plymouth | MCMLXXIII; 5-6 table of contents; 7-17 General Introduction, by C. J. Fox and Robert T. Chapman; 18 Acknowledgements; [19]-222 text.

Bound in light brown V cloth-patterned boards, stamped in gold on spine: [*running down spine:*] Wyndham Lewis UNLUCKY FOR PRINGLE [*running across bottom of spine:*] VISION | . Issued in white coated paper dustjacket, printed in blue and black, with design by Lewis (Michel 196) printed in blue and black on front. All edges trimmed and unstained. Wove unwatermarked paper.

Notes. Published May, 1973 in an edition of 1500 copies, and sold at £3.40.

This anthology contains seven previously unpublished stories and eight published stories by Lewis. The stories are divided into five sections, each of which has a sectional introduction by the editors: I. The Common Circumstances of Life; II. The Cyclopean Dividing Wall; III. Chocolate-Cream Traps and Rustic Fools; IV. Play-Shapes; V. Imposters. The sections contain the following stories: I. "Unlucky for Pringle," pp. 23-38 (originally published in *The Tramp,* 1911, D10), "A Breton Innkeeper," pp. 39-44 (originally published in *The Tramp,* 1910, D6), "The Countryhouse Party, Scotland," pp. 45-49 (previously unpublished); II. "The French Poodle," pp. 53-59 (originally published in *The Egoist,* 1916, D52), "The King of the Trenches," pp. 60-72 (originally published in *Blasting and*

Bombardiering, A26); III. "Cantleman's Spring-Mate," pp. 77-84 (originally published in *The Little Review,* 1917, D76), "The War Baby," pp. 85-108 (originally published in *Art and Letters,* 1918, D83), "Junior," pp. 109-123 (previously unpublished), "Pish-Tush," pp. 124-142 (originally published in *Encounter,* 1956, D347); IV. "The Yachting Cap," pp. 147-151 (previously unpublished), "The Weeping Man," pp. 152-158 (previously unpublished), "The Man Who Was Unlucky With Women," pp. 159-168 (previously unpublished); V. "The Two Captains," pp. 171-192 (previously unpublished), "Children of the Great," pp. 193-202 (previously unpublished) and "Doppelgänger," pp. 203-222 (originally published in *Encounter,* 1954, D341).

In all copies examined the titles in running headlines for pp. 58-59 are mistakenly reversed so that the story title ("THE FRENCH POODLE") appears on a verso, and the book title ("UNLUCKY FOR PRINGLE") appears on the recto. The running headlines throughout the rest of the book give story titles on the rectos and book title on versos.

David Lewis Inc. published 500 sets of English sheets in 1973, altering publisher's name and price throughout.

A47a THE ROARING QUEEN [1973]

Limited, signed edition:

WYNDHAM LEWIS | The Roaring Queen | Edited and introduced by Walter Allen | SECKER & WARBURG · LONDON

8½" x 5¼". Collation: *1*^{14}, *2-5*^{16}, *6*^{14}; single sheet folded once to make two leaves, bearing limitation notice mounted to title between *1*^{1} and *1*^{2}, and single leaf with etching mounted against *recto* of second folio leaf. Pp. 184; endsheets.

[1] half-title; [*mounted folio, not paged, bearing notice of limitation and plate:*] [*i*] This edition of | THE ROARING QUEEN | by Wyndham Lewis | is limited to thirty copies numbered I to XXX | which are not for sale and one hundred copies | numbered 1 to 100 for sale to the public. Each | copy is signed by Mrs Wyndham Lewis, Walter | Allen and Michael Ayrton and contains an | original etching by Michael Ayrton | [*ornament*], [*ii*] [*beneath holograph signatures of Walter Allen, G. A. Wyndham Lewis, and Michael Ayrton, single rule*] | The etching by Michael Ayrton on the | facing page is entitled 'Mr Wyndham | Lewis regarding, with distaste and rancour, | the literary establishment of the 1930s' | [*rule*] | *This is copy no* [*number written in ink*], [*iii*] [*leaf of heavy white paper with etching, numbered and signed in pencil, mounted at top*]; [3] title; [4] First published in England 1973 by | Martin Secker &

Warburg Limited | 14 Carlisle Street, London WIV 6NN | Copyright © by the Estate of the late Wyndham Lewis | Introduction Copyright © 1973 by Walter Allen | [*registration number*] | *Printed in Great Britain by Cox and Wyman Ltd,* | *London, Fakenham and Reading;* 5-23 Introduction, by Walter Allen; 24-184 text.

Bound in maroon V cloth, stamped in gold on spine: [*running down spine*] WYNDHAM LEWIS ■ THE ROARING QUEEN [*running across spine, at foot*] SECKER & | WARBURG |. Issued in matching maroon cloth-covered slipcase. All edges trimmed and unstained. Laid unwatermarked paper.

Notes. Published July 30, 1973 in an edition of 130 copies, and sold at £30 (copies "I-XXX" not for sale).

The Roaring Queen (originally spelled "Quean" in early drafts) was offered first to Charles Prentice of Chatto & Windus in late June, 1930, and although Prentice proclaimed it "one of the best things of its kind I have ever read . . . ," it was also considered "too risky for Chatto's to do. Too many heads are cracked, & the result would be that the wounded would take it out on us, which means not just the partners in Chatto's, but their authors also" (ALS, Prentice to Lewis, July 2, 1930, NIC). Lewis read portions of the manuscript to Desmond Harmsworth and Winifred Henderson on April 29, 1932 in an effort to interest Harmsworth in publishing the novel; however it wasn't until early 1935 that the manuscript was accepted for publication, by Jonathan Cape, Ltd. Lewis received £30 advance on royalties before April, 1935.

On October 19, 1936, G. Wren Howard, director of Jonathan Cape, wrote Lewis to advise him that a set of proofs of *The Roaring Queen* had been submitted to the firm's lawyer, for consideration of the matter of possible libel. The reply Jonathan Cape had received was that the text was libellous, and that the manuscript should not be published. Howard then proceeded to explain that however much he regretted having to halt publication, the firm had determined, under the circumstances, that this is what would have to be done. Lewis protested, demanding explanation for the reasons the book was considered libellous, to which Wren replied: "The advice we received was to the effect that the restricted range of the *motif* coupled with the essentially allusive treatment of the subject matter of your book rendered it inherently dangerous from the point of view of libel" (TLS, Wren to Lewis, April 13, 1937, NIC).

Two copies of the suppressed proofs of *The Roaring Queen* have been located (Harvard and Cornell). Bibliographical description is given below (NIC):

THE | ROARING QUEEN | *by* | WYNDHAM LEWIS | [*publisher's device*] | JONATHAN CAPE | THIRTY BEDFORD SQUARE | LONDON

7⅜" x 5⅛". Collation A^8, B-Q^8. Pp. 256.

[1] half-title; [2] By the same author | [*list of nineteen titles*]; [3] title; [4] FIRST PUBLISHED 1936 | JONATHAN CAPE LTD. 30 BEDFORD SQUARE, LONDON | AND 91 WELLINGTON STREET WEST, TORONTO | PRINTED IN GREAT BRITAIN IN THE CITY OF OXFORD | AT THE ALDEN PRESS; [5] internal half-title; 7-256 text.

Bound in printed wrappers, all edges trimmed.

A47b *First trade edition:*

[*Title page transcription, measurements, collation, pagination and contents identical with signed, limited edition except limitation notice and Michael Ayrton etching not present* ([*i-iv*]) *in this edition.*]

Bound in dull black V cloth-patterned boards, stamped in gold on spine as limited, signed edition. Issued in white coated paper dustjacket, printed in black and red, with caricature of Arnold Bennett by Michael Ayrton printed in black on front. All edges trimmed and unstained. Wove unwatermarked paper.

Notes. Published July 30, 1973 in an edition of 3000 copies, and sold at £2.10.

A47c *First American edition:*

WYNDHAM LEWIS | The Roaring Queen | Edited and introduced by Walter Allen | LIVERIGHT · NEW YORK

Measurements, collation, pagination, contents same as English trade edition, but with verso of title ([4]) altered to read: First published in the U.S.A. in 1973 by | Liveright, 386 Park Avenue South, | New York, N.Y. 10016 | Copyright ©1973 by the Estate of the late Wyndham Lewis | Introduction copyright ©1973 by Walter Allen | All rights reserved. No part of this book may | be reproduced in any form without per- | mission in writing from the publisher. | [*catalogue registration*] | Library of Congress Card Number: 73-80783 | *Printed in Great Britain* |.

Bound in black V cloth, stamped in gold on spine as English trade edition. Issued in dustjacket identical to A47b, but with price and publisher's name altered.

Notes. Published August, 1973 in an edition of 1001 copies, and sold at $10.00 (994 additional copies were imported from England shortly thereafter).

A48 ENEMY SALVOES [1976]

First edition:

ENEMY SALVOES | *Selected Literary Criticism* | by | WYNDHAM LEWIS | Edited with Sectional Introductions and Notes by | C. J. FOX | General Introduction by | C. H. SISSON | VISION

8½" x 5⅜". Collation: A^{16}, B-H^{16}, I^{8}. Pp. 272; endsheets.

[1] half-title; [3] title; [4] Vision Press Limited | 11-14 Stanhope Mews West | London SW7 5RD | [*catalogue registration*] | © 1975 Anne Wyndham Lewis and Vision Press | *All rights reserved* | Printed in Great Britain by | Clarke, Doble & Brendon Ltd | Plymouth | MCMLXXV; 5-6 table of contents; 7-18 general introduction, by C. H. Sisson; 19 Preface, by C. J. Fox; [21]-265 text; 267-272 index.

Bound in red V cloth, stamped in gold running down spine: Wyndham Lewis ENEMY SALVOES Vision |. Issued in white coated paper dustjacket, printed in black, red and orange, with design by Lewis on front cover (Michel 627). All edges trimmed and unstained. Wove unwatermarked paper.

Notes. Published January, 1976 in an edition of 1350 copies, and sold at £4.95.

American edition published by Barnes & Noble on February 23, 1976 in an edition of 650 copies, sold at $17.50.

Contains "The Solitary Outlaw" (pp. 23-30, from *The Enemy, No. 1)*; "Truth and the Writer's Freedom" (pp. 31-34, from *The Writer and the Absolute)*; "The External Approach to Writing" (pp. 35-37, from *Men Without Art)*; "Satire Defended" (pp. 41-49, from "Studies in the Art of Laughter," *The London Mercury,* D215); "Shakespeare" (pp. 53-65, from *The Lion and the Fox)*; "George Bernard Shaw" (pp. 66-71, from *The Art of Being Ruled)*; "Cervantes" (pp. 75-76, from *The Lion and the Fox)*; "The Russians" (pp. 77-83, from ["The Puritans of the Steppes"] *Rude Assignment)*; "Russian Novelists and Trollope" (pp. 84-86, from " 'Detachment' and the Fictionist," *The English Review,* D217); "Henry James" (pp. 88-92, from *Men Without Art)*; "Virginia Woolf" (pp. 93-97, from *Men Without Art)*; "James Joyce" (pp. 99-111, from *Time and Western Man)*; "Gertrude Stein" (pp. 113-116, from *Time and Western Man)*; "D.H. Lawrence" (pp. 118-125, from *Paleface)*; "Sherwood Anderson" (pp. 127-131, from *Paleface)*; "Ernest Hemingway" (pp. 132-144, from *Men Without Art)*; "Ezra Pound" (pp. 161-171, from *Time and Western Man)*; "The Machine Poets" (pp. 174-175, from TM at NIC, later rewritten and published by Lewis as "Shropshire Lads and Robots," *New Britain,* D197); "Matthew Arnold" (pp. 179-182, from *The Times Literary Supplement,*

D342); "T.S. Eliot and I.A. Richards" (pp. 184-199, from *Men Without Art)*; "Gustave Flaubert" (pp. 203-206, from *Men Without Art)*; "Charles Péguy" (pp. 208-210, from *The Art of Being Ruled)*; "The War Writers" (pp. 212-216, from *The Old Gang and the New Gang)*; "The *transition* Writers" (pp. 217-225, from *The Diabolical Principle and the Dithyrambic Spectator)*; "André Malraux" (pp. 226-233, from *The Writer and the Absolute)*; "Camus and Sartre" (pp. 235-245, from *The Writer and the Absolute)*; "George Orwell" (pp. 246-262, from *The Writer and the Absolute)*; " 'Detachment' and the Writer" (pp. 263-265, from " 'Detachment' and the Fictionist," *The English Review,* D220).

A49 THE CODE OF A HERDSMAN 1977

First separate edition:

The Code of a Herdsman | Wyndham Lewis | Wyndham Lewis Society | 1977

8½" x 5⅞". 2 sheets folded once to make 4 unsigned leaves. Pp. 8; wrappers.

[1] title; [2] Published by the Wyndham Lewis Society | 148 Bellahouston Drive, Glasgow G52 1HL | Copyright 1977 Anne Wyndham Lewis; 3-7 text; [8] 'The Code of a Herdsman' was first published in the July, 1917 number | of *The Little Review,* where it was wrongly included in the 'Imaginary | Letters' series. A manuscript in the Wyndham Lewis Collection at | Cornell University shows that it belongs to the story 'The Crowd', | part of which was published in *Blast* No. 2 in 1915. | Text edited by Alan Munton. | Printed by Able Printers (T.U.) Reading.

Bound in heavy white wove paper wrappers, printed in black on front cover: The Code of a Herdsman | Wyndham Lewis | [*design by Lewis, Michel 106*] |. Text printed on off-white, coated paper. All edges trimmed and unstained; stapled.

Notes. Published October 24, 1977 in an edition of 300 copies, and distributed without charge to members of the Wyndham Lewis Society, loosely enclosed with *Lewisletter No.* 7. Separately sold at £2 as a set, along with *Imaginary Letters* (A50).

The Code of a Herdsman was originally published in *The Little Review* in July, 1917 (D71) and in *The Ideal Giant* in November, 1917 (A2). This is the first separate publication of the story.

A50 IMAGINARY LETTERS 1977

First separate edition:

Imaginary Letters | Wyndham Lewis | Wyndham Lewis Society | 1977

8¼" x 5⅞". 7 sheets folded once to make 14 unsigned leaves. Pp. 28; wrappers.

[1] title; [2] Published by the Wyndham Lewis Society | 148 Bellahouston Drive, Glasgow G52 1HL | Copyright 1977 Anne Wyndham Lewis; 3-25 text; [26] The 'Imaginary Letters' were first published in the *Little Review* as | follows: I May 1917; II June 1917; III-IV March 1918; V-VI April | 1918. | The form and manner of the 'Imaginary Letters' owe something to | Ivan Turgenev's story 'A Correspondence', which appeared in *The Diary* | *of a Superfluous Man Etc.*, published in a translation by Constance | Garnett in 1899. | Text edited by Alan Munton. | Printed by Able Printers (T.U.) Reading.

Bound in heavy white wove paper wrappers, printed in black on front cover: Imaginary Letters | Wyndham Lewis | [*design by Lewis, Michel 105*] |. Text printed on off-white coated paper. All edges trimmed and unstained; stapled.

Notes. Published October 24, 1977 in an edition of 300 copies, and distributed without charge to members of the Wyndham Lewis Society, loosely enclosed with *Lewisletter No.* 7. Separately sold at £2 as a set, along with *The Code of a Herdsman* (A49).

Originally published in *The Little Review* (D67, D69, D80 and D81). This is the first separate publication of the series.

A51 MRS. DUKES' MILLION 1977

First edition:

Mrs. Dukes' Million | WYNDHAM LEWIS | [*design by Lewis, Michel 47*] | THE COACH HOUSE PRESS | TORONTO · 1977

8¼" x 5½". Collation: [184] unsigned leaves. Pp. 368.

[1] half-title; [2] [*design by Lewis, Michel 47*]; [3] title; [4] Edited for the press by Frank Davey. | [*acknowledgements*] | Copyright ©1977 by Mrs. Anne Wyndham Lewis | This edition copyright ©1977 by The Coach House Press. | The cover drawing copyright ©1977 by Mrs. Anne Wyndham Lewis. | Typeset in Bembo and printed in Canada | in an edition of 2000 copies at | 401 (rear) Huron Street |

Toronto, Canada M5S 2G5; [5-7] table of contents; 9-365 text; [367-368] Editor's Note.

Perfect bound, glued in grey textured card cover, stamped in silver on front cover: *Mrs. Dukes' Million* | WYNDHAM LEWIS | [*design by Lewis, Michel 47, printed in dark grey*] |. Stamped in silver running down spine: WYNDHAM LEWIS *Mrs. Dukes' Million* [*publisher's device printed in dark grey across bottom of spine*] |. Youthful portrait of Lewis by Augustus John and blurb on rear cover, printed in dark grey. Blurb printed in dark grey on inside front cover. All edges trimmed and unstained. Laid unwatermarked paper.

Notes. Published December 16, 1977 in an edition of 2000 copies, and sold at $7.50.

Written between 1908-1910 this, Lewis's first novel, was submitted to the literary agent J.B. Pinker in 1910. Intended for publication under a pseudonym, Lewis suggested several alternate titles for the novel such as "Khan and Company" and "The Three Mrs. Dukes," but Pinker apparently considered the novel unmarketable and no attempt was made to publish it. The 518 page typescript (NIC) bears numerous revisions in both Lewis's and his mother's holograph, and has the pseudonym "John Lawrence" on a leaf. The text of this first publication of the novel was edited by Frank Davey.

In the *Coach House Press Newsletter,* no. 5 (February 1978) [1], the publishers state that "a limited number of line printer editions of [*Mrs. Dukes' Million*] were run off and sent out as advance review copies." These copies were printed on a General Electric TermiNet line printer, the first such printed by the publisher, and were mentioned in an article about recently acquired printing equipment, "Technotes: Line Printers." No example of this line printer edition seen.

Front cover of *Timon of Athens*, designed by Lewis (A1).

Back cover of *Timon of Athens*, designed by Lewis (A1).

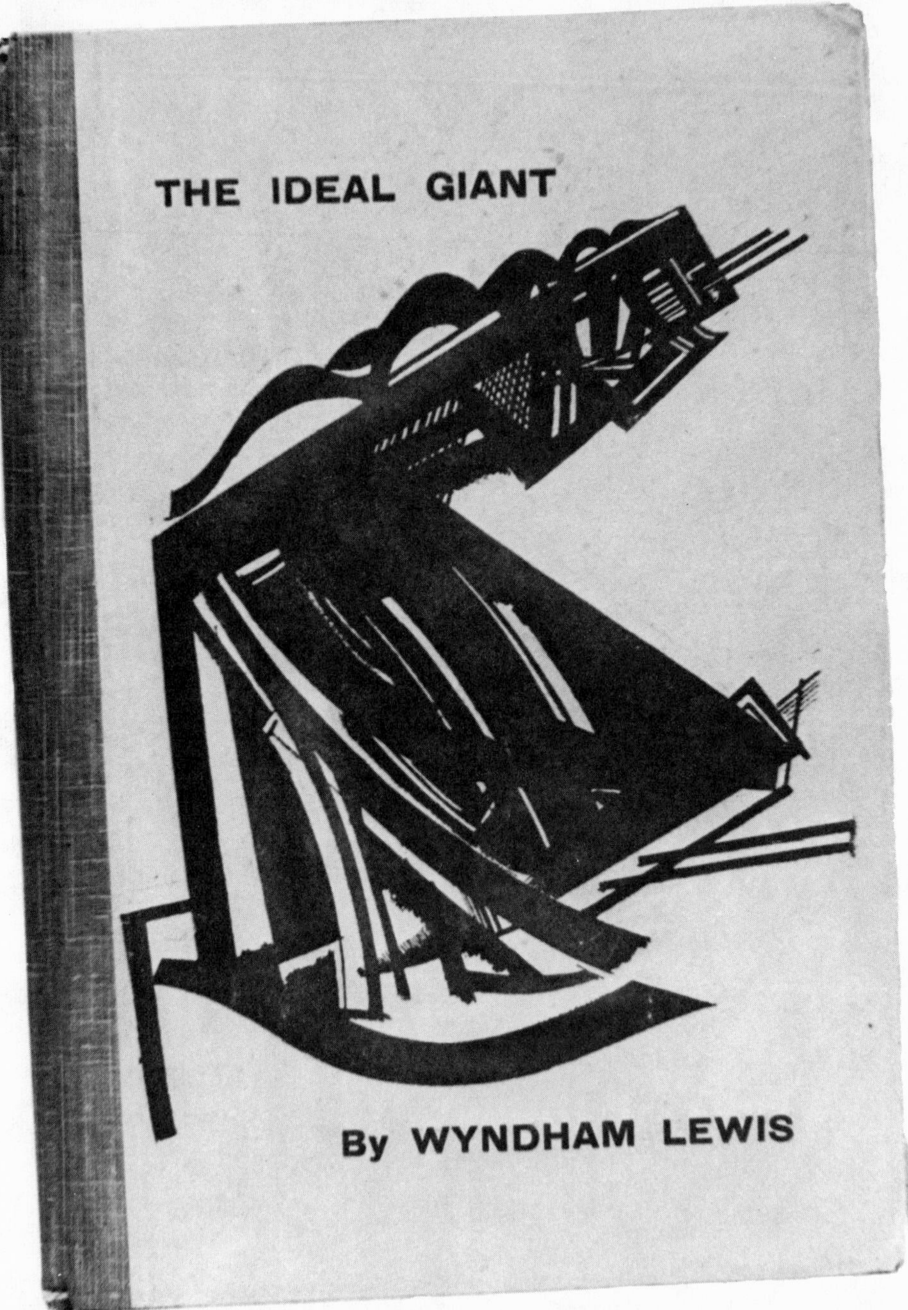

Front cover of *The Ideal Giant*, designed by Lewis (A2).

From left to right: first American edition of *Tarr*, first binding (A3a(1)), second binding (A3a(2)) and second American edition (A3c).

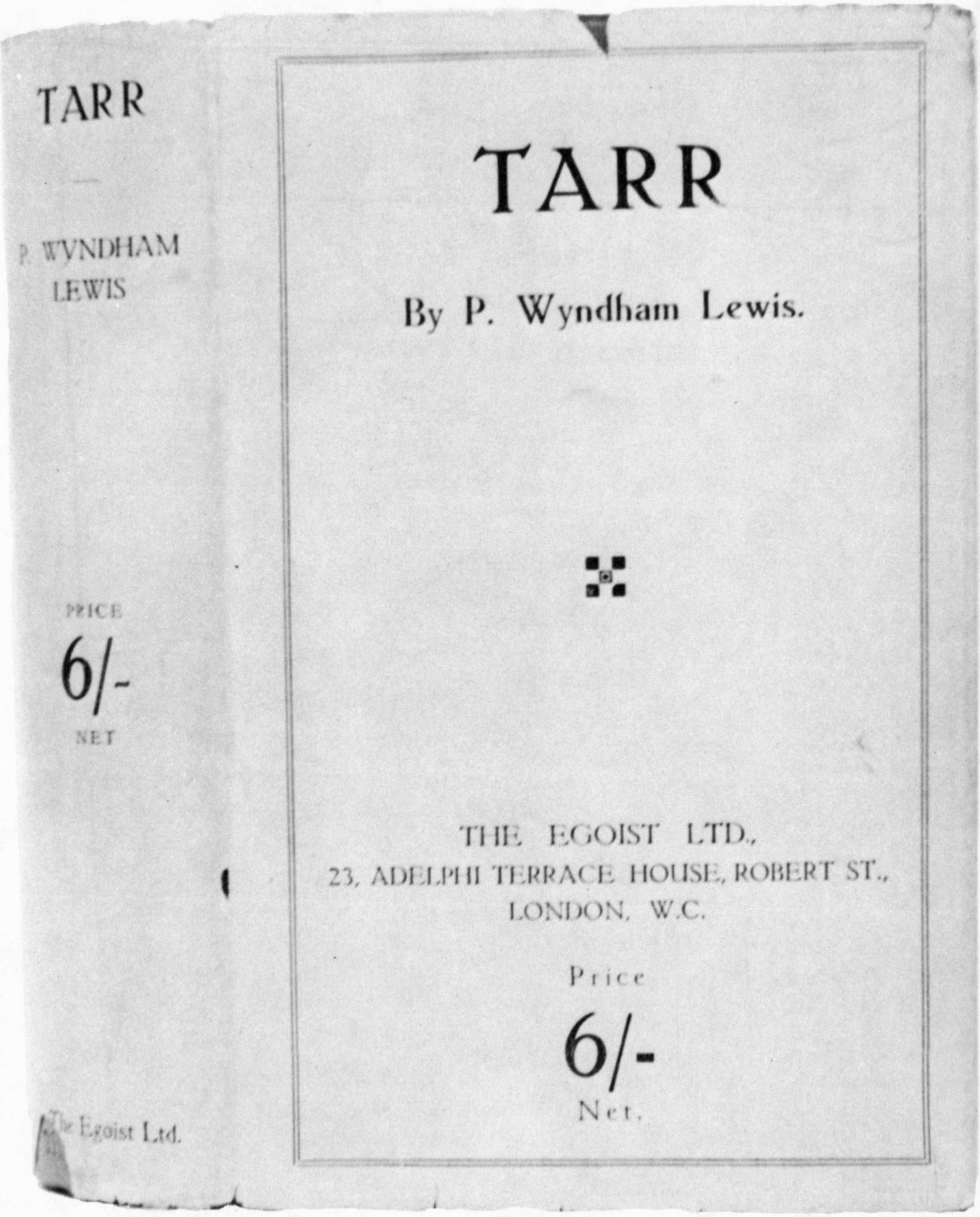

TARR

P. WYNDHAM LEWIS

PRICE

6/-

NET

The Egoist Ltd.

TARR

By P. Wyndham Lewis.

THE EGOIST LTD.,
23, ADELPHI TERRACE HOUSE, ROBERT ST.,
LONDON, W.C.

Price

6/-

Net.

Dustjacket for *Tarr*, first English edition (A3b).

Dustjacket for *Tarr*, second American edition (A3c).

Dustjacket for *Tarr*, first revised edition (A3d).

Dustjacket, designed by Lewis for second revised edition of *Tarr* (A3e).

Front cover of *The Caliph's Design* (A4).

Front cover of *Fifteen Drawings*, designed by Lewis (A5).

Dustjacket for *The Art of Being Ruled* (A6a).

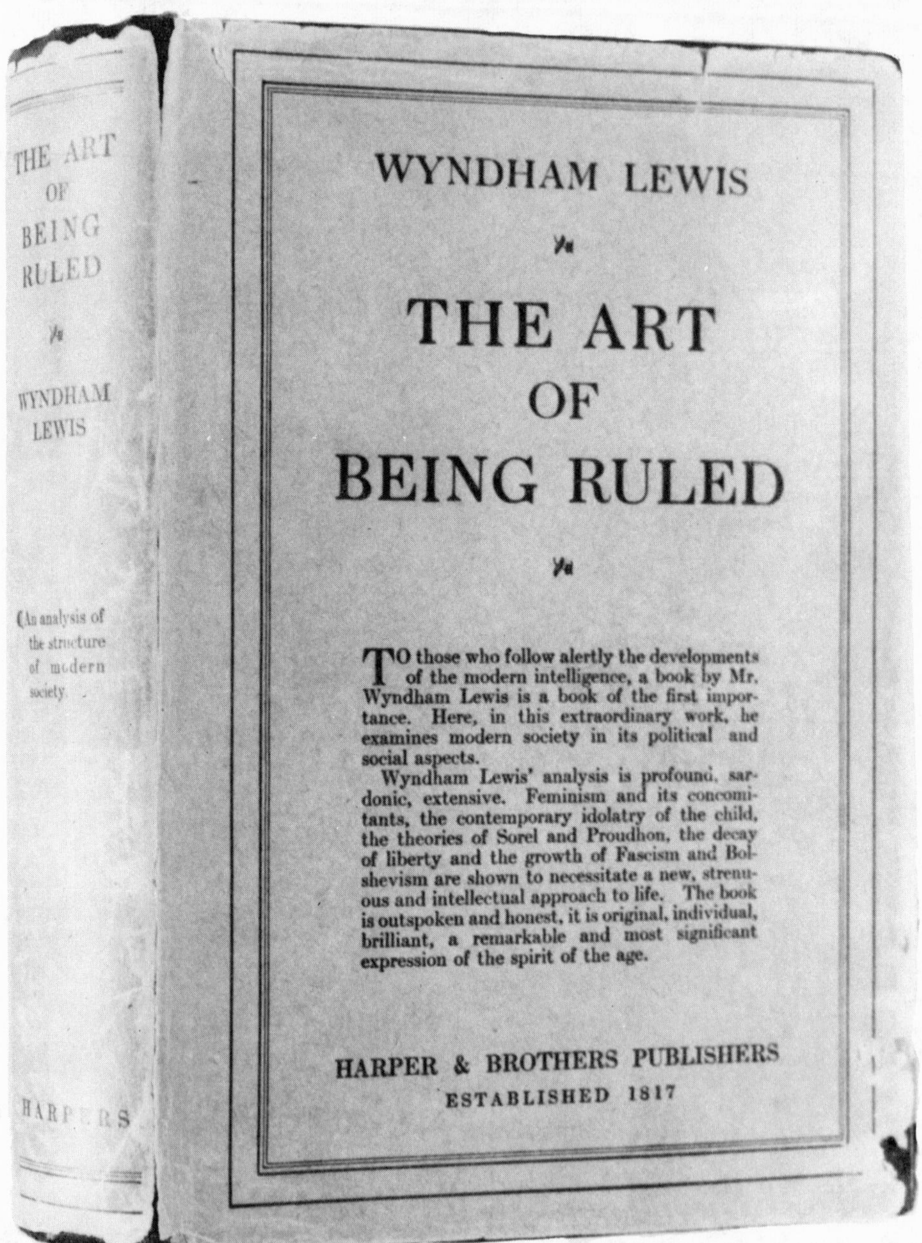

Dustjacket for *The Art of Being Ruled*, first American edition (A6b).

Dustjacket for *The Lion and the Fox* (A7a).

First American edition of *The Lion and the Fox* (A7b).

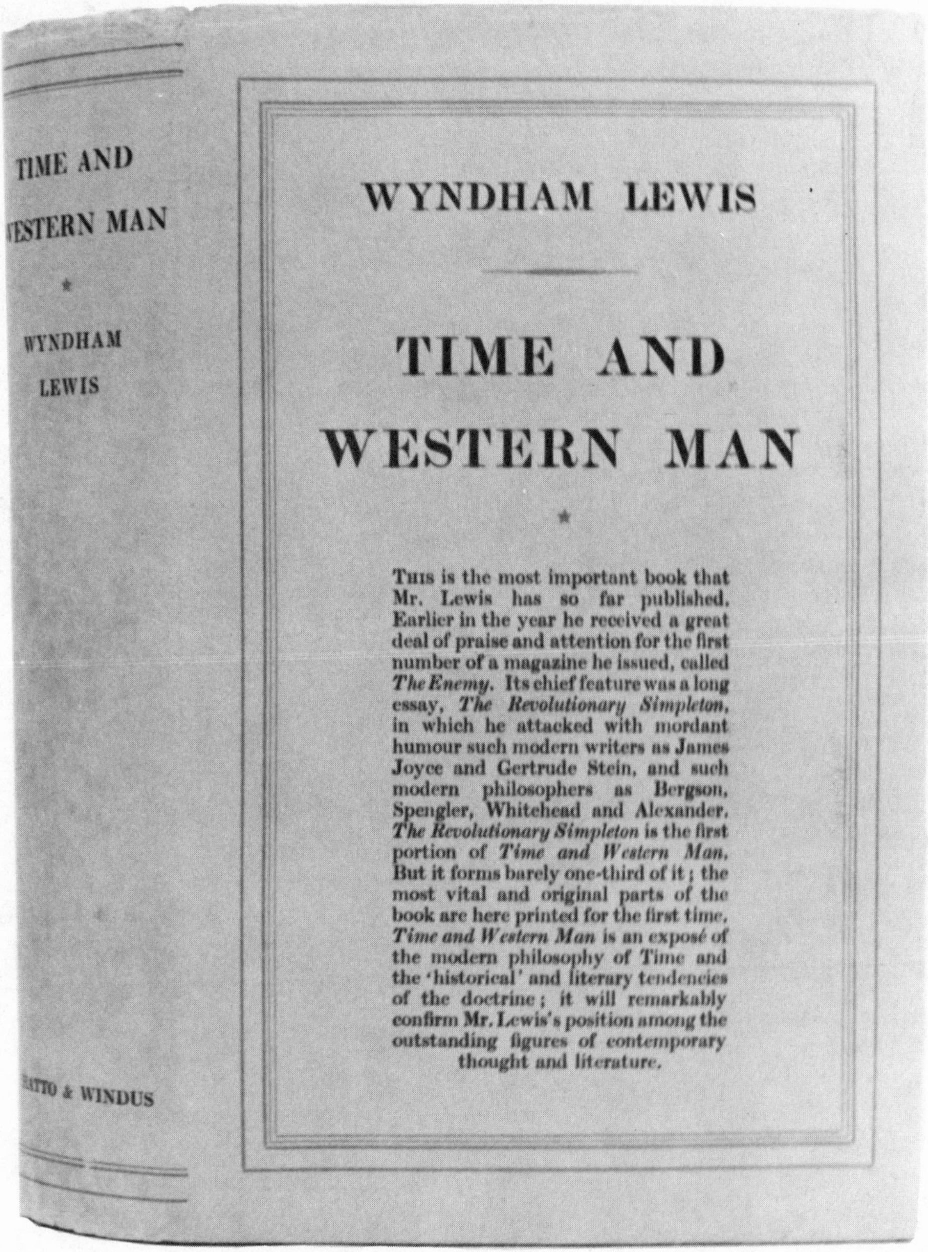

TIME AND
ESTERN MAN
*
WYNDHAM
LEWIS

ATTO & WINDUS

WYNDHAM LEWIS

TIME AND
WESTERN MAN

*

THIS is the most important book that Mr. Lewis has so far published. Earlier in the year he received a great deal of praise and attention for the first number of a magazine he issued, called *The Enemy*. Its chief feature was a long essay, *The Revolutionary Simpleton*, in which he attacked with mordant humour such modern writers as James Joyce and Gertrude Stein, and such modern philosophers as Bergson, Spengler, Whitehead and Alexander. *The Revolutionary Simpleton* is the first portion of *Time and Western Man*. But it forms barely one-third of it; the most vital and original parts of the book are here printed for the first time. *Time and Western Man* is an exposé of the modern philosophy of Time and the 'historical' and literary tendencies of the doctrine; it will remarkably confirm Mr. Lewis's position among the outstanding figures of contemporary thought and literature.

Dustjacket for *Time and Western Man* (A8a).

Dustjacket for *Time and Western Man*, first American edition, designed by Lewis (A8b).

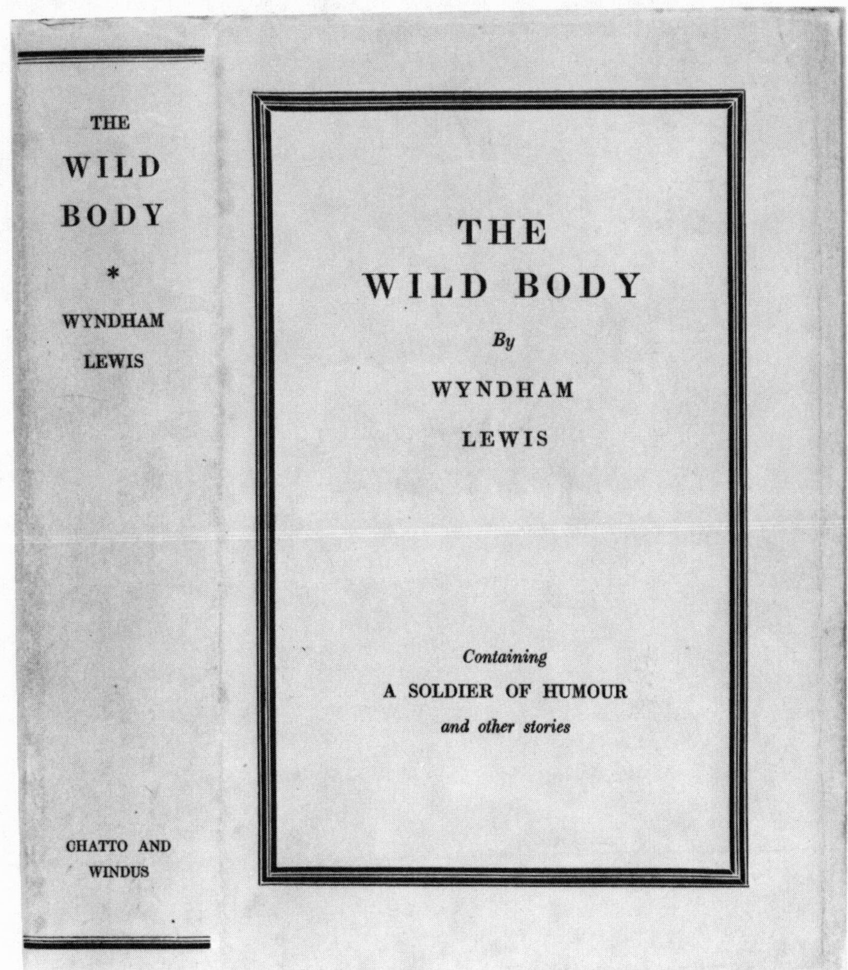

Dustjacket for limited, signed edition of *The Wild Body* (A9a).

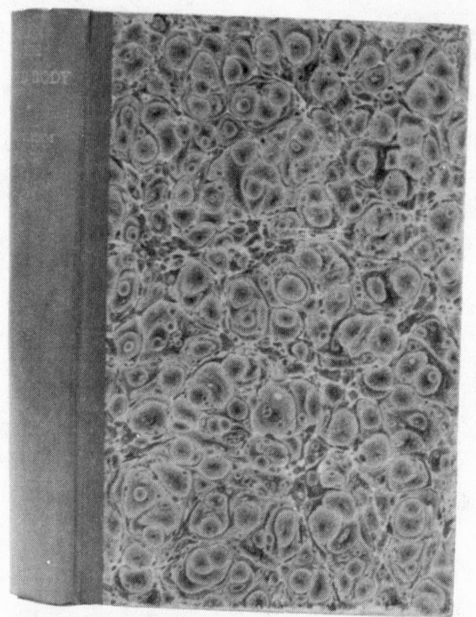

Limited, signed edition of *The Wild Body* (A9a).

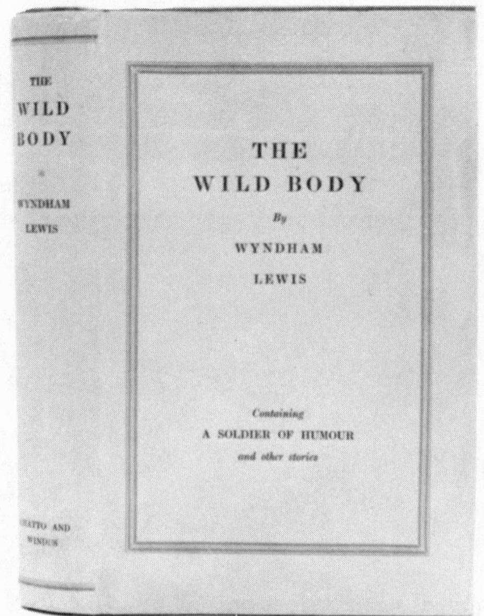

Dustjacket for first trade edition of *The Wild Body* (A9b).

Dustjacket for limited, signed edition of *The Childermass* (A10a).

Dustjacket for *The Childermass*, first trade edition (A10b).

Dustjacket for *The Childermass*, first American edition (A10c).

Dustjacket designed by Michael Ayrton for *The Human Age, Book 1, The Childermass* (A10d).

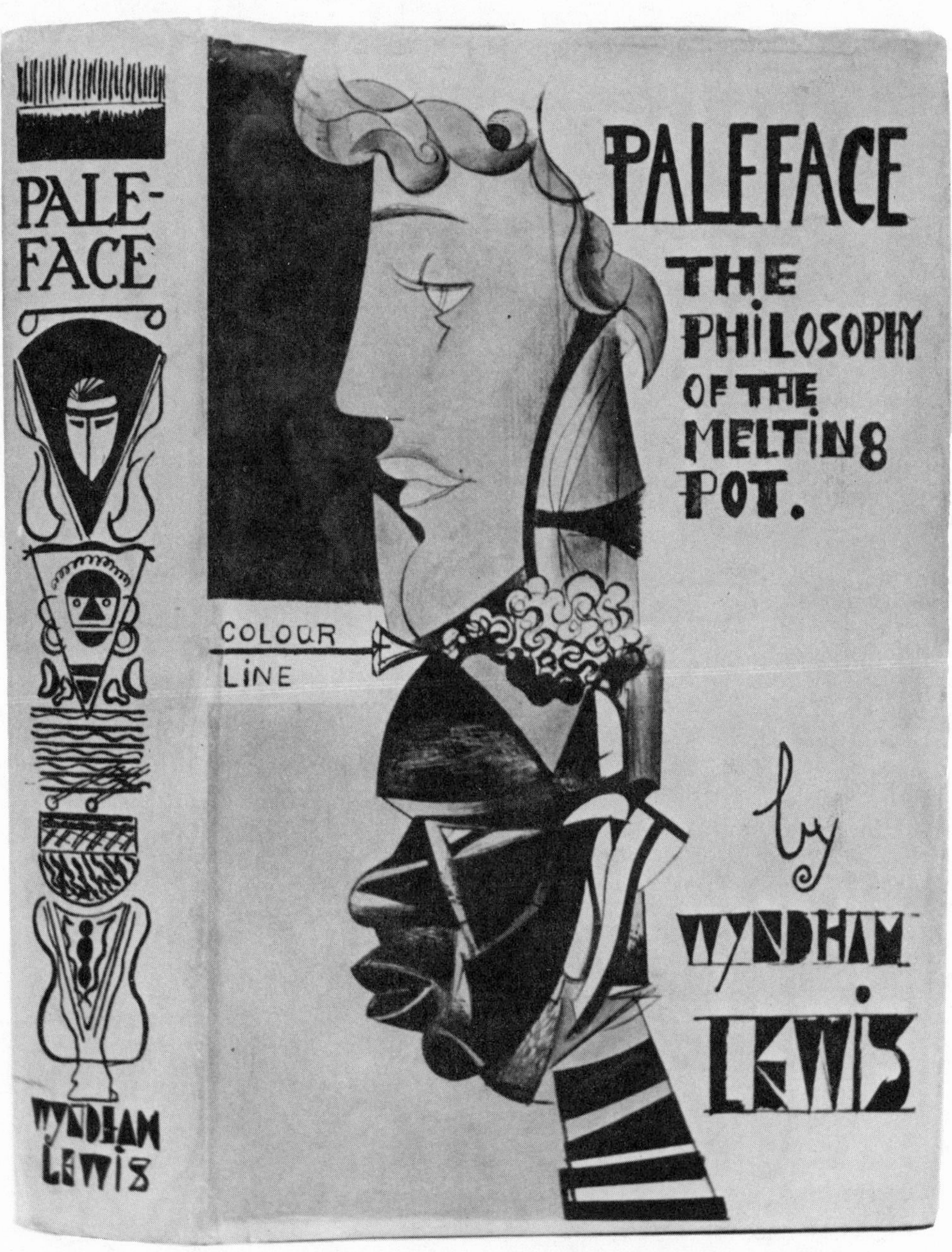

Dustjacket for *Paleface*, designed by Lewis (A11).

Top left: dustjacket for limited, signed edition of *The Apes of God*, designed by Lewis (A12a). Top right: first trade edition, designed by Lewis (A12b). Bottom: dustjacket designed by Michael Ayrton for limited, signed 25th Anniversary edition (A12d).

Dustjacket for *The Apes of God*, first American edition, with designs by Lewis (A12c).

Dustjacket for *Hitler*, designed by Lewis (A13).

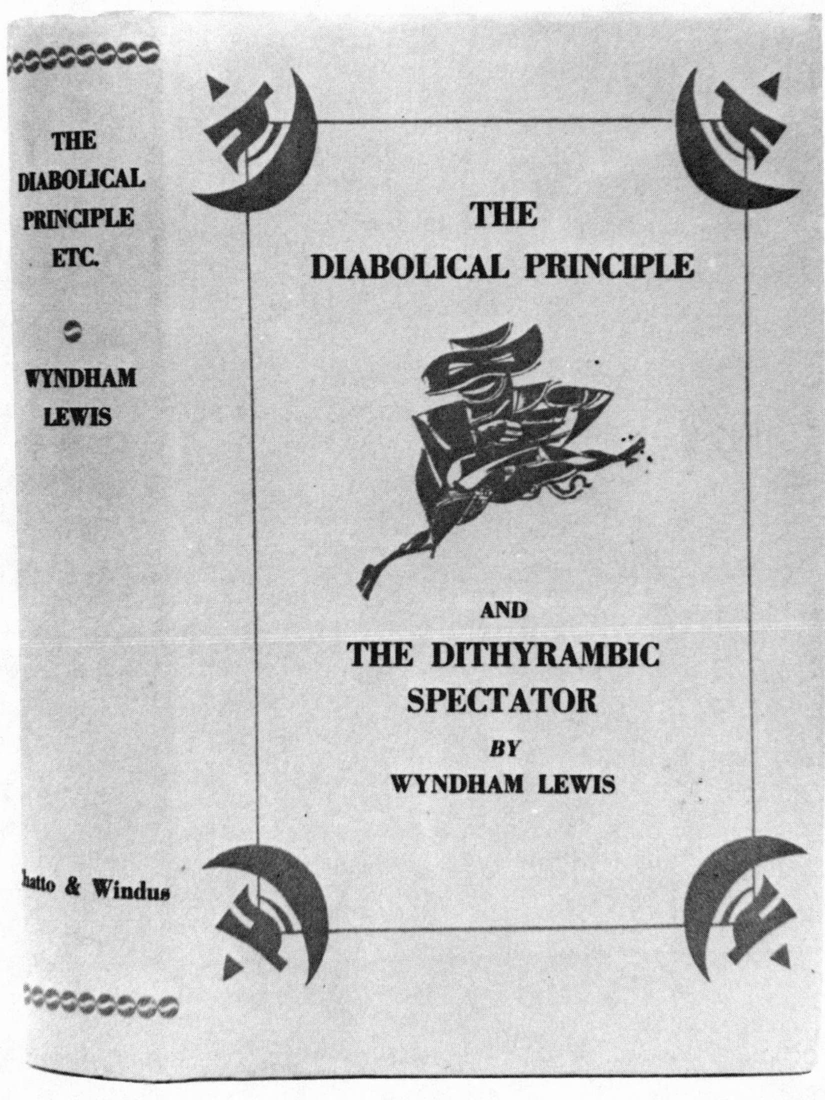

Dustjacket for *The Diabolical Principle and the Dithyrambic Spectator*, designed by Lewis (A14).

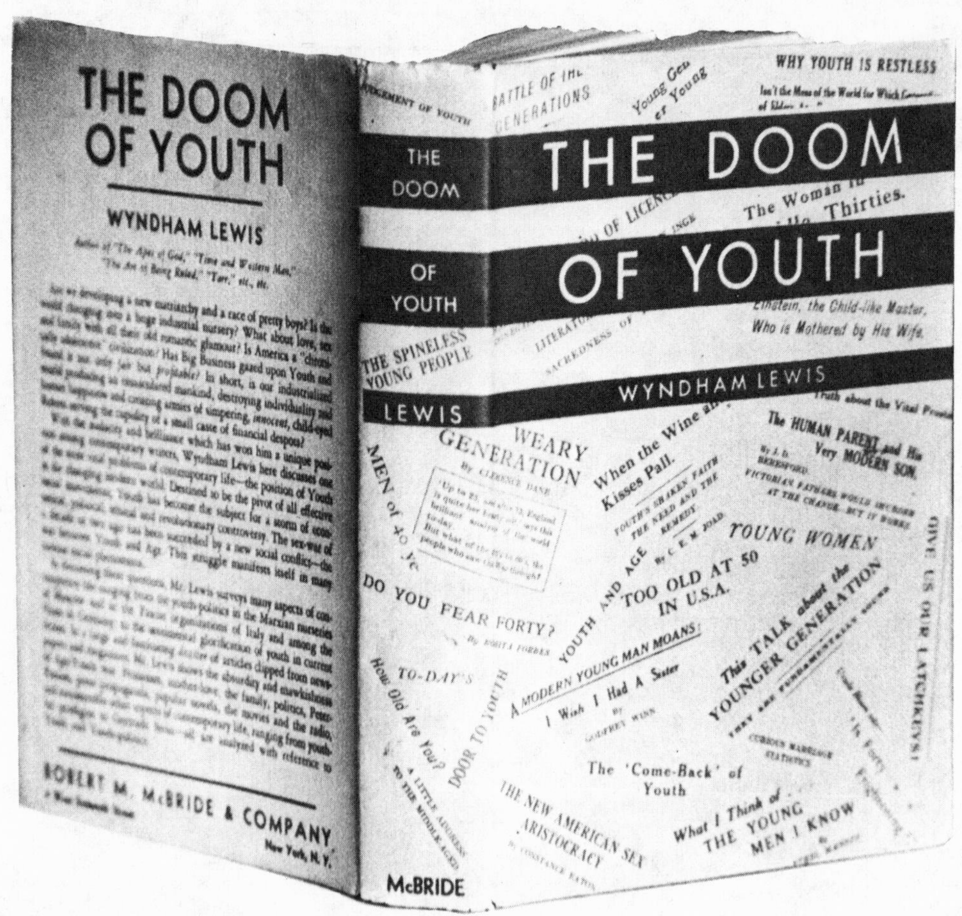

Dustjacket for *The Doom of Youth* (A15a).

Dustjacket for *Doom of Youth*, first English edition (A15b).

Dustjacket for *Filibusters in Barbary* (A16a).

Dustjacket for *Filibusters in Barbary*, National Travel Club edition (A16b).

Dustjacket for *Filibusters in Barbary*, first regular American trade edition (A16c).

From left to right: second variant binding on *The Enemy of the Stars* (A17(2)), first variant binding (A17(1)) and third variant binding (A17(3)). First and second variants in pictorial boards, designed by Lewis.

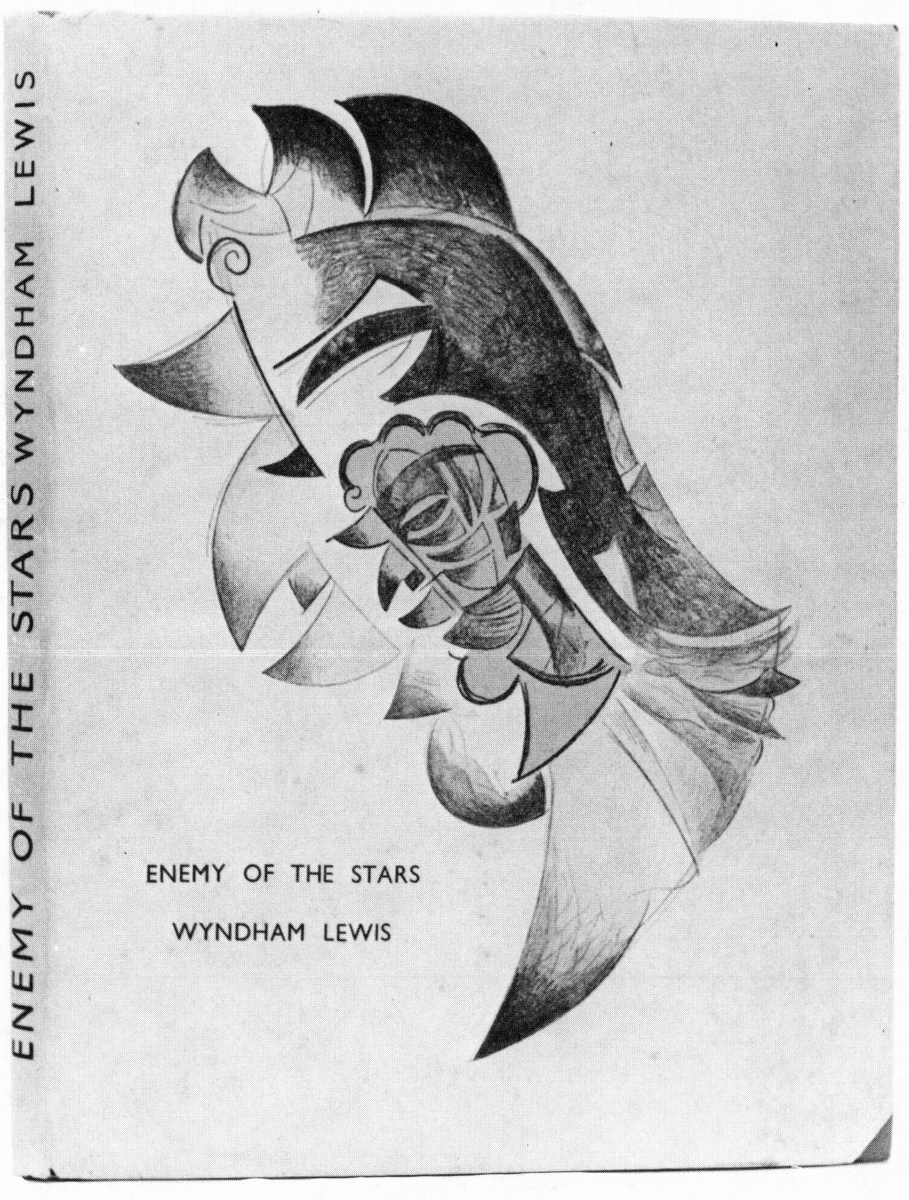

Dustjacket for *The Enemy of the Stars*, designed by Lewis (A17(1-3)).

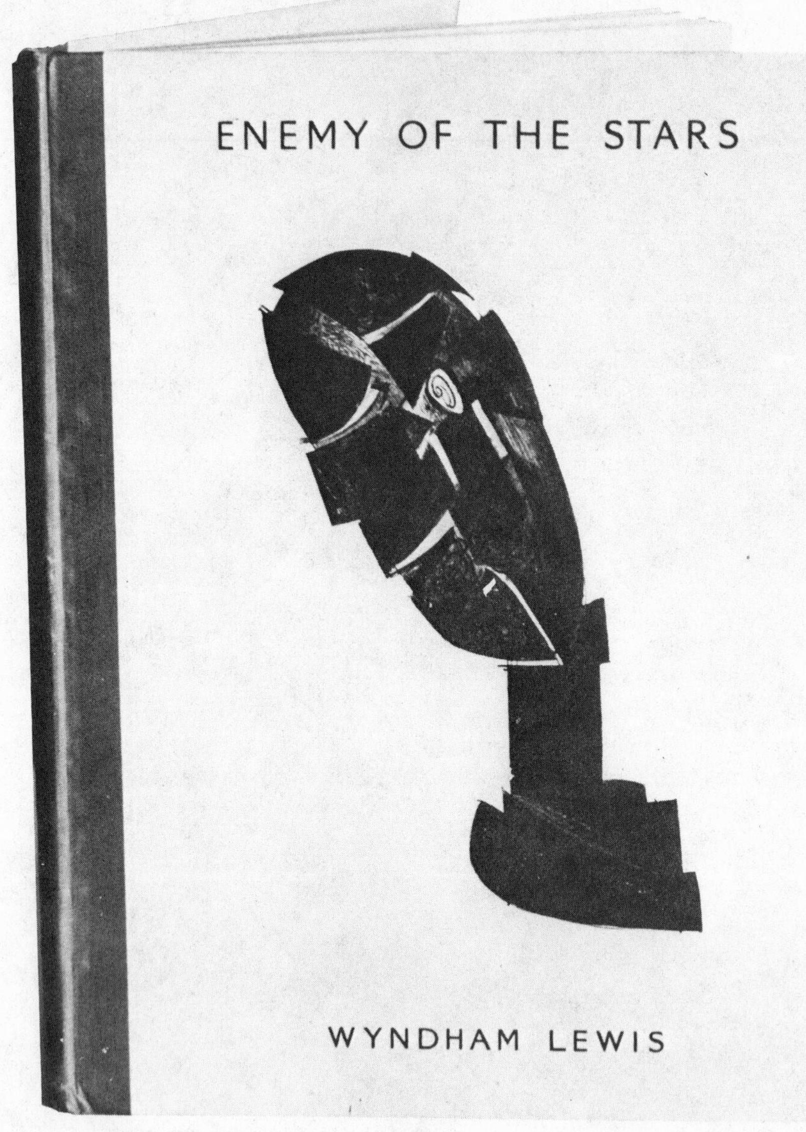

Front cover of first and second variant bindings of *The Enemy of the Stars*, designed by Lewis (A17(1-2)).

Dustjacket for *Snooty Baronet* (A18).

Front cover, title page and leaves of *Thirty Personalities and a Self-Portrait* (A19).

THE OLD GANG AND THE NEW GANG · WYNDHAM LEWIS

THE

OLD

GANG

AND

THE

NEW

GANG

BY

WYNDHAM

LEWIS

Dustjacket for *The Old Gang and the New Gang* (A20).

Limited, signed edition vellum binding of *One-Way Song* (A21a).

Dustjacket for *One-Way Song*, first trade edition, designed by Lewis (A21b).

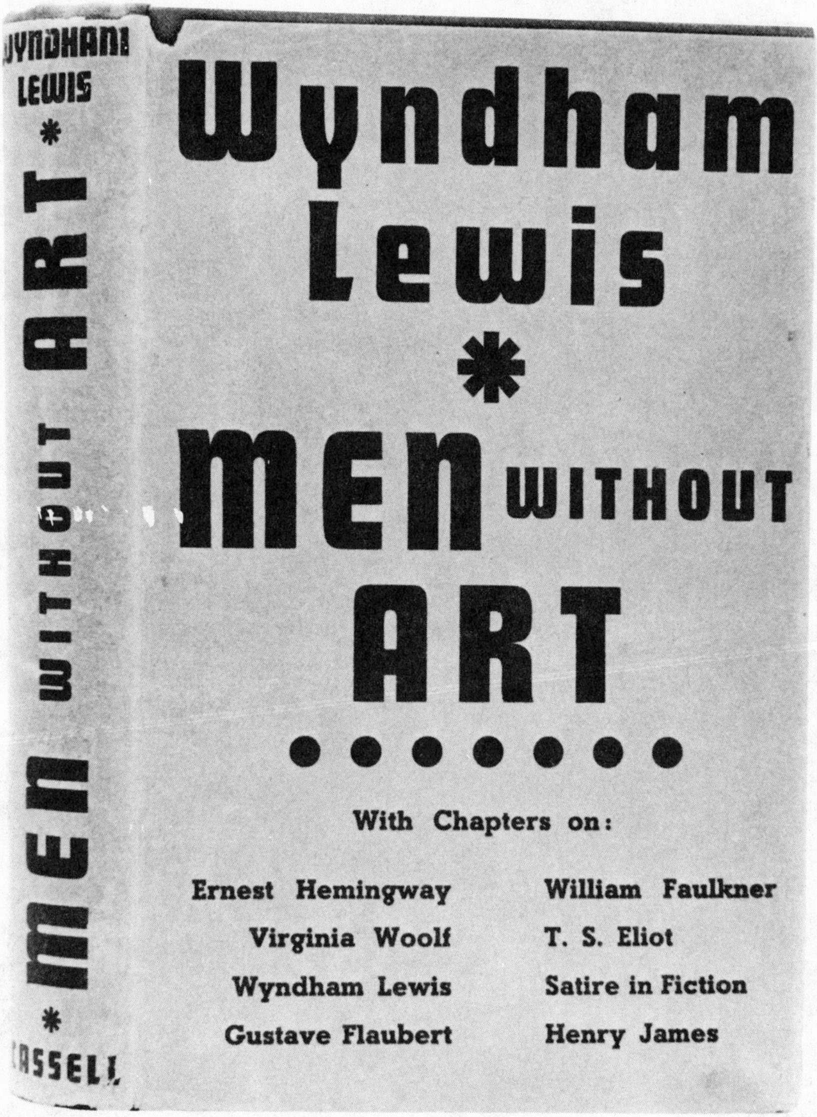

Dustjacket for *Men Without Art* (A22).

Dustjacket for *Left Wings Over Europe* (A23).

Dustjacket for *Count Your Dead: They Are Alive!*, designed by Lewis (A24).

Dustjacket for *The Revenge for Love* (A25a).

Dustjacket designed by Charles Handley-Read for *The Revenge for Love*, second English edition (A25b).

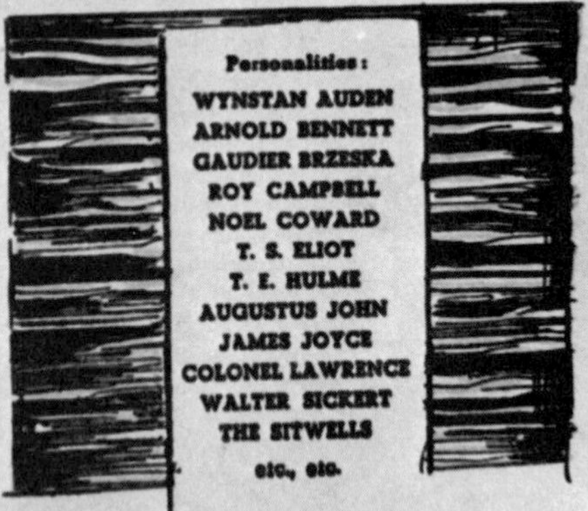

Dustjacket for *Blasting and Bombardiering*, with designs by Lewis (A26a).

Dustjacket designed by John Plant for *The Mysterious Mr Bull* (A27).

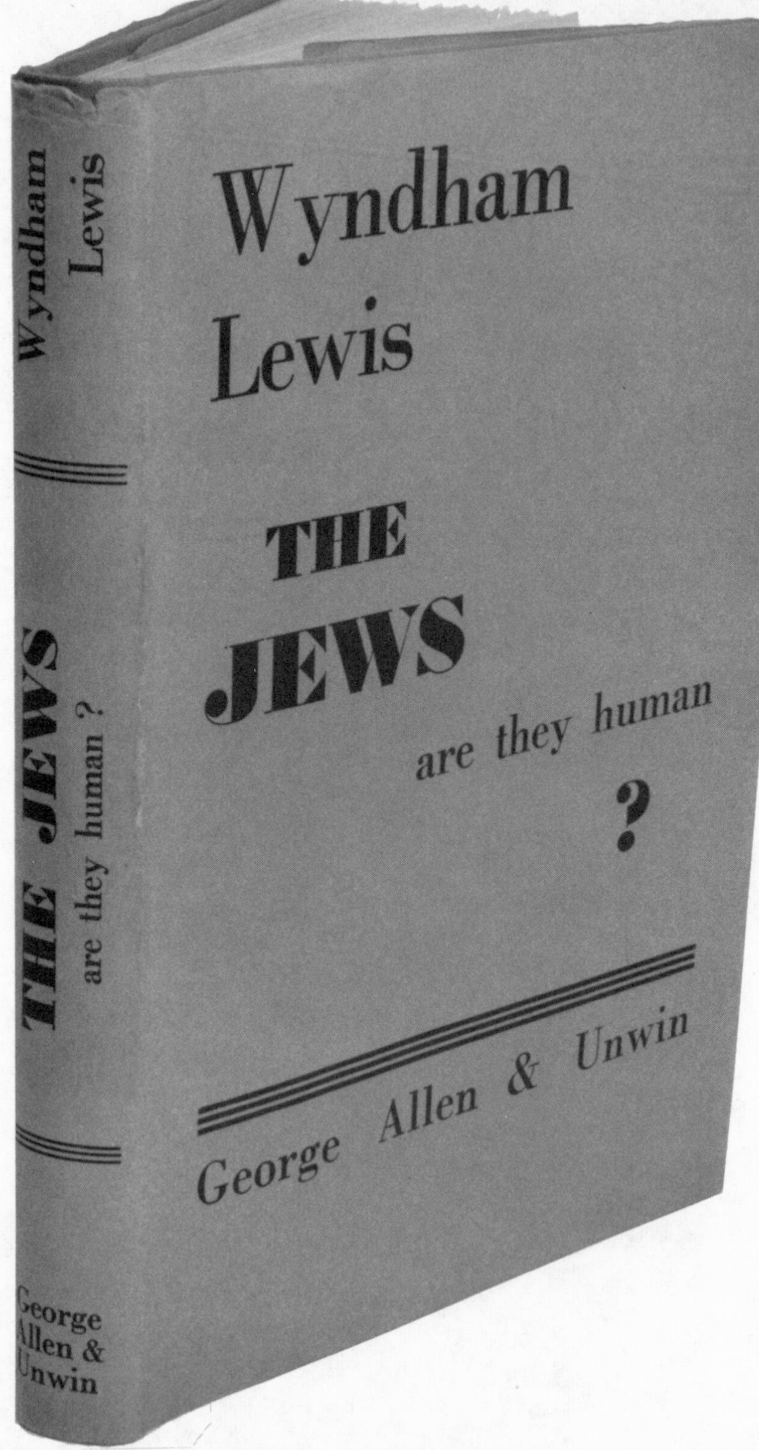

Dustjacket for *The Jews Are They Human?* (A28).

Dustjacket for *Wyndham Lewis the Artist From 'Blast' to Burlington House*, with designs by Lewis (A29).

THE HITLER CULT

and how it will end

by Wyndham Lewis

DENT

THE HITLER CULT and how it will end——by Wyndham Lewis

In this book Wyndham Lewis discusses the Hitler cult in all its bearings & foretells its catastrophic termin-

(continued on back of wrapper)

Dustjacket for *The Hitler Cult* (A30).

Dustjacket for *America, I Presume* (A31).

ANGLOSAXONY:
A League that Works

WYNDHAM LEWIS

ANGLOSAXONY: A League that Works — WYNDHAM LEWIS

Front cover of *Anglosaxony: A League that Works* (A32).

Dustjacket for *The Vulgar Streak* (A33).

Dustjacket for *America and Cosmic Man* (A34a).

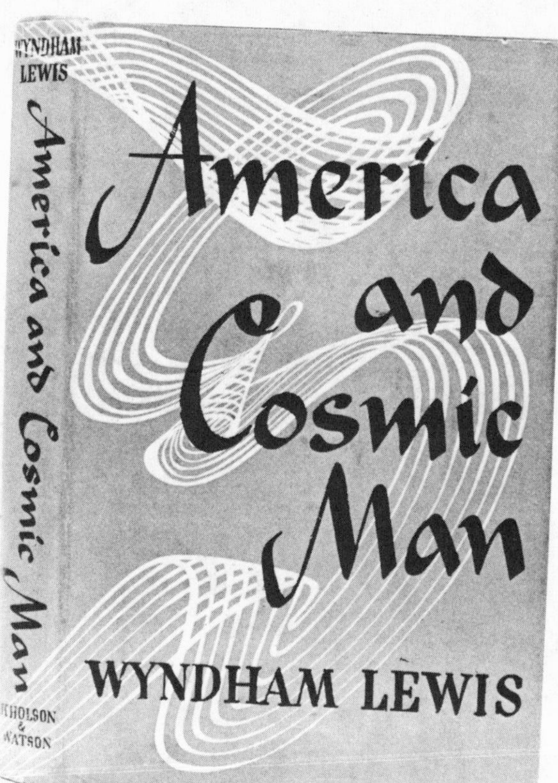

Dustjacket for *America and Cosmic Man*, first American edition (A34b).

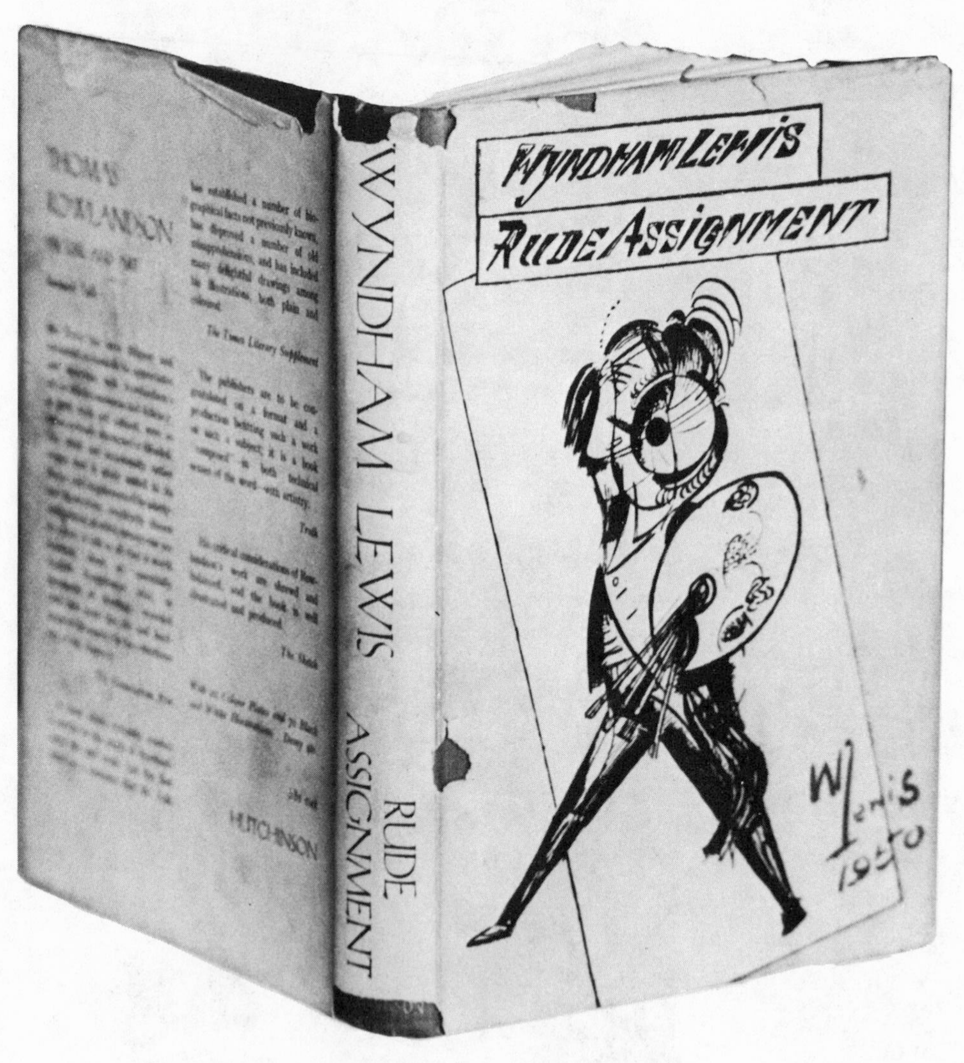

Dustjacket for *Rude Assignment*, designed by Lewis (A35).

Dustjacket for *Rotting Hill* (A36a).

Dustjacket for *Rotting Hill*, first American edition (A36b).

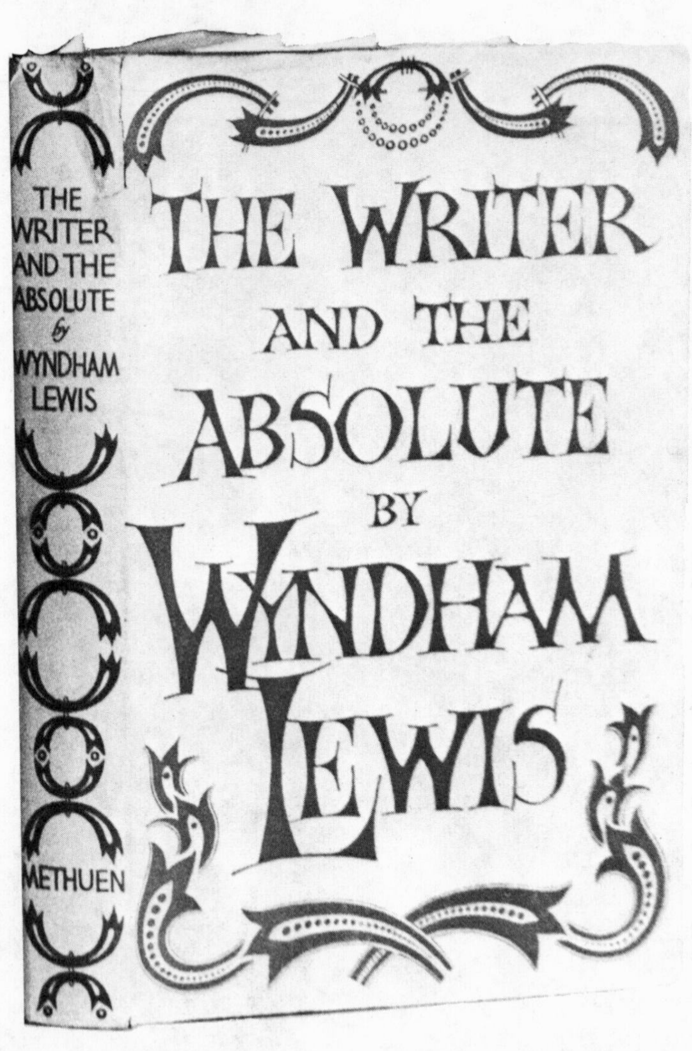

Dustjacket designed by Charles Handley-Read for *The Writer and the Absolute* (A37).

Dustjacket designed by Michael Ayrton for *Self Condemned* (A38a).

Dustjacket for *Self Condemned*, first American edition (A38b).

Dustjacket for *The Demon of Progress in the Arts* (A39a).

Dustjacket for *The Demon of Progress in the Arts*, first American edition (A39b).

Dustjacket designed by Michael Ayrton for *The Human Age, Books 2 and 3* (A40).

Dustjacket designed by Michael Ayrton for *The Red Priest* (A41).

B. Books, Pamphlets and Exhibition Catalogues with Contributions by Wyndham Lewis (including several graphic collaborations)

B1 THE CAVE OF THE GOLDEN CALF [1912]

[*At right of design by Lewis, Michel 32, printed in yellowish orange:*] Cabaret | Club | The Cave | of the | Golden | Calf | [*beneath design:*] 9, Heddon Street | Regent Street | W.

10⅞" x 8⅝". Two sheets folded to make 4 unpaged leaves, with single leaf mounted to verso of *A3*. Pp. [10]. Two separate leaves laid in all copies: (1). announcement of Sunday Theatre performances (printed in black on one side of orange sheet), (2). application form for joining The Cabaret Club (printed in orange on one side on white sheet). Heavy wove unwatermarked paper, printed entirely in yellowish orange, stapled.

Notes. Distributed in September, 1912 without charge.

Contains six designs by Lewis: [1], Michel 32; [2], Michel 35; [3], Michel 34; [5], Michel 36; [9], Michel 37; [10], Michel 38. This brochure announces the re-opening of the second season of The Cabaret Club on October 2, 1912.

B2 EXHIBITION OF ENGLISH POST-IMPRESSIONISTS, CUBISTS AND OTHERS 1913

County Borough of Brighton. | [*coat of arms of the borough*] | PUBLIC ART GALLERIES. | [*rule*] | CATALOGUE | OF AN | Exhibition of the Work of | English Post Impressionists, | Cubists and others. | [*rule*] | 3905 - 8/12/13 - 1000. C. Pell & Son, Typs., Brighton.

5⅜" x 4⅜". Pp. 32.

Bound in green wrappers, printed in black. All edges trimmed and unstained.

Notes. Published December 8, 1913 in an edition of 1000 copies, and distributed without charge at the exhibition.

Contains "The Cubist Room" by Lewis, one of the two forewords to the catalogue. The other foreword, by J. B. Manson, represents the more traditional artists whose works were shown with examples of *avant garde* work, whose spokesman in the catalogue is Lewis. Reprinted in *Wyndham Lewis on Art* and in Michel. See also D11.

B3 PROSPECTUS. THE REBEL ART CENTRE [1914]

[*Design by Lewis, over:*] PROSPECTUS. | [*double rule*] | THE REBEL ART CENTRE. | 38, GREAT ORMOND STREET, | Telephone: HOLBORN 457. | QUEEN'S SQUARE, W. C. | [*double rule*] | Fee for Membership . . . . 1 : 1s. | [*double rule*] | The Rebel Art Centre is under the personal management of Mr. Wyndham Lewis. | The Directors are Miss Lechmere and Mr. Wyndham Lewis. | [*text, describing intentions of the Rebel Art Centre and other information*]

13" x 8¼". Pp. [2] as follows: [1] title, as above; [2] text, design by Lewis at foot.

Notes. Printed and distributed without charge in April, 1914.

B4 EXHIBITION, LEEDS 1914

EXHIBITION, | LEEDS. | [*rule*] | MAY 16th, 1914.

Approximately 12" x 9½". Pp. [4]
[1] title; [2-4] Preface to exhibition catalogue, by Lewis.

Notes. Published about May 16, 1914.

Contains Preface to an exhibition which may have taken place in Leeds on that date, according to a proof copy, which is reprinted in Michel (p. 447). Photographed in *Vorticism and Abstract Art in the First Machine Age,* by Richard Cork. This text appeared with the same typography in *Blast No. 1*, under the title "Life is the Important Thing!" (p. 129).

B5 ANTWERP [1915]
BY FORD MADOX HUEFFER

[*Cover designed by Lewis, Michel 198*] ANTWERP | BY FORD MADOX HUEFFER | THE POETRY BOOKSHOP 3[D.] net

8⅜" x 6¾". Two sheets folded once to make 4 unpaged leaves. Pp. [8].
[1] title; [2-8] text, publisher's imprint beneath rule at foot of [8]: "London: The Poetry Bookshop, 35 Devonshire St., Theobalds Rd., W. C."
Issued as pamphlet, title design by Lewis printed in light raspberry-red [1], text and designs by Lewis printed in black. All edges untrimmed; leaves sewn with burgundy thread. Wove paper, watermarked "ANTIQUE DE LUXE."

Notes. Published early January, 1915 and sold at 3d.

Contains designs by Lewis on pp. [1] Michel 198, [4] and [8].

B6 VORTICIST EXHIBITION 1915

VORTICIST. | [*rule*] | EXHIBITION | [*rule over design*] | DORÉ GALLERIES, | 35, NEW BOND STREET, W. | [*rule*] | OPENING 10th JUNE, 1915.

8 ½" x 5 ½". Pp. [8].
Bound in orange wrappers, printed in black (front cover transcribed above). All edges trimmed and unstained.

Notes. Published June, 1915 and distributed without charge at the exhibition.

Contains "Note for Catalogue" by Lewis, an essay which defines briefly the meaning of Vorticism. This exhibition was the first devoted wholly to works by the Vorticist school. Catalogue divided into 3 sections: "Pictures," "Drawings" and "Sculpture." Reprinted in *Wyndham Lewis on Art* and in Michel.

B7 MAYVALE [1915]
BY H.E. CLIFTON AND JAMES WOOD

MAYVALE | BY | H.E. CLIFTON AND JAMES WOOD

8 ⅝" x 5 ⅛". Pp. iv, 48; endsheets.
Dark blue speckled V cloth, stamped in gold, blind-stamped double rule around

edges of front and back covers. Issued without dustjacket. All edges trimmed and unstained.

Notes. Published December, 1915 and sold at 5s.

Contains "Preface" by Lewis, p. [iv]. Originally printed in *The Cambridge Magazine* on December 4, 1915 (see D51). *Mayvale* is a short novella by Clifton and Wood.

B8 GUNS 1919

[*Title derived from front cover*] February, 1919. | [*rule*] | GUNS | By | WYNDHAM LEWIS. | WILLIAM MARCHANT & Co., | The Goupil Gallery, | 5 Regent Street, | London, S. W. I.

8" x 5¼". Pp. [8].
[1] Catalogue. | [*rule*] | GUNS | By | WYNDHAM LEWIS, | with Foreword | by the Artist.; [2] [*within single rule rectangular compartment*] THE EXHIBITS ARE FOR SALE, | AND THE PRICES OBTAINABLE | ON APPLICATION.; [3-4] Foreword; [5-8] catalogue listing 54 works by Lewis.
Issued in plain cream wrappers, printed in black, stapled.

Notes. Published early January, 1919 and distributed at exhibition.

Contains Foreword by Lewis, pp. [3-4], dated January, 1919. Reprinted in Michel (pp. 433-434) and *Wyndham Lewis on Art* (pp. [104]-106). Catalogue for Lewis's one-man show held at Goupil Gallery in London, in February, 1919.

B9 HAROLD GILMAN AN APPRECIATION 1919

Harold Gilman | An Appreciation | *By* | Wyndham Lewis | & | Louis F. Fergusson | *Illustrated* | London: Chatto & Windus | 1919

11½" x 9". Collation: A^4, B-D^4, E-M^4. Pp. 96; single leaf containing color frontispiece mounted between pp. [2] and [3], not included in collation; tissue leaf mounted between frontispiece and title; endsheets.
[1] half-title; [3] title; [4] PRINTED AT | THE COMPLETE PRESS | WEST NORWOOD | LONDON; [5-6] table of contents; [7] divisional half-title; [10] photograph of Harold Gilman; 11-15 "Harold Gilman," essay by Lewis; [17] divisional half-title; 19-32 "Harold Gilman," essay by Louis F. Fergusson; 33-95 plates, works by Harold Gilman, printed on rectos only.

Bound in smooth maroon V cloth, single rule frame blind-stamped on front cover (⅛" wide), and stamped in gold at top of front cover within frame: HAROLD [*small star*] GILMAN |. Stamped in gold running up spine: HAROLD [*small star*] GILMAN |. Top edge trimmed and unstained; fore- and bottom edges untrimmed. Printed on white coated paper; endsheets wove cream paper. No example of dustjacket located.

Notes. Published December 8, 1919 in an edition of 500 copies, and sold at 21s.

Contains "Harold Gilman" by Lewis, pp. 11-15. Lewis finally submitted his manuscript to the publishers between September 16 and 19, 1919, barely in time for its inclusion in the book. The memorial exhibition of paintings and drawings by Harold Gilman (1876-1919), which the volume was meant to accompany, took place later in September, 1919 (TLS, Chatto & Windus to Lewis, September 16, 1919, NIC).

B10 GROUP X 1920

GROUP | X | EXHIBITION | CATALOGUE | MANSARD GALLERY | MARCH 26—APRIL 24 | 1920 | ONE SHILLING

8½" x 5¼". 12 sheets folded once to make 24 leaves. Pp. 48. Printed light salmon wrappers, wove unwatermarked paper, stapled.

Notes. Published March 26, 1920 and sold at 1s.

Contains Foreword by Lewis, "Group X," pp. 3-6. Also, reproductions and list of Lewis's contributions to exhibition, pp. 28-29. Members of "Group X," founded by Lewis in 1920, included the painters Jessie Dismorr, Frederick Etchells, Charles Ginner, C. J. Hamilton, E. McKnight Kauffer, William Turnbull, Edward Wadsworth and the sculptor Frank Dobson, all of whose works were shown from March 26 through April 24, 1920 at Heal's Mansard Gallery. Reprinted in Michel (pp. 436-437) and *Wyndham Lewis on Art* (pp. [184]-186).

B11 TYROS AND PORTRAITS 1921

"TYROS AND PORTRAITS" | CATALOGUE OF AN EXHIBITION OF | PAINTINGS AND DRAWINGS | BY WYNDHAM LEWIS | ERNEST BROWN & PHILLIPS | LEICESTER GALLERIES | LEICESTER SQUARE, LONDON | APRIL, 1921

5¾" x 4½". Collation: A^8. Pp. 16. Issued in orange-brown wrappers printed in black, edges untrimmed, laid unwatermarked paper, stapled.

Notes. Published April, 1921 and distributed without charge.

Contains Foreword by Lewis, pp. 5-8. Catalogue of one-man show by Lewis, held in the Hogarth Room at Leicester Galleries; pp. 9-12 list works displayed (see Michel, p. 438). Reprinted in Michel (pp. 437-438) and *Wyndham Lewis on Art* (pp. [187]-188, 190).

B12 DOCTOR DONNE AND GARGANTUA, FIRST CANTO BY SACHEVERELL SITWELL 1921

Doctor Donne and | Gargantua | [*single line between two short rules*] FIRST CANTO | By | *Sacheverell Sitwell* | WITH A DRAWING BY | WYNDHAM LEWIS | AT | THE FAVIL PRESS | KENSINGTON | A. 1921 D.

7½" x 5¼". Pp. 16.
[1] half-title; [2] design by Lewis (Michel 448); [3] title; [4] quotation; [5]-14 text; [15] limitation page with signature of author in red ink, advertisement; [16] printer's imprint, date, device.
Bound in marbled paper wrappers, sewn. All edges untrimmed. White paper label on front cover, printed in black.

Notes. Privately published in October, 1921 in an edition of 106 copies (80 for sale, 21 for author's use, 5 for printer's file and copyright files).

Contains frontispiece design by Lewis (Michel 448), p. [2].

B13 JOB LE PAUVRE BY JEAN DE BOSSCHÈRE [1923]

Jean de BOSSCHÈRE | Job le Pauvre | *With English translation* | Avec un portrait par | —Wyndham Lewis— | traduction des poèmes | en anglais, et quatorze | ~~gravures noires~~ | John Lane The Bodley Head Limited | London, 1922

8" x5⅞". Collation: A^2, B-H^8. Pp. {vi}, 126 (15 plates); no endsheets. Bound in black boards, paper label on spine, printed in black: Jean | de Boss | chère | {*double rule*} | Job | le | pau- | vre | {*double rule*} | 1922 | {*double rule*} |. Issued without dustjacket. Edges untrimmed; laid paper.

Notes. Published February, 1923 {*sic*} in a special edition of 50 copies numbered and signed by the author (12 of which were issued with the plates hand-colored by the author), and sold at 30s.

Contains special frontispiece portrait of Jean de Bosschère by Lewis (Michel 523) printed on light grey paper and mounted, p. {v}. Trade edition, published March 8, 1923 {*sic*} in an edition of 450 copies, and sold at 15s. Some copies published with the following imprint on title page, using the same sheets and binding: Collection d'Art "La Cible" | Jacques Povolzky {or, "Pavolosky"} & Cie, Éditeurs | 13, rue Bonaparte, PARIS |.

B14 MADNESS IN SHAKESPEARIAN TRAGEDY {1929} BY HENRY SOMERVILLE

MADNESS IN | SHAKESPEARIAN | TRAGEDY | BY | H. SOMERVILLE | MEMBER OF THE ROYAL MEDICO-PSYCHOLOGICAL ASSOCIATION | AUTHOR OF VARIOUS PAPERS IN ABNORMAL PSYCHOLOGY | WITH A PREFACE BY | WYNDHAM LEWIS | {*publisher's device*} | LONDON | THE RICHARDS PRESS LTD. | PUBLISHERS

8½" x 6¼". Collation: π^4, A-N^8. Pp. viii, 207; endsheets.
Bound in green V cloth, stamped on front cover and spine in black. No example of dustjacket examined. Top edge trimmed and stained green; fore-edge trimmed; bottom edge untrimmed.

Notes. Published July 14, 1929 in an edition of 1000 copies, and sold at 6s.

Contains "Preface" by Lewis, pp. 1-8. Reprinted in *Wyndham Lewis an Anthology* (A44) and by Folcroft Press, Inc., 1969.

B15 WRITERS AT WORK 1931

WRITERS AT WORK | *By* | LOUISE MORGAN | [*design*] | LONDON | CHATTO & WINDUS | 1931

7¼" x 5". Collation: π^4, A-E^4, F^2. Pp. viii, 76; endsheets.
[i] half-title; [ii]advertisements; [iii] title; [iv] PRINTED IN GREAT BRITAIN | BY T. AND A. CONSTABLE LTD. | AT THE UNIVERSITY PRESS | EDINBURGH | ALL RIGHTS RESERVED | FIRST PUBLISHED | 1931; [v] table of contents; [vi] dedication; vii-viii Preface, by Louise Morgan; 1-71 text; [72] printer's imprint; [73-76] advertisements.
Bound in light tan textured boards, decorated and lettered ornately in orange. Issued in cream dustjacket, lettering and decorations printed in blue. All edges trimmed and unstained. Laid unwatermarked paper. Wove endsheets.

Notes. Published on September 17, 1931 in an edition of 3000 copies, and sold at 2s.

Reprints an interview with Lewis, pp. 43-53, originally published in *Everyman,* March 19, 1931, "Wyndham Lewis: the Greatest Satirist of our Day" (D161).

B16 MORE FROM THE ENEMY [1932]

more from | [*design by Lewis, Michel 634*] | THE ENEMY

8¾" x 5⅝". Two sheets folded to make 4 unsigned leaves. Pp. 8.
Pamphlet published by Desmond Harmsworth, announcing forthcoming publications of *The Enemy of the Stars* (A15), *The Old Gang and the New Gang* (A18) and *A Tip from the Augean Stable* (unpublished, see G2): [1] title, as above; [3] Three New Books by | WYNDHAM LEWIS | [*advertisements*] | DESMOND HARMSWORTH | 44 GREAT RUSSELL STREET, W.C. 1; 4-8 descriptions of *The Enemy of the Stars, The Old Gang and the New Gang* and *A Tip from the Augean Stable,* and (7-8) review extracts of *The Apes of God.*
Pamphlet printed on wove unwatermarked paper; sewn.

Notes. Published late April, 1932 and distributed without charge.

"The Old and the New Gang, or The Great Blank of the Missing Generation" (5-6) and "A Tip from the Augean Stable. Description" (6-7) are by Lewis. "Enemy of the Stars" (4-5) is extracted from Hugh Gordon Porteus, *Wyndham Lewis: A Discursive Exposition* (F403). Michel erroneously dates this pamphlet 1927; however, the publication dates, formats and prices of the three books advertised in the pamphlet had not been determined until April, 1932. Futhermore, *The Apes of God* is advertised as being in "its third edition"—that is, the second printing of the second English edition, published by Grayson & Grayson in March, 1932 (A12b)—a fact which makes publication of the pamphlet at a date earlier than March, 1932 impossible.

B17 THIRTY PERSONALITIES 1932

THIRTY | PERSONALITIES | by | [*in red*] WYNDHAM LEWIS | [*in blue*] *October, 1932* |ALEX. REID & LEFEVRE, LTD. | (THE LEFEVRE GALLERIES) | la, KING STREET, ST. JAMES'S | LONDON, S.W.1

8½" x 5¾". Pp. 4. Bound in light blue wove paper wrappers, printed in blue and red. Text printed in blue on unwatermarked laid paper.

Notes. Published October, 1932 and distributed without charge.

Contains Preface by Lewis, pp. [1-2]. Published in conjunction with exhibition of Lewis's works at Lefevre Galleries, October, 1932. List of 30 portraits offered for sale, pp. [3-4], with advertisement for portfolio *Thirty Personalities and a Self-Portrait* (A19). This Preface is textually at variance with the introduction published in the portfolio in September (pp. 3-5), and is reprinted in Michel (p. 439).

B18 BEGINNINGS [1935]

BEGINNINGS | *by* | ADRIAN ALINGTON | L.E.O. CHARLTON A.E. COPPARD A.J. CRONIN | E.M. DELAFIELD LOUiS GOLDING | WYNDHAM LEWIS V.S. PRITCHETT | V. SACKVILLE-WEST | BEATRICE KEAN SEYMOUR HELEN SIMPSON | L.A.G. STRONG ALEC WAUGH | MALACHI WHITAKER | THOMAS NELSON & SONS LTD | LONDON EDINBURGH | PARIS TORONTO NEW YORK

7½" x 5". Collation: A^8, B-N^8. Pp. viii, 200; endsheets.

[i] half-title; [iii] title; [iv] reservation of rights, publisher's address, publication date; v table of contents; vii Foreword; 1-200 text, publisher's imprint at foot of 200.

Bound in light orange V cloth, stamped in blue on spine: BEGINNINGS | *by* | [*list of fourteen authors' names as title*] | NELSON |. Issued in yellow dustjacket, printed in blue. Top edge trimmed and stained orange; other edges trimmed and unstained. Laid unwatermarked paper.

Notes. Published March 27, 1935 and sold at 5s.

Contains untitled autobiographical essay by Lewis, pp. 91-103.

B19 BEYOND THIS LIMIT BY NAOMI MITCHISON [1935]

BEYOND THIS | LIMIT | Pictures by | WYNDHAM LEWIS | and | Words by | NAOMI MITCHISON | [*publisher's device*] | JONATHAN CAPE | 30 BEDFORD SQUARE LONDON

10" x 7". Collation: A^8, B-F^8. Pp. 90, 3 blank leaves; endsheets.
[3] half-title; [4] *Books by Wyndham Lewis* | [*list of thirteen titles by Lewis*] | *Books by Naomi Mitchison* | [*list of ten titles by Naomi Mitchison*]; [6] frontispiece design by Lewis, Michel 810; [7] title; [8] FIRST PUBLISHED 1935 | JONATHAN CAPE LTD. 30 BEDFORD SQUARE, LONDON | AND 91 WELLINGTON STREET WEST, TORONTO | PRINTED IN GREAT BRITAIN IN THE CITY OF OXFORD | AT THE ALDEN PRESS | PAPER MADE BY JOHN DICKINSON & CO., LTD. | BOUND BY A.W. BAIN & CO., LTD.; [9]-[89] text (for plates by Lewis see below).
Bound in three-quarter smooth black V cloth on spine and along length of fore-edge of boards, shiny silver foil boards, stamped in silver running up spine: [*publisher's device*] BEYOND THIS LIMIT [*triple-rule, center rule longer than outer rules*] WYNDHAM LEWIS & NAOMI MITCHISON |. Issued in cream dustjacket with design by Lewis (Michel 825) printed in black on front cover, and printed in red and black. Top edge trimmed and stained black; fore-edge trimmed; bottom edge untrimmed. Wove unwatermarked paper.

Notes. Published Spring, 1935 and sold at 7s. 6d.

Contains thirty-two designs by Wyndham Lewis, executed in close collaboration with Naomi Mitchison, who wrote the text, most of which were completed by December, 1934 (see Rose, *Letters*, p. 232): [6], Michel 810; [10], Michel 811; [13], Michel 812; [17], Michel 813; 19, Michel 814; [21], Michel 815; 23, Michel 816; 24, Michel 817; [25], Michel 818; 27, Michel 819; 28, Michel 820; [29], Michel 821; 31, Michel 822; [33], Michel 823; [37], Michel 824; [41], Michel 825; [45], Michel 826; 47, Michel 827; [49], Michel 828; 51, Michel 829;

[53], Michel 830; 55, Michel 831; [57], Michel 832; 59, Michel 833; [61], Michel 834; [65], Michel 835; [71], Michel 836; 75, Michel 837; [77], Michel 838; [81], Michel 839; [85], Michel 840; [89], Michel 841. All unnumbered pages with designs are full-page illustrations, and with the exception of p. [10] all versos of full-page illustrations are blank.

B20 B·B·C ANNUAL 1935 [1935]

B·B·C | ANNUAL 1935 | *[design]* | THE PROGRAMME PERIOD COVERED BY | THIS BOOK IS FROM 1 NOVEMBER 1933 TO | 31 DECEMBER 1934 | THE BRITISH BROADCASTING | CORPORATION | BROADCASTING HOUSE | LONDON·W1

9¾" x 7⅜". Collation: *1*[8], 2-12[8]. Pp. 192; endsheets.

[1]title; [2] prefatory note, publisher's imprint; 3-4 table of contents; 5-[192] text.

Bound in blue V cloth, lettering stamped in gold running up spine: B.B.C. ANNUAL 1935 |. All edges trimmed and unstained. Coated paper. Issued without dustjacket.

Notes. Published April, 1935.

Contains "Art and Patronage (1)" by Lewis, pp. 184-187. (Part (2) of the essay is by Charles Nevinson.) Excerpts reprinted in *Wyndham Lewis on Art* (A45).

B21 FREEDOM [1936]

FREEDOM | *by* | SIR ERNEST BENN | J. L. GARVIN | THE RT. HON. | HERBERT MORRISON | J. A. SPENDER | WYNDHAM LEWIS | THE RT. HON. | LORD EUSTACE PERCY | SIR THOMAS D. BARLOW | THE RT. HON. | SIR WILLIAM JOWITT | THE RT. REV. | THE LORD BISHOP OF DURHAM | PROF. E. SCHRODINGER | JOHN MOORE | G. K. CHESTERTON | GEORGE BERNARD SHAW | *[rule]* | GEORGE ALLEN & UNWIN LTD

7¼" x 4¼". Collation: *A*[8], B-I[8], K[4]. Pp. 152; endsheets.

[1-2] publisher's advertisements; [3] half-title; [5] title; [6] FIRST PUBLISHED IN 1936 | *This book is based on a series of* | *Broadcast Talks, which were considered* | *too valuable to be allowed to fade* | *away on the ether. They have been* | *preserved with the*

helpful co-operation | *of the B.B.C.* | *All rights reserved* | PRINTED IN GREAT BRITAIN BY | UNWIN BROTHERS LTD., WOKING; 7 table of contents; 9-149 text; [151-152] publisher's advertisements.
Bound in grey V cloth, decorations and lettering printed in blue. Issued in white dustjacket printed in purple, with purple on spine and front cover printed in white. All edges trimmed and unstained.

Notes Published January 30, 1936, and sold at 4s. 6d.

Contains broadcast talk "Freedom that Destroys Itself," pp. 50-59. Originally broadcast by the B.B.C. National Service on April 30, 1935 at 10:00 PM, and printed in *The Listener* in May, 1935 (D179). Lewis contracted with Allen & Unwin for inclusion of this essay in the collection on September 3, 1935.

B22 PAINTINGS AND DRAWINGS BY WYNDHAM LEWIS 1937

CATALOGUE OF AN EXHIBITION | OF PAINTINGS AND DRAWINGS | BY WYNDHAM LEWIS | ERNEST BROWN & PHILLIPS, Ltd. | (Directors: CECIL L. PHILLIPS, OLIVER F. BROWN) | THE LEICESTER GALLERIES | LEICESTER SQUARE, LONDON | DECEMBER, 1937 | EXHIBITION NO. 663.

5¾" x 4½". Pp. 16.
Bound in brownish orange wrappers, printed in black, stapled. All edges trimmed and unstained

Notes. Published December, 1937 and distributed at the exhibition.

Contains "Foreword" by Lewis, briefly commenting upon several paintings shown in the exhibition. Reprinted in Michel, pp. 439-440.

B23 LONDON GUYED BY WILLIAM KIMBER 1938

LONDON GUYED | *Edited by* | WILLIAM KIMBER | [*rule*] | JAMES AGATE | K. R. G. BROWNE | ANTHONY GIBBS | DOUGLAS JERROLD | WYNDHAM LEWIS | A. G. MACDONELL | J. B. MORTON | L. A. PAVEY | EDWARD SHANKS | STEVIE SMITH | HUMBERT WOLFE | Illustrations by | IAN FENWICK | [rule] | HUTCHINSON & CO. (*Publishers*) LTD.

8" x 5⅜". Collation : A^8, B-Q^8. Pp. 256; endsheets.
[1] half-title; [2] frontispiece; [3] title; [4] PRINTED IN GREAT BRITAIN | BY WILLIAM BRENDON AND SON LTD | AT THE MAYFLOWER PRESS PLYMOUTH | SET IN MONOTYPE PERPETUA; 5 table of contents; [7] anonymous quotation from the *Evening Standard*; [9]-[256] text.
Bound in half light green smooth V linen, green and white heavy B cloth boards, stamped in gold on spine: London | Guyed | Edited by | William | Kimber | Hutchinson | . Issued in dustjacket (not seen). All edges trimmed; top edge stained green. Wove paper, watermarked:"Cambrian Parchment."

Notes. Published October 20, 1938 in an edition of 3000 copies, and sold at 8s. 6d.

Contains "The Zoo" by Lewis, pp. [165]-188 (illustration for the article by Ian Fenwick on p. [166]).

B24 WHO IS WYNDHAM LEWIS? 1943

[*At right of photograph of Lewis:*] WHO IS WYNDHAM LEWIS? | [*biographical sketch and extracts from comments about Lewis*]

5½" x 3½". Printed postcard announcing on verso Lewis's participation in the Heywood Broun Memorial Lecture series, at Assumption College, Windsor, Ontario, in Autumn, 1943. Green heavy card, printed in black.

Notes. Published about November 14, 1943 and distributed without charge.

Contains autobiographical sketch by Lewis on recto of card. Lewis's lecture topic is given as "Concept of Liberty from the Founding Fathers of the U.S.A. Till Now."

B25 THE PAVILION [1946]

THE PAVILION | A CONTEMPORARY COLLECTION OF BRITISH ART & ARCHITECTURE | *Edited by Myfanwy Evans* | published by | I. T. PUBLICATIONS LTD. | and distributed for them throughout the world by | GERALD DUCKWORTH LTD. | 3 Henrietta Street, London, W.C.2

12" x 9¾". Pp. [iv], 80.
[i] title; [ii] acknowledgements; [iii] table of contents; [iv]-80 text.

Bound in ochre wrappers printed in black on front cover only: THE PAVILION |. All edges trimmed.

Notes. Published December, 1946 in an edition of 1500 copies, and sold at 12s. 6d.

Contains "Towards an Earth Culture or the Eclectic Culture of the Transition" by Lewis, pp. 3-12 (includes plates of paintings and drawings by Lewis).

See A45 for reprint.

B26 T. S. ELIOT A SYMPOSIUM 1948

T. S. ELIOT | A symposium from Conrad Aiken, Luciano Anceschi, | G. B. Angioletti, W. H. Auden, George Barker, Mont- | gomery Belgion, Clive Bell, John Betjeman, Amalendu | Bose, Ronald Bottrall, E. Martin Browne, Emilio Cecchi, | Nevill Coghill, Ernst Robert Curtius, Bishnu Dey, Ashley | Dukes, Lawrence Durrell, William Empson, George | Every, G. S. Fraser, Henri Fluchère, Michael Hamburger, | Desmond Hawkins, John Heath-Stubbs, Pierre Jean | Jouve, Wyndham Lewis, E. F. C. Ludowyk, Louis | MacNeice, Claude Edmonde Magny, Richard March, | Eugenio Montale, Marianne Moore, Nicholas Moore, | F. V. Morley, Edwin Muir, Norman Nicholson, | Hugh Gordon Porteus, Mario Praz, Kath- | leen Raine, James Reeves, Anne Rid- | ler, George Seferis, Edith Sitwell, | Stephen Spender, Tambi- | muttu, Ruthven Todd, | Vernon Watkins | Compiled by Richard March and Tambimuttu | PL | Editions Poetry London | 1948

8½" x 5½". Collation: A^{10}, B-H^{16}, I^{8}. Pp. 260; endsheets. 8 leaves of plates. [1] half-title; [3] title; [4] All Rights Reserved | First Published 1948 | by PL Editions Poetry London Limited, 26 Manchester | Square, London, W1 | Typography | by Anthony Froshaug MSIA | Setting | by Monotyping Service Limited, 10 Gough Square, London, | EC4 | Printed in Great Britain | by Henry Ling Limited, The Dorset Press, Dorchester; 5-10 table of contents; 11-12 Foreword; [13] internal half-title; 15-259 text.

Bound in light tan B cloth, stamped in gold on spine over brown fields at top and bottom of spine: [*at top:*] [*decorative rule*] | T. S. | ELIOT | [*decorative rule*] | A Symposium | compiled by | Richard | March | and | Tambimuttu | [*at bottom:*] PL |. Issued in white coated paper dustjacket, front and spine red, lettering and decoration in white and black. Top edge trimmed and stained burgundy; other edges trimmed and unstained. Printed on wove unwatermarked paper.

Notes. Published September, 1948 in an edition of 2500 copies, and sold at 10s. 6d. Contains Lewis's "Early London Environment," pp. 24-32.

B27 WYNDHAM LEWIS [1949]

[*Within double rule frame*] WYNDHAM LEWIS | REDFERN GALLERY | 20 CORK STREET · BURLINGTON GARDENS | LONDON · W · 1

10" x 7½". Pp. [16], yellow printed wrappers, stapled.

Notes. Published May 5, 1949 and sold at 1s.

Contains "Introduction" by Lewis, pp. [4] and [7]. Also, reproduces works by Lewis on pp. [2], [5], [6], [11], [12], [15]. One-man show of Lewis's paintings and drawings from May 5 through May 28, 1949 (for list of works shown, not included in this catalogue, see Michel, pp. 440-441). Reprinted in Michel, pp. 439-440, and under the title "The 1949 Retrospective Exhibition" in *Wyndham Lewis on Art,* pp. [449]-450.

B28 EZRA POUND [1950]

EZRA POUND | *A collection of essays edited by* | *Peter Russell to be presented* | *to Ezra Pound on his sixty-fifth* | *birthday* | PETER NEVILL LIMITED | *London New York*

8⅜" x 5⅜". Collation: *1-15*^{8}, *16*^{6}, *17*^{8}. Single leaf mounted facing title. Pp. 268; endsheets.

[1] half-title; [3] title; [4] PETER NEVILL LIMITED | 50 Old Brompton Road | London SW7 and | 122 East 55th Street | New York 22 NY | Made and Printed in Great Britain by | WM CARLING AND COMPANY LIMITED | EXPRESS PRINTING WORKS HITCHIN | MCML; 5 table of contents; 6 Acknowledgements; 7 Preface; 9-266 text; 267-268 select bibliography of Ezra Pound.

Bound in tan B cloth stamped in blue and gold on spine: [*double rule*] | EZRA POUND | *Edited by* | PETER RUSSELL | [*double rule*] | PETER NEVILL | [*double rule*] |. Issued in cream dustjacket printed in blue and black. Top edge trimmed and stained brown; other edges trimmed and unstained. Wove unwatermarked paper. Later bindings bound in green or grey paper boards, stamped identically in black; top edge unstained.

Notes. Published October 16, 1950 in an edition of 2000 copies, and sold at 12s. 6d.

Contains "Ezra Pound *by* Wyndham Lewis [1948]," pp. 257-266. Published in the United States by New Directions under the title *An Examination of Ezra Pound: A Collection of Essays Edited by Peter Russell* in an edition of 1500 copies and sold at $3.75. Originally appeared under the title "Ezra: The Portrait of a Personality" in the *Quarterly Review of Literature* (1949), see D312. Translated into French under the title "Ezra Pound" in *Ezra Pound* (Paris: Les Cahiers de l'Herne, 1965), see E3. See also F781.

B29 THE PENGUIN BOOK OF CONTEMPORARY VERSE [1950]

The Penguin Book of | CONTEMPORARY | VERSE | [*ornament*] | SELECTED WITH AN | INTRODUCTION AND NOTES BY | *Kenneth Allott* | PENGUIN BOOKS | HARMONDSWORTH · MIDDLESEX

7⅛" x 4⅜". Collation: A^{16}, B-I^{16}. Pp. 272.
[1] half-title; [3] title; [4] publication information and dedication; [5]-10 table of contents; 11-266 text; 267-270 index.
Bound in yellow wrappers, printed in green and black. All edges trimmed and unstained. Wove paper.

Notes. Published October, 1950 in an edition of approximately 100,000 copies and sold at 1s. 6d.

Contains notes on the writing of *One-Way Song* and on verse satire (printed from a letter written to Kenneth Allott by Lewis), pp. [60]-61; and selections from "If So the Man You Are, 14" (pp. 61-62), and *One-Way Song,* XXIV (pp. 62-63). Reprinted in 1951, 1953, 1954, 1956, 1957, 1959. See F773.

B30 THE LITTLE REVIEW ANTHOLOGY 1953

THE LITTLE REVIEW | ANTHOLOGY | *Edited by* MARGARET ANDERSON | HERMITAGE HOUSE, INC. | New York, 1953

8½" x 6". Pp. 384; endsheets.
[1] half-title; [2] Other Books by Margaret Anderson | [*list of two titles*]; [3] title; [4] *Copyright, 1953, by Margaret Anderson* | *All rights reserved* | *Manufactured in the*

United States of America; 5-8 table of contents; 9-10 acknowledgements; 11-12 Preface; 13-383 text.
Bound in grey-green boards stamped in black on front cover, with grey V cloth spine stamped in black. Issued in white dustjacket, printed in green and black. Top edge stained green; fore-edge untrimmed; bottom edge trimmed. Wove unwatermarked paper.

Notes. Published on January 19, 1953, and sold for $3.95.

Contains "Imaginary Letters" (D67, D69, D71, D80, D81), pp. 110-128; "Cantleman's Spring-Mate" (D76), pp. 137-143; and Lewis's "Answer to a Questionnaire" included in the final number of *The Little Review* (D144), p. 370.

B31 WYNDHAM LEWIS AND VORTICISM [1956]

WYNDHAM LEWIS AND VORTICISM | A TATE GALLERY EXHIBITION CIRCULATED BY | THE ARTS COUNCIL

9½" x 6¾". Pp. 24 (two leaves containing plates not included in paging, stapled in). Bound in cranberry wrappers, printed in black, stapled.

Notes. Published July 6, 1956 and sold at 3s.

Contains an Introduction by Lewis, pp. 3-4. Also contains essay on Lewis by John Rothenstein, "Wyndham Lewis and Vorticism," pp. 5-7. Reprinted in Michel pp. 443-444 (list of paintings and drawings shown, pp. 444-446) and under the title "The 1956 Retrospective at the Tate Gallery" in *Wyndham Lewis on Art,* pp. [451]-453. Exhibition shown from July 6 through August 19, 1956.

B32 GOLDEN SECTIONS BY MICHAEL AYRTON [1957]

MICHAEL AYRTON | GOLDEN SECTIONS | *With an Introduction by* | WYNDHAM LEWIS | METHUEN & CO LTD | 36 ESSEX STREET, LONDON WC2

8½" x 5½". Collation: A^8, B-O^8. Pp. 224; eleven leaves of plates mounted, not included in collation; endsheets.
[1] half-title; [3] title; [4] First published in 1957 | Printed in Great Britain by | The Shenval Press, Hertford & Harlow | [*registration*]; [5] dedication; 7 table of contents; 9-10 table of illustrations; 11 acknowledgements; 13-16 Foreword, by Lewis; 17-219 text.

Bound in light red V cloth, geometric line design on front cover in gold, and stamped in gold on spine: [*triple rule*] | Golden Sections | [*triple rule*] | MICHAEL AYRTON |Methuen |. Issued in white dustjacket with design by Michael Ayrton printed in pink, yellow and black on front, back and spine; lettering printed in black and yellow. All edges trimmed and unstained. Wove unwatermarked paper.

Notes. Published October 3, 1957 in an edition of 1500 copies, and sold for 25s.

Contains "Foreword" by Lewis, pp. 13-16, which originally appeared as "A Note on Michael Ayrton" in *Spectrum* (D351). Ayrton, whose work Lewis greatly admired, asked Lewis to write the foreword to this collection of essays on art and artists in a letter dated July 24, 1956 (NIC): "Apropos my occasional writings, I think I mentioned some months ago that I was putting together a number of essays on various subjects, which White of Methuens is publishing. Both he and I are anxious that, if you have time and inclination, you should contribute an introduction. I hope that you are still willing . . . Whether you wish to plough through it all I don't know: you may prefer to do a sort of general note on my book and myself but that is up to you." Ayrton's portrait of Lewis faces p. 145. Lewis's foreword to *Golden Sections* is his last completed written work.

B33 WYNDHAM LEWIS PAINTINGS AND DRAWINGS [1971]

WYNDHAM LEWIS | *Paintings and Drawings* | WALTER MICHEL | *with an introductory essay by* | HUGH KENNER | [*publisher's device*] |THAMES AND HUDSON · LONDON

11" x 9". Collation: *1-20*^{8}, *21*^{4}, *22-29*^{8} *(11-20*^{8}, *21*^{4} printed on coated paper). Pp. 456 ([159-330] unnumbered); endsheets.

Bound in heavy light grey BD cloth, stamped in gold on chocolate brown rectangular field on spine: [*double rule, thick over thin*] | WYNDHAM | LEWIS | PAINTINGS AND | DRAWINGS | · | WALTER MICHEL | ESSAY BY | HUGH KENNER | [*double rule, thin over thick*] |[*at base of spine, below brown field:*] CALIFORNIA |. Issued in coated paper dustjacket, printed in brown, red, yellow and blue, reproducing painting by Lewis on front cover (Michel P76). All edges trimmed and unstained; black endsheets. White false headband and tailband. Illustrated with 781 plates, 16 of which are reproduced in color. Wove unwatermarked paper (text); coated paper (plates).

Notes. Published March 29, 1971 and sold at £12.60. Number of copies not disclosed. First American edition published by University of California Press on April 12, 1971 in an edition of 2000 copies, sold at $35.00 ($30.00 before publication).

Contains "The '1917 List' [Paintings Drawings *etc.* (For the Information of my Mother)]" by Lewis, pp. 447-448. Contains reprints of forewords to exhibition catalogues: "The Cubist Room [*Exhibition of the work of English Post-Impressionists, Cubists and Others,* Public Art Galleries, Brighton, December 1913-January 1914]" (430-431), "Note for Catalogue [*Vorticist Exhibition,* Doré Galleries, June 1915]" (432-433), "Foreword [*Vorticist Exhibition,* Penguin Club, New York, January 1917]" (433-434), "Foreword [*Group X,* Mansard Gallery, March 1920]" (436-437), "Foreword [*Tyros and Portraits,* Leicester Galleries, April 1921]" (437-438), "Preface [*Thirty Personalities,* Lefevre Galleries, October 1932]" (439), "Foreword [*Paintings and Drawings by Wyndham Lewis,* Leicester Galleries, December 1937]" (439-440), "Introduction [*Wyndham Lewis,* Redfern Gallery, May 1949]" (441-442), "Introduction [*Wyndham Lewis and Vorticism,* Tate Gallery, July—August 1956] (443-444) and "Leeds, 1914 [uncertain whether this exhibition was held]" (447). Also contained in this volume, besides Walter Michel's discussion of Lewis's art work (43-158), is an essay by Hugh Kenner, "The Visual World of Wyndham Lewis" (11-40).

Paintings refered to in the present bibliography are described in some detail by Michel in the catalogue (P1-P127; 333-346); drawings and watercolors are catalogued in a second section (1-1127 [dated], 1128-1219 [undated]; 347-421, 421-425); pictures executed in an "unknown" medium (not refered to in the present bibliography) are described (U1-U19; 426); and an addenda section is included (not assigned catalogue numbers, listed only by date; 427).

B34 WYNDHAM LEWIS IN CANADA [1971]

WYNDHAM LEWIS | IN CANADA | *edited by* | GEORGE WOODCOCK | *with an introduction by* | JULIAN SYMONS | University of British Columbia | Publications Centre | *Vancouver*

9¾" x 8¾". Pp. VIII, 112.
[I] half-title; [II] *Canadian Literature Series* | George Woodcock, general editor | *The Sixties,* GEORGE WOODCOCK, *editor;* [III] title; [IV] [*copyright information, acknowledgements, printer's imprint*]; [V] table of contents; VII Biographical Note; 1-103 text; 105-107 Notes on Contributors; 108-110 Selected Bibliography.

Perfect bound in coated white paper wrappers, printed on covers and spine in violet and black. All edges trimmed and unstained. Wove unwatermarked paper.

Notes. Published December 30, 1971 in an edition of 800 copies, and sold at $4.00.

Contains "On Canada" (pp. 24-29), "Nature's Place in Canadian Culture" (pp. 49-59) and "HILL 100: Outline for an Unwritten Novel" (pp. 90-96) by Lewis. This is an expanded and revised version of F1481.

B35 WYNDHAM LEWIS A DESCRIPTIVE CATALOGUE BY MARY DANIELS 1972

WYNDHAM LEWIS | A DESCRIPTIVE CATALOGUE | of the | Manuscript Material | in the | Department of Rare Books | Cornell University Library | Compiled by Mary F. Daniels | [*design by Lewis, Michel 945*] | Cornell University Library | Ithaca, New York | 1972

12" x 9". Pp. viii, 172.

Perfect bound, glued into heavy white paper wrappers, designs by Lewis on front (Michel 1107) and back (Michel 68) covers in black, lettering printed in red. All edges trimmed and unstained. Wove unwatermarked paper. Contains reproductions of designs by Lewis: Michel 253 (frontispiece), Michel 92 (24), Michel 1470 (74), Michel 1124 (117), Michel 369 (124).

Notes. Published July 31, 1972 in an edition of 500 copies, and sold at $6.00.

Contains "Autobiographical fragment . . . 1908" ([3]), "Holograph and typescript text of an unpublished poem" ([14]), "Synopsis of a Novel [*Chateau Rex*, i.e. *Self Condemned*]" ([18]) in facsimile, reproducing the original texts. Also contains an extensive catalogue of Wyndham Lewis manuscript materials and graphic works, acquired by Cornell University in 1960 largely through the work of W. K. Rose. Included in the catalogue are all materials acquired by Cornell from 1960-1972.

B36 MORLEY CALLAGHAN 1975

CRITICAL VIEWS ON CANADIAN WRITERS [*over rule*] | MORLEY | CALLAGHAN | Edited and with an Introduction by | BRANDON CONRON | McGRAW-HILL RYERSON LIMITED | TORONTO · MONTREAL · NEW YORK · LONDON · SYDNEY

8½" x 5½". Collation: *1-2*^{16}, *3*^{18}, *4-5*^{16}. Pp. vi, 158; endsheets.
[i] half-title; [ii] list of titles published in series; [iii] title; [iv] MORLEY CALLAGHAN | Copyright © McGraw-Hill Ryerson Limited, 1975 | [*reservation of rights, acknowledgements, publication information*]; v table of contents; 1-16 Introduction; 17-154 text; 155-156 Bibliography.
Bound in smooth dark green V cloth, stamped in silver running down spine: Conron MORLEY CALLAGHAN McGraw-Hill Ryerson |. Stamped in silver on back cover, running downwards: ISBN 0-07-082146-1 |. Dustjacket. All edges trimmed and unstained. Wove unwatermarked paper.

Notes. Published February 8, 1975 in an edition of 1500 copies, and sold at $9.95.

Contains "What Books for Total War?," pp. 55-59. See D270. A paperback edition was published simultaneously in an edition of 2000 copies, at $4.95.

C. Periodicals and a Pamphlet edited by Wyndham Lewis

C1 BLAST, No. 1 1914

No. 1. June 20th, 1914. | BLAST | Edited by WYNDHAM LEWIS. | [*rule*] | REVIEW OF THE GREAT ENGLISH VORTEX. | [*rule*] | 2/6 Published Quarterly. | 10/6 Yearly Subscription. | London: | JOHN LANE, | The Bodley Head. | New York: John Lane Company. | Toronto: Bell & Cockburn.

12" x 9". Collation: A^4, B-K^8, L^4, M^2 (22 leaves of plates not included in collation). Pp. 164 ([44] pp. not included in pagination).

[1] title; [3] distribution information and printer's imprint ("Printed by Leveridge and Co. (T. U.), St. Thomas' Road, Harlesden."); [4] unacknowledged design and errata list; [5] table of contents; [6] list of illustrations; [7-8] "Long Live the Vortex!" by Lewis, with design by Lewis (Michel 127) on [8]; [9]-28 "Manifesto" by Lewis, with designs on [9], 12 and 20 (all the same design of cone intersected by line down center, signifying a vortex) by Lewis [?]; 29 plate, "Newcastle" by Edward Wadsworth; 30-43 "Manifesto" by Lewis, Aldington, Arbuthnot, Atkinson, Gaudier-Brzeska, Dismorr, Hamilton, Pound, Roberts, Saunders, Wadsworth; 45-50 "Poems" by Ezra Pound, including "Salutation the Third" (45), "Monumentum Ære, Etc." (46), "Come my Cantilations" (46), "Before Sleep" (47), "His Vision of a Certain Lady Post Mortem" (48), "Epitaphs" (48), "Fratres Minores" (48)*, "Women Before a Shop" (49), "L'Art" (49), "The New Cake of Soap" (49), "Meditatio" (49) and "Pastoral" (50); [51]-85 "The Enemy of the Stars" by Lewis; 87-97 "The Saddest Story" by Ford Maddox [*sic*] Heuffer; 98-117 "Indissoluble Matrimony" by Rebecca West; 118 design (probably by Lewis, not in Michel); 119-125 "Inner Necessity" by [Wassily] Kandinsky, excerpts translated from *Ueber das Geistige in der Kunst* by Edward Wadsworth, design on 125 by Lewis (Michel 126); [126] design by Lewis (Michel 127); [127]-149 "Vorteces and Notes" by Lewis, including "Life is the Important Thing!" (129-131), "Futurism, Magic and Life" (132-135), "Note [on some

German Woodcuts at the Twenty-One Gallery]" (136), "Policeman and Artist" (137), "Fêng Shui and Contemporary Form" (138), "Relativism and Picasso's Latest Work" (139-140), "The New Egos" (141), "Orchestra of Media" (142), "The Melodrama of Modernity" (143-144), "The Exploitation of Vulgarity" (145), "The Improvement of Life" (146) and "Our Vortex" (147-149), with designs by Lewis on [127] (Michel 128), [128] and 149 (same as p. [9]); 150 "Frederick Spencer Gore" by Lewis; 151-152 "To Suffragettes" by Lewis, design by Lewis on 152 (same as p. [9]); 153-154 "Vortex" by [Ezra] Pound; 155-158 "Vortex" by [Henri] Gaudier-Brzeska, with design by Lewis on 158 (same as p. [9]); 159-[164] advertisements.

Plates. 22 plates printed on heavy coated paper, printed in monochrome on rectos of leaves only, all versos blank, sewn between pages indicated below:

(48/49) i. "Cape of Good Hope" by Edward Wadsworth; ii. "A Short Flight" by Edward Wadsworth; iii. "March" by Edward Wadsworth; iv. "Radiation" by Edward Wadsworth.

([56]/[57]) v*a*[.] "Plan of War" by Lewis (Michel P12); v. "Timon of Athens" by Lewis (Michel 154); vi. "Slow Attack" by Lewis (Michel P13); vii. "Decoration for the Countess of Drogheda's House" by Lewis (Michel P10a); viii. "Portrait of an Englishwoman" by Lewis (Michel 146); viii*a*[.] "The Enemy of the Stars" by Lewis (Michel 143). The numbering of plates v*a* and viii*a* suggests that "Plan of War" and "The Enemy of the Stars" were added after the printing of the other plates was completed.

(88/89) ix. "Head" by Frederick Etchells; x. "Head" by Frederick Etchells; xi. "Patchopolis" by Frederick Etchells; xii. "Dieppe" by Frederick Etchells.

(96/97) xiii. "Dancers" by W[illiam]. Roberts; xiv. "Religion" by W[illiam]. Roberts.

(120/121) xv. "Drawing" by Jacob Epstein; xvi. "Drawing" by Jacob Epstein.

([128]/129) xvii. "Stags" by [Henri] Gaudier[-]Brzeska (photograph of sculpture); xviii. "Group" by Cuthbert Hamilton.

(152/153) xix. "Brighton Pier" by Spencer Gore; xx. "Richmond Houses" by Spencer Gore.

Bound in bright pinkish violet wrappers, with "BLAST" printed in black (3¼+" x 11½+") at angle running down front cover, and in reverse running down back cover. Text printed in black on heavy brown wove paper, unwatermarked. Plates printed in black on heavy white coated paper. All edges trimmed and unstained; sewn.

Notes. Published about June 20, 1914 and sold at 2s. 6d. (sold at 65¢ in United States).

The first of two numbers of *Blast,* founded and edited by Lewis, intended to be issued quarterly at an annual subscription rate of 10s. 6d. ($2.50 in United States) and to function as the "official" journal of English Vorticists. Initially announced for April publication in full-page advertisements in *The Egoist* (April 1 and April 15), *Blast, No. 1* was delayed until June in order that additional material could be included (for example, see note above concerning numbering of plates v*a* and viii*a*).

"Long Live the Vortex!," "Manifesto" (pp. 30-43), "Vorteces and Notes," "Frederick Spencer Gore" reprinted in *Wyndham Lewis on Art* (A45). "Vorteces and Notes" slightly revised and reprinted in *Wyndham Lewis the Artist* (A29), with additional notes by Lewis, omitting "The Melodrama of Modernity." "The Enemy of the Stars" completely rewritten for *The Enemy of the Stars* (A17), adding a postlude "The Physics of the Not-Self." Also, passage from "The Enemy of the Stars" reprinted in *Wyndham Lewis. An Anthology.*

*Most copies of *Blast* bear censor's inked cancellations of the first and last two lines of Ezra Pound's poem "Fratres Minores" (48).

A prospectus for *Blast* was sent out by the publisher in June, 1914: [*Within single rule frame:*] FIRST VOLUME NOW READY OF ALL BOOKSELLERS | [*single word in large type:*] BLAST | *A NEW ILLUSTRATED QUARTERLY* | EDITED BY WYNDHAM LEWIS | Royal Quarto (12 x 9 ¾) | 2/6 net | [*text, with publisher's imprint at foot*]. 10" x 8¼". Single leaf, not folded, printed on both ([2 pp.]) sides, as follows: [1] title and text, as above; [2] [*within single rule frame:*] text, order form, publisher's imprint. Text prints passage from "Long Live the Vortex!" Unwatermarked laid paper, printed in black.

See D20, D21, D22, D23, D24, D25 and D26.

C2 **BLAST, No. 2** 1915

No. 2. July, 1915. | BLAST | Edited by WYNDHAM LEWIS. | [*rule*] | REVIEW OF THE GREAT ENGLISH VORTEX. | [*rule*] | Price 2/6. Post free 2/10. | Yearly Subscription 11/4 post free. | London: | JOHN LANE, | The Bodley Head. | New York : John Lane Company. | Toronto: Bell & Cockburn.

11¾" x 9¾". Collation: A^4, B-G^8, H^2. Pp. 108.

[1] title; [3] table of contents; [4] list of illustrations and printer's imprint ("Printed by Leveridge and Co. (T.U.), St. Thomas' Road, Harlesden."); 5-6 "Editorial" by Lewis; [7] "Notice to Public" by Lewis; [8] design, "Island of Laputa" by [Helen] Sanders [*sic*]; 9-10 "The God of Sport and Blood," by Lewis, with design by Lewis [?] on 10; 11 "Constantinople Our Star" by Lewis; 12 "Mr. Shaw's Effect on my Friend" by Lewis; 13-14 "A Super-Krupp—or War's End" by

Lewis, design by Lewis [?] on 14; 15-16 "The European War and Great Communities" by Lewis, with design by Lewis [?] on 16; 17 design, "Hyde Park" by [Frederick] Etchells; 19-22 "Poems" by Ezra Pound, including "Dogmatic Statement on the Game and Play of Chess" (19), "The Social Order" (20), "Ancient Music" (20), "Gnomic Verses" (21), "Our Contemporaries" (21), "Our Respectful Homages to M. Laurent Tailhade" (21), "Ancient Music, rather cosmic" (22) and "Et Faim Sallir le Loup des Boys" (22); 23-24 "Artists and the War" by Lewis; 24 "The Exploitation of Blood" by Lewis; 25-26 "The Six Hundred, Verestchagin and Uccello" by Lewis; 26 "Marinetti's Occupation" by Lewis; 27 design, "The Engine" by [Jessie] Dismorr; 29 design, "Design" by [Jessie] Dismorr; 31 design, "Types of the Russian Army" by [Jacob] Kramer; 33-34 "Vortex Gaudier-Brzeska. (Written from the Trenches)." by [Henri] Gaudier-Brzeska, with unsigned obituary notice within single-rule frame on 34; 35 design, "Snow Scene" by [Dorothy] Shakespeare; 37 "The Old Houses of Flanders" by Ford Madox Hueffer; 38-47 "A Review of Contemporary Art" by Lewis, with design by D[orothy]. S[hakespeare]. on 47; 48-49 "Poems" by T. S. Eliot, including "Preludes" (48-49) and "Rhapsody of a Windy Night" (50-51), with general title on 50, design by Lewis (Michel 126) on 49; 53 design, "Progression" by [Frederick] Etchells; 55 design, "Combat" by [William] Roberts; 57 design, "Atlantic City" by [Helen] Sanders; 59 design, "Rotterdam" by [Edward] Wadsworth; 61 design, "War-Engine" by [Edward] Wadsworth; 63 design, "Design for 'Red Duet' " by Lewis (Michel 204); 65 "Monologue" by Jessie Dismorr; 66 "London Notes" by [Jessie Dismorr]; 67-68 "June Night" by [Jessie Dismorr]; 69 "Promenade," "Payment" and "Matilda" by [Jessie Dismorr], with design by Lewis (Michel 128) on 69; 70-72 "The Art of the Great Race" by Lewis; 73-74 "A Vision of Mud" by [Helen Saunders], with design by Lewis [?] on 74; 75 design, "Design for Programme Cover—Kermesse" by Lewis (Michel 52); 77-82 "Five Art Notes" by Lewis, including "The London Group" (77-79), "Modern Caricature and Impressionism" (79), "History of the Largest Independent Society in England" (80-81), "Life has no Taste" (82), "American Art" (82), with design by Lewis (Michel 127) on 82; 84 photograph of "Head of Eza [*sic*] Pound," sculpture by [Henri] Gaudier-Brzeska, printed on coated paper within single-rule frame and mounted; 85-86 "Chronicles" by E[zra]. P[ound].; 87 design, "Drawing" by [William] Roberts; 89 design, "On the way to the Trenches" by [C. R. W.] Nevinson; 91 "Wyndham Lewis Vortex No. 1. Art Vortex. Be Thyself" by Lewis; 92-93 "Blast [and] Bless" by Lewis; 94-102 "The Crowd Master. 1914. London, July." by Lewis; [103-108] advertisements.

Bound in heavy off-white wrappers, front cover printed in black, designed by Lewis (Michel 200). Printed on heavy wove, unwatermarked paper; all edges trimmed and unstained. Sewn.

Notes. Published late July, 1915 and sold at 2s. 6d.

This "War Number" of *Blast,* edited by Lewis, was the second and final issue of the journal. The appearance of *Blast, No. 2,* which had been announced for publication in Autumn, 1914, was delayed primarily due to the war and Lewis's occasional illnesses during this period. Ford Madox Ford's "The Saddest Story" which was partially published in *Blast, No. 1* was to be continued in *Blast, No. 2.* However, this first section of "The Saddest Story" was revised by Ford between issues of *Blast* and was published with the conclusion of the text on March 17, 1915 as *The Good Soldier* (London: John Lane, 1915). Lewis expresses his regret that circumstances prevented him from publishing "the whole of this admirable story" in "Notice to Public" ([7]). In Lewis's explanation for the delay in publication, he also points out that "as this paper is run chiefly by Painters . . . and they are only incidentally Propagandists, they do their work first, and, since they must, write about it afterwords (sic)" ([7]).

Announced for the third number of *Blast,* which was never published, were the following: poems and a story by Ezra Pound, poems and "vortices" by Jessie Dismorr, reproductions of drawings and paintings by the Vorticists (Dismorr, Etchells, Gaudier-Brzeska, Kramer, Roberts, Saunders, Wadsworth and Lewis), and "The Crowd-Master" [II] and "War Notes" by Lewis. In his "Notice to Public" ([7]), Lewis also indicated that letters to the editor would be printed in *Blast, No. 3.*

"A Review of Contemporary Art" (38-47) and "The Art of the Great Race" (70-72) reprinted with variations in *Wyndham Lewis the Artist* (A29). "A Review of Contemporary Art" (38-47), "The Art of the Great Race" (70-72), "The London Group" (77-79), "History of the Largest Independent Society in England" (80-81), "Life has no Taste" (82) reprinted with some minor alterations in *Wyndham Lewis on Art* (A45). "The Crowd-Master" incorporated in *Blasting and Bombardiering* (A26).

See D30, D31, D32, D33, D34, D35, D36, D37, D38, D39, D40, D41, D42, D43, D44, D45, D46, D47, D48, D49 and D50.

C3 THE TYRO [No. 1] [1921]

[*Design by Lewis extending length of page at right of typepage, Michel 451*] THE TYRO | A REVIEW OF | THE ARTS | OF PAINTING | SCULPTURE | AND DESIGN. | EDITED BY | WYNDHAM | LEWIS. | TO BE PRODUCED AT INTERVALS | OF TWO OR THREE MONTHS. | Publishers: | THE EGOIST PRESS, | 2, ROBERT STREET, ADELPHI. | PUBLISHED AT 1s. 6d. | Subscription for 4 numbers, 6s. 6d. with | postage. | [*beneath fine rule, in smaller type*] Printed by Bradley & Son, Ltd., Little Crown Yard, Mill Lane, Reading.

14¾" x 9¾". Three sheets (19½" x 14¾") folded once to make 6 unsigned leaves, stapled. Pp. 12.

[1] title; 2 "Note on Tyros" and "The Objects of this Paper" by Lewis, table of contents; 3 "The Children of the New Epoch" and "Roger Fry's rôle of Continental Mediator" by Lewis; [4] "The Romantic Englishman, the Comic Spirit, and the Function of Criticism" and "The Lesson of Baudelaire" by T. S. Eliot; [5] design by Lewis (Michel 449); 6 "Song to the Opherian" by Guz Krutzsch [i.e., T. S. Eliot], "White Males" by Robert McAlmon, "Cafe Cannibale" by John Adams and "Will Eccles" by Lewis; [7] design by Lewis (Michel 470) and untitled dialogue between "Mr. Segando" and "Phillip" by Lewis; 8 "Mr. Segando in the Fifth Cataclysm" by John Rodker; [9] two designs, "The Exit" by David Bomberg and "Dancers" by William Patrick Roberts; 10 "Emotional Æsthetics" by O. Raymond Drey; [11] photograph of sculpture "Dancing Figures," by Frank Dobson and design by Lewis (Michel 467); 12 "Critics in Arabia" by Herbert Read and "The Wild Boar" by Robert McAlmon.

White light-weight machine finished paper, attached by two staples. Printed in black.

Notes. Published April, 1921 and sold at 1s. 6d.

The first of two numbers of *The Tyro* (see C4), founded and edited by Lewis.

"Note on Tyros" reproduces a postscript in the introduction to the catalogue of the exhibition "Tyros and Portraits" (B11), reprinted in *Wyndham Lewis on Art* (A45) pp. 188-190; "The Objects of this Paper," "The Children of the New Epoch" and "Roger Fry's rôle of Continental Mediator" reprinted in *Wyndham Lewis on Art* (A45) pp. 193-194, 195-196 and 197-199; "Will Eccles," subtitled "A Serial Story," was not continued in *The Tyro, No. 2*, but became with revisions the opening pages of "You Broke My Dream" (see A9a). Both numbers of *The Tyro* reprinted in one volume by Frank Cass, London, in 1970 at £5.
See D96, D97, D98, D99, D100 and D101.

C4 THE TYRO, No. 2 [1922]

[*Thick rule*] | NO. 2 THE | [*ten lines at right of design by Lewis, Michel 494*] TYRO | A REVIEW | OF THE ARTS | OF PAINTING | SCULPTURE | AND DESIGN | 2/6 | THE EGOIST PRESS | 2 ROBERT ST: | ADELPHI.LONDON

9¾" x 7⅛". Collation: A^2, *B-G*^{8}, *H*^{1}. Pp. [iv], 98; wrappers.

[i-iv] advertisements; [1] THE TYRO. | Edited by WYNDHAM LEWIS. | Publishers—The Egoist Press, 2, Robert Street, Adelphi, London, W.C. | [*rule*] |

No. 2. Two Shillings and Sixpence. | [*rule*] | [*table of contents*] | [*rule*] | BRADLEY & SON, LTD., PRINTERS & PUBLISHERS, LITTLE CROWN YARD, MILL LANE, READING. | COPYRIGHT U.S.A.; [2] list of plates; 3-10 "Editorial" by Lewis; 11-13 "The Three Provincialities" by T. S. Eliot; 14-18 "Abstract Painting and Some Analogies" by O. Raymond Drey; 19-[20] "Some Russian Artists" by Jessie Dismorr, with design by Cedric Morris on [20]; [21]-37 "Essay on the Objective of Plastic Art in Our Time" by Lewis; 38-40 "Bugs" by Stephen Hudson; 41-42 "Grotesques Walking" by John Adams, with "Pieta" by John Rodker on 42; 43-45 "A Note on Imagination" by Herbert Read, with "Southern Syncopated Singers" by John Rodker on 45; 46-49 "Tyronic Dialogues.—X. and F." [by Lewis]; 50-52 "Lettre de Paris" by Waldeman George (in French); 53-63 "Bestre" by Lewis; [65] plate, "Conversation" by [Jessie] Dismorr; [67] plate, "Sculpture" by [Jacques] Lipschitz; [69] plate, "Room No. 59" by Lewis (Michel 505); [71] plate, "Red and Black Olympus" by Lewis (Michel 474); [73] plate, "Women" by Lewis (Michel 518); [75] plate, "Girl Reading" by Lewis (Michel 464); [77] plate, "Sensibility" by Lewis (Michel 483); [79] plate, "Drawing for Jonathan Swift" by Lewis (Michel 526); [81] plate, "Women descending from Bus" by [Austin] Dobson; [83] plate, "Family" by [Austin] Dobson; [85] plate, "Cornish Arabesque" by [Frederick] Etchells; [87] plate, "Gunwalloe" by [Frederick] Etchells; [89] plate, "Porthleven" by [Frederick] Etchells; [91] plate, "Portland" by [Edward] Wadsworth; [93] plate, "Port" by [Edward] Wadsworth; [95] plates (2), "Mudros" by [Edward] Wadsworth; [97] plate, "Mudros" by [Edward] Wadsworth.

Bound in heavy white textured paper wrappers, glued along spine, printed in black on front cover (transcription above) and in black on back inner cover and back cover (advertisements). Spine unlettered. All edges trimmed and unstained. Wove unwatermarked paper.

Notes. Published March, 1922 and sold at 2s. 6d.

The second of two numbers of *The Tyro* (see C3), founded and edited by Lewis. "Essay on the Objective of Plastic Art in Our Time" reprinted with slight revisions in *Wyndham Lewis the Artist* (A29) and *Wyndham Lewis on Art* (A45); "Bestre" reprinted in *The Wild Body* (A9a). See D106, D107, D108 and D109.

C5 THE ENEMY, Vol. 1 1927

THE ENEMY | *A review of art and literature* | [*ornamental rule*] | *Editor–* Wyndham Lewis | Author of *The Art of Being Ruled* | VOL. 1. JANUARY, 1927 | [*ornamental rule*] | PUBLISHED BY | THE ARTHUR PRESS.

11⅛" x 7⅜". Collation: A^6, B-N^8, O^{10}. Pp. *xii,* xvi, 196 (*xii* pages of advertisements not included in pagination).

i-xii advertisments; [i] [*within rectangular frame of dots*] *Note.*—"THE ENEMY" was to have appeared in | January, as indicated on the cover; but owing to | miscalculation as to the time required to prepare | it, it is appearing in February instead. Numbers | uniform as regards format will appear from time to | time during the year, longer or shorter according | to circumstances.; [ii] extract from review of *The Tyro* over design by Lewis (Michel 629); [iii] title; [iv] quotation from Plutarch's *Moralia* over design by Lewis (Michel 630); v-vi table of contents; vii-viii "Preliminary Note to Public" by Lewis; ix-xv "Editorial" by Lewis; 1-7 "The Position of Beethoven in the Modern World" by J. W. N. Sullivan; 9-14 "Giorgio di Chirico" by W[ilfrid]. Gibson; 15-17 "A Note on Poetry and Belief" by T.S. Eliot; 19-23 "What's in a Namesake" [by Lewis]; 25-192 "The Revolutionary Simpleton" by Lewis (design by Lewis on 25, Michel 640); 193-195 Index; [196] THE BLACKFRIARS PRESS LTD. | 17-23 ALBION ST., LEICESTER, *and* [*sic*] | 32 FURNIVAL ST., LONDON, E.C.4.

Issued in heavy mustard paper wrappers, glued along spine, front cover white with lettering and design by Lewis: THE ENEMY | A REVIEW OF ART AND | LITERATURE | JAN. 1927 | [*design by Lewis, Michel 620*] |. Lettering on front cover printed in grey-green, design printed in black, brown, blue, red, green and yellow. Top and fore-edges trimmed and unstained; bottom edge untrimmed. Printed on wove unwatermarked paper; sewn. In some copies the publisher's address is rubber-stamped in violet ink on the title, below publisher's imprint: "113a, WESTBOURNE GROVE, W."; also, some copies have the price, 2/6, rubber-stamped on front cover.

Plates. Four plates reproducing designs by Lewis, printed on coated paper, unpaged leaves mounted facing following pages: viii "Magellan" (Michel 636), in black; 14 "Figures in Air" (Michel 635), in black, brown, green, yellow, red and violet; [18] "The Sibyl" (Michel 624), in black; [24] "Self-portrait" (Michel 641), in black.

Notes. Published February, 1927 in an edition of 1500 copies, and sold at 2s. 6d. A few copies specially signed by Lewis on the title page, were sold at 30s.

This is the first of three numbers of *The Enemy* (see C6 and C7), founded, edited and published by Lewis between February, 1927 and January, 1929. Subtitled "A Review of Art and Literature," *The Enemy* was founded by Lewis (who during this period styled himself as "The Enemy") as a vehicle for "serious unpartisan criticism" of society, from a position of objective distance ("in solitary schism"). These intentions, outlined by Lewis in his initial "Editorial," were immediately carried out by the publication of his well-known attack on the "romanticism" of Joyce, Pound, Stein, McAlmon, Charlie Chaplin, the Russian Ballet and *This Quarter* in "The Revolutionary Simpleton" (25-192), reprinted in *Time and Western Man* (A8).

The Arthur Press was established by Lewis in late 1926 to undertake the publication of the *The Enemy*. An office was maintained at 13A Westbourne Grove (later moved to 53 Ossington Street, Bayswater), which was occupied by Lewis and a secretary only. Besides *The Enemy,* Lewis used this imprint for *The Apes of God* (A12a) and *Satire & Fiction* (C8), as well as several publicity broadsides. Although Geoffrey Wagner asserts that the name of Lewis's publishing house—The Arthur Press—was chosen because Arthur "is the same in all languages" (*A Portrait of the Artist as Enemy,* p. 23; see F1067), W. K. Rose denies this, stating that the name was selected because of the "proximity of the office to The Arthur Stores" (*The Letters,* p. 171; see A42). After the publication of *Satire & Fiction,* The Arthur Press ceased to function.

A prospectus was sent out by The Arthur Press just prior to publication of *The Enemy, No. 1*:
THE ENEMY | *A Review of Art and Literature* | Editor: WYNDHAM LEWIS | [*fine rule over text*]. 10½" x 8¼". Single leaf, printed on both sides, unfolded to make [2] pp., as follows: [1] title and text, as above; [2] text, publisher's address. This prospectus announces the founding of "Free West Publications" (later renamed "The Arthur Press"), Lewis's publishing firm. The purpose of "Free West Publications" is also set forth in the text of the prospectus, citing the need for "an organisation [dedicated to] . . . the publishing of pamphlets." Also, a general description of *The Enemy* is given. Wove unwatermarked paper, printed in black.

A broadside measuring 8¾" x 5½", printed on one side only in black, giving six extracts from reviews of *The Enemy, No. 1* was issued in March, 1927: Some extracts from | first notice of . . . *The Enemy* No. 1 | [*extracts*] |.

See D129, D130, D131 and D132.

C6 THE ENEMY, No. 2 1927

THE ENEMY No. 2 | *A review of art and literature* | [*ornamental rule*] | *Editor*–Wyndham Lewis | Author of *The Art of Being Ruled; The Lion and the Fox;* | *Time and Western Man; The Wild Body* | PRICE—3*s*. 6*d*. | (POSTAGE 6*d*.) | [*ornamental rule*] | PUBLISHED BY | THE ARTHUR PRESS | 113A Westbourne Grove, London, W. | *Telephone*—Park 7986

11⅛" x 7⅜". Collation: $1\text{-}11^8$, 12^{10} ($1^2\text{-}11^2$ signed 1A-11A, 12^2 signed 12*, 12^3 signed 12A). Pp. *xvi,* xl, 140.

i-xvi advertisements; [i] title; ii quotation from Plutarch's *Moralia* over double rule over list of booksellers and agents handling *The Enemy*; iii-v table of contents; vii-x "Notes Regarding Details of Publication and Distribution" by Lewis; xi-xxxi "Editorial Notes" by Lewis; xxxiii-xl "Editorial" by Lewis; [1] design by Lewis (Michel 638); 3-112 "Paleface or 'Love? What ho! Smelling Strangeness' " by Lewis; [113] design by Lewis (Michel 396); 115-137 "Towards Reintegration" by Henry John; [138] *Printed by* | *Hazell, Watson & Viney, Ld.,* [*sic*] | *52, Long Acre, London, W.C.2* | 7838-27.

Bound in heavy white coated paper wrappers, glued along spine, front cover designed by Lewis printed in black, yellow and red. All edges trimmed and unstained. Regular paper copies printed on wove, unwatermarked paper (paper bulk, 9/16"); large paper copies printed on heavier white wove paper, watermarked "—BASINGWERK PARCHMENT—" (paper bulk, ¾"); sewn.

Notes. Published late September, 1927 in an edition of 5000 copies, and sold at 3s. 6d. Special large paper edition printed on Basingwerk Parchment consisted of 150 copies numbered, dated and signed by Lewis, sold at 21s. Titlepage of this limited edition was altered to read "*Price*—One Guinea net" from "PRICE—3*s*. 6*d*." in the regular edition. Copies of the Special edition on Basingwerk Parchment, signed by Lewis, examined in the collections of Hugh Anson-Cartwright (copy #74) and University of California at Santa Barbara (copy #51). Published simultaneously.

The second of three numbers of *The Enemy* (see C5 and C7), founded, edited and published by Lewis. See D135, D136, D137 and D138.

C7 THE ENEMY, No. 3 1929

THE ENEMY No. 3 | *A review of art and literature* | [*ornamental rule*] | *Editor*– Wyndham Lewis | Author of *The Art of Being Ruled; The Lion and the Fox; Time* | *and Western Man; The Wild Body; The Childermass,* etc. | [*design by Lewis, Michel 633*] | FIRST QUARTER, 1929. | [*ornamental rule*] | PUBLISHED BY | THE ARTHUR PRESS | 113A Westbourne Grove, London, W. | *Telephone* Park 7986 | 2/6.

11¼" x 7⅜". Collation: A^8, B^9, C-G^8, H^4 (single leaf inserted after B4 included in pagination, unsigned). Pp. *xx*, [i] ii-viii, [9-10] 11-84, [2 unpaged pages], 85-100. Roman to arabic paging is continuous after viii; single unpaged leaf at *84*bis included in collation (given below as *84*bis_r and *84*bis_v).

i-xx advertisements (note below review extracts on *xvii* is by Lewis); [i] title; [ii] quotation from Plutarch's *Moralia* over rule over list of booksellers and agents handling *The Enemy;* iii-iv table of contents; [v] photograph captioned "A recent photograph of the Enemy, Mr. Wyndham Lewis."; vii-viii "Enemy Bulletin" by Lewis; [9]-84 "The Diabolical Principle" by Lewis (design by Lewis on [9], Michel 652); *84*bis$_r$ design by Lewis (Michel 667); 85-88 "The Albatross" by Roy Campbell; 88-89 "Fine Fellow Son of a Poor Fellow" by Laura Riding; 90 "Details regarding publication and distribution" by Lewis; 91-100 "Notes" by Lewis.

Bound in heavy white paper wrappers, glued along spine, front cover (Michel 633) printed in black and yellow, back cover (Michel 649) printed in black. Top and fore-edges trimmed and unstained; bottom edge untrimmed. Wove unwatermarked paper; sewn.

Notes. Published about March, 1929 and sold at 2s. 6d.

The third of three numbers of *The Enemy* (see C5 and C6), founded, edited and published by Lewis. That a fourth number of *The Enemy* was planned is evident from Lewis's note (4) on p. 90: "The next number of the *Enemy,* which it is hoped will be available early in the New Year, will contain a long essay by Mr. Wyndham Lewis. It will deal with contemporary literature in England, with regard especially to its technical evolution: or if the notes for that are not completed in time, it will be the essay on the *Youth Movement,* already announced in no. 2." The three numbers of *The Enemy* were reprinted in 2 volumes by Frank Cass, London, in 1968 at £12. See D139, D140, D141 and D142.

C8 SATIRE & FICTION 1930

SATIRE & FICTION | *By* | WYNDHAM LEWIS | PRECEDED BY | THE HISTORY OF A | REJECTED REVIEW | *By* | ROY CAMPBELL | THE ARTHUR PRESS | 53. OSSINGTON STREET | LONDON. W.2.

11" x 8¼". Collation: 16 sheets folded once to make 32 unsigned leaves. Pp. 64 (pp. 3-4 signed "iii-iv"); wrappers.

[1] title; [2] quotation from Plutarch's *Moralia;* iii-iv table of contents; [5] divisional half-title; 7-8 "A Storm in that Tea-Cup called London" by Lewis; 9-12 "Letter to Mr. Wyndham Lewis" by Roy Campbell; 13-14 "Reviewer's Preface" by Roy Campbell; 15-16 "A Rejected Review" by Roy Campbell; 17-21 "General Editorial Comments" by Lewis; 22 "Circular Letter Issued by The Arthur Press" by Lewis; 23-29 letters to Lewis from Richard Aldington, Montgomery Belgion, J. D. Beresford, Meyrick Booth, Augustus John, H. G. Wells, W. B. Yeats; "A Reader's Report for an American Publisher" by Montgomery Belgion; 32-40 extracts from reviews of *The Apes of God,* "An Alibi!" on 40 is by Lewis; [41]

divisional half-title; 43-62 "Satire and Fiction" by Lewis; 63 extracts from reviews of *The Apes of God.*

Bound in heavy white coated paper wrappers, printed in black and red on front cover, and in black on inner front cover and back cover. Printed on wove unwatermarked smooth finished paper; attached with two staples. Edges trimmed and unstained.

Notes. Published September, 1930 and sold at 1s. 6d.

Subsequent to Lewis's controversial novel, *The Apes of God* (A12), which came out in June, 1930, *Satire & Fiction* was published as "Enemy Pamphlets No. 1" largely to promote further interest in the novel. Although by numbering the pamphlet Lewis suggests that further issues will follow, *Satire and Fiction* was the only "Enemy Pamphlet" published.

A prospectus was sent out by The Arthur Press just prior to publication of *Satire & Fiction:*

SATIRE & FICTION | *by Wyndham Lewis.* [*at left:*] PRICE | 1/6 | [*at right:*] *Preceded by* | [*below:*] HISTORY OF A REJECTED REVIEW | *by Roy Campbell.* | [*rule*] | *Letters from Augustus John, H G. Wells, W. B. Yeats, and other* | *distinguished people.* | SCANDAL of an attempt to SABOTAGE A | GREAT WORK OF ART! | [*rule*] | THE ARTHUR PRESS, 53, OSSINGTON ST., LONDON, W.2. | Telephone: PARK 0667. Postage 3d.

4½" x 7". Single leaf, unfolded, printed on one side only, as above, in black. Cream wove paper, watermarked: "WYNYARD | BOND."

Reprinted by Folcroft Press in 1967 at $7.50.

See D148, D149, D150, D151 and D152.

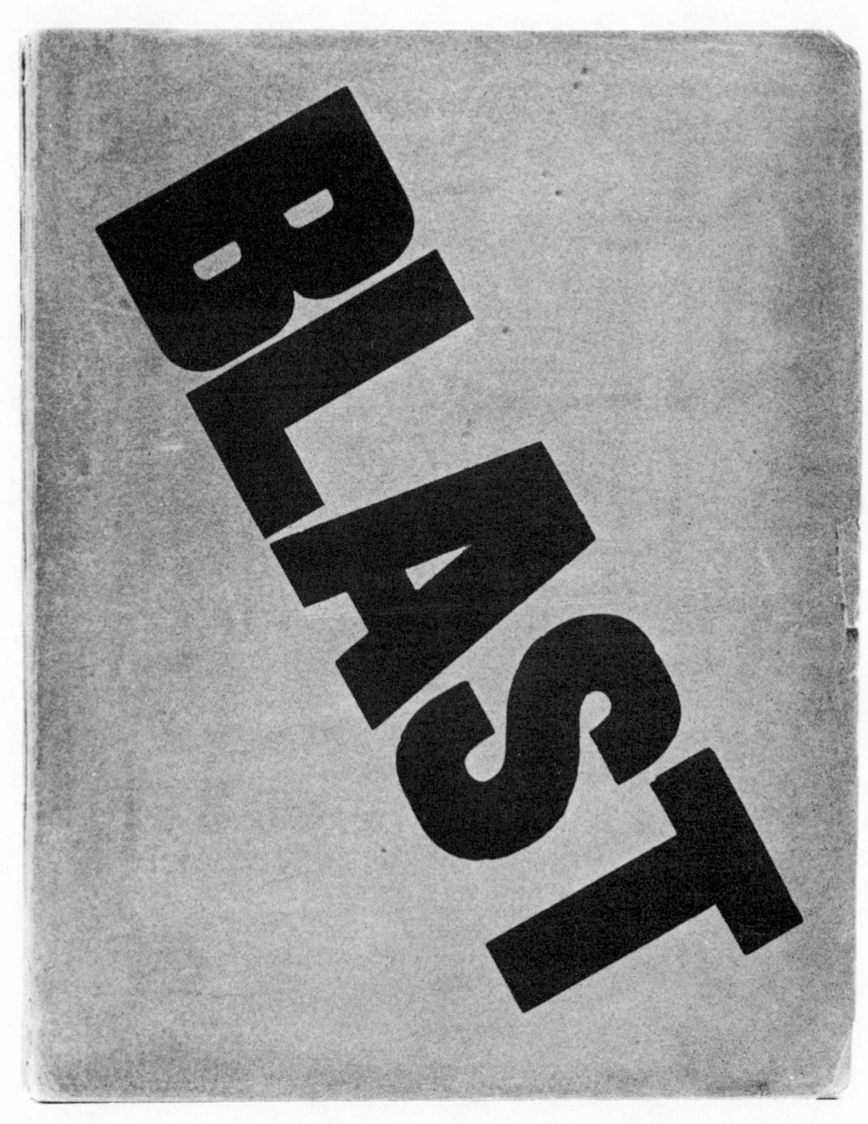

Front cover of *Blast, No. 1* (C1).

Front cover of *Blast, No. 2*, designed by Lewis (C2).

THE TYRO

A REVIEW OF THE ARTS OF PAINTING SCULPTURE AND DESIGN.

EDITED BY

WYNDHAM LEWIS.

TO BE PRODUCED AT INTERVALS OF TWO OR THREE MONTHS.

Publishers:
THE EGOIST PRESS,
2, ROBERT STREET, ADELPHI.

PUBLISHED AT 1s. 6d.

Subscription for 4 numbers, 6s. 6d. with postage.

Printed by Bradley & Son, Ltd., Little Crown Yard, Mill Lane, Reading.

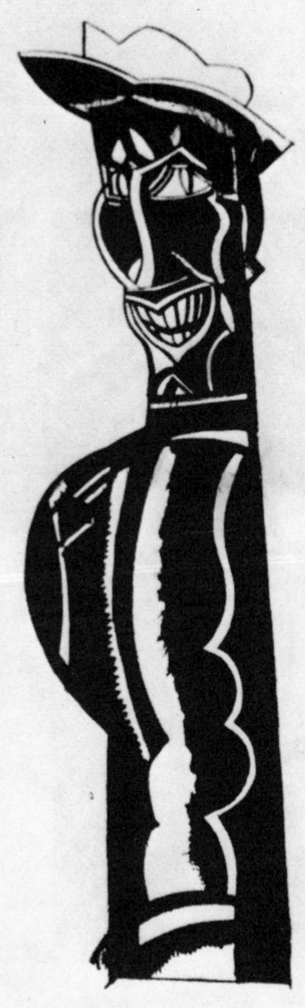

Front cover of *The Tyro, No. 1*, designed by Lewis (C3).

Front cover of *The Tyro, No. 2*, designed by Lewis (C4).

ENEMY PAMPHLETS No. 1.

SATIRE & FICTION

Price
1/6

by Wyndham Lewis.

'THE APES OF GOD' *explained by the author*

ALSO — *HAVE WITH YOU TO GREAT QUEEN STREET!*

THE HISTORY OF A REJECTED REVIEW, By ROY CAMPBELL.

SCANDAL OF AN ATTEMPT TO SABOTAGE A GREAT WORK OF ART!

Letters concerning 'The Apes of God' from
RICHARD ALDINGTON
MONTGOMERY BELGION
J. D. BERESFORD
DR. MEYRICK BOOTH
AUGUSTUS JOHN
H. G. WELLS
W. B. YEATS

A NOVEL BY WYNDHAM LEWIS
APES OF GOD

PREFACE TO A REJECTED REVIEW
by ROY CAMPBELL

NOTES ON THE SATIRE OF *The Apes of God*
by WYNDHAM LEWIS

THE ARTHUR PRESS
53. OSSINGTON STREET
BAYSWATER.—LONDON. W.

TELEPHONE PARK. 0667.

Front cover of *Satire & Fiction*, designed by Lewis (C8).

THE "ENEMY" IS THE NOTORIOUS AUTHOR, PAINTER AND PUBLICIST, MR. WYNDHAM LEWIS. HE IS THE DIOGENES OF THE DAY: HE SITS LAUGHING IN THE MOUTH OF HIS TUB AND POURS FORTH HIS INVECTIVE UPON ALL PASSERS-BY, IRRESPECTIVE OF RACE, CREED, RANK OR PROFESSION, AND SEX. THIS PAPER, WHICH APPEARS OCCASIONALLY, IS THE PRINCIPAL VEHICLE OF HIS CRITICISM. ⁝ FOR CONTENTS OF THIS ISSUE SEE BACK COVER.

WYNDHAM LEWIS
Editor.

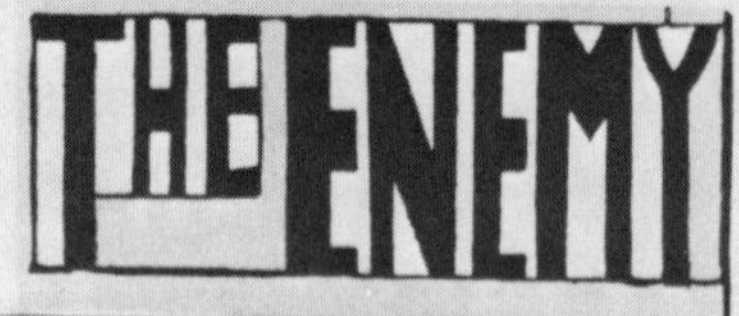

Front cover of *The Enemy. No. 3*, designed by Lewis (C7).

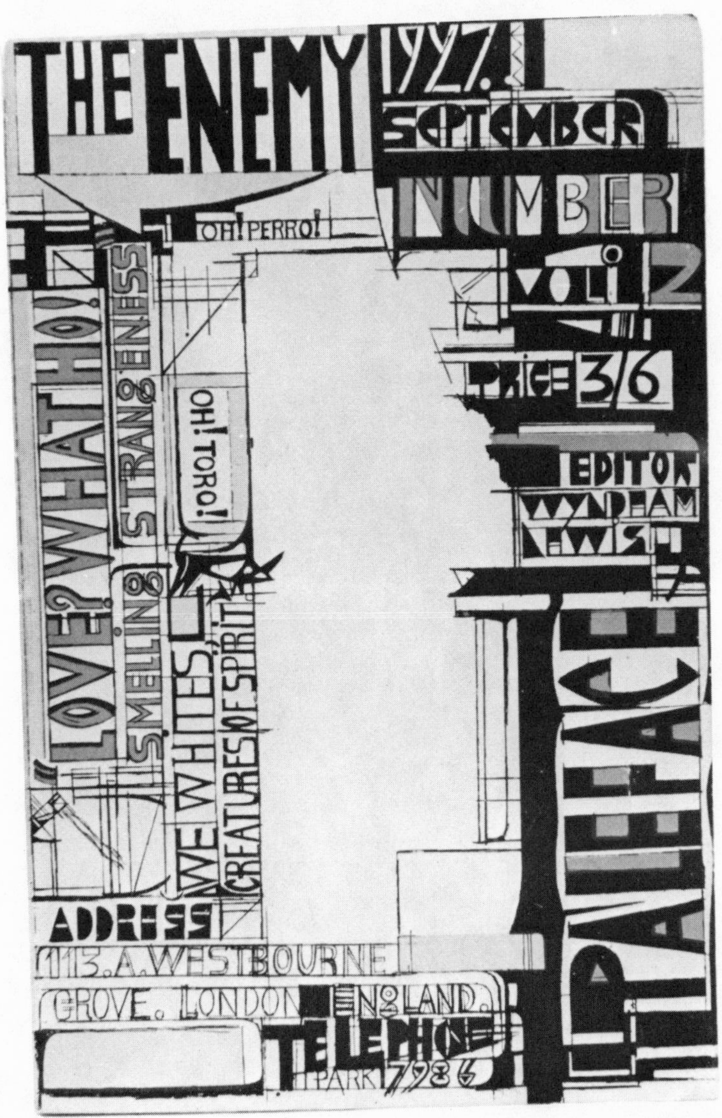

Front cover of *The Enemy, No. 2*, designed by Lewis (C6).

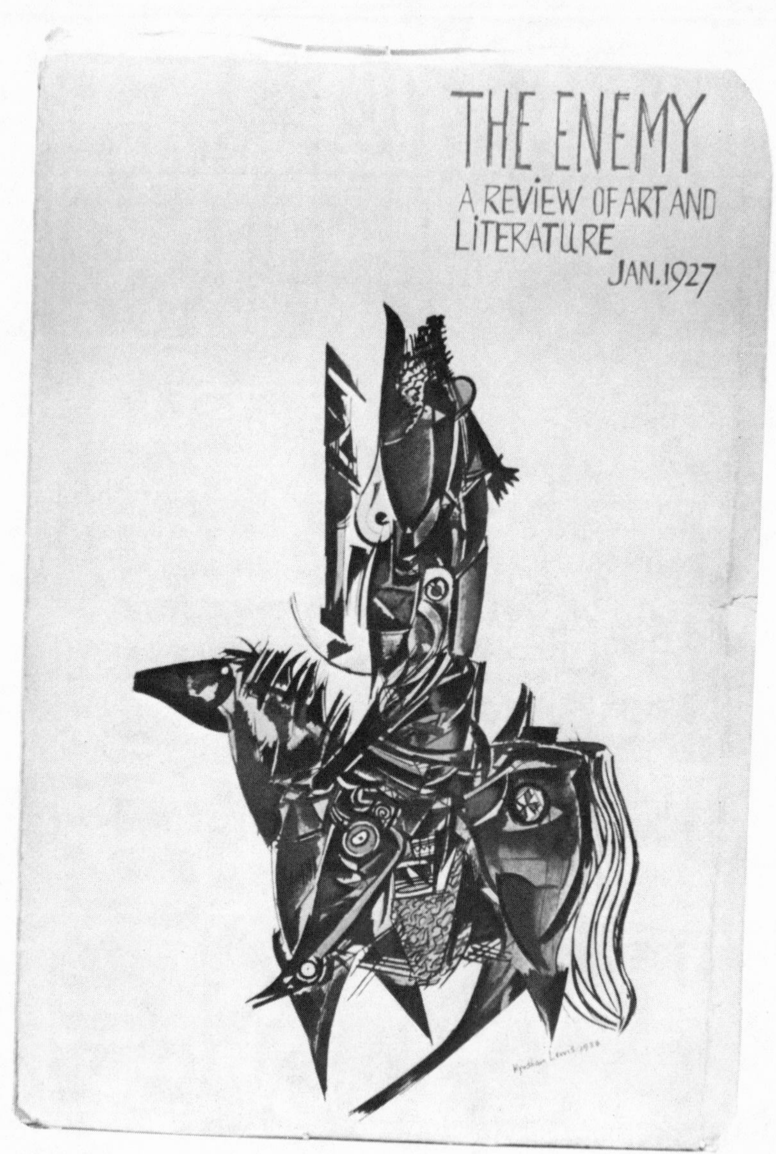

Front cover of *The Enemy, No. 1*, designed by Lewis (C5).

D. Contributions to Periodicals

1909

D1 THE POLE. *The English Review,* II (May) 255-256.

Revised version published under the title "Beau Séjour" in *The Wild Body* (A9). Lewis's first appearance in print. Signed: "P. Wyndham Lewis."

D2 SOME INNKEEPERS AND BESTRE. *The English Review,* II (June) 471-484.

Revised version of "Bestre" passage (479-484), omitting the theoretical introduction (471-479), published in *The Tyro, no. 2* (C4). Further revised version published in *The Wild Body* as "Bestre" (A9).

D3 LES SALTIMBANQUES. *The English Review,* III (August) 76-87.

Revised version published under the title "The Cornac and his Wife" in *The Wild Body* (A9). Signed: "P. Wyndham Lewis."

1910

D4 OUR WILD BODY. *The New Age,* II, no. 1 (May 5) 8-10.

Essay marking Lewis's first attempt to expound the meaning of the "Wild Body."

D5 A SPANISH HOUSEHOLD. *The Tramp: an Open Air Magazine,* I (June-July) 356-360.

Contrary to Wagner's assertion in *Portrait of the Artist as Enemy* (see F1067, p. 322), this text was neither incorporated nor expanded in *The Wild Body* (A9). Final paragraph sheds light on a rather enigmatic unpublished story, *Crossing the Frontier* (see Mary Daniels, *Descriptive Catalogue,* p. 6).

D6 A BRETON INNKEEPER. *The Tramp: an Open Air Magazine,* I (August) 411-414.

Reprinted in *Unlucky for Pringle* (A46).

D7 LE PÈRE FRANÇOIS (A FULL-LENGTH PORTRAIT OF A TRAMP). *The Tramp: an Open Air Magazine,* I (September) 517-521.

Revised version published in *The Wild Body* under the title "Franciscan Adventures" (see A9). Signed: "P. Wyndham Lewis."

D8 GRIGNOLLES (BRITTANY). *The Tramp: an Open Air Magazine,* II (December) 246.

The only poem Lewis published besides *One-Way Song* (A21).

1911

D9 BROBDINGNAG. *The New Age,* VIII (Literary Supplement), no. 10 (January 5) 2-3.

Revised version published in *The Wild Body* (A9) under the title "Brotcotnaz."

D10 UNLUCKY FOR PRINGLE. *The Tramp: an Open Air Magazine,* II (February) 404-414.

Illustrated by F. Gregory Brown. Reprinted in *Unlucky for Pringle* (A46).

1914

D11 THE CUBIST ROOM. *The Egoist,* I, no. 1 (January 1) 8-9.

Reprints *The Cubist Room,* foreword to *Exhibition of English Post-Impressionists, Cubists and Others,* Public Art Galleries, Brighton, December 1913-January 1914 (B2). Reprinted in *Wyndham Lewis on Art* (A45) and Michel (B33).

D12 EPSTEIN AND HIS CRITICS, OR NIETZSCHE AND HIS FRIENDS. *The New Age,* XIV, no. 10 (January 8) 319.

Letter to the editor concerning the Hulme-Lodovici controversy (see F22 seq.). Reprinted in *The Letters* (A42a).

D13 MR. ARTHUR ROSE'S OFFER. *The New Age,* XIV, no. 15 (February 12) 479.

Letter to the editor, reprinted in *The Letters* (A42a).

D14 MODERN ART. *The New Age,* XIV, no. 22 (April 2) 703.

Letter to the editor in response to a letter from Walter Sickert (see F32 and F47).

D15 REBEL ART IN MODERN LIFE. *The Daily News and Leader,* XXI, no. 240 (April 7) 14.

Interview and photograph of Lewis at the Rebel Art Center, by M. M. B. Excerpts reprinted in Cork, *Vorticism* (I), see F1833.

D16 A MAN OF THE WEEK. MARINETTI. *The New Weekly,* I, no. 11 (May 30) 328-329.

Also, prints caricature of Lewis by Kapp (p. 331).

D17 FUTURISM. *The New Weekly,* I, no. 13 (June 13) 406.

Also printed in *The Observer* and *The Egoist* (see D18 and D19), this is a collective letter signed by Aldington, Bomberg, Etchells, Pound, Wadsworth, Atkinson, Gaudier-Brzeska, Hamilton, Roberts and Lewis, in response to *Futurism and English Art (The Observer,* IV, no. 420 (June 7)), a manifesto associating them with Futurism. Reprinted in *The Letters* (A42a) and Wees's *Vorticism* (F1671).

D18 FUTURISM. *The Observer,* VI, 421 (June 14) 9.

Same as D17.

D19 FUTURISM. *The Egoist,* I, no. 12 (June 15) 239.

Same as D17.

D20 LONG LIVE THE VORTEX! *Blast,* 1 (June 20) 7-8.

Blast, No. 1 edited by Lewis (see C1). Reprinted in *Wyndham Lewis on Art* (A45), this *credo* briefly defines the meaning of Vorticism and the intentions of *Blast.* See D21, D22, D23, D24, D25 and D26.

D21 MANIFESTO. *Blast,* 1 (June 20) 9-28.

"Blasts" and "Blesses" by Lewis. See C1 and D20.

D22 MANIFESTO [II]. *Blast,* 1 (June 20) 30-43.

Collective manifesto signed by Aldington, Arbuthnot, Atkinson, Gaudier-Brzeska, Dismorr, Hamilton, Pound, Roberts, Saunders, Wadsworth and Lewis. Reprinted in *Wyndham Lewis on Art* (A45). See C1, D17 and D20.

D23 ENEMY OF THE STARS. *Blast,* 1 (June 20) 51-85.

Heavily revised version published in *The Enemy of the Stars* (A17). See C1 and D20.

D24 VORTECES AND NOTES. *Blast,* 1 (June 20) 127-149.

Reprinted in *Wyndham Lewis the Artist* (A29) and *Wyndham Lewis on Art* (A45). See C1 and D20.

D25 FREDERICK SPENCER GORE. *Blast,* 1 (June 20) 150.

Obituary notice about Gore (1878-1914). Reprinted in *Wyndham Lewis on Art* (A45). See C1 and D20.

D26 TO SUFFRAGETTES. *Blast,* 1 (June 20) 151-152.

Warns suffragettes to "leave works of art alone." See C1 and D20.

D27 AUTOMOBILISM. *The New Weekly,* II, no. 1 (June 20) 13.

This article marks Lewis's dissociation from the Futurists.

D28 FUTURISM AND THE FLESH. A FUTURIST'S REPLY TO MR. G. K. CHESTERTON. *T. P.'s Weekly,* XXXIV, no. 609 (July 11) 49.

Rebuttal of Chesterton's "mid-Victorian" article on Futurism, "The Asceticism of Futurism" (July 4) though Lewis no longer considered himself a Futurist (see D27). Includes photograph of Lewis, p.49.

D29 KILL JOHN BULL WITH ART. *The Outlook,* XXXIV, no. 74 (July 18) 74.

Nationalism viewed as "the national enemy of each nation." Includes photograph of Lewis.

1915

D30 EDITORIAL. *Blast,* 2 (July) 5-6.

Blast, No. 2 edited by Lewis (see C2). See D31, D32, D33, D34, D35, D36, D37, D38, D39, D40, D41, D42, D43, D44, D45, D46, D47, D48, D49 and D50.

D31 NOTICE TO PUBLIC. *Blast,* 2 (July) 7.

Includes list of contents for *Blast, No. 3* (not published). See C2 and D30.

D32 THE GOD OF SPORT AND BLOOD. *Blast,* 2 (July) 9-10.

Satirical essay about German statesmanship. See C2 and D30.

D33 CONSTANTINOPLE OUR STAR. *Blast,* 2 (July) 11.

Humorous discussion enumerating why those interested in Art should "pray" that Russia will "get" Constantinople. See C2 and D30.

D34 MR. SHAW'S EFFECT ON MY FRIEND. *Blast,* 2 (July) 12.

Discussion about English manners and Shaw's "Common Sense." See C2 and D30.

D35 A SUPER-KRUPP—OR WAR'S END. *Blast,* 2 (July) 13-14.

Discussion about the war, stating that "nobody but Marinetti, the Kaiser, and professional soldiers WANT War." See C2 and D30.

D36 THE EUROPEAN WAR AND GREAT COMMUNITIES. *Blast,* 2 (July) 15-16.

Essay on the nature of war, stating that wars will continue to occur: "Murder and destruction is man's fundamental occupation." Satirical view of war between "large communities." See C2 and D30.

D37 ARTISTS AND THE WAR. *Blast,* 2 (July) 23-24.

See C2 and D30.

D38 THE EXPLOITATION OF BLOOD. *Blast,* 2 (July) 24.

See C2 and D30.

D39 THE SIX HUNDRED, VERESTCHAGIN AND UCCELLO. *Blast,* 2 (July) 25-26.

See C2 and D30.

D40 MARINETTI'S OCCUPATION. *Blast,* 2 (July) 26.

See C2 and D30.

D41 A REVIEW OF CONTEMPORARY ART. *Blast,* 2 (July) 38-47.

Reprinted in *Wyndham Lewis the Artist* (A29) omitting the introductory note; reprinted with introductory note in *Wyndham Lewis on Art* (A45). General survey of Expressionism, Cubism, Futurism, Vorticism and other modern art movements. See C2 and D30.

D42 THE ART OF THE GREAT RACE. *Blast,* 2 (July) 70-72.

Essay about artists and æsthetics, delineating various Vorticists' doctrines. Reprinted with minor revisions and an introductory note in *Wyndham Lewis the Artist* (A29); also reprinted in *Wyndham Lewis on Art* (A45). See C2 and D30.

D43 THE LONDON GROUP. *Blast,* 2 (July) 77-79.

Review of the second exhibition of the London Group, held at Goupil Gallery in March, 1915. Reprinted in *Wyndham Lewis on Art* (A45). See C2 and D30.

D44 MODERN CARICATURE AND IMPRESSIONISM. *Blast,* 2 (July) 79.

Included with D38, D40, D41 and D42 under the general title "Five Art Notes." See C2 and D30.

D45 HISTORY OF THE LARGEST INDEPENDENT SOCIETY IN ENGLAND. *Blast,* 2 (July) 80-81.

Discussion about the Allied Artists' Association, founded by Frank Rutter, which held large exhibitions at Albert Hall between 1908-1919. Reprinted in *Wyndham Lewis on Art* (A45). See C2 and D30.

D46 LIFE HAS NO TASTE. *Blast,* 2 (July) 82.

Brief *credo* explaining why the "best artist is an imperfect artist." Reprinted in *Wyndham Lewis on Art* (A45). See C2 and D30.

D47 AMERICAN ART. *Blast,* 2 (July) 82.

See C2 and D30.

D48 WYNDHAM LEWIS VORTEX NO. 1. ART VORTEX. BE THYSELF. *Blast,* 2 (July) 91.

Brief Vorticist *credo.* See C2 and D30.

D49 BLAST [AND] BLESS. *Blast,* 2 (July) 92-93.

Essentially a satirical valuation of various social, political and artistic groups which are either "blasted" or "blessed" by Lewis. See C2 and D30.

D50 THE CROWD-MASTER. *Blast,* 2 (July) 94-102.

First version of this story, the manuscript of which (NIC) contains "The Code" later published in *The Ideal Giant* (A2). See C2 and D30. See also D71.

D51 PREFACE. *The Cambridge Magazine,* V, no. 8 (December 4) 173.

Preface to "Mayvale," a story by H. E. Clifton and James Wood. See B7.

1916

D52 THE FRENCH POODLE. *The Egoist,* III, no. 3 (March) 39-41.

Includes drawing of Lewis by Roald Kristian. Reprinted in *Unlucky for Pringle* (A46).

D53 A YOUNG SOLDIER. *The Egoist,* III, no. 3 (March) 46.

Prose vignette similar to *Cantleman's Spring-Mate.*

D54 TARR. *The Egoist,* III, no. 4 (April 1) 54-63.

First instalment in the serial publication of Lewis's first published novel, probably completed in November 1915, according to the date given at the end of the Epilogue (see D77). This instalment corresponds to Part I, Chaps. 1-3, with numerous textual differences (see A3a and A3b). See also D55, D56, D57, D58, D59, D60, D61, D62, D63, D64, D65, D66, D68, D70, D72, D73, D75 and D77.

D55 TARR. *The Egoist,* III, no. 5 (May 1) 72-79.

Corresponds to Part I, Chap. 4 of *Tarr.* See D54.

D56 TARR. *The Egoist,* III, no. 6 (June 1) 90-94.

Corresponds to Part II, Chaps. 2-5 of *Tarr,* with "considerable excisions." See D54.

D57 TARR. *The Egoist,* III, no. 7 (July 1) 107-110.

Corresponds to Part III, Chap. 1 of *Tarr.* See D54.

D58 TARR. *The Egoist,* III, no. 8 (August) 122-125.

Corresponds to Part III, Chap. 2 of *Tarr,* the beginning "deleted for want of space." See D54.

D59 TARR. *The Egoist,* III, no. 9 (September) 139-143.

Corresponds to Part IV, Chaps. 1-4 of *Tarr.* See D54.

D60 TARR. *The Egoist,* III, no. 10 (October) 155-158.

Corresponds to Part IV, Chaps. 5-7 of *Tarr.* See D54.

D61 TARR. *The Egoist,* III, no. 11 (November) 170-173.

Corresponds to Part IV, Chaps. 8-9 of *Tarr.* See D54.

D62 TARR. *The Egoist,* III, no. 12 (December) 184-186.

Corresponds to Part IV, Chaps. 10-11 of *Tarr.* See D54.

1917

D63 TARR. *The Egoist,* IV, no. 1 (January) 10-15.

Corresponds to Part V, Chaps. 1-4 of *Tarr.* See D54.

D64 TARR. *The Egoist,* IV, no. 2 (February) 29-30.

Corresponds to Part V, Chaps. 5-6 of *Tarr.* See D54.

D65 TARR. *The Egoist,* IV, no. 3 (April) 39-41.

Corresponds to Part V, Chap. 7 of *Tarr.* See D54.

D66 TARR. *The Egoist,* IV, no. 4 (May) 60-61.

Corresponds to Part V, Chap. 8 of *Tarr.* See D54.

D67 IMAGINARY LETTERS I (SIX LETTERS OF WILLIAM BLAND TO HIS WIFE). *The Little Review,* IV, no. 1 (May) 19-23.

The beginning of a fictive epistolary chronicle, in which Ezra Pound participated (letters IV, V and VI). From an examination of typed manuscripts at Cornell, it appears that the first two *Imaginary Letters* were written in late 1916 or early 1917. Completed sequence reprinted in *The Little Review*

Anthology (B30) and in *Lewisletter,* nos. 6 and 7 (see F1905 and F1916). See D69, D71, D80 and D81. See also A50.

D68 TARR. *The Egoist,* IV, no. 5 (June) 75-78.

Corresponds to Part VI, Chaps. 1-2 of *Tarr.* See D54.

D69 IMAGINARY LETTERS II. (SIX LETTERS OF WILLIAM BLAND TO HIS WIFE). *The Little Review,* IV, no. 2 (June) 22-26.

Contains *Imaginary Letter,* no. 2. See D67.

D70 TARR. *The Egoist,* IV, no. 6 (July) 93-95.

Corresponds to Part VI, Chap. 5 of *Tarr,* omitting first part of chapter. See D54.

D71 IMAGINARY LETTERS. THE CODE OF A HERDSMAN. *The Little Review,* IV, no. 3 (July) 3-7.

Although the title indicates that this is part of the *Imaginary Letters* sequence, it is probable that "The Code of a Herdsman" forms instead part of the "Cantleman Saga," as is made clear by the "Cantleman" manuscripts at Cornell. This would explain why although only six *Letters* were announced in the first two instalments (see D62 and D64), seven *Letters* ultimately appeared; furthermore "The Code" was reprinted with "Cantleman's Spring-Mate" in *The Ideal Giant* (see A2). It is possible that Pound, acting as editor of the series, used this text (which had been completed long before 1917) in the sequence as a stop-gap measure, since Lewis was unable to maintain the original schedule because of war responsibilities. "The Code" is incorporated in the story "The Crowd" in manuscript (Cornell), a part of which was published in *Blast, No. 2* (see C2). Reprinted in A2, A49 and E4. See D67.

D72 TARR. *The Egoist,* IV, no. 7 (August) 106-109.

Corresponds to Part VI, Chap. 6 of *Tarr.* See D54.

D73 TARR. *The Egoist,* IV, no. 8 (September) 123-127.

Corresponds to Part VII, Chaps. 1-2 of *Tarr.* See D54.

D74 INFERIOR RELIGIONS. *The Little Review,* IV, no. 5 (September) 3-8.

Revised version reprinted in *The Wild Body* (A9) and in *A Soldier of Humor* (A43).

D75 TARR. *The Egoist,* IV, no. 9 (October) 138-141.

Corresponds to Part VII, Chaps. 3-5 of *Tarr.* See D54.

D76 CANTLEMAN'S SPRING-MATE. *The Little Review,* IV, no. 6 (October) 8-14.

Slightly revised version reprinted in *The Ideal Giant* (A2). The 1917 texts spell the character's name either "Cantleman" or "Cantelman," but in *Blasting and Bombardiering* (A26) Lewis uses "Cantleman." This issue of *The Little Review* was suppressed by United States postal authorities on grounds of obscenity in "Cantleman's Spring-Mate"; the editor, Margaret Anderson, contested the suppression in court but lost her case. The case is discussed in the December issue of *The Little Review* (pp. 46-48), printing excerpts from Judge Augustus N. Hand's decision, probably the first critical appraisal of the story. "Cantleman's Spring-Mate," along with *Tarr* the most frequently reprinted of all Lewis's writings, was reprinted with various textual alterations in *The Little Review Anthology* (B30), *A Soldier of Humor* (A43), *Blasting and Bombardiering* (A26b), *Cantleman's Spring-Mate* (bilingual text based on *The Ideal Giant* (A2) text but printing textual variants included in D76 and A26b, see E4), and *Unlucky for Pringle* (A46). It should also be noted that "Cantleman" appears to be Lewis's "mask" in *Blasting and Bombardiering* (II, "Declaration of War") and in the unfinished novel, *Cantleman-Crowd Master,* excerpts of which were published in *Unlucky for Pringle* (A46).

D77 TARR: AND EPILOGUE. *The Egoist,* IV, no. 10 (November) 152-153.

Corresponds to Part VII, Chap. 6 and Epilogue in *Tarr.* The Epilogue, dated "November 1915," was considerably modified in 1918 editions (see A3a and A3b). See D54.

D78 A SOLDIER OF HUMOUR. PART I. *The Little Review,* IV, no. 8 (December) 32-46.

Corresponds to Parts I and II of *The Wild Body* (A9), though the later version was considerably revised. See D79.

1918

D79 A SOLDIER OF HUMOUR. PART II. *The Little Review,* IV, no. 9 (January) 35-51.

Corresponds to Part III of *The Wild Body* (A9), the later version having been revised slightly with the excision of several paragraphs. Reprinted with D78 in *A Soldier of Humor* (A43).

D80 IMAGINARY LETTERS (WILLIAM BLAND BURN TO HIS WIFE). *The Little Review,* IV, no. 11 (March) 23-30.

Contains *Imaginary Letters* IV and V; see D67.

D81 IMAGINARY LETTERS (WILLIAM BLAND BURN TO HIS WIFE). *The Little Review,* IV, no. 12 (April) 50-54.

Contains *Imaginary Letters* VI and VII, concluding the series. The fact that the text of *Letter* VII is followed by an announcement that the series is "to be concluded" must have been in anticipation of Pound's intention to make a further contribution; see D67.

D82 THE IDEAL GIANT. *The Little Review,* VI, no. 1 (May) 1-18.

Originally titled "Miss Godd and the Ideal Giant," this play had originally been published in *The Ideal Giant* (A2) and was reprinted in *A Soldier of Humor* (A43).

D83 THE WAR BABY. *Art and Letters,* II, no. 1 (Winter) 14-41.

Includes drawing by Lewis (Michel 269). Probably written before 1917 at the same time as its companion story, "Cantleman's Spring-Mate," which would explain why, though described as being "in the possession of Ezra Pound and Miss Saunders," it was not published by *The Little Review*, especially after the suppression of "Cantleman's Spring-Mate" (see D71). Reprinted in *Blasting and Bombardiering* (A26b) and *Unlucky for Pringle* (A46).

1919

D84 THE MEN WHO WILL PAINT HELL. MODERN WAR AS A THEME FOR THE ARTIST. *The Daily Express*, no. 5877 (February 10) 4.

Reprinted in *Wyndham Lewis on Art* (A45).

D85 MR. WADSWORTH'S EXHIBITION OF WOODCUTS. *Art and Letters*, II, no. 2 (Spring) 85-89.

Article primarily concerned with correcting misconceptions about abstract art.

D86 WHAT ART NOW? *The English Review*, XXVIII (April) 334-338.

Analysis of the pre-war artistic revolution. Reprinted in *Wyndham Lewis on Art* (A45).

D87 PREVALENT DESIGN. I. NATURE AND THE MONSTER OF DESIGN. *The Athenæum*, no. 4673 (November 21) 1230-1231.

The first of a series of four articles (see D88, D89 and D90), this essay attempts to establish the difference between art derived directly from nature and art which dispenses with direct observation of nature.

D88 PREVALENT DESIGN. II. PAINTING THE SOUL. *The Athenæum*, no. 4676 (December 12) 1343.

Continuation of D87. See also D89 and D90.

D89 PREVALENT DESIGN. III. THE MAN BEHIND THE EYES. *The Athenæum*, no. 4678 (December 26) 1404.

Discusses the relation between intellect, vision and pleasure. See also D87, D88 and D90.

1920

D90 PREVALENT DESIGN. IV. THE BULLDOG EYE'S DEPREDATIONS. *The Athenæum*, no. 4681 (January 16) 84-85.

Discusses the differences between "realism" and "fancy" in modern art. This series of four articles (D87, D88, D89 and D90) reprinted in *Wyndham Lewis on Art* (A45).

D91 MR. EZRA POUND. *The Observer*, no. 6713 (January 18) 5.

Letter to the editor defending Ezra Pound's *Quia Pauper Amavi*, which had been adversely criticized by Robert Nichols in *The Observer*, January 11.

D92 MR. CLIVE BELL AND 'WILCOXISM.' *The Athenæum,* no. 4689 (March 12) 349.

Letter to the editor in answer to Clive Bell's "Wilcoxism" (*The Athenæum,* March 5). Reprinted in *The Letters* (A42); see also D93, F151 and F152.

D93 MR. CLIVE BELL AND 'WILCOXISM.' *The Athenæum,* no. 4691 (March 26) 425.

Letter to the editor in response to Clive Bell's letter (*The Athenæum,* March 19). See D92, F151 and F152.

D94 SIGISMUND. *Art and Letters,* III, no. 1 (Winter) 14-31.

Reprinted in *The Wild Body* (A9).

1921

D95 WHY PICASSO DOES IT. *The Daily Mail* (January 10) 6.

Defense of Picasso, exhibiting at the Leicester Galleries; includes a self-portrait of Lewis (Michel 425).

D96 NOTE ON TYROS. *The Tyro,* I ([April]) 2.

The first of six articles published in *The Tyro,* I, edited by Lewis. See C3, D97, D98, D99, D100 and D101.

D97 THE OBJECTS OF THIS PAPER. *The Tyro,* I ([April]) 2.

Introduction to the first number of Lewis's journal, *The Tyro.* Reprinted in *Wyndham Lewis on Art* (A45). See C3 and D96.

D98 THE CHILDREN OF THE NEW EPOCH. *The Tyro,* I ([April]) 3.

Announces the emergence of a new Post-War intellectual order, "*whose interests lie all ahead,* whose credentials are in the future." Reprinted in *Wyndham Lewis on Art* (A45). See C3 and D96.

D99 ROGER FRY'S ROLE OF CONTINENTAL MEDIATOR. *The Tyro,* I ([April]) 3.

Reprinted in *Wyndham Lewis on Art* (A45). See C3 and D96.

D100 WILL ECCLES. *The Tyro,* I ([April]) 6.

See C3 and D96.

D101 [DIALOGUE BETWEEN MR. SEGANDO AND PHILLIP.] *The Tyro,* I ([April]) 7.

See C3 and D96.

D102 DEAN SWIFT WITH A BRUSH. THE TYROIST EXPLAINS HIS ART. *The Daily Express,* no. 6548 (April 11) 5.

Interview with Lewis; includes Tyro design by Lewis (Michel 492).

D103 THE COMING ACADEMY. *The Sunday Express,* no. 121 (April 24) 3.

Lewis's first attack on the Royal Academy. Reprinted in *Wyndham Lewis on Art* (A45).

D104 PARIS VERSUS THE WORLD. *The Dial,* LXXI, no. 1 (July) 22-27.

Concerns Lewis's decision to live and work in London rather than Paris after World War I.

1922

D105 THE CREDENTIALS OF THE PAINTER—I. *The English Review,* XXXIV (January) 33-38.

The first instalment in a series, analyzing the painter's relation to life in comparison with writers and musicians. See D110.

D106 EDITORIAL. *The Tyro,* 2 ([March]) 3-10.

Editorial for the second and final number of Lewis's journal, *The Tyro.* See C4, D107, D108 and D109.

D107 ESSAY ON THE OBJECTIVE OF PLASTIC ART IN LIFE. *The Tyro,* 2 ([March]) 21-37.

Lengthy essay on art and æsthetics, subdivided into the following sections: "Art subject to laws of life," "Art and games," "Standards in Art," "A third method, between subject and object," "The sense of the future" and "The function of the eye." Reprinted in *Wyndham Lewis the Artist* (A29) and *Wyndham Lewis on Art* (A45). See C4 and D106.

D108 TYRONIC DIALOGUES.—X. AND F. *The Tyro,* 2 ([March]) 46-49.

Unsigned fantastic dialogue between two "tyros." See C4 and D106.

D109 BESTRE. *The Tyro,* 2 ([March]) 53-63.

Newly revised version of the story, originally published in 1909 as "Some Innkeepers and Bestre" (D2). This version reprinted with minor changes in *The Wild Body* (A9). See C4 and D106.

D110 THE CREDENTIALS OF THE PAINTER—II. *The English Review,* XXXIV (April) 391-396.

Defense of art and the relativity of "taste." Reprinted with D105 in *Wyndham Lewis on Art* (A45).

D111 THE LONG AND THE SHORT OF IT. MR. WYNDHAM LEWIS SETTLES THE WAR OF THE SKIRT. *The Evening Standard,* no. 30,499 (April 28) 3.

Lewis's satirical views of female fashion, accompanied by two sketches by Lewis (Michel 531 and 532). See D117.

D112 THE WORSE-THAN-EVER ACADEMY. *The Sunday Express,* no. 174 (April 30) 5.

Unfavorable review of the summer Royal Academy exhibition.

1924

D113 MR. ZAGREUS AND THE SPLIT-MAN. *The Criterion,* II, no. 6 (February) 124-142.

Part XI of *The Apes of God* (A12), prefaced with the note "these few pages . . . belong to a book which will be finished I hope by next autumn" (p. 124). Along with D116, this passage from *The Apes of God* was enthusiastically received by the editor, T. S. Eliot (see letters and Rose's comments in *The Letters,* pp. 134 et seq.).

D114 THE STRANGE ACTOR. *The New Statesman,* XXII, no. 563 (February 2) 474-476.

Lewis's first openly political essay, associating the "Wild Body" and the "arch political animal"—the result of remarks about collectivism, Jewish ideology, individualism and utopianism.

D115 THE YOUNG METHUSELAH. *The New Statesman,* XXII, no. 567 (March 1) 601-602.

Lewis's first discussion of the "youth cult."

D116 THE APES OF GOD. *The Criterion,* II, no. 7 (April) 300-310.

The cover announces "The Apes of God—I," though *The Criterion* published no sequel to this section of the novel, which was later published with numerous revisions as Part III of *The Apes of God* (A12). See D113.

D117 THE DRESS-BODY-MIND AGGREGATE. *The New Statesman,* XXIII, no. 579 (May 24) 191.

Discussion of modern fashion and "epicene obsession" (see also D111).

D118 ART CHRONICLE. *The Criterion,* II, no. 8 (July) 447-482.

Discussion of the role of the public, in relation to the alleged decline of the artist-population (see D119).

D119 ART CHRONICLE. *The Criterion,* II, no. 9 (October) 107-113.

Reviews *Living Art* and *Raymond Duchamp-Villon: Sculpteur (1876-1918).* Partially reprinted in *Wyndham Lewis on Art* (A45).

1925

D120 BOOKS OF THE QUARTER. RECENT ANTHROPOLOGY. *The Criterion,* III, no. 10 (January) 311-315.

Reviews G. Elliot Smith, *Essays on the Evolution of Man,* G. Elliot Smith and Warren R. Dawson, *Egyptian Mummies* and W. H. R. Rivers, *Medicine, Magic and Religion.* Smith's work is further discussed in "The Dithyrambic Spectator" (see D121 and D122).

D121 THE DITHYRAMBIC SPECTATOR: AN ESSAY ON THE ORIGINS AND SURVIVALS OF ART. INTRODUCTION. *The Calendar of Modern Letters,* I, no. 2 (April) 89-107.

Reprinted with revisions in *The Diabolical Principle and the Dithyrambic Spectator* (A14). Partially reprinted in *Wyndham Lewis. An Anthology of his Prose* (A44) and *Wyndham Lewis on Art* (A45). See D120.

D122 THE DITHYRAMBIC SPECTATOR: AN ESSAY ON THE ORIGINS AND SURVIVALS OF ART. PART II. *The Calendar of Modern Letters,* I, no. 3 (May) 194-213.

Reprinted with revisions in *The Diabolical Principle and the Dithyrambic Spectator* (A14). See D120.

D123 THE POLITICS OF ARTISTIC EXPRESSION. *Artwork,* I, no. 4 (May-August) 223-226.

Discussion of art and the declining market.

D124 THE FOXES' CASE. *The Calendar of Modern Letters,* II, no. 8 (October) 73-90.

Essay divided in seven sections: Section 3, "Science, Puritanism and the Feminine," reprinted with minor revisions in *The Art of Being Ruled,* Part VII, Chap. 7 (A6); Sections 6 and 7, "The Hero and His Adversary in Shakespeare's Plays" and "The Transformed Shaman," reprinted with revisions in *The Lion and the Fox,* Part V, Chap. 4 ("Othello as the Typical Colossus") and Part VI, Chap. 4 ("Falstaff").

D125 THE PHYSICS OF THE NOT-SELF. *The Chapbook (A Yearly Miscellany),* London: Jonathan Cape, no. 40, 68-77.

Contains prefatory note to "The Physics of the Not-Self" and the essay itself which was revised and reprinted in *The Enemy of the Stars* (A17). Partially reprinted in *Wyndham Lewis. An Anthology of his Prose* (A44).

1926

D126 NOTES AND REVIEWS. BRITONS NEVER SHALL BE BEES. *The Calendar of Modern Letters,* II, no. 11 (January) 360-362.

Reviews Lord Beaverbrook's *Politicians and the Press.*

D127 THE NEW ROMAN EMPIRE. *The Calendar of Modern Letters,* II, no. 12 (February) 411-420.

Satiric article proposing the formation of a new Roman Empire (including Britain, France and Italy) under the leadership of Mussolini.

D128 CREATURES OF HABIT AND CREATURES OF CHANGE. *The Calendar of Modern Letters,* III, no. 1 (April) 17-44.

Essay discussing what Lewis termed "the Not-Self of Communism," "Progress and Variety" and "The Game and the Reality." Section II partially reprinted in *Time and Western Man* (A8). Section III analyzes Bradley from the same angle as *Time and Western Man,* III, Chap. 3, but this material was not directly incorporated.

1927

D129 PRELIMINARY NOTE TO THE PUBLIC. *The Enemy,* I ([February]) vii-viii.

Editorial announcements by Lewis, inviting correspondence and contributions to *The Enemy,* and outlining upcoming books by Lewis to be published by his Arthur Press. This is the first of three numbers of *The Enemy,* founded, edited and published by Lewis. See C5, D130, D131 and D132.

D130 EDITORIAL. *The Enemy,* I ([February]) ix-xv.

Editorial, discussing objectives and defining the meaning of *The Enemy,* in which Lewis dissociates himself from any "movement": "Outside I am freer." See C5 and D129.

D131 WHAT'S IN A NAMESAKE. *The Enemy,* I ([February]) 19-23.

Humorous essay in which P. Wyndham Lewis discusses D. B. Wyndham Lewis. See C5 and D129.

D132 THE REVOLUTIONARY SIMPLETON. *The Enemy,* I ([February]) 25-192.

Reprinted in *Time and Western Man* (A8), revised and rearranged. See C5 and D129.

D133 THE HYPOCRITE IN THE DRAWING-ROOM. *The Evening Standard,* no. 32,056 (May 6) 11.

Letter to the editor in response to Arnold Bennett's review of *The Enemy,* I (see F230). Reprinted in *The Letters* (A42a).

D134 THE VALUES OF THE DOCTRINE BEHIND 'SUBJECTIVE' ART. *The Monthly Criterion,* VI, no. 1 (July) 4-13.

Outlines why more "attention should be given to the intellectual principles behind a work of art." Reprinted in *Paleface,* Introduction, Part II (A11) and *Wyndham Lewis on Art* (A45).

D135 NOTES REGARDING DETAILS OF PUBLICATION AND DISTRIBUTION. *The Enemy,* 2 (September) vii-x.

Various announcements concerning price, distribution, contents and objectives of *The Enemy,* edited by Lewis. See C6, D136, D137 and D138.

D136 EDITORIAL NOTES. *The Enemy,* 2 (September) xi-xxxi.

Subdivided under the following headings: "Forthcoming 'Enemy' Campaigns," "Mother India," "*The Paris Address. (a)* The France that does not come out of Mother France," "*(b)* Art and 'Radical' Doctrines," "*(c)* The Psychology of 'Youth-Movements,' and how the 'Radical' has no claim to their Monopoly or Patent," "*(d)* How to 'Defend the West.' " See C6 and D135.

D137 EDITORIAL. *The Enemy,* 2 (September) xxxiii-xl.

Reaffirmation of Lewis's intentions in publishing *The Enemy.* See C6 and D135.

D138 PALEFACE OR "LOVE? WHAT HO! SMELLING STRANGENESS." *The Enemy,* 2 (September) 3-112.

Reprinted with numerous revisions in *Paleface* (A11). See C6 and D135.

1929

D139 ENEMY BULLETIN. 1929 (FIRST QUARTER). *The Enemy,* 3 (January 25) vii-viii.

Brief editorial note by Lewis, reaffirming his position as "Enemy." The third of three numbers of *The Enemy,* edited and published by Lewis. See C7, D140, D141 and D142.

D140 THE DIABOLICAL PRINCIPLE. *The Enemy,* 3 (January 25) 9-84.

Revised and reprinted in *The Diabolical Principle and the Dithyrambic Spectator* (A14), this long essay is subdivided in three parts: "The Political Philistine," "New Nihilism" and "Conclusion." See C7 and D139.

D141 DETAILS REGARDING PUBLICATION AND DISTRIBUTION. *The Enemy,* 3 (January 25) 90.

Various announcements about price, contributions, distribution and the contents of the next number of *The Enemy* (not published). See C7 and D139.

D142 NOTES. *The Enemy,* 3 (January 25) 91-100.

Comments on Shaw's *The Childermass,* Norman Douglas's *South Wind,* publishing schedules for Lewis's books and other topics. See C7 and D139.

D143 A WORLD ART AND TRADITION. *Drawing and Design,* V, no. 32 (February) 29-30, 56.

Survey of post-war art, and includes three drawings by Lewis (Michel 637, 639 and 643). Reprinted in *Wyndham Lewis on Art* (A45).

D144 [ANSWER TO A QUESTIONNAIRE.] *The Little Review,* XII, no. 2 (May) 49.

Response to questionnaire. Reprinted in *The Little Review Anthology* (B30).

D145 *** !! — ...? *** !!! *The Daily Herald,* no. 9200 (October 25) 10.

Discussion of censorship, in connection with Richard Aldington's *The Death of a Hero* in which "obscene words" were suppressed by the publisher. Includes photograph of Lewis.

D146 THE FUTURE OF AMERICAN ART. *The Studio,* 98, no. 439 (October) 687-690.

Discussion of the "Americanisation" of art and the inevitable future influence of a "Negro strain." Also printed in *Creative Art: a Magazine of Fine and Applied Art*, V, no. 4 (October) 687-688, 690.

1930

D147 OUR SHAM SOCIETY—AN INTERVIEW WITH WYNDHAM LEWIS BY DR. MEYRICK BOOTH. *Everyman,* III, no. 75 (July 3) 707.

Interview concerned primarily with *The Apes of God.* Includes self-portrait by Lewis, "hitherto unpublished" (Michel 642). See F337.

D148 A STORM IN THAT TEA-CUP CALLED LONDON. *Satire & Fiction,* 1 (September) 7-8.

Discusses the controversy which followed the publication of *The Apes of God* (A12) and announces the intentions in publishing *Satire & Fiction* (edited and published by Lewis, this was the only number published). See C8, D149, D150, D151 and D152.

D149 GENERAL EDITORIAL COMMENTS. *Satire & Fiction,* 1 (September) 17-21.

Discusses Lewis's deliberate stance as "The Enemy" and his role as pamphleteer. See C8 and D148.

D150 CIRCULAR LETTER ISSUED BY THE ARTHUR PRESS. *Satire & Fiction,* 1 (September) 22.

Reprints a form letter enclosed with copies of *The Apes of God* which were sent to prominent authors, painters and critics, inviting comments about the novel. See C8 and D148.

D151 AN ALIBI! *Satire & Fiction,* 1 (September) 40.

Rebuttal of Frank Swinnerton's complaint that Lewis has not identified those satirized in *The Apes of God:* "I should have preferred . . . less mysteriousness in the matter of identification." See C8 and D148.

D152 SATIRE & FICTION. *Satire & Fiction,* 1 (September) 43-62.

Essay on the principles of satire and the implementation of these principles in *The Apes of God* (A12). Includes "The Taxi-Cab-Driver Test" reprinted in *Men Without Art* (A22). See C8 and D148.

D153 AN "AGONY" SURPRISE FOR CHELSEA. ONE ARTIST AND ANOTHER ARTIST'S PAINTINGS. "FOR SALE." *The Daily Express,* no. 9466 (September 4) 1.

An interview following Richard Wyndham's advertisement in *The Times,* September 3, 1930. Wyndham had identified himself with a character in the newly published *The Apes of God* and advertised two paintings by Lewis for sale at absurdly low prices by way of revenge. Quoted in *A Stop-Press Explosion* (A12a(c)).

1931

D154 HITLERISM—MAN AND DOCTRINE: THE WEIMAR REPUBLIC AND THE DRITTE REICH. *Time and Tide,* XII, no. 3 (January 17) 59-60.

Corresponds to Part I, Chap. 1 in *Hitler* (A13). The foreword states that although the editor is not in agreement with Lewis's attitude towards the National Socialist Party the series of Hitler articles will be published because "they are of such unusual interest." See D155, D156, D157, D158 and D159; collected with textual revisions in *Hitler* (see A13).

D155 HITLERISM—MAN AND DOCTRINE: BERLIN IM LICHT! *Time and Tide,* XII, no. 4 (January 24) 87-88.

Corresponds to Part I, Chap. 2 in *Hitler* (A13). See D154.

D156 HITLERISM—MAN AND DOCTRINE: THE ONENESS OF 'HITLERISM' AND OF HITLER. *Time and Tide,* XII, no. 5 (January 31) 119-120.

Corresponds to Part II, Chaps. 1 and 2 in *Hitler* (A13), with numerous textual revisions in the final seven paragraphs of Chap. 2. See D145.

D157 HITLERISM—MAN AND DOCTRINE: THE DOCTRINE OF THE BLUTSGEFÜHL. *Time and Tide,* XII, no. 6 (February 7) 151-152.

Corresponds to Part V, Chaps. 1 and 2 in *Hitler* (A13) with numerous revisions in later text. See D154.

D158 MR. WYNDHAM LEWIS REPLIES TO HIS CRITICS. *Time and Tide,* XII, no. 6 (February 7) 159.

Letter to the editor answering the criticism provoked by the second Hitler article (D155), see F367, F368 and F369. Reprinted in *The Letters* (A42a). See D154.

D159 HITLERISM—MAN AND DOCTRINE: CREDITCRANKERY RAMPANT. *Time and Tide,* XII, no. 7 (February 14) 182,184-185.

Corresponds with some modifications to Part VI, Chap. 4 in *Hitler* (A13). See D154.

D160 NEBULAE IN BRUSSELS SPROUTS. *Time and Tide,* XII, no. 9 (February 28) 255-256.

Critical review of *Hunger and Love,* by Lionel Britton.

D161 WYNDHAM LEWIS: THE GREATEST SATIRIST OF OUR DAY. *Everyman,* V, no. 112 (March 19) 231-233.

An interview with Louise Morgan, reprinted in *Writers at Work* (B15), in which Lewis states that all serious writers should be taught to paint and draw. Also reproduces "Wyndham Lewis in a Basque beret. From a hitherto unpublished self-portrait" (not in Michel). See also F365.

D162 THE SON OF WOMAN. *Time and Tide,* XII, no. 16 (April 18) 470-472.

Review of *Son of Woman,* by John Middleton Murry.

D163 YOUTH POLITICS. FOREWORD: THE EVERYMANS. *Time and Tide,* XII, no. 24 (June 13) 703-704.

Corresponds to the Foreword in *Doom of Youth* (A15). The first of seven instalments which were later revised and incorporated in the book; see D164, D166, D167, D168, D169 and D170. Reprinted in *Wyndham Lewis. An Anthology of his Prose* (A44).

D164 YOUTH-POLITICS. THE AGE COMPLEX. *Time and Tide,* XII, no. 25 (June 20) 738-740.

Corresponds with numerous revisions to the Introduction and passages in Chap. V of *Doom of Youth* (A15). Partially reprinted in *Wyndham Lewis. An Anthology of his Prose* (A44). See D163.

D165 BRITAIN'S MOST ADVANCED PAINTER LEADS A RETURN TO NATURALISM, BUT IT IS A NEW NATURALISM. *The World of Art Illustrated,* I, no. 8 (June) 6-7.

An interview.

D166 YOUTH-POLITICS. YOUTH-POLITICS UPON THE SUPER-TAX PLANE. *Time and Tide,* XII, no. 26 (June 27) 770-772.

Corresponds with numerous differences to Part I, Chap. 4 of *Doom of Youth* (A15). See D163.

D167 YOUTH POLITICS. THERE IS *NOTHING* BIG BUSINESS CAN'T RATION. *Time and Tide,* XII, no. 27 (July 4) 798-800.

Corresponds to Part I, Chap. 1 and passages in Chap. 2 of *Doom of Youth* (A15). See D163.

D168 YOUTH-POLITICS. THE *CLASS-WAR* OF PARENTS AND CHILDREN. *Time and Tide,* XII, no. 28 (July 11) 826-828.

Corresponds to Part I, Chap. 12 of *Doom of Youth* with numerous modifications (see A15). See D163.

D169 YOUTH-POLITICS. GOVERNMENT BY INFERIORITY COMPLEX. *Time and Tide,* XII, no. 29 (July 18) 854-855.

Corresponds to Part V, Chap. 1 of *Doom of Youth* (A15). See D163.

D170 YOUTH-POLITICS. HOW YOUTH-POLITICS WILL ABOLISH YOUTH. *Time and Tide,* XII, no. 30 (July 25) 883-884.

Incorporated in *Doom of Youth* (A15), Part V, Chap. 1. See D163.

D171 FILIBUSTERS IN BARBARY. HIGH TABLE: THE PACKET TO AFRICA. *Everyman,* VI, no. 144 (October 29) 437-438.

The first of seven articles which were later revised and incorporated in *Filibusters in Barbary* (A16). Corresponds to Book I, I, Chap. 3 in *Filibusters in Barbary;* reproduces design by Lewis (Michel 722). See D172, D173, D174, D175, D176 and D177.

D172 THE BLUE SULTAN. *The Graphic,* CXXXIV, no. 3230 (November 7) 180.

Corresponds with revisions to Book II, Chaps. 11 and 14 in *Filibusters in Barbary;* reproduces design by Lewis (Michel 719). See D171.

D173 FILIBUSTERS IN BARBARY. TURNING DARKS INTO WHITES. *Everyman,* VI, no. 146 (November 12) 492.

Corresponds to Book I, I, Chap. 7 in *Filibusters in Barbary* (A16); reproduces design by Lewis (Michel 715). See D171.

D174 FILIBUSTERS IN BARBARY. ISLAMIC SENSATIONS. *Everyman,* VI, no. 148 (November 26) 583.

Corresponds to Book I, I, Chap. 8 in *Filibusters in Barbary* (A16); reproduces design by Lewis (Michel 713). See D171.

D175 FILIBUSTERS IN BARBARY. A DESERTED AFRICAN LIDO. *Everyman,* VI, no. 150 (December 10) 660. See D171.

D176 FILIBUSTERS IN BARBARY. PETROL-TIN TOWN. *Everyman,* VI, no. 152 (December 24) 724, 726.

Corresponds to Book I, I, Chap. 12 in *Filibusters in Barbary* (A16); reproduces design by Lewis (Michel 716). Reprinted in *Wyndham Lewis. An Anthology of his Prose* (A44). See D171.

1932

D177 FILIBUSTERS IN BARBARY. THE MOUTH OF THE SAHARA. *Everyman*, II, no. 154 (January 7) 793-794.

Corresponds to Book I, II, Chap. 1 in *Filibusters in Barbary* (A16); reproduces design by Lewis (Michel 729). See D171.

D178 A TIP FROM THE AUGEAN STABLE. *Time and Tide,* XIII, no. 12 (March 19) 322-324.

The first part of a two-part article which discusses, in a manner similar to *The Roaring Queen,* "the gangs" which run "the Literary Racket." This title was announced for publication by Desmond Harmsworth in April, 1932 in *More from The Enemy* (B16) and in May, 1932 on the dustjacket of *Enemy of the Stars* (A17) but was in fact never separately published. See also D179 and G2.

D179 A TIP FROM THE AUGEAN STABLE. *Time and Tide,* XIII, no. 13 (March 26) 348-349.

The second part of a two-part article (see D178).

D180 THE ARTIST AS CROWD. *The Twentieth Century,* III, no. 14 (April) 12-15.

Commentary on views expressed in *The Twentieth Century* on "Prometheanism" by Porteus and Pendle, and on "individualism" in *Axel's Castle,* by Edmund Wilson.

D181 ARNOLD BENNETT AS CRITIC: MR. WYNDHAM LEWIS REPLIES. *Time and Tide,* XIII, no. 16 (April 16) 423-424.

Lewis's answer to Henry Alder's defense of Arnold Bennett, which had been published in the April 2 number of *Time and Tide;* Lewis had attacked Bennett in "A Tip from the Augean Stable" (see D178, D179, F415 and F417). Reprinted in *The Letters* (A42a).

D182 WHAT IT FEELS LIKE TO BE AN ENEMY. *Daily Herald,* no. 5082 (May 30) 8.

Reply to Maurice Dekobra's article "The Art of Making Enemies" which had been published on May 21 in the *Daily Herald* (see F421). Reproduces a "self-sketch" by Lewis (Michel 782). Reprinted in *Wyndham Lewis on Art* (A45).

D183 FILIBUSTERS IN AGADIR. *Travel,* XII, no. 16 (June) 59.

D184 FÉNELON AND HIS VALET. *Time and Tide,* XIII, no. 25 (June 18) 673-674.

Reprinted in *Men Without Art* (A22).

D185 THE ARTIST AND THE NEW GOTHIC. *Time and Tide,* XIII, no. 26 (June 25) 707-708.

Reprinted in *Men Without Art* (A22).

D186 FLAUBERT AS A MARXIST. *Time and Tide,* XIII, no. 27 (July 2) 737-738.
Reprinted in *Men Without Art* (A22) and *Enemy Salvoes* (A48).

D187 NOTES ON THE WAY. *Time and Tide,* XIII, no. 41 (October 8) 1072-1073.
Discusses "bidonvilles" in Morocco and New York, President Hoover, Stendhal and pugilism.

D188 NOTES ON THE WAY. *Time and Tide,* XIII, no. 42 (October 15) 1098-1100.
Discusses the destruction of Europe in the "next war," various political parties, fiction and poetic diction.

D189 NOTES ON THE WAY. *Time and Tide,* XIII, no. 43 (October 22) 1129-1132.
Discusses the ban affecting *Snooty Baronet,* book censorship and the ambiguous nature of all fiction.

D190 A HISTORICAL CLOSE-UP. *Time and Tide,* XIII, no. 43 (October 22, Autumn Book Supplement) 1154.
Favorable review of *Just the Other Day,* by John Collier and Iain Lang.

D191 NOTES ON THE WAY. *Time and Tide,* XIII, no. 44 (October 29) 1174-1175.
Discusses unemployment, Rosamund Lehmann, peace and fiction in a "coarse" age.

D192 WYNDHAM LEWIS AND COMRADE GOLLANCZ. *Time and Tide,* XIII, no. 45 (November 5) 1214-1215.
Letter to the editor answering criticism from Winifred Holtby, and blaming Gollancz for his methods of salesmanship (see F442 and F445).

1933

D193 THE KASBAHS OF THE ATLAS. *The Architectural Review,* LXXIII, no. 434 (January 6) 73-74.
Detailed analysis of Berber architecture, not included in *Filibusters in Barbary* (A16). Reproduces two designs by Lewis and another related drawing (Michel 707, 711 and 717). Reprinted in *Wyndham Lewis on Art* (A45).

D194 POOR BRAVE LITTLE BARBARY. *The Daily Herald,* no. 5508 (October 10) 10.

D195 ONE WAY SONG. *New Britain,* II, no. 30 (December 13) 121.
Letter to the editor in response to a review of *One-Way Song* (A21) by Herbert Palmer (see F478) in which Lewis denies that *One-Way Song* satirizes poets published in *New Signatures.* Reprinted in *The Letters* (A42a). See also F489.

D196 WHAT ARE THE BERBERS? *The Bookman,* LXXXV, no. 507 (December) Special Christmas Number, 183-186.
Discusses the Celtic origins of the Berbers.

1934

D197 SHROPSHIRE LADS OR ROBOTS? *New Britain,* II, no. 33 (January 3) 194.

The first of a two-part article about the *New Signature* poets. Originally intended for publication in *Everyman* under the title "The Machine Poets" (see Mary Daniels's *A Descriptive Catalogue,* p. 11). Excerpts from the TM at Cornell published in *Enemy Salvoes* (A48). See D198.

D198 SHROPSHIRE LADS OR ROBOTS AGAIN. *New Britain,* II, no. 34 (January 10) 226-227.

Second of a two-part article (see D197).

D199 WHAT IS 'DIFFICULT' POETRY? *New Britain,* II, no. 42 (March 7) 482-483.

Discussion of "meaning" in poetry, centered on Mallarmé and T. S. Eliot's *Wasteland.*

D200 THE DUMB OX: A STUDY OF ERNEST HEMINGWAY. *Life and Letters,* X, no. 52 (April) 33-45.

This, probably Lewis's most well-known critical piece, was reprinted in *The American Review* (D203), *Men Without Art* (A22), *A Soldier of Humor* (A43), *Enemy Salvoes* (A48) and translated into Polish (E18).

D201 IN PRAISE OF OUTSIDERS. *The New Statesman and Nation,* VII, no. 168 (May 12) 709-710.

Discussion of "internalism" as opposed to "externalism" in art (an argument repeated in *Men Without Art,* II, Chap. 2, see A22).

D202 A MORALIST WITH A CORN COB: A STUDY OF WILLIAM FAULKNER. *Life and Letters,* X, no. 54 (June) 312-328.

Study of Faulkner, reprinted in *Men Without Art* (A22) and *Enemy Salvoes* (A48).

D203 THE DUMB OX: A STUDY OF ERNEST HEMINGWAY. *The American Review,* III, no. 3 (June) 189-212.

See D200.

D204 DEMOS DEFIED. *The Spectator,* CLII, no. 5528 (June 8) 892.

Favorable review of *Defy the Foul Fiend,* by John Collier.

D205 THE ENGLISH SENSE OF HUMOUR. *The Spectator,* CLII, no. 5529 (June 15) 915-916.

Discussion of English humor, associating it with Moslem fatalism: "a sort of philosophic rot."

D206 ART IN A MACHINE AGE. *The Bookman,* LXXXVI, no. 514 (July) 184-187.

Abstract of an address "delivered in the autumn of 1933 to a newly-founded society in the University of Oxford" (MS at Buffalo); reproduces a design by Lewis (Michel 782). Passages incorporated in various sections of *Men Without Art* (A22). Reprinted in *Wyndham Lewis on Art* (A45).

D207 THE PROPAGANDIST IN FICTION. *Current History,* (August) 567-572.

Discussion of commitment and detachment of the modern writer. Passages incorporated in various sections of *Men Without Art* (A22).

D208 KEYSERLING. *Time and Tide,* XV, no. 31 (August 4) 984-985.

Review of *Problems of Personal Life,* by Count Herman Alexander Keyserling.

D209 THE SATIRIST AND THE PHYSICAL WORLD. *The Spectator,* CLIII, no. 5537 (August 10) 196.

Discussion of "the present anti-satiric dispositions of the English."

D210 ROUSSEAU. *Time and Tide,* XV, no. 33 (August 18) 1034-1035.

Review of *Rousseau and the Modern State,* by Alfred Cobban.

D211 NATIONALISM. *The Bookman,* LXXXVI, no. 516 (September) 276-278.

Discussion of the various aspects of nationalism, particularly German nationalism.

D212 A COMMUNIST ABROAD. *Time and Tide,* XV, no. 37 (September 15) 1141-1142.

Review of *In All Countries,* by John Dos Passos.

D213 TRADESMEN, GENTLEMEN AND ARTISTS. *The Listener,* XII, no. 298 (September 26) 545.

Review of *Art,* by Eric Gill.

D214 'CLASSICAL REVIVAL' IN ENGLAND. *The Bookman,* LXXXVII, no. 517 (October) 8-10.

Discussion of the fallacies of a revival of "classicism" in England, linking Christianity and romanticism. Revised passages incorporated in *Men Without Art* (A22).

D215 STUDIES IN THE ART OF LAUGHTER. *The London Mercury,* XXX, no. 180 (October) 509-515.

Partially prints the end of "The Greatest Satire is Non-Moral" from *Men Without Art* (A22) Part II, Chap. 1 published the same month. Most of the article is reprinted in *Enemy Salvoes* (A48).

D216 AN ENQUIRY. *New Verse.* no. 11 (October) 7-8.

Answer to a questionnaire about poetry.

D217 DETACHMENT AND THE FICTIONIST. *The English Review,* LIX (October) 441-452.

First of a two-part article discussing the necessity of political detachment for the writer of fiction (see D220).

D218 ONE PICTURE IS MORE THAN ENOUGH. *Time and Tide,* XV, no. 41 (October 13) 1252-1253.

Criticizes the elimination of modern art in the "Ideal Modern Home." See D221.

D219 POWER-FEELING AND MACHINE-AGE ART. *Time and Tide,* XV, no. 42 (October 20) 1312-1314.

Refers to D218 and traces "machine-mindedness" to Marinetti and Magnetogorsk, asserting the incompatibility of art and "the sentiment of power." Reprinted in *Wyndham Lewis on Art* (A45). See D206.

D220 DETACHMENT AND THE FICTIONIST. *The English Review,* LIX (November) 564-573.

Second part of two-part article, see D217. Brief excerpt reprinted in *Enemy Salvoes* (A48).

D221 PLAIN HOME-BUILDER: WHERE IS YOUR VORTICIST? *The Architectural Review,* LXXVI, no. 456 (November) 155-158.

Discusses the same topic as "One Picture is More Than Enough" (D218) and claims that Vorticism had "aimed essentially at an *architectural* reform." Reprinted in *Wyndham Lewis on Art* (A45).

D222 THE CRITICISM OF MR. WYNDHAM LEWIS. *The Spectator,* CLIII, no. 5549 (November 2) 675.

Letter to the editor in response to Stephen Spender's review of *Men Without Art* (see F501). Reprinted in *The Letters* (A42a).

D223 ART IN INDUSTRY. *Time and Tide,* XV, no. 45 (November 10) 1410-1412.

Critical survey of decorative arts.

D224 SITWELL CIRCUS. *Time and Tide,* XV, no. 46 (November 17) 1480.

Unfavorable review of *Aspects of Modern Poetry,* by Edith Sitwell. See F487.

D225 ART AS LIFE. *The Spectator,* (Literary Supplement), CLIII, no. 5552 (November 23) 6, 8.

Review of *Art as Experience,* by John Dewey.

D226 MR. LEWIS AND MR. MURRY. *The Times Literary Supplement,* XXXIII, no. 1713 (November 29) 856.

Letter to the editor concerning an unsigned review which compared *Men Without Art* (A22) with *Middleton Murry: A Study in Excellent Normality,* by Rayner Heppenstall. Excerpts reprinted in *The Letters* (A42a). See D228, F504 and F508.

D227 [LETTER TO THE EDITOR.] *The New Statesman and Nation,* VIII, no. 199 (new series) (December 15) 900.

Letter to the editor following the controversy over a review by Lewis of Edith Sitwell's *Aspects of Modern Poetry* (see D224). Reprinted in *The Letters* (A42a).

D228 MR. LEWIS AND MR. MURRY. *The Times Literary Supplement,* XXXIII, no. 1716 (December 20) 909.

Letter to the editor concerning the controversy about Murry and *Men Without Art.* See D226, F504 and F508. Excerpts reprinted in *The Letters* (A42a).

1935

D229 NOTES ON THE WAY. *Time and Tide,* XVI, no. 9 (March 2) 304-306.

The first of a new series of five articles entitled "Notes on the Way" (see D231, D232, D233 and D234), this is a clear exposition of Lewis's views on the "Left-Wing orthodoxy" as it manifests itself in the world of letters and journalism.

D230 WYNDHAM LEWIS ASKS WHAT IS INDUSTRIAL ART? *Commercial Art and Industry,* XVIII, no. 105 (March 6) 83-86.

Reviews current exhibition at Burlington House, "Art in Industry," asserting that the essential quality of "machine-age art" is slickness.

D231 NOTES ON THE WAY. *Time and Tide,* XVI, no. 10 (March 9) 332-334.

Analysis of the irresponsibility of the British Parliamentary system, the threat of war and the general disregard of freedom. See D229.

D232 NOTES ON THE WAY. *Time and Tide,* XVI, no. 11 (March 16) 390-392.

Continuation of D231. See D229.

D233 NOTES ON THE WAY. *Time and Tide,* XVI, no. 12 (March 23) 425-427.

Continuation of D232 with comments on Hitler's denunciation of the Treaty of Versailles and criticism of the hostility towards Germany, viewing it as the perseverance of Disrealian politics. See D229.

D234 NOTES ON THE WAY. *Time and Tide,* XVI, no. 13 (March 30) 456-458.

Concludes the series of five articles (see D229) with a discussion of the dangers of a Franco-Russian hegemony following a defeat of Germany.

D235 FIRST AID FOR THE UNORTHODOX. *The London Mercury,* XXXII, no. 187 (May) 27-32.

Denunciation of the "leftwingism" of the English *intelligentsia.*

D236 FREEDOM THAT DESTROYS ITSELF. *The Listener,* XIII, no. 330 (May) 793-794.

Text of talk broadcast by the B.B.C. National Service on April 30, 10:00 PM discussing the loss of personal freedom to monopolies and orthodoxies. Reprinted in *Freedom* (B21). See also F537.

D237 AMONG THE BRITISH ISLANDERS—ART AND LITERATURE. *The Listener,* XIII, no. 337 (June 26) 1108-1109.

Subtitled "A Martian Reviews our Books," Shaw, Wells, Lawrence and Joyce are humorously attacked in this essay on British contradictions. See F533, F534 and D238.

D238 MARTIAN OPINIONS. *The Listener,* XIV, no. 340 (July 17) 125.
Letter to the editor in response to criticism of D237.

1936

D239 MR. ERVINE AND THE POETS. *The Observer,* no. 7549 (February 2) 13.
Letter to the editor. Reprinted in *The Letters* (A42, see p. 235 note).

D240 LEFT-WINGISM. *The New Statesman and Nation,* XI, no. 279 (June 27) 1024.
Letter to the editor in response to an unfavorable review of *Left Wings Over Europe* (A23). See F545.

D241 THE BIG SOFT "CENTRE." *The English Review,* LXIII, no. 1 (July) 27-34.
Discussion of the tendency of "centre-governed" nations, such as England, to sink into decline. The same concept is outlined in *Left Wings Over Europe,* Part I, Chap. 1 (A23).

1937

D242 "LEFT WINGS" AND THE C3 MIND. *The British Union Quarterly,* I, no. 1 (January/April) 22-34.
Discussion of the Spanish Civil War and the British *intelligentsia,* denouncing Marxism as the "dark apotheosis of Imperialism."

D243 MY REPLY TO MR. ALDINGTON. A DEFENCE OF STYLE: THE NOVEL AND THE NEWSPAPER. *John O'London's Weekly and the Outline,* XXXVII, no. 952 (July 9) 555-556.

D244 COUNT YOUR DEAD—THEY ARE ALIVE: WYNDHAM LEWIS'S NEW TRACT FOR THE TIMES. *The American Review,* XIX, no. 2 (Summer) 266-295.
Excerpts from *Count Your Dead* (A24).

D245 REBEL AND ROYALIST. *The Spectator,* no. 5701 (October 1) 553.
Review of *Georgian Adventure. The Autobiography of Douglas Jerrold,* by Douglas Jerrold. See F562.

D246 LETTER TO THE EDITOR. *Twentieth Century Verse*, (Wyndham Lewis Double Number), nos. 6-7 (November/December) 3-5.
Prefatory letter to Julian Symons, editor and founder of *Twentieth Century Verse*, dated November 21, 1937. Reprinted in *The Leters* (A42a). A prospectus (10" x 8", printed on recto only) announcing this special number was issued in early November. See F577-F596.

1938

D247 PICTURES AS INVESTMENTS: A STRAIGHT TALK; SOME POSSIBLE GOLD MINES OF TOMORROW. *John O'London's Weekly,* XXXVIII, no. 985 (February 25) 852, 858.

Recommends work of Henry Moore, Augustus John, Jacob Epstein and Stanley Spencer as good investments.

D248 ROYAL ACADEMY ATTACKED. "PREJUDICE AGAINST ART OF TO-DAY." WYNDHAM LEWIS'S CRITICISMS. *The Daily Telegraph,* no. 25, 861 (April 22) 16.

Interview with Lewis following news of the Royal Academy's rejection of Lewis's portrait of T. S. Eliot (as reported in *The Daily Telegraph,* April 21, p. 15). Also, photograph of Lewis with Eliot portrait (Michel P80), p. 18. See D249, D250, D251, D252, D253, D254, F618, F619, F620, F621, F622, F623, F624 and F626.

D249 THE ACADEMY AND MODERN ART. IS BURLINGTON HOUSE TOO ADVANCED? *The Daily Telegraph,* no. 25,864 (April 25) 14.

Letter to the editor answering remarks made by a member of the Royal Academy's "Hanging Committee" in *The Daily Telegraph,* April 23 (F618). Reprinted with slight textual variants in *The Letters* (A42a). See D248.

D250 MR. AUGUSTUS JOHN RESIGNS FROM ACADEMY. *The Daily Telegraph,* no. 25,865 (April 26) 18.

Article containing Lewis's comments on Augustus John's resignation from the Royal Academy in protest of their rejection of Lewis's portrait of T. S. Eliot (Michel P80). See D248.

D251 THE REJECTED PORTRAIT. POLICY OF THE ROYAL ACADEMY. ART AND NATURE. *The Times,* no. 47,983 (May 2) 17.

Letter to the editor in response to *The Times* editorial (April 30) and a review of the exhibition in the same issue, see F622 and F629. Reprinted in *The Letters* (A42a). See D248.

D252 THE REJECTED PORTRAIT. *The Times,* no. 47,985 (May 4) 10.

Letter to the editor commenting on Winston Churchill's "passionate advocacy of platitude" in his speech at the Royal Academy banquet, printed in full in *The Times* (May 2), see F624. Reprinted in *The Letters* (A42a). See D248.

D253 THE REJECTED PORTRAIT. *The Times,* no. 47,988 (May 7) 8.

Letter to the editor commenting on letters from W. R. M. Lamb (see F626) and Sir William Nicholson (see F628). Reprinted in *The Letters* (A42a). See D248.

D254 AFTER NINE YEARS: AUGUSTUS JOHN. *The Listener,* XIX, no. 489 (May 25) 1105-1107

Discusses John's resignation from the Royal Academy. See D248.

D255 WHEN JOHN BULL LAUGHS. *The Listener,* XIX, no. 495 (July 7) 38-39.
Originally a radio address broadcast on June 29, 1938 (TM in Cornell).

1939

D256 W. B. YEATS. *New Verse,* I, no. 2 (May) 45-46.
An obituary note.

D257 THE NUDE IS DYING OUT. *Lilliput,* IV, no. 5 (May) 441-444.
Discussion of the nude in modern art. Signed: "P. Wyndham Lewis."

D258 BRITAIN'S MOST ADVANCED PAINTER LEADS A RETURN TO NATURALISM, BUT—IT IS A NEW NATURALISM. *The World of Art Illustrated,* I, no. 8 (June 7) 6-7.
Interview in "The Personality of the Week" series. Lewis discusses Vorticism and defines his art as "supernatural as opposed to super-real."

D259 TRADITIONAL VERSUS MODERN ART. A TELEVISED DISCUSSION. *The Listener,* XXI, no. 543 (June 8) 1191-1195, 1223.
Debate mediated by Sir William Rothenstein between the modernists (Lewis and Geoffrey Grigson) and the traditionalists (A.K. Lawrence, R.A. and Sir Reginald Blomfield, R.A.). See Fox's "Two Pioneer Broadcasts" (F1882).

D260 THE LIFE OF AN ARTIST. *Lilliput,* V, no. 1 (July) 19-22.
Recollections of Lewis's first artistic efforts, with remarks on the social status of artists in England. Signed: "P. Wyndham Lewis."

1940

D261 PICASSO. *The Kenyon Review,* II, no. 2 (Spring) 196-211.
Discussion of Picasso, viewed as "a cultural alembic" rather than a creative artist. Reprinted in *Wyndham Lewis on Art* (A45).

D262 THE END OF ABSTRACT ART. *The New Republic,* CII, no. 14 (April 1) 438-439.
Part of Lewis's "Back to Nature Campaign" this essay announces that "abstract art died of acute *boredom.*" See D263 and D264.

D263 ABSTRACT ART TURNS OVER. *The New Republic,* CII, no. 21 (May 20) 675.
Letter to the editor in response to letters published in *The New Republic* reviewing "The End of Abstract Art" (D262). See F669. Reprinted in *The Letters* (A42a).

D264 AFTER ABSTRACT ART. *The New Republic,* CIII, no. 2 (July 8) 51-52.
Continuing the controversy begun with Lewis's article, "The End of Abstract Art" (D262), this article reiterates his denunciation of abstract art. Excerpts printed in D265 and D295. Reprinted in *Wyndham Lewis on Art* (A45).

D265 END OF ABSTRACTION. *Art and Reason,* VI, no. 68 (August) 3-4.
Prints excerpts from "After Abstract Art" (see D264).

1941

D266 LITTLE MAGS, WHAT NOW? *The New Republic,* CIV, no. 13 (March 31) 424.

Discussion about the tendency of little magazines to publish materials which are not social-realistic.

D267 HOW WOULD YOU EXPECT THE ENGLISH TO BEHAVE? *Saturday Night: The Canadian Weekly,* LVII, no. 4 (October 4) 18-19.

D268 REASONS WHY AN ENGLISHMAN IS AN ENGLISHMAN. *Saturday Night: The Canadian Weekly,* LVII, no. 10 (November 15) 34b.

1942

D269 THAT 'NOW-OR-NEVER' SPIRIT. *Saturday Night: The Canadian Weekly,* LVII, no. 40 (June 13) 6.

D270 WHAT BOOKS FOR TOTAL WAR? *Saturday Night: The Canadian Weekly,* LVII, no. 5 (October 10) 16.

Favorable review of *Now That April's Here,* by Morley Callaghan. Reprinted in *Morley Callaghan* (B36).

1945

D271 THE COSMIC UNIFORM OF PEACE. *The Sewanee Review,* LIII, no. 4 (Autumn) 507-531.

With revisions this essay was incorporated in *America and Cosmic Man* (A34), sections I, II and III becoming, respectively, Chaps. 21, 22 and 23. Section IV was entirely rewritten and incorporated as Chap. 26.

1946

D272 CANADIAN NATURE AND ITS PAINTERS. *The Listener,* XXXVI, no. 920 (August 29) 267-268.

Contrary to what is stated in "Notes on Contributors" in *Wyndham Lewis in Canada* (F1481, p. 105), the article entitled "Nature's Place in Canadian Culture" is not in fact a new essay as it incorporates, with numerous revisions, the present article. See Mary Daniels's *Descriptive Catalogue,* p. 12. Reprinted in *Wyndham Lewis on Art* (A45).

D273 DE TOCQUEVILLE AND DEMOCRACY. *The Sewanee Review,* LIV, no. 4 (Autumn) 555-575.

Reprinted in *The Mint* (D297).

D274 AMERICAN MELTING POT. *Contact Books,* II ("Britain East and West") George Weidenfeld and Nicolson Ltd. (October) 56-59.

D275 THE ART OF GWEN JOHN. *The Listener,* XXXVI, no. 926 (October 10) 484.

Subtitled "The First of Two Articles by Wyndham Lewis reviewing Current Exhibitions," this is a favorable review of John's work. See D276.

D276 MOORE AND HEPWORTH. *The Listener,* XXXVI, no. 927 (October 17) 505-506.

Reviews Henry Moore's new exhibition at Leicester Galleries, and recent work of Barbara Hepworth. Partially reprinted in *Wyndham Lewis on Art* (A45).

1947

D277 ROUND THE ART GALLERIES. *The Listener,* XXXVII, no. 944 (February 13) 283.

Discusses recent work of Jacob Epstein, John Strachey and Robert Colquhoun, and reviews *Sandro Botticelli: The Nativity,* by Pope-Hennessy. Passages about Epstein and Colquhoun reprinted in *Wyndham Lewis on Art* (A45).

D278 PURITANS OF THE STEPPES. *The Listener,* XXXVII, no. 949 (April 3) 508-509.

Originally broadcast talk entitled "A Crisis of Thought," March 16, 1947, 8:00-8:20 PM, London, B.B.C. Third Programme. Revised and incorporated in *Rude Assignment* (A35), Part III, Chap. 27.

D279 SATIRE IN THE TWENTIES. *The Times Literary Supplement,* XLVI, no. 2382 (September 27) 493.

Letter to the editor concerning a discussion of *Tarr* published in *TLS,* September 13 (see F721). Reprinted in *The Letters* (A42a). See D280.

D280 SATIRE IN THE TWENTIES. *The Times Literary Supplement,* XLVI, no. 2383 (October 4) 507.

Letter to the editor in which Lewis expresses regret for having doubted the reviewer's accuracy about *Tarr* (see D279).

D281 ROUND THE ART EXHIBITIONS. *The Listener,* XXXVIII, no. 978 (October 23) 736.

Reviews work by Robert Colquhoun and a Welsh exhibition at the St. George's Gallery. Partially reprinted in *Wyndham Lewis on Art* (A45).

1948

D282 THE BROTHERHOOD. *The Listener,* XXXIX, no. 1004 (April 22) 672.

Review of "The Pre-Raphaelites" exhibition held at Whitechapel Art Gallery, April 8-May 12, 1948. Largely reprinted in *Wyndham Lewis on Art* (A45). See D283.

D283 THE PRE-RAPHAELITE BROTHERHOOD. *The Listener,* XXXIX, no. 1006 (May 6) 743.

Letter to the editor responding to R. L. Megroz's criticism of "The Brotherhood" (D282), published in *The Listener,* April 21 (see F731).

D284 AUGUSTUS JOHN AND THE ROYAL ACADEMY. *The Listener*, XXXIX, no. 1007 (May 13) 794.

Reviews Augustus John exhibition at Leicester Galleries, Royal Academy exhibition and other recent shows. John exhibition review reprinted in *Wyndham Lewis on Art* (A45)

D285 ROUND THE ART GALLERIES. *The Listener*, XXXIX, no. 1011 (June 10) 944.

Subtitled "The First of Two Articles by Wyndham Lewis," this reviews the Courtauld Memorial Exhibition and other recent shows. Courtauld review reprinted in *Wyndham Lewis on Art* (A45). See D287, D288, D289, D290, D291, F732, F733, F734, F735 and F736.

D286 ROUND THE LONDON ART GALLERIES. *The Listener*, XXXIX, no. 1012 (June 17) 980.

Subtitled "The Second of Two Articles by Wyndham Lewis," this reviews the Edouard Vuillard exhibition at the Wildenstein Galleries. Reprinted in *Wyndham Lewis on Art* (A45).

D287 STANDARDS OF ART CRITICISM. *The Listener*, XXXIX, no. 1013 (June 24) 1009.

A controversy arose from Lewis's criticism of Seurat's "Une Baignade" in the Courtauld Memorial Exhibition (D285). This letter to the editor responds to an article by Ralph Edwards, one of the Keepers at the Victoria and Albert Museum (F733), which cites the lack of common standards among critics, mentioning Herbert Read's favorable review of the Seurat painting. Reprinted in *The Letters* (A42a). See D285.

D288 STANDARDS IN ART CRITICISM. *The Listener*, XL, no. 1014 (July 1) 22.

Letter to the editor answering criticism by A. C. Sewter, Senior Lecturer in the History of Art at the University of Manchester (see F735). Reprinted in *The Letters* (A42a). See D285.

D289 STANDARDS IN ART CRITICISM. *The Listener*, XL, no. 1015 (July 8) 61-63.

Letter to the editor concerning the controversy begun by Lewis with "Round the Art Galleries" (D285). Reprinted in *The Letters* (A42a).

D290 STANDARDS IN ART CRITICISM. *The Listener*, XL, no. 1016 (July 15) 99-100.

Letter to the editor responding to A. C. Sewter's letter of July 8 (F738). Reprinted in *The Letters* (A42a). See D285.

D291 STANDARDS IN ART CRITICISM. *The Listener*, XL, no. 1017 (July 22) 133.

Letter to the editor replying to a letter from Ralph Edwards, July 15 (F739). See D285.

D292 MR. RUSSELL AND THE VORTEX. *The Times Literary Supplement*, XLVII, no. 2430 (August 28) 485.

Letter to the editor in which Lewis complains that his "initiative of 1913-14 [i.e. Vorticism] not only was not recognized" but was "very successfully occulted" and asserts that he was "one of the first two or three in Europe to sever all connexion, visually, with environing nature," many years before the artists of the 1930's who "took on quite the air of pioneers."

D293 ROUND THE LONDON ART EXHIBITIONS. *The Listener,* XL, no. 1029 (October 14) 572.

Reviews a number of current art exhibitions. Passages reviewing recent work of Austin Cooper, Henry Moore and Ceri Richards reprinted in *Wyndham Lewis on Art* (A45).

D294 AMERICA AND COSMIC MAN. *The Times Literary Supplement,* XLVII, no. 2437 (October 16) 583.

Letter to the editor following an unfavorable review of *America and Cosmic Man* entitled "Salvation from the West" (see F741 and F742).

D295 END OF ABSTRACTION. *Art and Reason,* XIV, no. 166 (October) 11-12.

Reprinted excerpts from "End of Abstraction" (D265).

D296 THE ROT: A NARRATIVE. *Wales,* VIII, no. 30 (November) 574-589.

Reprinted with minor revisions in *The Sewanee Review* (D309), *The American Mercury* (D339) and *Rotting Hill* (A36).

D297 DE TOCQUEVILLE'S DEMOCRACY IN AMERICA. *The Mint,* no. 2 (Fall) 121-137.

Reprints D273 with some minor revisions.

1949

D298 THE CHANTREY COLLECTION AT THE ACADEMY. *The Listener,* XLI, no. 1042 (January 13) 65.

Critical review of the Chantrey Bequest paintings and drawings exhibition at the Tate. Reprinted in *Wyndham Lewis on Art* (A45).

D299 ROUND THE LONDON GALLERIES. *The Listener,* XLI, no. 1050 (March 10) 408.

Reviews current exhibitions of Ivon Hitchens and the "Borough Group" led by David Bomberg, and comments on the official opening of a new room at the Tate. Passages on Hitchens and Bomberg reprinted in *Wyndham Lewis on Art* (A45).

D300 PAINTING IN AMERICA. *The Listener,* XLI, no. 1054 (April 7) 584.

Review of *Milestones of American Painting in our Century,* by Frederick Wright. Lewis mentions that conditions in the United States are not favorable "for the development of the visual arts," citing John Marin as "the most perfect of living American artists."

D301 ROUND THE LONDON ART GALLERIES. *The Listener,* XLI, no. 1059 (May 12) 811-812.

Discusses shows of Francis Bacon, Giorgio de Chirico, Robert Colquhoun and others. Reprint of passages on Bacon and de Chirico in *Wyndham Lewis on Art* (A45).

D302 THE CASE AGAINST ROOTS. *Saturday Review of Literature,* XXXII, no. 21 (May 21) 7-8, 32-33.

Passage from *America and Cosmic Man,* Part II, Chap. 13. Includes photograph of Lewis, p. 7.

D303 WHITE FIRE. *Time,* (Atlantic Overseas edition), LIII, no. 22 (May 30) 32.

Interview concerned with Lewis's second portrait of T. S. Eliot exhibited at the Redfern Gallery. Contains a "written statement" by Lewis accompanied by reproductions of both Eliot portraits (Michel P80 and P124). Wagner suggests that the author of the article might be Marvin Barrett (see Wagner, *Portrait of the Artist as Enemy,* p. 347, F1067).

D304 THE LONDON ART GALLERIES. *The Listener,* XLI, no. 1063 (June 9) 988.

Discussion of works by Michael Ayrton, Edward Burra and Massimo Campigli. Reprinted in *Wyndham Lewis on Art* (A45).

D305 EDWARD WADSWORTH: 1889-1949. *The Listener,* XLI, no. 1066 (June 30) 1107.

Obituary note. Reprinted in *Wyndham Lewis on Art* (A45).

D306 THE LONDON GALLERIES. *The Listener,* XLII, no. 1068 (July 14) 68.

Discussion of works by Kofi Antubam, Dennis Williams and Mark Gertler (memorial exhibition); also exhibition of "The Traditional Art of the British Colonies." Reprint of the Gertler passage in *Wyndham Lewis on Art* (A45).

D307 WYNDHAM LEWIS COMMENTS. *Saturday Review of Literature,* XXXII, no. 31 (July 30) 24.

Letter to the editor in which Lewis expresses appreciation for copies of the article "The Case Against Roots" (D302), and comments on the fact that *America and Cosmic Man* "had the worst reception any book of mine has ever received in England," and that he expects no better reception in the United States.

D308 BREAD AND BALLYHOO. *The Listener,* XLII, no. 1076 (September 8) 407.

Essay on the deteriorating economic condition among artists in Great Britain. Reprinted in *Wyndham Lewis on Art* (A45).

D309 THE ROT. *The Sewanee Review,* LVII, no. 4 (October) 541-549.

See D296 and D339.

D310 ROUND THE ART GALLERIES. *The Listener,* XLII, no. 1082 (October 20) 686.

Reviews current exhibitions by Gerard David, Thomas Rowlandson and Josef Herman. Sections about David and Herman reprinted in *Wyndham Lewis on Art* (A45).

D311 ROUND THE LONDON ART GALLERIES. *The Listener,* XLII, no. 1086 (November 17) 860.

Reviews exhibitions of works by Ethel Walker, Francis Bacon, Victor Pasmore, Augustus John, William Roberts and Bateson Mason. Sections about Bacon, Pasmore and John reprinted in *Wyndham Lewis on Art* (A45). See D313.

D312 EZRA: THE PORTRAIT OF A PERSONALITY. *Quarterly Review of Literature,* V, no. 2 (December) 136-144.

Reprinted under the title "Ezra Pound *by* Wyndham Lewis [1948]," in *Ezra Pound. A collection of essays edited by Peter Russell to be presented to Ezra Pound on his sixty-fifth birthday* (see B27). Translated into French (see E3).

D313 ROUND THE LONDON ART GALLERIES. *The Listener,* XLII, no. 1088 (December 1) 959.

Letter to the editor answering the correspondence provoked by Lewis's article in *The Listener,* November 17. See D311, F769 and F770.

1950

D314 ROUND THE LONDON GALLERIES. *The Listener,* XLIII, no. 1095 (January 19) 116.

Reviews current exhibitions of work by John Minton, Ivon Hitchens, Theodore Garman, Alan Clutton-Brock and comments on the Howard Bliss collection. Passages about Minton, Garman, Clutton-Brock and the Bliss collection reprinted in *Wyndham Lewis on Art* (A45).

D315 ROUND THE LONDON ART GALLERIES. *The Listener,* XLIII, no. 1099 (February 16) 298.

Reviews exhibitions of works by Eric Peskett, Desmond Morris, Cyril Hamersma, Barbara Hepworth and Rolf Durig, with comments on Henry Fuseli and Edward Lear. Passages on Hepworth, Hamersma and Fuseli are reprinted in *Wyndham Lewis on Art* (A45).

D316 FERNAND LÉGER AT THE TATE GALLERY. *The Listener,* XLIII, no. 1101 (March 2) 396.

Review of the Arts Council show. Lewis views Léger as "a *popular* genius." Reprinted with one paragraph deleted in *Wyndham Lewis on Art* (A45).

D317 ROUND THE LONDON GALLERIES. *The Listener,* XLIII, no. 1104 (March 23) 522.

Remarks on Julian Trevelyan, Frederick Spencer Gore, Jacob Epstein and a show at the Institute of Contemporary Art, with a denunciation of André Malraux's high opinion of Aeply Replicas. Passages on Trevelyan, Epstein and Hepworth reprinted in *Wyndham Lewis on Art* (A45).

D318 CONTEMPORARY ART AT THE TATE. *The Listener,* XLIII, no. 1106 (April 6) 610-611.

Favorable review of an exhibition staged at the Tate by the Contemporary Art Society. Reprinted in *Wyndham Lewis on Art* (A45).

D319 ROUND THE LONDON GALLERIES. *The Listener,* XLIII, no. 1108 (April 20) 685.

Reviews a number of current exhibitions, with remarks about the Paris School (Derain, Bonnard, Dufy, Tal Coat and others).

D320 ROYAL ACADEMY. *Contact,* I, no. 1 (May/June) 22-25.

Critical discussion of the Royal Academy.

D321 ROUND THE LONDON ART GALLERIES. *The Listener,* XLIII, no. 1112 (May 18) 878-879.

Discusses the Rothenstein memorial exhibition at the Tate and the Royal Academy annual show, whose only good works are by Augustus John and Stanley Spencer. Passages about John and Spencer reprinted in *Wyndham Lewis on Art* (A45).

D322 ROUND THE LONDON GALLERIES. *The Listener,* XLIV, no. 1120 (July 13) 62.

Discusses the difference between the Paris and London galleries, Italian exhibition at the Tate, Graham Sutherland and others. Reprinted partially under the title "Criticism or Propaganda?" in *Wyndham Lewis on Art* (A45).

D323 A NOTE ON MICHAEL AYRTON. *Nine,* II, no. 3 (August) 184-185.

Reviews Ayrton's series of four paintings titled "The Passion of the Vine" (illustrated).

D324 ROUND THE LONDON ART GALLERIES. *The Listener,* XLIV, no. 1129 (September 21) 388.

Discusses Francis Bacon ("the most astonishingly sinister artist in England"), Colquhoun and "Children's Art 1950" (this final section reprinted in *Wyndham Lewis on Art* (A45).

D325 ROUND THE LONDON ART GALLERIES. *The Listener,* XLIV, no. 1132 (November 9) 508.

Reviews recent work by the Camden Town Group, Claude Monet, Henry Moore and Ivon Hitchens. Reprinted in *Wyndham Lewis on Art* (A45). See D326.

D326 HENRY MOORE'S 'HEAD OF A CHILD.' *The Listener,* XLIV, no. 1135 (November 30) 647.

Letter to the editor in response to Lord Brand's criticism (see F790) of Lewis's review of the sculpture "Head of a Child" by Henry Moore, published in the November 9 issue of *The Listener* (D325). The controversy continued for two months (see D329, D330, D331, D332, D333, D335, F793, F795, F796, F813, F815, F816, F817). Reprinted with deletions in *The Letters* (A42a).

D327 ROUND THE LONDON ART GALLERIES. *The Listener,* XLIV, no. 1135 (November 30) 650.

Reassertion of Lewis's admiration for Colquhoun, followed by a discussion of Sir William Russell Flint and Picasso, whom he describes as "incontinent" and "mechanical."

D328 A NEGRO ARTIST. *The Listener,* XLIV, no. 1136 (December 7) 696.

Reviews exhibition of Denis Williams. Reprinted in *Wyndham Lewis on Art* (A45).

D329 NATURE AND ART. *The Listener,* XLIV, no. 1137 (December 14) 745.

Response to a letter from Harold Speed published in the December 7 issue of *The Listener* (see D326, F793 and F817).

D330 NATURE AND ART. *The Listener,* XLIV, no. 1139 (December 28) 839.

Letter to the editor in response to a letter from J. Evleigh and H. M. Robson which appeared in December 21 issue of *The Listener* (see D326 and F795). Reprinted in *The Letters* (A42a).

1951

D331 NATURE AND ART. *The Listener,* XLV, no. 1140 (January 4) 22.

Letter to the editor in response to a letter from A. K. Lawrence, R.A., which appeared in December 28 issue of *The Listener* (see D326 and F796). Reprinted in *The Letters* (A42a).

D332 NATURE AND ART. *The Listener,* XLV, no. 1141 (January 11) 63.

Letter to the editor in response to another letter from Lord Brand which appeared in January 4 issue of *The Listener* (see D326 and F813).

D333 NATURE AND ART. *The Listener,* XLV, no. 1142 (January 18) 106.

Letter to the editor in response to a new letter from A. K. Lawrence, R.A., which appeared in January 11 issue of *The Listener* (see D326 and F815). Reprinted in *The Letters* (A42a).

D334 ROUND THE LONDON ART GALLERIES. *The Listener,* XLV, no. 1142 (January 18) 110.

Reviews a number of current exhibitions briefly, concentrating on the work of Alexander Calder. Announces an article on the École de Paris, which never appeared due to Lewis's increasing blindness. Passage on Calder reprinted in *Wyndham Lewis on Art* (A45).

D335 NATURE AND ART. *The Listener,* XLV, no. 1143 (January 25) 145.

Letter to the editor in response to letters from Lord Brand and Harold Speed which appeared in January 8 issue of *The Listener* (see D326, F816 and F817).

D336 THE ROCK DRILL. *The New Statesman and Nation,* XLI, no. 1048 (April 7) 398.

Favorable review of *The Letters of Ezra Pound,* ed. by D. D. Paige. See F779.

D337 THE SEA-MISTS OF THE WINTER. *The Listener,* XLV, no. 1158 (May 10) 765.

Valedictory in which Lewis announces his total blindness. Reprinted in *Wyndham Lewis. An Anthology of his Prose* (A44). Abbreviated version translated into German broadcast by B.B.C. German Service on June 23, 1951 (TLS, B. H. Alexander to Lewis, May 24 and 29, 1951, NIC).

1952

D338 AUGUSTUS JOHN LOOKS BACK. *The Listener,* XLVII, no. 1203 (March 20) 476-479.

Favorable review of *Chiaroscuro: Fragments of an Autobiography,* by Augustus John.

D339 ROT. *The American Mercury,* LXXIV, no. 340 (April) 91-106.

See D296 and D309. See also *Rotting Hill* (A36b).

1953

D340 THE REBELLIOUS PATIENT. *Shenandoah,* IV, nos. 2/3 (Summer/Autumn) "Wyndham Lewis Number," 3-16.

Short story. See F897.

NOTE. A special issue of 3 copies, hardbound and signed by Lewis, was presented to the editors, Ashley Brown, Thomas Carter and Hugh Kenner.

1954

D341 DOPPELGÄNGER: A STORY. *Encounter,* II, no. 1 (January) 23-33.

Short story. Reprinted in *Unlucky for Pringle* (A46).

D342 MATTHEW ARNOLD. *The Times Literary Supplement,* LIII, no. 2740 (August 6) xxii.

Reviews *Matthew Arnold: Poetry and Prose,* ed. John Bryson. Excerpts reprinted in *Enemy Salvoes* (A48).

D343 MEREDITH AS A NOVELIST. *Time and Tide,* XXXV, no. 39 (September 25) 1269-1270.

Review of *The Ordeal of George Meredith,* by Lionel Stevenson.

1955

D344 MONSTRE GAI. *The Hudson Review,* VII, no. 4 (Winter) 502-521.

Corresponds to *The Human Age. Book II: Monstre Gai,* Chap. 1 (A40). See D345 and D346.

D345 MONSTRE GAI. *The Hudson Review,* VIII, no. 1 (Spring) 28-56.

Reprinted in *The Human Age. Book II: Monstre Gai* (A40). See D344 and D346.

D346 A VERY SINISTER OLD LADY. *Shenandoah,* VII, no. 1 (Autumn) 3-14.

Reprinted as Chap. 2 in *The Human Age. Book II: Monstre Gai* (A40). See D344 and D345.

1956

D347 PISH-TUSH. *Encounter,* VI, no. 2 (February) 40-50.
Short story. Reprinted in *Unlucky for Pringle* (A46).

D348 WITH GLINTING IRONY . . . WITH GAY SAVAGERY . . . AND A SLOGGING PENCIL. THE BLIND OUTSIDER BATTLES ON AT 72. *The Daily Mail* (September 6) 4.

Interview with Lewis about Notting Hill, his future books and the condition of young writers. Lewis interviewed by Richard Evans.

D349 THE VORTICISTS. *Vogue,* CXII, no. 9 (September) 216, 221.

Survey of the Vorticist movement. Reprinted in *Wyndham Lewis on Art* (A45).

D350 PERSPECTIVES ON LAWRENCE. *The Hudson Review,* VIII, no. 4 (Winter) 596-608.

Review of *Lawrence of Arabia. A Biographical Enquiry,* by Richard Aldington, and *The Home Letters of T. E. Lawrence and his Brothers.*

1957

D351 A NOTE ON MICHAEL AYRTON. *Spectrum,* V, no. 2 (Spring/Summer) 15-18.
Preface to Michael Ayrton's *Golden Sections,* published later in 1957 (see B32).

1960

D352 WYNDHAM LEWIS AND THE ARCHANGEL MICHAEL. *Spectrum,* IV, no. 3 (Autumn) 176-191.

Includes first printings of numerous excerpts of letters sent from Lewis to David Kahma. Passages reprinted in *The Letters* (A42a).

1968

D353 WYNDHAM LEWIS AT WINDSOR. *Canadian Literature,* no. 35 (Winter) 9-19.
Includes five hitherto unpublished letters from Lewis to J. Stanley Murphy, C.S.B. dated September 12, 1942; March 4, 1943; May 2, 1944; May 23, 1944 and August 28, 1944. "Wyndham Lewis in Canada" issue of *Canadian Literature;* see also D354, D355, D356, F1481.

D354 ON CANADA. *Canadian Literature,* no. 35 (Winter) 20-25.

Essay discussing reasons for Lewis's residence in Canada and opinions about Canada. Reprinted in *Wyndham Lewis in Canada* (B34). Untitled AMS in Cornell.

D355 HILL 100. OUTLINE FOR AN UNWRITTEN NOVEL. *Canadian Literature,* no. 35 (Winter) 37-43.

Passages from unfinished novel (AMS entitled "Hill One Hundred" in Cornell). Reprinted in *Wyndham Lewis in Canada* (B34).

D356 EXILE'S LETTERS. *Canadian Literature,* no. 35 (Winter) 64-73.

Includes extracts from letters to W. K. Rose not included in *The Letters* (A42). Rose asserts that Lewis's Canadian correspondence forms an "epistolary proto-novel."

1969

D357 FURTHER NOTE. *Agenda,* VII-VIII, nos. 3-1 (Autumn/Winter) 184-186.

Afterword to an unfinished novel (AMS in Cornell). See "Excerpts from *The Man of the World*" by Hugh Kenner (F1544). This issue of *Agenda* is "Wyndham Lewis Special Issue," see also D358, D359, D360, D361, F1521.

D358 FROM HOODOPIP. *Agenda,* VII-VIII, nos. 3-1 (Autumn/Winter) 187-196.

Excerpts from *Hoodopip,* an unfinished novel written by Lewis in the 1920's. See "Note on *Joint*" by Hugh Kenner (F1546). AMS in Cornell. See also D359 and D360.

D359 FROM JOINT. *Agenda,* VII-VIII, nos. 3-1 (Autumn/Winter) 198-208.

Passage from *Joint.* See D358.

D360 FROM THE INFERNAL FAIR. *Agenda,* VII-VIII, nos. 3-1 (Autumn/Winter) 209-215.

Passage from *Joint.* See D358.

D361 THE DO-NOTHING MODE. AN AUTOBIOGRAPHICAL FRAGMENT. *Agenda,* VII-VIII, nos. 3-1 (Autumn/Winter) 216-221.

Memoirs of Lewis's father.

1970

D362 FIFTY YEARS OF PAINTING: SIR WILLIAM ROTHENSTEIN'S EXHIBITION. *Apollo,* XCI, no. 97 (March) 218-223.

An article written for *The London Mercury* in 1938 on the occasion of the exhibition of Sir William Rothenstein's paintings at the Leicester Galleries.

1977

D363 THE STURGE MOORE LETTERS. *Lewisletter,* no. 7 (October) 8-23.

Contains fifteen previously unpublished letters from Lewis to T. Sturge Moore, covering a period from about July 1909 through December 1933, edited with an introduction and notes by Victor M. Cassidy.

E. Translations

FRENCH

E1 ASPECTS DE LA LITTERATURE ANGLAISE DE 1918 A 1940. *Fontaine,* no. 37/40 (1944) 310-314.

Contains two excerpts from *The Art of Being Ruled* (Part XI, Chaps. 8 and 10) translated by "XXX."

E2 HOMAGE A ROY CAMPBELL. F.-J. TEMPLE * ROB LYLE * RICHARD ALDINGTON * LAWRENCE DURRELL * ALAN PATON * EDITH SITWELL * MAURICE OHANA * ALISTER KERSHAW * CILETTE OFAIRE * ARMAND GUIBERT * UYS KRIGE * WYNDHAM LEWIS * HENRI CHABROL * CHARLES DE RICHTER * FREDERIC MISTRAL, NEVEU * CATHERINE ALDINGTON * F. DE FREMINVILLE. [Paris: Société Cevenole du Mercou], 1958. Pp. 148; 5 plates. Pictorial wrappers. Published December, 1958 in an edition of 700 copies.

Contains a passage from *Snooty Baronet* (Chap. VIII) translated by Armand Guibert, pp. 89-93 ("Extract de 'Snooty Baronet,' dans lequel Wyndham Lewis met en scène Roy Campbell sous le nom de Rob McPhail," 93).

E3 EZRA POUND. *Ezra Pound–1.* Paris: Les Cahiers de l'Herne, 1965.

Contains translation of "Ezra Pound" by Pierre Alien, pp. 128-133. See D312.

E4 CANTLEMAN'S SPRING MATE CODE OF A HERDSMAN CANTLEMAN ET LA SAISON DES AMOURS LE CODE D'UN BOUVIER. Paris: M. J. Minard, 1968. Pp. 88. Blue and white wrappers printed in black. Published early 1968 in an edition of 1392 copies, 6 fr.

Bilingual edition, with translations of "Cantleman's Spring Mate" and "Code of a Herdsman" by Bernard Lafourcade. Contains three designs by Lewis (Michel 629, 631 and 652), with an introduction by the translator.

E5 TARR. [Paris]: Christian Bourgois Editeur, [1970]. Pp. 576. Cream wrappers printed in black and violet, tissue dustjacket. Published November, 1970 in an edition of 4241 copies, 40.65 fr.

Includes introduction by the translator, Bernard Lafourcade (7-10), Prologue from the 1918 edition of *Tarr* (549-553), "Le Schicksal: Tarr et les Allemands" from *Rude Assignment,* Chap. 28 (555-565), "A Propos de Tarr" (letter in French from Lawrence Durrell, pp. 567-568) and Lafourcade's translation of *Tarr.*

GERMAN

E6 NIETZSCHE ALS POPULARPHILOSOPH. *Der Querschnitt,* VII, no. 2 (1927) 90-96.

Contains a translation of "Nietzsche as a Vulgarizer" from *The Art of Being Ruled* (Part IV, Chap. 5). Translator unacknowledged.

E7 HITLER UND SEIN WERK IN ENGLISCHER BELEUCHTUNG . . . EINZIG BERECHTIGTE DEUTSCHE AUSGABE. Berlin: Verlag von Reimar Hobbing, 1932. Pp. 168. 3.60 DM. Half black cloth binding, lettered in red on spine, photo-montage covers depicting various Nazi propaganda scenes; gothic type.

Translation of *Hitler* (A13) by Max Sylge.

E8 INSEL UND WELTREICH. *Europäische Revue,* XIII, no. 9 (September 1937) 699-707.

Largely a translation from *The Mysterious Mr Bull* (Book VI, Chap. 6), A27. Translator unacknowledged.

E9 LAWRENCE VON ARABIEN. *Europäische Revue,* XIV, no. 3 (March 1938) 200-205.

Article about T. E. Lawrence translated by Hans Wilfert.

E10 DER TOD DES ANKOU. *Europäische Revue,* XIV, no. 3 (March 1938) 215-224.

Translation of "The Death of the Ankou" from *The Wild Body* (A9) by the editor, Joachim Moras.

E11 DIE RACHE FÜR LIEBE. Essen: Essener Verlagsanstalt, 1938. Pp. 420. 6.50 DM. Yellow cloth, stamped in black and red, issued in white pictorial dustjacket printed in black, red, yellow and green.

Translation of *The Revenge for Love,* by Hans Rudolf Rieder.

E12 JOHN BRIGHT UND DIE ENGLISCHE AUSSENPOLITIK. *Europäische Revue,* XV, no. 4 (April 1939) 358-364.
Translation of "John Bright and Foreign Policy" from *The Mysterious Mr Bull* (Book V, Chap. 2), by Hans Rudolf Rieder. See E13.

E13 DER MYSTERIÖSE JOHN BULL. EIN TUGENDSPIEGEL DES ENGLÄNDERS. Essen: Essener Verlagsanstalt, 1939. Pp. 329. 5.20 DM. (clothbound edition). 3.50 DM. (paperbound edition).

Translation of *The Mysterious Mr Bull,* by Hans Rudolf Rieder. Reprints "John Bright und die englische Aussenpolitik" (see E12).

ITALIAN

E14 ANARCHIA DEL SESSO. Roma: Jandi-Sapi, 1948. Vol. XXXV of "Le Najadi, collezione di grandi narratori." Pp. 351. Lire 550.
Translation of *Tarr,* by Francesco Valori ("unica traduzione autorizzata").

E15 EZRA POUND. UN SAGGIO E TRE DISEGNI DI WYNDHAM LEWIS. Milano: All'insegna del pesce d'oro, 1958. Pp. 20; 2 plates. Cream wrappers printed in black, design by Lewis on front cover. Edition of 1000 copies on July 9, 1958. Lire 400.
Translation of "Ezra Pound," by Mary de Rachewiltz.

E16 TARR. Milano: Feltrinelli Editore, [1959]. Vol. 4 of "Biblioteca di letteratura diretta da G. Bassani. I classici moderni." Pp. 448. Tan boards printed in black, dustjacket. Published September, 1959. Lire 2000.
Translation of *Tarr,* by Enzo Siciliano.

NORWEGIAN

E17 FREMSKRITTETS DEMON I KUNSTEN. Olso: J.W. Cappelens Forlag, 1956. Pp. 88; one plate inserted between pp. 8-9. Yellow wrappers printed in red. Published September, 1956 in an edition of 1200 copies.
Translation of *The Demon of Progress in the Arts,* by Louise Bohr Nilsen.

POLISH

E18 HEMINGWAY W. OCZACH KRYTYKI ŚWIATOWEJ. [Edited by] Leszek Elektorowicz. Warsaw: Pańtwowy Instytut Wydawniczy, 1968.
Contains "Ernest Hemingway: Tępy Wól" (117-148), a translation of "The Dumb Ox: a Study of Ernest Hemingway" from *Men Without Art*, by Ewa Krasnowolska.

F. Books and Periodicals About Lewis

1912

F1 Fry, Roger. *The Nation,* XI, no. 16 (July 20) 583-584 (review of the AAA exhibition stating that only Lewis with "Kermesse" (Michel P4) "has risen to the occasion").

F2 B., C., [i.e. Clive Bell]. "The London Salon at the Albert Hall," *The Athenaeum,* no. 4422 (July 27) 98-99 (review of the AAA exhibition with a fairly favorable description of Lewis's "large picture"; reprinted in *Pot-Boilers* (London: Chatto and Windus, 1918).

F3 "Exhibition at the Albert Hall," *The Times* (July 30) 8 (favorable review of "Creation").

F4 Bell, Clive. "The English Group," *Second Post-Impressionist Exhibition* (catalogue introduction, Grafton Galleries, October 5-December 31).

F5 Fry, Roger. "Introduction," *ibid.*

F6 "The Grafton Galleries," *The Athenaeum,* no. 4433 (October 12) 422 (review of the Second Post-Impressionist Exhibition with a favorable comment on Lewis's drawings).

F7 "The Camden Town Group," *The Athenaeum,* no. 4442 (December 14) 737-738 (review of the third exhibition of the Camden Town Group with a favorable review of "Danse," Michel P3).

1913

F8 Fry, Roger. *The Nation,* XIII, no. 18 (August 2) 676-677 (review of the AAA's Summer Salon; "Group" (Michel P8) is described as Lewis's "most completely realized painting").

F9 Rutter, Frank. *Post-Impressionist and Futurist Exhibition* (foreword to the catalogue of the exhibition held at The Doré Galleries, London, October).

F10 "Post-Impressionist Pictures. Exhibition at the Doré Gallery," *The Times* (October 16) 12 (favorable review of "Kermesse," Michel P4).

F11 "Decoration at the Ideal Home Show," *Journal of the Royal Society of Arts* (London), October 24, 1062.

F12 [*Unsigned review.*] *The Graphic,* LXXXVIII, no. 2291 (October 25) 748 (caustic review of the Post-Impressionist and Futurist Exhibition).

F13 Bell, Clive. "The New Post-Impressionist Show," *The Nation,* XIV, no. 4 (October 25) 172-173 (review of the Post-Impressionist and Futurist exhibition favorably comparing "Kermesse" (Michel P4) to Delaunay's "The Cardiff Football Team"; reprinted in *Pot-Boilers* (London: Chatto and Windus, 1918).

F14 Cournos, John. "The Battle of the Cubes," *The New Freewoman,* I, no. 11 (November 13) 214-215.

1914

F15 Bell, Clive. *Art.* London: Chatto and Windus, passim (Lewis among the Futurists; reprinted, London: Chatto and Windus, 1949).

F16 Eddy, A. J. *Cubists and Post-Impressionists,* London: Grant Richards, passim ("Wyndhover Lewis" labeled an English "Fauve").

F17 Pound, Ezra. *Preliminary Announcement of the College of Art,* London: Complete Press (proposal for an educational institution in London staffed by Lewis among others; published also in *The Egoist,* November 2, 1914).

F18 Aldington, Richard. "Books, Drawings, and Papers," *The Egoist,* I, no. 1 (January 1) 11-12 (favorable review of *Timon of Athens).*

F19 C., R. H. [i.e. A. R. Orage]. "Readers and Writers," *The New Age,* XIV, no. 10 (January 8) 307 (claims that *Blast* is not likely to be the "independent arena necessary to encourage discussion").

F20 [*Unsigned review.*] *The Athenaeum,* no. 4498 (January 10) 70 (review of the Grafton Group exhibition at the Alpine Club Gallery, London, mentioning the defection of Lewis and his friends).

F21 Hulme, T. E. "Modern Art I.—The Grafton Group," *The New Age,* XIV, no. 11 (January 15) 341-342 (after the departure of Lewis and his friends "Mr. Fry and his group are nothing but a kind of backwater"; reprinted in *Further Speculations,* F941).

F22 Ludovici, Anthony M. "Mr. Wyndham Lewis's Methods," *ibid.,* 351 (response to Lewis's letter, D12).

F23 Hulme, T. E. "Modern Art II.—A Preface Note and Neo-Realism," *The New Age,* XIV, no. 15 (February 12) 469 (review of the Grafton Group exhibition at the Alpine Club; reprinted in *Further Speculations,* F941).

F24 "Exhibitions," *The Athenæum,* no. 4506 (March 7) 348-349 (review of "Lady Drogheda's Dining-Room," in which Lewis showed "great cleverness").

F25 Konody, P. G. "Art and Artists: the London Group," *The Observer* (March 18) 7 (review of the show at the Goupil Gallery, London).

F26 "The London Group," *The Athenæum,* no. 4507 (March 14) 387 (review of the exhibition at the Goupil Gallery).

F27 Fry, Roger. "Two Views of the London Group," *The Nation,* XIV, no. 24 (March 14) 998-999 (review of the London Group exhibition with a comment on Lewis's "close reasoning" but lack of feeling).

F28 [*Anonymous.*] *Ibid.,* 999-1001 (adverse view of the modern revolt and of Lewis's "patchwork").

F29 Pound, Ezra. "Exhibition at the Goupil Gallery," *The Egoist,* I, no. 6 (March 16) 109 (discusses Lewis's painting, "Christopher Columbus," Michel P9).

F30 "Lady Drogheda's Futurist Dining Room Decorations," *The Sketch,* March 24 (includes photographs of the room).

F31 Hulme, T. E. "Modern Art III.—The London Group," *The New Age,* XIV, no. 1 (March 26) 661-662 (Lewis's works have "always certain qualities of dash and decision," but "they do not produce a whole"; reprinted in *Further Speculations,* F941).

F32 Sickert, Walter Richard. "On Swiftness," *The New Age,* XIV, no. 21 (March 26) 655-656 (discusses "Creation" and how "non-representation is forgotten when it comes to the sexual organ"; Lewis answers this attack, D14).

F33 "Centre for Revolutionary Art—Cubist Pictures and Curtains," *Daily Mirror* (March 30) 7 (commentary on photographs taken in the Rebel Art Centre).

F34 Hulme, T. E. "Contemporary Drawings," *The New Age,* XIV, no. 22 (April 2) 688 (beginning of a series which includes drawings by Lewis; reprinted in *Further Speculations,* F941).

F35 Rutter, Frank. "Art and Artists—The English Cubists," *The New Weekly,* I, no. 3 (April 4) 85 (announces the opening of the Rebel Art Centre).

F36 Rutter, Frank. "A School for Cubists," *Sunday Times* (April 5) 7 (rather satirical view of "Eisteddfod," Michel P11).

F37 B., M. M. "Rebel Art in Modern Life," *Daily News and Leader*, XXI, no. 240 (April 7) 14 (interview with Lewis, see D15).

F38 "The Home of the Cubist Artists at 38, Great Ormond Street," *The Graphic* (April 25) 726 (includes a photograph of a Lewis painting).

F39 Rodker, John. "The New Movement in Art," *The Dial Monthly*, II, no. 17 (May) 176.

F40 Rutter, Frank. "Art and Artists," *The New Weekly*, I, no. 10 (May 23) 311 (review of Whitechapel Art Gallery Exhibition).

F41 Gaudier-Brzeska, Henri. "Allied Artists' Association, Ltd," *The Egoist*, I, no. 12 (June 15) 117-118 (a favorable review of Lewis's contribution to the Allied Artists' Salon).

F42 Pound, Ezra. "Wyndham Lewis," *The Egoist*, I, no. 12 (June 15) 233-234 (reprinted in Ezra Pound's *Instigations*, see F142; Lewis proclaimed by Pound as "one of the greatest masters of design yet born in the occident").

F43 Brookfarmer, Charles [i.e. Bechhöfer]. "Futile-ism," *The New Age*, XV, no. 7 (June 18) 154 (reports on Marinetti's lecture and Nevinson defining Lewis as "one of the great Futurist painters").

F44 Nevinson, C. R. W. *The New Weekly*, II, no. 1 (June 20) 18 (discusses the rift between Vorticists and Futurists).

F45 Rutter, Frank. "Art and Artists," *The New Weekly*, II, no. 1 (June 20) 19 (review of the AAA Salon).

F46 Redmon-Howard, L. G. "The Futurist Note in Interior Decoration," *Vanity Fair* (June 25) 32, 74 (favorable review of Lady Drogheda's dining-room).

F47 Sickert, Walter. "Democracy in Esse at Holland Park," *The New Age*, XV, no. 8 (June 25) 177 (critical attack on Lewis, dismissing his work as that of a "superannuated art-student . . . trying to paint like coastguardsmen," see D14 and F32).

F48 Sickert, Bernhard. "Democratic Painting and the 'Desophistication' of the Eye," *The English Review*, XVII, no. 65 (June) 325-338 (views non-representational art such as Lewis's as "aristocratic," which escapes condemnation as bad art by not being art at all).

F49 Eliot, T. S. "Contemporanea," *The Egoist*, V, 6 (June/July) 84-85 (includes a review of *Tarr*).

F50 "Blast!" *Pall Mall Gazette* (July 1) 7 (review of *Blast*).

F51 Aldington, Richard. "Blast," *The Egoist*, I, no. 13 (July 1) 248 (reviews *Blast*, "the most amazing, energised, stimulating production I have ever seen").

F52 "Blast. The Vorticists' Manifesto," *The Times* (July 1) 8 (favorably compares *Blast* to the Futurist manifesto).

F53 "Fine Art Gossip," *The Athenæum*, no. 4523 (July 4) 26 (unfavorable review of *Blast*).

F54 Ford, Ford Madox. "Mr. Wyndham Lewis and 'Blast,' " *The Outlook*, XXXIV (July 4) 15-16 (review of *Blast* and record of Lewis's famous first visit, incorporated in *Return to Yesterday*, see F399).

F55 [Orage, A. R.]. "Readers and Writers," *The New Age*, XV, no. 11 (July 16) 253 (describes "The Enemy of the Stars" as "an extraordinary piece of work, full of almost grandiose ideas . . . felt rather than thought").

F56 Phillips, Stephen. "Views and Reviews," *Poetry Review*, V (July) 48 (unfavorable review of *Blast*).

F57 [*Unsigned review.*] *Burlington Magazine*, XXV, no. 137 (August) 317-318 (review of *Blast*).

F58 "Vorticism, the Latest Cult of Rebel Artists," *The New York Times*, 5 (August 9) 10 (unfavorable review of *Blast*).

F59 Pound, Ezra. "Edward Wadsworth, Vorticist," *The Egoist*, I, no. 16 (August 15) 306-307 (a comparison of Lewis and Wadsworth, "the two best Vorticist painters").

F60 Tietjens, Eunice. "Blast," *The Little Review*, I, no. 5 (September) 33-34 (reviews *Blast*).

F61 Pound, Ezra. "Vorticism," *The Fortnightly Review*, XCVI, no. 573 (September 1) 461-471.

F62 [*Unsigned review.*] *Poetry*, V, no. 1 (October) 44-45 (favorably reviews *Blast* as "the height of sophistication").

1915

F63 Ford, Ford Madox. *The Good Soldier.* London: John Lane, passim (preface XVIII-XVIX; see also C2).

F64 Pound, Ezra. "Affirmations II. Vorticism," *The New Age,* XVI, no. 11 (January 14) 277-278 (compares Lewis favorably with Kandinsky and Picasso).

F65 Pound, Ezra. "Affirmations IV. As for Imagisme," *The New Age,* XVI, no. 13 (January 28) 349-350 (comments on the "energy" of *Timon of Athens;* reprinted in *Selected Prose).*

F66 Pound, Ezra. "Affirmations V. Gaudier-Brzeska," *The New Age,* XVI, no. 14 (February 4) 380-382 (refers to "Vortex Gaudier-Brzeska" in *Blast).*

F67 Pound, Ezra. "Synchronism," *ibid.,* 389-390 (a letter arguing that there is no trace of Futurism in *Timon of Athens).*

F68 Pound, Ezra. "Affirmations VI. Analysis of this Decade," *The New Age,* XVI, no. 15 (February 11) 409-411 (discusses Lewis's "great faculty of design" and "sense of dynamics").

F69 "Junkerism in Art: the London Group at the Goupil Gallery," *The Times* (March 10) 8 (Lewis's reply appears in C2, pp. 78-79).

F70 Storer, Edward. "The London Group," *The New Witness,* March 11 (Marinetti as the "St. Augustine" of the English rebels).

F71 Denver, Frank. "The London Group," *The Egoist,* II, no. 4 (April 1) 60-61 (favorable comment on "The Crowd," Michel P17).

F72 Flint, F. S. "The History of Imagism," *The Egoist,* II, no. 5 (May 1) 70-71 (discusses Pound's contradiction in terms when he assimilates Imagism and pictures by Lewis).

F73 "Which is Blackpool? How a Vorticist Sees It," *Daily Mirror* (June 11) 12.

F74 "The Vorticists, A New Group of Artists," *Glasgow Herald* (June 11) 8 (review of the Vorticist Exhibition at the Doré Gallery, London, June).

F75 "Vorticists and Others," *Westminster Gazette,* June 18 (a review of the Doré Gallery exhibition).

F76 "Vorticist Exhibition at the Doré Galleries," *The Athenæum,* no. 4573 (June 19) 556-557 (expresses respect for Lewis but states that Lewis's introduction to the Catalogue of the exhibition is not very enlightening, see B6).

F77 Gwennett, Gunn. "Vorticism and Mysticism," *Drawing and Design,* I, no. 2 (June) 56 (a review of the Doré Gallery exhibition).

F78 Konody, P. G. "The Vorticists at the Doré Gallery," *The Observer* (July 4) 9 (Vorticist experiments transmit "no emotion" and have therefore "no raison d'être").

F79 Pound, Ezra. "Et Faim Sallir le Loup des Boys," *Blast, No. 2* (July) 22 (poem expressing faith in Lewis).

F80 Pound, Ezra. "Chronicles," *ibid.,* 85-86 (on the reception of *Blast, No. 1).*

F81 Douglas, James. *The Star* (July 23) 4 (review of *Blast, No. 2,* see F83).

F82 C., R. H. [i.e. A. R. Orage] "Readers and Writers," *The New Age,* XVII, no. 13 (July 29) 309 (favorable review of *Blast, No. 2;* reprinted in *Orage as Critic).*

F83 Ford, Ford Madox. "On a Notice of Blast," *The Outlook,* XXXVI, no. 913 (July 31) 143-144 (discussion of James Douglas's review, see F81; includes favorable review of *Blast, No. 2).*

F84 "Art of Yester-Year. A War-Number of the Weird and Unwonted," *Daily Graphic* (July 31) 12 (review of *Blast, No. 2,* stating that nobody is interested in Vorticism, but quoting from Lewis approvingly).

F85 "Our Library Table," *The Athenæum,* no. 4579 (July 31) 78 (favorable review of *Blast, No. 2).*

F86 "Vorticist Exhibition," *Colour,* II (July) 198 (reviews the Doré Gallery exhibition).

F87 "Periodical not Received," *The Egoist,* II, no. 8 (August 2) 131 (mildly favorable review of *Blast, No. 2* seen as better than *Blast, No. 1,* "but wholly negative").

F88 Konody, P. G. " 'Blast' and the Vorticists," *The Observer* (August 1) 5 (reviews *Blast, No. 2).*

F89 Eagle, Solomon [i.e. Sir J. C. Squire]. "Books in General," *The New Statesman,* V, no. 123 (August 14) 449 (short review of *Blast, No. 2).*

F90 Ellwood, G. M. "Futurism in Design," *Drawing and Design,* I, no. 5 (September 1) 109.

F91 Gwennett, Gunn. "Blast," *Drawing and Design,* II, no. 8 (December) 30 (views *Blast* as "easily the premier comic publication of the day").

F92 Pound, Ezra. "Rémy de Gourmont," *The Fortnightly Review,* MCXXII (December) 1159-1166 (proposes that "intelligence" may triumph because of Joyce, Eliot and "the more normal part of Mr. Wyndham Lewis's narrative writings").

1916

F93 Pound, Ezra. *Gaudier-Brzeska: a Memoir, including the published writings of the sculptor, and a selection from the letters.* London: John Lane, The Bodley Head, passim.

F94 "Restaurant Art," *Colour,* IV, no. 3 (April) 14 (describes favorably Lewis's decoration at the Restaurant de la Tour Eiffel).

F95 Rothery, Guy Cadogan. "Futurism in Furnishing," *Colour,* IV, no. 4 (May), (reservedly favorable comment on the Dining Room at the Restaurant de la Tour Eiffel).

F96 Pound, Ezra. "Ezra Pound Files Exceptions," *Reedy's Mirror,* XXV, no. 32 (August 18) 535-536 (letter on Vorticism stating that "Lewis supplied the volcanic force"; reprinted in Pound, *Pavannes and Divisions).*

F97 "Art Which Makes for Emotion," *The Literary Digest,* LIII, no. 22 (November 25) 1406 (review of Vorticism, following the Vorticist Exhibition at the Penguin Club in New York, January).

F98 "At Last the Vorticists," *Vanity Fair,* VII, no. 3 (November) 72 (announces the Vorticist Show at the Penguin Club).

1917

F99 Cournos, John. "The Death of Futurism," *The Egoist,* IV, no. 1 (January) 6-7 (discusses Vorticism and the philosophy of *Tarr).*

F100 Marquis, Don. "The First Intelligent Answer," *Art World,* II (May) 166 (a sarcastic definition of Vorticism).

F101 Bell, Clive. "Contemporary Art in Britain," *Burlington Magazine,* XXXI, no. 172 (July) 30-37 (defines Vorticism as a kind of backwater, reprinted in *Pot Boilers* (London: Chatto and Windus, 1918).

F102 P., E. [i.e. Ezra Pound]. "Editor's Note," *The Little Review,* IV, no. 5 (September) 3, 7 (an introduction and footnote to Lewis's "Inferior Religions," D74).

F103 Winans, Walter. "The Ugly Side of the Cubist-Futurist-Vorticist Craze," *Quest,* IX, no. 1 (October) 144-149.

1918

F104 E., T. S. [i.e. T. S. Eliot]. "Literature and the American Courts," *The Egoist,* V, no. 3 (March) 39 (discusses the suppression of the issue of *The Little Review* because it printed "Cantleman's Spring-Mate," see D76).

F105 Pound, Ezra. "Tarr," *The Little Review,* IV, no. 11 (March) 35 (reprinted in *Instigations* and in *The Literary Essays of Ezra Pound).*

F106 C., R. H. [i.e. A. R. Orage]. "Readers and Writers," *The New Age,* XXIII, no. 1343 (June 6) 89 (survey of *The Little Review* stating that Lewis and Joyce are getting "too clever"; reprinted in *Readers and Writers* and in *Orage as Critic).*

F107 [Clutton-Brock, A.]. "A Scientific Experiment," *The Times Literary Supplement*, XVII, no. 860 (July 11) 323 (reviews *Tarr* as a Dostoievskyan *reductio ad absurdum).*

F108 "Tarr," *Glasgow Herald* (July 11) 3 (favorable review).

F109 H., F. "Purple Cows," *The New Republic*, XV, no. 193 (July 15) 322-323 (reviews *Tarr*, stressing "its exasperated self-consciousness").

F110 "New Fiction," *Morning Post* (July 26) 2 (favorable review of *Tarr*, termed an "extreme" novel).

F111 H., F. M. [i.e. Ford Madox Ford]. "Mr. Wyndham Lewis's First Novel," *The Outlook*, XLII, no. 1069 (July 27) 85-87 (favorable review of *Tarr*, seen as an "elaborated *Trilby").*

F112 Pound, Ezra. "A Shakedown," *The Little Review*, V, no. 4 (August) 9-41 (reprinted in *The Literary Essays of Ezra Pound).*

F113 West, Rebecca. "Tarr," *The Nation*, XXIII, no. 19 (August 10) 506-508 (reprinted in *Agenda*, F1529).

F114 "Literary Digest," *The Cambridge Magazine*, VII, no. 45 (August 17) 947 (reviews *Tarr* as "an interesting and instructive document").

F115 [*Unsigned review.*] *The Nation*, CVII, no. 2772 (August 17) 176 (unfavorably reviews *Tarr* as "dull rigamarole").

F116 [*Unsigned review.*] *The Athenæum*, no. 4632 (August) 366 (*Tarr* seen as "off the trodden paths of fiction").

F117 Nichols, Robert. *The New Witness*, XII, no. 305 (September 6) 371 (enthusiastic review of *Tarr*, "the forerunner of the prose . . . to come").

F118 [*Unsigned review.*] *The New Age*, XXXIII, no. 21 (September 19) 338 (hostile review of *Tarr*, pointing out the contradictions in its message and concluding that the author "befouls life").

F119 "Tarr," *The English Review*, XXVII (September) 238 (reviews *Tarr* as "baffling and fascinating").

F120 Eliot, T. S. "Tarr," *The Egoist*, V, no. 8 (September) 105-106 (reprinted in *Shenandoah* "Wyndham Lewis Number"; *Tarr* expresses "the thought of the modern and the energy of the cave-man").

F121 Pound, Ezra. "Tarr," *Future*, II, no. 9 (September) 237-239 (*Tarr* reviewed "as a huge act of scavenging").

F122 Fuller, Henry B. "A Literary Swashbuckler," *The Dial*, LXV, no. 774 (October 5) 261-262 (favorably reviews *Tarr* as "a dashing and bizarre experiment").

F123 "Tarr. Extracts from Press Notices," *The Egoist*, V, no. 9 (October) 124 (a full page of extracts from reviews published by *The Nation, The Times, Morning Post, Manchester Guardian, Glasgow Herald, Scotsman, English Review, New Witness, Future, The Outlook, Everyman, Southport Guardian, Eastern Morning News, Westminster Gazette, Weekly Dispatch, Observer, Birmingham Post, Aberdeen Journal, Cambridge Magazine, Athenæum, Sketch* and *Daily News).*

F124 [*Unsigned review.*] *The Mask*, (Florence) VIII, nó. 12 (December) 53 (sees *Tarr* as the work of "a young artist packed full of the signs of genius").

1919

F125 Brinton, Christian. "Introduction," *War Paintings and Drawings by British Artists* (exhibited under the auspices of the Ministry of Information, London). New York: Redfield-Kendrick-Odell, passim.

F126 Pound, Ezra. "The War Paintings of Wyndham Lewis," *The Nation*, XXIV, no. 19 (February 8) 546-547 (compared with Goya's and Uccello's treatment of war, "Mr Lewis's pictures are the most thoughtful exposition of the war that any painter has yet given us").

F127 Dias, H. B. [i.e. Ezra Pound]. "Wyndham Lewis at the Goupil Gallery," *The New Age*, XXIV, no. 16 (February 20) 263-264 (reprinted in Ezra Pound's *Selected Prose).*

F128 Pound, Ezra. "The Death of Vorticism, *The Little Review*, V, nos. 10-11 (February-March) 45-51.

F129 "The Canadian War Memorial Exhibition," *The Burlington Magazine,* XXXIV, no. 190 (February) 79 (favorable estimation of Lewis's war paintings).

F130 "Tis" [i.e. Herbert E. A. Furst]. "About Wyndham Lewis," *Colour*, no. 10 (March) 24-27 (survey of Lewis's artistic production, favorable to *Blast* and the war paintings).

F131 Cournos, John. "The Death of Vorticism," *The Little Review,* VI, no. 2 (June) 47-48 (discussion of why "the war was bound to kill Futurism and Vorticism").

F132 "Mr. Wyndham Lewis on Art," *The Athenæum,* no. 4670 (October 31) 1127 (review of "Modern Tendencies in Art," a lecture given by Lewis on October 22 in the Conference Hall, Central Buildings, Westminster, chaired by G. B. Shaw, concluding that Lewis was "incoherent").

F133 [*Unsigned review.*] *The Athenæum,* no. 4670 (October 31) 1137 (review of *The Caliph's Design).*

F134 "An Artist on the State of War," *The Times Literary Supplement,* XVIII, no. 930 (November 13) 646 (review of *The Caliph's Design).*

F135 Murry, John Middleton. "Our Art Executioner," *The Athen*æum, no. 4672 (November 14) 1181-1182 (favorable review of *The Caliph's Design).*

F136 "Some Books of the Week," *The Spectator,* LXXIII, no. 4772 (December 13) 829 (review of *The Caliph's Design,* deploring Lewis's "crabbedness").

F137 "Harold Gilman," *The Times Literary Supplement,* XVIII, no. 935 (December 18) 768 (favorable review of *Harold Gilman).*

F138 "Look Here," *The Sketch,* CIX, no. 1405 (December 31) 5.

F139 "Goupil Gallery Salon 1919," *Burlington Magazine,* XXXV, no. 201 (December) 278 (favorable comment on Lewis's portrait of Ezra Pound).

1920

F140 Goldring, Douglas. *Reputations. Essays in Criticism.* New York: Thomas Seltzer, 135-144 (includes a survey of Lewis's literary works).

F141 Marriott, Charles. *Modern Movements in Painting.* London: Chapman and Hall (New York: Scribner's, 1921) 159-163, passim (discusses "Modern Tendencies in Art" a lecture given by Lewis in the Conference Hall, Central Buildings, Westminster, London, October 22, 1919).

F142 Pound, Ezra. *Instigations of Ezra Pound.* New York: Boni and Liveright, passim.

F143 W., R. H. [i.e. Reginald Howard Wilenski]. "Mr. Lewis as Draughtsman," *The Athenæum,* no. 4679 (January 2) 19-20 (favorable review of *Fifteen Drawings,* seeing the drawings as the products of a man "abnormally sane").

F144 W., R. H. [i.e. Reginald Howard Wilenski]. "The Moral Factor in Art," *The Athenæum,* no. 4680 (January 9) 52 (favorable review of *Harold Gilman).*

F145 Wilenski, Reginald Howard. *The Athenæum,* no. 4681 (January 16) 85 (announces exhibition of drawings by Lewis at the Adelphi Gallery).

F146 Hannay, Howard. "Photography and Art," *The London Mercury,* I, no. 5 (January) 301-311 (mentions *The Caliph's Design).*

F147 "Wyndham Lewis's Drawings," *The Times Literary Supplement,* XIX, no. 940 (January 22) 47 (detailed, favorable analysis of *Fifteen Drawings).*

F148 "America in Wyndham Lewis," *Drawing and Design,* X, no. 55 (January) 66-67 (hostile review of *The Caliph's Design).*

F149 Hannay, Howard. "War Pictures at Burlington House," *The London Mercury,* I, no. 4 (February) 503-504 (Vorticism termed "a mechanical cul-de-sac").

F150 Goldring, Douglas. "Modern Critical Prose," *The Chapbook,* II, no. 8 (February) passim (mentions *The Caliph's Design* and Lewis as a "modern" novelist).

F151 Bell, Clive. "Wilcoxism," *The Athenæum*, no. 4688 (March 5) 311-312 (reprinted in *Since Cézanne;* Lewis answered this criticism of the exhibition of Imperial War Pictures with "Mr. Clive Bell and 'Wilcoxism,'" see D92, D93 and F152).

F152 Bell, Clive. "Wilcoxism," *The Athenæum*, no. 4690 (March 19) 379 (satirical attack of Lewis's letter, see F151, D92 and D93).

F153 Collings, Ernest H. R. *Ibid.*, 379 (letter supporting Lewis's demand for more encouragement of the arts, see D92).

F154 "The Art of Group X," *The Daily Graphic* (March) 25.

F155 "Spurious Art," *The Connoisseur*, LVI, no. 223 (March) 138.

F156 "New Pictures: Principles of the X Group; 'Literary' Painting,'" *The Times* (April 1) 14 (favorably reviews the exhibition at the Mansard Gallery, but claims that Lewis makes objects "look too large").

F157 Constable, W. G. "Wyndham Lewis," *The New Statesman*, XV, no. 367 (April 24) 73-74 (analysis of Lewis's use of two media).

F158 Wilenski, Reginald Howard. "Lettre de Londres," *L'Amour de l'Art*, I (Mai-Décembre) 223.

F159 Hannay, Howard. "Tyros and Portraits by Wyndham Lewis," *The London Mercury*, IV, no. 20 (June) 204-205.

F160 [*Unsigned review.*] *Burlington Magazine*, XXXVII, no. 208 (July) 49 (favorable review of *Harold Gilman*).

1921

F161 Hind, C. Lewis. *Art and I.* London: John Lane, The Bodley Head, passim (analysis of Lewis's "post-impressionism").

F162 Manly, John and Edith Rickert (revised by Fred B. Millett). *"Contemporary British Literature,"* New York: Harcourt, Brace, passim (a checklist of press notices).

F163 Defries, Amelia. "Notes and News," *Drawing and Design*, no. 9 (January) 272 (advocates "free-mindedness" as opposed to Lewis's "bigotry").

F164 Defries, Amelia. "Notes and News," *Drawing and Design*, no. 10 (February) 325 (Lewis derided as a self-publicizing stunt artist).

F165 Drey, O. R. "Exhibitions of the Week," *The Nation and Athenæum*, XIX, no. 3 (April 16) 106-108 (review of the Tyro exhibition seeing the Tyros as adult *enfants terribles*, stressing "the immense zest and brilliance" of the catalogue introduction).

F166 Sitwell, Osbert. "Wyndham Lewis as a Tyro," *The Sketch*, LXIV, no. 1473 (April 20) 89.

F167 S., H. "Art," *The Spectator*, CXXVI, no. 4844 (April 30) 555 (analysis of the Tyros).

F168 "The Picasso Exhibition, and Others," *Drawing and Design*, no. 13 (May) 423-428 (Lewis termed "more or less a plagiarist").

F169 Defries, Amelia. "Notes and News," *Drawing and Design*, no. 14 (June) 480 (mentions Lewis's Tyros).

F170 Parker, Kineton. "Tyronnics," *ibid.*, 464.

F171 Hannay, Howard. "Tyros and Portraits by Wyndham Lewis," *The London Mercury*, IV, no. 20 (June) 204-205.

F172 Pantaloo. "Caffey Royalties," *Drawing and Design*, no. 16 (August) 555 (discusses "Tyrotechnics").

F173 "The New Spirit in Art," *Drawing and Design*, no. 19 (November) 637-639 (refusal to advertise the self-advertising Lewis).

1922

F174 Bell, Clive. *Since Cézanne.* London: Chatto and Windus, passim (reprints "Wilcoxism," see D92, D93, F151 and F152).

F175 Orage, A. R. *Readers and Writers (1917-1921).* New York: Alfred A. Knopf, passim (expresses "mystified bewilderment" at Lewis's "cleverness"; incorporates F106).

F176 Rutter, Frank. *Some Contemporary Artists.* London: Leonard Parsons, 179-193 (survey of Lewis's artistic career).

F177 Hind, C. Lewis. *More Authors and I.* London: John Lane, The Bodley Head, passim (reminiscences of Ford and Lewis).

F178 Stephen, R. A. "Art Notes," *The New Age,* XXX, no. 23 (April 6) 300 (reviews Lewis's drawings as "very tame").

F179 Ford, Ford Madox. "A Haughty and Proud Generation," *The Yale Review,* XI, no. 4 (July) 703-717.

F180 Sickert, Walter Richard. *The Burlington Magazine,* XLI, no. 135 (October) 200 (favorable review of *The Tyro).*

1923

F181 Pound, Ezra. "On Criterion in General: et qu'on me laisse tranquille," *The Criterion,* I, no. 2 (January) 151.

F182 "Arts League of Service," *"Drawing and Design*, III, no. 34 (February) (about portfolios including one by Lewis).

F183 Eliot, T. S. *The Dial,* LXV, no. 5 (November) 480-483 (a review of Joyce's *Ulysses).*

1924

F184 Furst, Herbert. *The Modern Woodcut.* London: John Lane, 182 (Wadsworth's association with "the Lewis group").

F185 Bertram, Anthony. "London Exhibitions (Winter 1923-1924)," *The Transatlantic Review,* I, no. 3 (March) 109-111 (discusses the "heritage of Lewis" and William Roberts).

F187 Pound, Ezra. "George Antheil," *The Criterion,* II, no. 7 (April) 321-331 (proposes an analogy between Antheil's music and *Timon of Athens).*

F188 Wilenski, Reginald Howard. "London Art Chronicle," *The Transatlantic Review,* I, no. 6 (June) 487-488 (discusses artistic stagnation in London, "the crucial exception" being Lewis).

F189 "The Art League of Service Travelling Portfolios of Pictures," *Artwork,* I, no. 2 (October) 70-75 (see F182; includes two drawings by Lewis, one of which, "The God in the Car," is not listed in Michel).

1925

F190 Laver, James. *Portraits in Oil and Vinegar.* London: John Castle, 191-196 (includes a self-portrait by Lewis, favorable survey of Lewis's career, stressing that he is a writer rather than a painter).

F191 Rickword, Edgell. "The Returning Hero," *The Calendar of Modern Letters,* I, no. 6 (August) 472-474 (mentions Lewis in connection with the vanishing hero in painting).

F192 Mortimer, Raymond, "London Letter," *The Dial*, LXXVIII, no. 5 (May) 405-410 (praises *The Caliph's Design).*

F193 Wellington, Hubert (Deutsch von Margarete Mauthner). "Die Neuste Malerei in England, II," *Kunst und Künstler,* XXIII, no. 12 (September) 464-466.

1926

F194 Forbes, Watson (editor). *The John Quinn Collection of Paintings, Watercolours, Drawings and Sculptures.* New York: Huntington, 152.

F195 Higginbottom, W. Hugh. *Frightfulness in Modern Art.* London: Cecil Palmer, passim (hostile review of Lewis's work).

F196 Hunt, Violet. *I Have This to Say. The Story of My Flurried Years.* New York: Boni and Liveright, passim (recollections of Lewis).

F197 Rodker, John. *The Future of Futurism.* London: Kegan Paul, Trench, Trubner, passim.

F198 Nash, Paul. "Modern English Textiles," *Artwork,* II, no. 6 (January-March) 83 (mentions Lewis in connection with the Omega Workshop).

F199 McBride, H. *The Dial,* LXXX, no. 2 (February) 150-152 (review of Laver's *Portraits in Oil and Vinegar,* with hostile remarks about Lewis as a painter).

F200 "New Books at a Glance," *The Saturday Review,* CXLI, no. 3672 (March 13) 339 (review of *The Art of Being Ruled).*

F201 [Sullivan, J. W. N.]. "An Analysis of Society," *The Times Literary Supplement,* XXV, no. 1264 (April 8) 258 (favorable account of *The Art of Being Ruled,* "an extremely well written book").

F202 "Aristotle Up To Date," *The Nation and the Athenæum,* XXXIX, no. 3 (May 29) 210 (review of *The Art of Being Ruled,* seen as "a highly intelligent cross-word puzzle comparable to Samuel Butler's *Notebooks).*

F203 "A Commentary," *The Criterion,* IV, no. 3 (June) 419-420 (reviews *The Art of Being Ruled).*

F204 Aldington, Richard. "Mr. Lewis on Everything," *The Saturday Review of Literature,* III, no. 4 (July 31) 4 (reviews *The Art of Being Ruled* as "a magnificent amateur construction").

F205 [*Unsigned review.*] *The New York Herald Tribune Weekly Book Review* (September 12) 17 (reviews *Tarr).*

F206 Lovett, Robert M. "Mr. Wyndham Lewis's Ulysses," *The New Republic,* XLVIII, no. 616 (September 22) 124-125 (detailed description of *The Art of Being Ruled,* comparing Lewis and Nordau).

F207 Beard, Charles A. "Wyndham Lewis Takes Stock," *The New York Herald Tribune Weekly Book Review* (September 26) 1-2 (descriptive review of *The Art of Being Ruled).*

F208 Beard, Charles A. *Boston Transcript* (September 26) 4 (reviews *The Art of Being Ruled).*

F209 Krutch, Joseph Wood. "The New Asceticism," *The Nation,* CXXIII, no. 3195 (September 29) 299 (review of *Tarr,* "a prophetic novel").

F210 Rickword, Edgell. "The Art of Being Ruled," *The Calendar of Modern Letters,* III, no. 3 (October) 247-250 (favorable review of *The Art of Being Ruled).*

F211 Thorpe, W. A. "Books of the Quarter," *The New Criterion,* IV, no. 4 (October) 758-764 (favorable, detailed review of *The Art of Being Ruled).*

F212 Aldington, Richard. *The Springfield Republican* (November 15) 6 (reviews *The Art of Being Ruled).*

F213 Shuster, George N. *The Commonweal,* V, no. 3 (November 24) 83-84 (favorably reviews *The Art of Being Ruled,* in spite of its "atrocious style").

F214 Ferguson, Charles W. "Outline of Everything," *The Bookman,* LXIV, no. 4 (December) 510-511 (unfavorable review of *The Art of Being Ruled,* termed a "potpourri").

1927

F215 Furst, Herbert. *Portrait Painting.* Plymouth: Mayflower Press, passim (a comparison of Futurism, Cubism and Vorticism).

F216 Rutter, Frank. *Since I was 25.* London: Constable and Co., passim (pre-war recollections of Lewis).

F217 Vines, Sherard. *Movements in Modern English Poetry and Prose.* London: Oxford University Press, 200-208, passim (discusses *Blast, The Caliph's Design* and *The Lion and the Fox).*

F218 Wells, H. G. "The Story of the Last Trump," *The Short Stories of H. G. Wells.* London: Ernest Benn, 666.

F219 A., A. M. *The Liverpool Post* (January 6) (review of *The Lion and the Fox,* termed the work of "a man of brilliant but illogical mentality").

F220 Woolf, Leonard. "Shakespeare and Machiavelli," *The Nation and the Athenæum,* XL, no. 15 (January 15) 539 (favorable review of *The Lion and the Fox).*

F221 "Shakespeare Again," *The Saturday Review,* CXLIII, no. 3717 (January 22) 121-122 (review of *The Lion and the Fox,* applauding Lewis's contribution to the destruction of "the dummy Shakespeare of the school-room").

F222 "Shakespeare's Heroes, *The Spectator,* CXXXVIII, no. 5144 (January 29) 159-160 (mildly favorable review of *The Lion and the Fox).*

F223 Holms, J. F. " 'Composition as Explanation' by Gertrude Stein," *The Calendar,* III, no. 4 (January) 229-232 (quotes Lewis on Stein).

F224 "The Lion and the Fox," *The Times Literary Supplement,* XXVI, no. 1306 (February 10) 89 (favorable review of *The Lion and the Fox).*

F225 The Journeyman [i.e John Middleton Murry]. "The Lion and the Fox," *The Adelphi,* IV, no. 8 (February) 510-514 (a review finding *The Lion and the Fox* "swarming with ideas" but incoherent, comparing Lewis with Chapman).

F226 Affable Hawk [i.e. Desmond McCarthy]. "Books in General," *The New Statesman,* XXVIII, no. 724 (March 12) 667 (most favorably reviews *The Enemy* and *The Lion and the Fox,* stressing the non-academic richness of Lewis's work).

F227 [*Unsigned review.*] *The Times Literary Supplement*, XXVI, no. 1311 (March 17) 198 (favorable review of *The Enemy, No. 1).*

F228 Taylor, Rachel Annand. "Machiavelli and the Elizabethans," *The Bookman,* LXXI, no. 426 (March) 329-330 (review stressing the uneven quality of *The Lion and the Fox).*

F229 Krutch, Joseph Wood. "Wyndham Lewis," *The Nation,* no. 3224 (April 20) 446-448 (very favorable review of *The Art of Being Ruled* and *The Lion and the Fox* seen as examples of the anti-liberal movement).

F230 Bennett, Arnold. "Books and Persons. An Artist Turned Author: Mr. Wyndham Lewis," *The Evening Standard* (April 28) (generally favorable review of *The Enemy,* though teeming with hostile remarks about Lewis; reprinted in *Arnold Bennett: The Evening Standard Years,* 1974).

F231 Holms, J. F. "Notes and Reviews," *The Calendar,* IV, no. 1 (April) 62-67 (detailed critical review of *The Lion and the Fox).*

F232 Gilder, Rosamond. *The Theatre Arts Monthly,* XI, no. 55 (May) 372 (favorable review of *The Lion and the Fox).*

F233 Chew, Samuel. "A Machiavellian Shakespeare," *The New York Herald Tribune Weekly Book Review* (June 26) 13 (description of *The Lion and the Fox* termed a "brilliant and stimulating book").

F234 Dobrée, Bonamy. "Recent Books," *The Criterion,* V, no. 3 (June) 339-343 (favorable review of *The Lion and the Fox,* praising it as a revolutionary piece of Shakespearean criticism).

F235 Blackmur, R. P. "Hubris," *The Hound and Horn,* I, no. 1 (September) 42-47 (favorable review attempting to discover the fundamental concepts underlying *The Lion and the Fox).*

F236 [*Unsigned review.*] *The Hound and Horn,* I, no. 1 (September) 67-68 (favorably reviews *The Enemy).*

F237 Gill, Eric. "An Enemy for Friendship's Sake," *Pax,* no. 84 (Autumn) 263-265 (reviews *The Enemy).*

F238 Belgion, Montgomery. "In Memory of T. E. Hulme," *The Saturday Review of Literature,* IV, no. 10 (October 1) 155-156 (references to Lewis).

F239 Spencer, Hazelton. "Shakespeare (Himself)," *The New Republic,* LII, no. 670 (October 5) 181 (reviews *The Lion and the Fox,* as "stimulating but hard to read").

F240 Wolfe, Humbert. "Time and Western Man," *The Observer* (October 9) (highly favorable review which calls Lewis "one of the best natural metaphysicians that England has produced").

F241 "A Defense of Intellect," *The Liverpool Post* (October 12) 4 (favorable review of *Time and Western Man).*

F242 [*Unsigned review.*] *The Spectator,* CCXXXIX, no. 5182 (October 22) 675 (short critical review of *Time and Western Man).*

F243 [*Unsigned review.*] *The Times Literary Supplement,* XXVI, no. 1343 (October 27) 760 (favorable reviews of *Time and Western Man* and *The Enemy, No. 1).*

F244 " 'Time-Philosophy' and the Artist," *The Saturday Review,* CXLIV, no. 3757 (October 29) 587-588 (reviews *Time and Western Man).*

F245 Palmer, Arnold. "Books," *The Sphere,* CXI, no. 1449 (October 29) 217 (favorable review of *The Enemy, No. 2).*

F246 "An Enemy Worth Having," *The Nation,* CXXV, no. 3254 (November 16) 535 (favorable review of *The Enemy,* seen as the product of "an intelligent conservative").

F247 Read, Herbert. "Time and Mr. Wyndham Lewis," *The Nation and Athenæum,* XLII, no. 7 (November 19) 282-284 (very favorably reviews *Time and Western Man).*

F248 Le Gallienne, Richard. *The New York Times* (November 20) 9 (review of *The Lion and the Fox).*

F249 Berdan, John. "A Shakespeare Hunt," *The Saturday Review of Literature,* IV, no. 18 (November 26) 342 (hostile review of *The Lion and the Fox* stressing its "academic imperfections").

F250 Taylor, Rachel Annand. "Some Modern Pessimists," *The Spectator,* CXXXIX, no. 5188 (December 3) 1016-1019 (review of *The Wild Body,* stressing Lewis's "French romantic" taste for monsters).

F251 Campbell, Roy. "The Emotional Cyclops," *The New Statesman and Nation,* XXX, no. 762 (December 3) Supplement X-XII (highly critical review of *Time and Western Man* whose author is labelled "time-obsessed").

F252 Krutch, Joseph Wood. "Plastic and Temporal in Art," *The Nation,* CXXV, no. 3257 (December 7) Holiday Book Section, Supplement 643-645 (detailed account of *Time and Western Man,* a "sub specie æternitatis" product of a classical mind).

F253 "The Wild Body," *The Times Literary Supplement,* XXVI, no. 1349 (December 8) 930 (favorable review of *The Wild Body).*

F254 Jolas, Eugene, Elliot Paul and Robert Sage. "First Aid to the Enemy," *transition,* no. 9 (December) 161-176 (review of *The Enemy* and answer to "Analysis of the Mind of James Joyce").

F255 Hartley, L. P. "New Fiction," *The Saturday Review,* CXLIV, no. 3764 (December 17) 862-863 (favorable review of *The Wild Body,* though it finds the author tormented and confused).

F256 "Myth and Sentiment," *Glasgow Herald* (December 22) 4 (favorable review of *The Wild Body,* objecting to the essays accompanying the stories).

F257 Brittain, Vera. "New Fiction," *Time and Tide,* VIII, no. 51 (December 23) 1159-1160 (unfavorable review of *The Wild Body* which claims Lewis "never succeeds in getting anywhere").

F258 Muir, Edwin. "Fiction," *The Nation and Athenæum,* XLII no. 12 (December 24) 488-489 (*The Wild Body* viewed as "both brilliant and disappointing").

F259 Connolly, Cyril. "New Novels," *The New Statesman,* XXX, no. 765 (December 24) 358-359 (favorable review of *The Wild Body* whose only fault is that it does not apply "the religion of the grotesque" to "a beautiful creature").

F260 D'Arcy, M. C. "A Critic Among the Philosophers," *The Month,* CL, no. 76 (December) 511-515 (highly favorable review of *Time and Western Man,* which shows, however, a "curious unsteadiness" when it comes to religion).

F261 [*Unsigned review.*] *The Hound and Horn,* 1, no. 2 (December) 178-179 (favorable review of *The Enemy, No. 2).*

F262 R., G. R. [i.e. G. R. Reitlinger]. "Reviews," *Drawing and Design,* III, no. 18 (December) 190 (reservedly favorable review of *The Enemy, No. 2).*

F263 Saintsbury, Geoffrey. "Anti-Spengler," *The Adelphi,* (December) 162-167 (a grudgingly favorable review of *Time and Western Man* seen as a piece of "destructive" criticism).

1928

F264 Aragon, Louis. *Traité du Style.* Paris: Gallimard, 152-153 (approves of Lewis's analysis of the effects of the time-cult, but finds the basis of his philosophy to be "pro-British").

F265 Campbell, Roy. "Contemporary Poetry." *Scrutinies by Various Writers,* collected by Edgell Rickword. London: Wishart and Company, passim.

F266 Isaacs, Jakob. "England." *Contemporary Movements in European Literature* (Jakob Isaacs and William Rose, editors). London: George Routledge, passim.

F267 Riding, Laura. *Anarchism is not Enough.* London: Jonathan Cape, 41-133 (a detailed, witty discussion of Lewis's "objective hardness").

F268 Thorpe, W. A. "Recent Books," *The Monthly Criterion,* VII, no. I (January) 70-73 (favorably reviews *Time and Western Man,* though it stresses that Lewis's Aristotelianism is "prejudice rather than philosophy").

F269 Ward, Leo. *The Catholic Times* (January 6) 6 (favorable account of *Time and Western Man).*

F270 Aiken, Conrad. *The New York Evening Post* (February 25) 12 (review of *Time and Western Man,* "the most confused and restless and peaceless of contemporary books of philosophy" and the product of a "dyed-in-the-wool romantic"; reprinted in *A Reviewer's ABC,* see F290 and F999).

F271 Praz, Mario. "Wyndham Lewis," *English Studies,* X, no. I (February) 1-8 (survey mostly discussing *Time and Western Man* and Lewis's attacks against Croce; *The Lion and the Fox* seen as a "hasty production").

F272 Bates, Ernest Sutherland. "The Road to Rome," *The Saturday Review of Literature,* IV, no. 35 (March 24) 700-701 (sympathetic review of *Time and Western Man* which, in spite of its "destructiveness," tends to Neo-Scholasticism).

F273 Mumford, Lewis. "The Case Against Time," *The New Republic,* LIV, no. 692 (March 7) 102-103 review of *Time and Western Man).*

F275 Blackmur, R. P. "The Enemy," *The Hound and Horn,* I, no. 3 (March) 270-272 (favorable review of *Time and Western Man,* comparing Lewis to Ramon Fernandez, Henri Massis, Babbitt and the Neo-Thomists).

F276 Robinson, M. "Sex and Sanity," *The Adelphi,* I, no. 3 (March) 266-269 (favorable analysis of *The Wild Body).*

F277 Gorman, Herbert. "Mr. Lewis Laughs," *New York Herald Tribune Weekly Book Review* (April 1) 3-4 (reviews *The Wild Body* favorably, defining *Tarr* as "an immensely important gesture of defiance in the history of the English novel").

F278 Cowley, Malcolm. *The New Republic,* LIV, no. 697 (April 11) 253 (favorable review of *The Wild Body* suggesting readers "will demand that character should result in action").

F279 Aiken, Conrad. *The New York Evening Post* (April 14) 14 (review of *The Wild Body* which calls Lewis "a first rate narrator" who is also "less fortunately a theorist"; contradicts Eliot's praise of "Inferior Religions").

F280 Levine, I. "Time and Western Man," *The Sociological Review,* XX (April) 162-163 (a review of *Time and Western Man).*

F281 [*Unsigned review.*] *The Bookman,* LXVII, no. 4 (June) 463 (a review of *The Wild Body).*

F282 Mortimer, Raymond. "New Novels," *The Nation and Athenæum,* XLIII, no. 13 (June 23) 396 (reviews *The Childermass* as "incomprehensible" though "wider in scope than *Ulysses").*

F283 "Tales by Wyndham Lewis," *The New York Times Book Review* (July 1) 13 (critical review of *The Wild Body* concluding that "a multiplication of Wyndham Lewises would mean a sterilization of fiction").

F284 Connolly, Cyril. "Chang," *The New Statesman and Nation,* XXXI, no. 793 (July 7) 426-427 (detailed and finally favorable review of *The Childermass* praising Lewis's "brave stand against modernity" which he fights "with its own weapons").

F285 "The Childermass," *The Times Literary Supplement,* XXVII, no. 1381 (July 19) 534 (review of *The Childermass;* seen as "a difficult and disjointed book . . . extravagantly expressive").

F286 Hartley, L. P. "New Fiction," *The Saturday Review,* CXLVI, no. 3796 (July 28) 126 (review of *The Childermass* exasperated by its "abstract, mental . . . unintelligibility").

F287 [*Unsigned review.*] *The Booklist,* XXIV, no. 9 (July) 344 (favorable review of *Time and Western Man).*

F288 Carter, Huntly. " 'Sociology' in the New Literature," *The Sociological Review,* XX, no. 3 (July) 250-255 (describes Lewis as "an individualist and Thomist intellectual").

F289 [*Unsigned review.*] *Pittsburg Modern Bulletin,* XXXIII (July) 68 (review of *Time and Western Man).*

F290 Aiken, Conrad. "Mr. Lewis and the Time-Beast," *The Dial,* LXXXV, no. 20 (August) 168-171.

F291 Hull, Robert R. "The Comic Cosmos," *The Commonweal,* VIII, no. 13 (August 1) 335-337 (detailed analysis of *The Wild Body).*

F292 Lindsay, Jack. "The Modern Consciousness. An Essay Towards an Integration," *The London Aphrodite,* no. 1 (August) 3-24 (discusses Lewis's stand against Time, Nietzsche and D. H. Lawrence).

F293 Belgion, Montgomery. "Wyndham Lewis, Alias the Enemy," *The Bookman,* LXVIII, no. 1 (September) 56-60 (survey of Lewis's career).

F294 Krutch, Joseph Wood. "Wyndham Lewis Made Easier," *New York Herald Tribune Weekly Book Review* (September 2) 1, 4 (detailed favorable review of *The Childermass).*

F295 Trilling, Lionel. *New York Evening Post* (September 22) 5 (reviews *The Childermass).*

F296 Davin, Tom. *New York World* (September 23) 9 (reviews *The Childermass).*

F297 Pound, Ezra. "Data," *The Exile,* 4 (Autumn) 104-117 (bibliographical information, incorporated in "On Wyndham Lewis," see F898).

F298 Bates, Ernest Sutherland. "A Cathedral of Gargoyles," *The Saturday Review of Literature,* V, no. 11 (October 6) 181-182 (reviews *The Childermass* and *The Wild Body).*

F299 [*Unsigned review.*] *Saint Louis,* XXVI (October) 322 (review of *Time and Western Man).*

F300 Powys, John Cowper. "The God of Time," *The Dial,* LXXXV, no. 5 (November) 416-419 (review of *Time and Western Man).*

F301 Rascoe, Burton. "Contemporary Reminiscences: An American Garden Party for Wyndham Lewis," *Arts and Decoration,* no. 80 (November) 98, 100 (gossip about a party Donald Friede gave on July 4 in Larchmont).

F302 Morris, L. S. "The Gist of Wyndham Lewis," *The New Republic,* LVII, no. 732 (December 12) 111-112 (mixed review of *The Childermass,* "the tempestuously ineffective work" of "one of the most invigorating writers alive").

F303 Beresford, J. D. "The Strange Necessity," *The Adelphi,* II, no. 2 (December 1928-February 1929) 173-174 (review of *The Childermass,* finding it superior to Joyce's *Ulysses).*

1929

F304 Barney, Nathalie C. "Adventures de l'Esprit," Paris: Editions Emile Paul Frères (Lewis appears in "Salon de l'Amazone entre 1900 et 1930"; reproduced in *Selected Writings by Nathalie Clifford Barney.* London: Adam Books, 1963).

F305 Goldring, Douglas. *People and Places.* Boston: Houghton Mifflin, passim (recollections of Lewis and Ford).

F306 Beckett, Samuel [et al.]. *Our Exagmination round his Factification for Incamination of Work in Progress.* Paris: Shakespeare and Company (direct and indirect answers to *Time and Western Man* and its criticism of Joyce).

F307 Taupin, René. *L'Influence du Symbolisme sur la Poésie Américaine (1910-1920).* Paris: Champion (discusses *Blast* and *The Little Review).*

F308 Thieme-Becker (Ulrich Thieme and Felix Becker). *Allgemeines Lexikon der bildenden Künstler, 23.* Leipzig: Verlag von E. A. Seeman (contains a list of reproductions of Lewis's works).

F309 Wickham, Harvey. *The Impuritans.* New York: The Dial Press (London: Allen and Unwin) 92-93 (mentions Lewis on primitivism).

F310 Connolly, Cyril. "New Novels," *The New Statesman,* XXXII, no. 819 (January 5) 412-413 (short review of *Tarr* seen as "an arid and untidy little picture").

F311 Powys, John Cowper. "The Childermass—Part I," *The Dial,* LXXXVI, no. 2 (January) 163 (favorable review of *The Childermass).*

F312 [Eliot, T. S.]. "A Commentary: The Politics of Men of Letters," *The Criterion,* VIII, no. 32 (April) 378-380 (on Shaw, Wells and Lewis described as "fascists").

F313 "The Poor White: Mr. Wyndham Lewis's Paradox," *The Times* (May 17) 19 (mixed review of *Paleface,* describing it as being at once "an entertainment, a scourge and an apocalypse").

F314 West, Rebecca. "On Making Due Allowance for Distortion," *Time and Tide,* X, no. 21 (May 24) 623-625 (review of *Paleface* using it to criticize Spengler's *Decline of the West* but regretting Lewis's inability "to assume his rightful authority").

F315 "Readers' Reports," *Life and Letters,* II, no. 12 (May) 393-394 (favorable review of *Tarr* and "its rhinocerous vigour").

F316 "A Brief for the White," *The Times Literary Supplement,* XXVIII, no. 1426 (May 30) 432 (favorable review of *Paleface).*

F317 Five. "Wyndham Lewis's 'Enemy'," *The Experiment,* no. 3 (May) 2-5 (review of *The Enemy, No. 3* analyzing Lewis's attitude towards politics).

F318 [*Unsigned review.*] *The Times Literary Supplement,* XXVIII, no. 1427 (June 6) 459 (reviews *The Enemy, No. 2.* as "subtle and powerful").

F319 Porter, Alan. "The Poor White," *The Spectator,* CXLII, no. 5267 (June 8) 904-905 (favorable review of *Paleface).*

F320 Slater, Montagu. "Journalism and Art: VI—P. Wyndham Lewis," *Arts and Crafts,* III, no. 1 (June) 14-17 (survey of Lewis's career).

F321 Campbell, Roy. "White Laughter," *The New Statesman,* XXXIII, no. 847 (July 20) 473-474 (favorable review of *Paleface* which, however, criticizes Lewis for treating "the colour question as if it were *one* universal problem").

F322 Ransome, John Crowe. "Flux and Blur in Contemporary Art," *The Sewanee Review,* XXXVII, no. 3 (July-September) 353-365 (detailed and critical analysis of *Time and Western Man).*

F323 Cournos, John. "An *Enfant Terrible* of Philosophy," *The Yale Review,* XVIII, no. 18 (Winter) 393-394 (favorably reviews *Time and Western Man).*

1930

F324 Anderson, Margaret. *My Thirty Years' War.* New York: Alfred A. Knopf, passim (Lewis and *The Little Review).*

F325 Fletcher, Ifan Kyrle. *Ronald Firbank: a Memoir.* London: Duckworth, passim.

F326 Gilbert, Stuart. *James Joyce's "Ulysses." A Study.* London: Faber and Faber, passim (Lewis's opinion of "the silent monologue" and the Circe episode in *Ulysses).*

F327 Orage, A. R. *The Art of Reading*. New York: Farrar and Rinehart, passim (unfavorable evaluation of Vorticism, deriding Lewis's "Welshness").

F328 Pound, Ezra. *Imaginary Letters*. Paris: Black Sun Press (Pound's contribution to the sequence originated by Lewis, see D67).

F329 Ward, A. C. *The Nineteen-Twenties. Literature and Ideas in the Post-War Decade*. London: Methuen, 67-68 (discusses *Time and Western Man*).

F330 Waugh, Evelyn. *Vile Bodies*. London: Chapman and Hall (*Blast* mentioned in a footnote and one of the characters is named "Mrs. Ape").

F331 Wilenski, Reginald Howard. *The Modern Movement in Art*. London: Faber and Faber, passim (views Lewis as the only artist in England who understood Cubism).

F332 Pound, Ezra. "Epstein, Belgion, and Meaning," *The Criterion*, IX, no. 36 (April) 471.

F333 Burdett, Osbert. "Mr. Lewis's Satire," *The Saturday Review*, CXLIX, no. 3894 (June 14) 759-760 (criticizes *The Apes of God;* partly reprinted in *Satire and Fiction*, p. 37).

F334 Aldington, Richard. "A Stream of Satire," *The Sunday Referee* (June 22) (highly favorable review of *The Apes of God*, reprinted in *Satire and Fiction*, pp. 32-33).

F335 "The Apes of God," *The Times Literary Supplement*, XXIX, no. 1483 (July 3) 552 (hostile review of *The Apes of God*, "one of the tundras of modern literature"; partly reprinted in *Satire and Fiction*, p. 34).

F336 Mitchison, Naomi. "Anna and the Apes," *Time and Tide*, XI, no. 26 (June 28) 835-836 (favorably reviews *The Apes of God;* partly reprinted in *Satire and Fiction*, p. 33).

F337 Booth, Meyrick. "Our Sham Society—An Interview with Wyndham Lewis," *Everyman*, III, no. 75 (July 3) 707 (see D147; partly reprinted in *Satire and Fiction*, pp. 33-34).

F338 Mais, S. P. B. "Recent Fiction," *The Daily Telegraph* (June 20) 6 (review of *The Apes of God* regretting that Lewis "should waste his giant strength and venom on such unworthy adversaries"; partly reprinted in *Satire and Fiction*, p. 34).

F339 Lynd, Sylvia. *The Daily News* (June 9) 4 (unfavorable review of *The Apes of God* partly reprinted in *Satire and Fiction*, p. 34).

F340 "A Cubist Telephone Book," *The Spectator*, no. 5324 (July 12) 59 (favorable review of *The Apes of God;* partly reprinted in *Satire and Fiction*, p. 36).

F341 "These Be Your Gods. Figures of Cosmic Mirth," *The Glasgow Herald* (June 26) 4 (favorable review of *The Apes of God;* partly reprinted in *Satire and Fiction*, p. 38).

F342 West, Douglas. "Cult of Childishness. Mr. Lewis and the Bright Young People. But Why a Limited Edition?" *The Daily Mail* (June 27) 6 (favorable review of *The Apes of God;* partly reprinted in *Satire and Fiction*, p. 38).

F343 Hartley, L. P. *The Week End Review*, II, no. 21 (August 2) 168 (review of *The Apes of God*, "a most remarkable book" by "a mind preoccupied by the body"; partly reprinted in *Satire and Fiction*, p. 37).

F344 Roberts, R. Ellis. "Ways of Fiction," *The New Statesman*, XXXV, no. 903 (August 16) 597-598 (generally favorable review of *The Apes of God;* but see *Satire and Fiction*, pp. 7-16).

F345 Wyndham, Richard. *The Times* (September 3) (an advertisement, see "A Stop-Press Explosion," A12a(c)).

F346 Campbell, Roy. "Letter to Mr. Wyndham Lewis," *Satire and Fiction*, I (September) 8 (see F347-F358 and C8).

F347 Roberts, Ellis. *Ibid.*, 10-12 (photographic reproduction of letter about *The Apes of God* sent to Roy Campbell).

F348 Campbell, Roy. "Reviewer's Preface," *ibid.*, 13-14.

F349 Campbell, Roy. "The Rejected Review," *ibid.*, 15-16.

F350 Aldington, Richard. *Ibid.*, 23 (letter to Lewis).

F351 Belgion, Montgomery. *Ibid.*, 24 (letter to Lewis).

F352 Beresford, J. D. *Ibid.*, 25 (letter to the Arthur Press).

F353 Booth, Meyrick. *Ibid.*, 26 (letter to the Arthur Press).

F354 John, Augustus. *Ibid.*, 27 (letter to Lewis).

F355 Wells, H. G. *Ibid.*, 28 (letter to the Arthur Press).

F356 Wells, H. G. *Ibid.*, 28 (letter to Lewis).

F357 Yeats, W. B. *Ibid.*, 29 (letter to Lewis).

F358 Belgion, Montgomery. "A Reader's Report for an American Publisher," *ibid.*, 30-31.

F359 Jebb, Gladwyn. "Off the Rails," *The Adelphi*, I, no. 1 (October) 74-76 (hostile review of *The Apes of God*, "a compound of envy, hatred and malice").

1931

F360 Campbell, Roy. *The Georgiad. A Satirical Fantasy in Verse*. London: Boriswood, 54 (refers to Campbell's suppressed review of *The Apes of God*, see C8)

F361 D'Arcy, M. C. *The Nature of Belief*. London: Sheed and Ward, 21-23 (concerns Lewis's opposition to the Time-Cult).

F362 Dilly Tante. [i.e. S. J. Kunitz]. *Living Authors, a Book of Bibliographies*. New York: H. W. Wilson, 226-227.

F363 Hughes, Glenn. *Imagism and the Imagists. A Study in Modern Poetry*. Stanford: Stanford University Press (London: Bowes and Bowes, 1960), passim.

F364 Melville, Cecil F. *The Truth About the new Party (and much else besides concerning Sir Oswald Mosley's political aims, the "Nazi" movement of Herr Adolph Hitler, and the adventure in political philosophy of Mr. Wyndham Lewis)*. London: Wishart, passim (Lewis is seen as "barking the right ideas up the wrong tree").

F365 Morgan, Louise. *Writers at Work*. London: Chatto and Windus, 42-53 (reprints "Wyndham Lewis: the Greatest Satirist of our Day," an interview, see D161).

F366 Rickword, Edgell (editor) "Wyndham Lewis." *Scrutinies*. [Vol. II.] London: Wishart, 139-161.

F367 Voigt, Frederick A. "Hitlerism—Man and Doctrine," *Time and Tide*, XII, no. 5 (January 31) 126-127 (letter following Lewis's first articles on Hitler, concluding that Lewis "has simply been stuffed with Nazi propaganda"; for Lewis's reply see D158).

F368 Hamilton, Cicely. *Ibid.*, 127 (letter in which the author declares that unlike Lewis she "saw no depravity in Berlin"; for Lewis's answer, see D158; see also F372).

F369 Melville, C. F. *Ibid.*, 127 (letter reviewing Lewis's Hitler articles, "very interesting, very brilliantly done"; for Lewis's answer, see D158).

F370 Pound, Ezra. "After Election," *The New Review*, I, no. 1 (January-February) 53-55.

F371 Chambers, W. J. *Time and Tide*, XII, no. 6 (February 7) 159-160 (refering to Lewis's Hitler articles, this letter advocates British fascism which would be "a synthesis of the Italian and German models").

F372 Hamilton, Cicely. "Hitlerism," *Time and Tide*, XII, no. 7 (February 14) (reply to Lewis's answer to F368; see D158).

F373 Voigt, Frederick A. "Hitlerism," *Time and Tide*, XII, no. 8 (February 21) 221 (letter repeating that Lewis "had his leg pulled in grandiose manner," see F367 and F375).

F374 The Walrus. *Ibid.*, 221-222 (letter stating that Lewis "does not know what he is talking about").

F375 Voigt, Frederick A. *Time and Tide*, XX, no. 9 (February 28) 249 (a fresh attack on Lewis making use of the letter sent by "the Walrus," see F374).

F376 Bronovski, J. "D. H. Lawrence," *The Experiment*, no. 7 (Spring) 5-13 (discusses Lewis's evaluation of D. H. Lawrence in *Paleface*).

F377 Wilkinson, Clennell. "Wyndham Lewis on Hitler," *Everyman*, V, no. 114 (April 2) 303 (unfavorable review of *Hitler*, "unsubstantial" and "carelessly written").

F378 Berkeley, Reginald. "The Dictators," *The Saturday Review*, CLI, no. 3937 (April 11) 535 (review of *Hitler*, "stimulating" but "exasperatingly facetious").

F379 "Hitler and his Movement," *The Times Literary Supplement*, XXX, no. 1524 (April 16) 296 (favorable review of *Hitler*).

F380 "Mr. Lewis Amongst the Nazis," *The Spectator*, CXLVI, no. 5634 (April 18) 642-643 (mixed review of *Hitler*).

F381 Simmonds, E. Hayles. "Son of Woman," *Time and Tide*, XII, no. 17 (April 25) 502 (indignant letter about Lewis's treatment of D. H. Lawrence, see D162).

F382 "The Diabolical Principle," *The Times Literary Supplement*, XXX, no. 1526 (April 30) 340 (unfavorable review of *The Diabolical Principle and the Dithyrambic Spectator*, "repetitive" and unconclusive").

F383 Mitchison, Naomi. "Keeping Us Awake," *Time and Tide*, XII, no. 20 (May 16) 596-597 (mixed review of *The Diabolical Principle and the Dithyrambic Spectator*).

F384 "Blutsgefühl," *The New Statesman and Nation*, I, no. 13 (May 23) 469 (reviews *Hitler* as valid as social philosophy, but inaccurate as a political analysis).

F385 "A First Glance at the New Books," *Everyman*, V, no. 122 (May 28) 561 (review of *The Diabolical Principle and the Dithyrambic Spectator*).

F386 "Shorter Notices," *The Adelphi New Series*, II, no. 2 (May) 180-182 (*Hitler* reviewed as no more than "a descriptive sketch").

F387 Lansbury, George. "Youth-Politics," *Time and Tide*, XII, no. 28 (July 11) 831-832 (reviews Lewis's "Doom of Youth" articles).

F388 Chesterton, G. K. "The Doom of Doom. A Reply to Mr. Wyndham Lewis's Articles on Youth-Politics," *Time and Tide*, XII, no. 31 (August 1) 910-913 (the first of two favorable articles, see F390).

F389 "Big Business, Youth and Age. Mr. Wyndham Lewis and Mr. Chesterton," *Time and Tide*, XII, no. 32 (August 8) 935-936.

F390 Chesterton, G. K. "The Doom of Doom," *Time and Tide*, XII, no. 32 (August 8) 935-936 (second of two articles expressing "admiration" for "the genius of Mr. Wyndham Lewis"; see F388).

F391 Porteus, Hugh Gordon. *The Twentieth Century*, I, no. 6 (August) 24-25 (favorable review of *Hitler* and *The Diabolical Principle*).

F392 Porteus, Hugh Gordon. "Wyndham Lewis," *The Twentieth Century*, II, no. 7 (September) 4-6.

F393 Barry, Iris. "The Ezra Pound Period," *The Bookman*, LXXIV, no. 2 (October) 159-171 (survey of Imagism and Vorticism).

F394 Cazamian, M. L. *Revue Anglo-Américaine*, IX, no. 2 (December) 177-179 (review of *Tarr*).

1932

F395 Baker, Ernest A. and James Packman. *A Guide to the Best Fiction*. London: Routledge, passim (discusses *Tarr* and *The Wild Body*).

F396 Booth, Meyrick. *Youth and Sex. A Psychological Study*. London: Allen and Unwin, passim (mentions *The Art of Being Ruled*, *Time and Western Man* and *Doom of Youth*).

F397 Coburn, Alvin Langdon. *More Men of Mark*. London: Duckworth, pl. 22 (includes a photograph of Lewis in front of a lost Vorticist painting, reproduced as frontispiece in Michel).

F398 Fehr, Bernhard. *Das England von heute: Kulturprobleme, Denkformen, Schrifttum*. Leipzig: Verlag von Bernhard Tauchnitz, 82-83, passim (discusses *Time and Western Man*).

F399 Ford, Ford Madox. *Return to Yesterday*. London: Victor Gollancz, passim (reprints "Mr. Lewis and Blast," see F54).

F400 Gawsworth, John [i.e. Terence Ian Fytton Armstrong]. *Apes, Japes and Hitlerism. A Study and Bibliography of Wyndham Lewis.* London: Unicorn Press, pp. 100 (the first book-length study of Lewis, including criticism and a bibliography; for reviews, see F436, F438 and F466).

F401 Hamnet, Nina. *Laughing Torso.* London: Constable, passim (biographical reminiscences of Lewis; 1914-15).

F402 Linati, Carlo. *Scrittori anglo americani d'oggi.* Milano: Corticelli, 21-40 (often mentioned by Lewis, this study defines him as "unclassificabile").

F403 Porteus, Hugh Gordon. *Wyndham Lewis: a Discursive Exposition.* London: Desmond Harmsworth, pp. 303 (important critical study of Lewis; for reviews see F463, F464, F466, F467, F468, F470 and F475).

F404 Rothenstein, Sir William. *Men and Memories, 1900-1922. Recollections of William Rothenstein,* II. London: Faber and Faber, 33.

F405 Rutter, Frank. *Evolution in Modern Art. A Study in Modern Painting.* London: George S. Harrap, passim (reviews Lewis's career from Vorticism to the Tyros).

F406 Scott-James, R. A. *The Making of Literature.* London: Martin Secker, 21 (reviews Lewis's early drawings).

F407 Vines, Sherard (editor). *Whips and Scorpions, Specimens of Modern Satiric Verse, 1914-1918.* London: Wishart, passim (Lewis discussed in preface).

F408 Porteus, Hugh Gordon. "Bombs for Bloomsbury," *The Twentieth Century,* II, no. 11 (January) 4-6 (first of two articles concerned with Roy Campbell's *The Georgiad* and Lewis's *The Apes of God;* see F411).

F409 R. R. *The Adelphi New Series,* III, no. 4 (January) 246-247 (reviews Campbell's *The Georgiad,* see F408).

F410 Rascoe, Burton. "The Other Wyndham Lewis," *New York Herald Tribune Weekly Book Review* (February 28) 7 (a review of *The Apes of God;* includes reproduction of "Self-Portrait" (Michel 642) described as "a caricature by himself").

F411 Porteus, Hugh Gordon. "Bombs for Bloomsbury (II)," *The Twentieth Century,* II, no. 12 (February) 13-15 (favorable review of *The Apes of God;* see F408).

F412 "Homo Sappyens," *Time,* XIX, no. 10 (March 7) 63 (short favorable review of *The Apes of God).*

F413 Stone, Geoffrey. *The Bookman,* LXXIV, no. 6 (March) 696-699 (review of *The Apes of God* ranking it as one of the three "greatest novels" of the twentieth century with *Ulysses* and *Remembrance of Things Past).*

F414 Quennell, Peter. *Life and Letters,* VIII (March-December) 362 (reviews *The Doom of Youth* as "almost dull").

F415 Adler, Henry. "Arnold Bennett as Critic," *Time and Tide,* XIII, no. 14 (April 2) 370 (letter defending Bennett, attacked by Lewis in the "Augean Stables" articles; see D178 and D179).

F416 Barry, Iris. "Too Young for Their Age," *New York Herald Tribune Weekly Book Review* (April 17) 6 (favorably reviews *Doom of Youth).*

F417 Adler, Henry. "Arnold Bennett as Critic," *Time and Tide,* XIII, no. 17 (April 23) 446-447 (response to Lewis's letter, see D181 and F415).

F418 Brooks, W. R. *The Outlook,* CLX (April) 230 (reviews *The Apes of God).*

F419 Marsh, E. T. *The New York Times* (April 17) 2 (reviews *The Apes of God).*

F420 Krutch, Joseph Wood. "Youth Also is Doomed," *The Nation,* CXXXIV, no. 3487 (May 4) 518 (favorable review of *Doom of Youth,* "eccentric . . . and brilliant").

F421 Dekobra, Maurice. "The Art of Making Enemies," *The Daily Herald,* no. 5075 (May 21) 8 (Lewis replied to this article with "What it Feels Like to Be an Enemy," see D182).

F422 Parkes, Henry Bamford. "Wyndham Lewis," *The New Republic,* LXXI, no. 914 (June 8) 105 (reviews of *The Apes of God,* seen as "Lewis's best achievement so far . . . the greatest piece of fiction since *Ulysses,"* and *Doom of Youth.*

F423 Porteus, Hugh Gordon. "Art for Politicians," *The Twentieth Century,* III, no. 16 (June) 20-24.

F424 "Doom of Youth," *The Times Literary Supplement,* XXXI, no. 1588 (July 7) 490 (reviews *Doom of Youth* as "interesting . . . and exasperating").

F425 "Mr. Wyndham Lewis in Barbary," *The Times* (July 5) 19 (analysis of *Filibusters in Barbary).*

F426 Vernon, Grenville. "The Savage Critic," *The Commonweal,* XVI, no. 11 (July 13) 294-295 (review of *The Apes of God* criticizing Lewis's manner of expressing valid ideas).

F427 "Half Morocco," *The Saturday Review,* CLIV, no. 4004 (July 23) 105 (favorable review of *Filibusters in Barbary).*

F428 Benson, Stella. "Wyndham Lewis," *Time and Tide,* XIII, no. 30 (July 23) 819-820 (fairly favorable review of *Filibusters in Barbary, Doom of Youth* and *The Enemy of the Stars).*

F429 Zukofsky, Louis. "The Transition," *The Saturday Review of Literature,* IX, no. 2 (July 30) 18 (review of *Doom of Youth).*

F430 Porteus, Hugh Gordon. "Doomsday Data," *The Twentieth Century,* III, no. 17 (July) 20-22 (review of *Doom of Youth,* "a book of singular importance").

F431 "Mr. Lewis in Barbary," *The Times Literary Supplement,* XXXI, no. 1592 (August 4) 553 (review of *Filibusters in Barbary,* proposing that Lewis has a "frustrated desire to be a filibuster").

F432 Pritchett, V. S. "Crabbed Youth," *The Spectator,* CXLIX, no. 5433 (August 13) 210-211 (review of *Doom of Youth,* finding Lewis "conspiratorial").

F433 Stonier, George Walter. "Air Raid," *The New Statesman and Nation,* IV, no. 77 (August 13) 179-180 (reviews of *Doom of Youth* and *Filibusters in Barbary).*

F434 Thost, H. W. "Does Hitler Mean War," *Time and Tide,* XII, no. 34 (August 22) 987-988 (letter, quoting Lewis, in defense of Hitler).

F435 Owen, Robert. "Lewisite," *The Week-End Review,* VI, no. 129 (August 27) (reviews *Doom of Youth* and *Filibusters in Barbary).*

F436 [*Unsigned review.*] *The Twentieth Century,* III, no. 18 (August) 25 (favorable review of John Gawsworth's *Apes, Japes and Hitlerism,* see F400).

F437 [*Unsigned review.*] *The Twentieth Century,* IV, no. 19 (September) 28 (favorable review of *Enemy of the Stars* and *Filibusters in Barbary).*

F438 "Apes, Japes and Hitlerism," *The Times Literary Supplement,* XXXI, no. 1597 (September 8) 626 (a review of John Gawsworth's *Apes, Japes and Hitlerism;* see F 400).

F439 Hartley, L. P. "Novels," *The Week-End Review,* VI, no. 134 (October 1) 379 (favorable review of *Snooty Baronet).*

F440 "A Comedy of Masks," *The New Statesman and Nation,* IV, no. 85 (October 8) 411 (review of *Snooty Baronet).*

F441 Blunt, A. "Plagiarism and Vulgarity," *The Spectator,* CXLIX, no. 5442 (October 15) 478 (favorable review of the "30 Personalities" exhibition at the Lefèvre Galleries, London).

F442 Holtby, Winifred. "Wyndham Lewis and Comrade Gollancz," *Time and Tide,* XIII, no. 44 (October 29) 1182 (letter marking the beginning of a controversy following Lewis's remarks on Gollancz in "Notes on the Way," see D192; see also F445, F446, F447 and F448).

F443 "Invective and Abuse," *The Bookman,* LXXV, no. 6 (October) 578-579 (review of *Filibusters in Barbary).*

F444 Ross, Patricia. "Wyndham Lewis and our Epoch," *Time and Tide,* XIII, no. 45 (November 5) 1213-1214 (critical letter to the Editor).

F445 Gollancz, Victor. "Wyndham Lewis and Comrade Gollancz," *Time and Tide,* XIII, no. 46 (November 12) 1250 (Gollancz's answer to Lewis's letter; see D192 and F442).

F446 Brittain, Vera. "Wyndham Lewis and Comrade Gollancz," *Time and Tide,* XIII, no. 46 (November 12) 1250 (letter in defence of Gollancz, see D192 and F442).

F447 Porteus, Hugh Gordon. "Wyndham Lewis and Comrade Gollancz," *Time and Tide,* XIII, no. 47 (November 19) (letter in support of Lewis and against "the oppressive respectability of revolution"; see D192 and F442).

F448 Gollancz, Victor. "Wyndham Lewis and Comrade Gollancz," *Time and Tide,* XIII, no. 48 (November 26) 1305 (letter criticizing Porteus's "lack of logic"; see D142 and F442).

F449 [*Unsigned review.*] *Apollo,* XVI, no. 95 (November) 252-253 (favorable review of *Thirty Personalities and a Self-Portrait,* accompanied by six reproductions).

F450 Gaunt, William. "Contemporary Personalities by Wyndham Lewis," *The London Studio,* CIV, no. 476 (November) 262-268 (favorable review of *Thirty Personalities and a Self-Portrait).*

F451 Simon, S. B. *The Adelphi,* V, no. 2 (November) 155-156 (unfavorable review of *Enemy of the Stars* seen as a collection of "Shavian tricks").

F452 Spender, Stephen. *The Twentieth Century,* IV, no. 21 (November) 27 (favorable review of *Snooty Baronet).*

F453 Bourbon, Diana. "Mr. Wyndham Lewis's Pipe Dream," *Time and Tide,* XIII, no. 50 (December 10) 1366.

F454 The Walrus. "Mr. Wyndham Lewis's Pipe Dream," *Time and Tide,* XIII, no. 51 (December 17) 1395.

F455 Schneider, Isidor. "Rummaging in Africa," *The Nation,* CXXXV, no. 3250 (December 21) 623 (review of *Filibusters in Barbary).*

F456 Garman, Douglas. "A Professional Enemy," *Scrutiny,* I, no. 3 (December) 279-282 (unfavorable reviews of *Doom of Youth, Filibusters in Barbary* and *Enemy of the Stars* marked by their "slapdash carelessness in the writing").

1933

F457 Brodzky, Horace. *Henri Gaudier-Brzeska, 1891-1915.* London: Faber and Faber, 166.

F458 Charques, R. D. *Contemporary Literature and Social Revolution.* London: Martin Secker, 168 (Lewis's works contain no "incitement to violence").

F459 Ford, Ford Madox. *It Was the Nightingale.* Philadelphia: Lippincott (London: Heinemann) passim (recollections of Lewis).

F460 Pound, Ezra. *Active Anthology.* London: Faber and Faber (includes "Prefatio Aut Tumulus Cimicium"; reprinted in Ezra Pound's *Polite Essays,* 1937).

F461 Rutter, Frank. *Art in My Time.* London: Rich and Cowan, passim (discusses Lewis's pre-war abstract works).

F462 Stein, Gertrude. *The Autobiography of Alice B. Toklas.* London: John Lane, The Bodley Head, passim (hostile recollections of Lewis).

F463 "Mr. Wyndham Lewis," *The Times Literary Supplement,* XXXII, no. 1617 (January 26) 53 (review of Porteus's *Wyndham Lewis: a Discursive Exposition,* see F403).

F464 Hawkins, A. Desmond. *The Twentieth Century,* IV, no. 23 (January) 29-31 (favorable review of Porteus's *Wyndham Lewis: a Discursive Exposition,* see F403).

F465 Spender, Stephen. *The Criterion,* XII, no. 47 (January) 313-315 (review of *Enemy of the Stars,* stressing "its admirable integrity").

F466 "Visual and Visionary," *The Modern Scot,* III, no. 4 (Winter 1932-1933, January 1933) 364-366 (reviews of *Wyndham Lewis: a Discursive Exposition,* see F403, and *Apes, Japes and Hitlerism,* see F400).

F467 Bridson, D. G. "Wyndham Lewis, Pro and Con," *The New English Weekly,* II, no. 16 (February 2) 376-378 (review of *Wyndham Lewis: a Discursive Exposition,* see F403).

F468 Roberts, Michael. *The Adelphi,* V, no. 5 (February) 385-386 (review of *Wyndham Lewis: a Discursive Exposition,* see F403).

F469 [*Unsigned review.*] *The Times Literary Supplement*, XXXII, no. 1623 (March 9) 171 (non-committal review of *The Old Gang and the New Gang*).

F470 Barnes, T. R. *Scrutiny*, I, no. 4 (March) 400-401 (review of Porteus's *Wyndham Lewis*, see F403, reprinted in *A Selection from Scrutiny*, compiled by F. R. Leavis, Cambridge, 1968).

F471 Stonier, George Walter. "Gog-Magog," *Life and Letters*, IX, no. 49 (June) 191-205 (Lewis on *Ulysses* in *Time and Western Man;* reprinted in *Gog Magog and Other Critical Essays*. London: Dent, 1933).

F472 Wallace, Sarah A. "The Youth Movement Arraigned," *The South Atlantic Quarterly*, XXXII, no. 2 (April) 202-204 (favorable review of *Doom of Youth*).

F474 Pound, Ezra. "Murder by Capital," *The Criterion*, XII, no. 49 (July) 585-592 (remarks on Lewis and "unemployment" among modern artists; reprinted in *Selected Prose*, see F1926).

F475 Roberts, Michael. *The Criterion*, XII, no. 49 (July) 691-694 (favorable review of *Wyndham Lewis: a Discursive Exposition*, see F403).

F476 Stone, Geoffrey. "The Ideas of Wyndham Lewis," *The American Review*, I, no. 5 (October) 578-599 (first part of a detailed survey, see F477).

F477 Stone, Geoffrey. "The Ideas of Wyndham Lewis. Part II," *The American Review*, II, no. 1 (November) 82-96 (see F476).

F478 P., H. [i.e. Herbert Palmer]. "The Machine Poets," *New Britain*, II, no. 28 (November 29) 51 (review of *One-Way Song* attempting to analyze some of its "obscurity"; for Lewis's answer see D195).

F479 Spender, Stephen. "Wyndham Lewis as Poet," *The Spectator*, CLI, no. 5501 (December 1) 812 (favorable review of *One-Way Song*, seen as "constructive satire").

F480 Stonier, George Walter. "New Satires," *The New Statesman and Nation*, VI, no. 145 (December 2) 710-711 (review of *One-Way Song*, "a surprisingly successful performance").

F481 Spender, Stephen. "Politics and Literature in 1933," *The Bookman*, LXXXV, no. 507 (December) 147 (views *One-Way Song* as Lewis's attempt to refute admiration for Hitler).

1934

F482 Campbell, Roy. *Broken Record. Reminiscences*. London: Boriswood, 167, passim (recollections of Lewis).

F483 Dobrée, Bonamy. *Modern Prose Style*. Oxford: Clarendon Press, passim (analyzes passages from *The Wild Body* and *The Childermass*).

F484 Earp, T. W. *Augustus John*. London: Nelson, 58.

F485 Eliot, T. S. *After Strange Gods. A Primer of Modern Heresy*. New York: Harcourt Brace, 63 ("Lewis's brilliant exposure of Lawrence in *Paleface*").

F486 Pound, Ezra. *Make It New*. London: Faber and Faber, 311.

F487 Sitwell, Edith. *Aspects of Modern Poetry*. London: Duckworth, 38 (see D224).

F488 Wilenski, Reginald Howard. *Masters of English Painting*. Boston and New York: Hall, Cushman, and Flint, passim.

F489 Palmer, Herbert. "The Chaste Wand," *New Britain*, II, no. 34 (January 10) 227 (an ironical poem in answer to Lewis's letter; see D195 and F478).

F490 Armitage, Gilbert. "The New Wyndham Lewis," *New Verse*, no. 7 (February) 12-17 (favorable review of *One-Way Song*).

F491 "One-Way Song," *The Times Literary Supplement*, XXXIII, no. 1676 (March 15) 185 (favorable review of *One-Way Song*).

F492 Bramwell, James. "Poetry—II," *The London Mercury*, XXIX, no. 173 (March) 459-460 (favorable review of *One-Way Song*).

F493 Porteus, Hugh Gordon. *The Criterion*, XIII, no. 52 (April) 492-494 (review of *One-Way Song*, "a staggering achievement").

F494 Grigson, Geoffrey. "Art Non-Figuratif," *The Bookman,* LXXXVI, no. 511 (April) 36.

F495 Grigson, Geoffrey. "Modern Art and Official Art," *The Bookman*, LXXXVI, no. 514 (July) 195 (the Tate should not hide away its pictures by Lewis and others).

F496 Neuglass, James. "Angry Man," *The New Republic,* LXXX, no. 1029 (August 22) 53-54 (review of *One-Way Song,* which sees Lewis as "too brilliant for his own good").

F497 [*Unsigned review.*] *Life and Letters,* X, no. 56 (August) 629-631 (a review of Campbell's *Broken Record,* see F482; Lewis and Campbell labelled "outsiders").

F498 Leavis, F. R. "Mr. Eliot, Mr. Wyndham Lewis and Lawrence," *Scrutiny,* III, no. 2 (September) 184-191 (review of Eliot's *After Strange Gods,* see F485, rejecting Lewis's view of Lawrence as expressed in *Paleface).*

F499 Stonier, George Walter. "Personal Appearance Artist," *The New Statesman and Nation,* VIII, no. 189 (October 6) 438-439 (favorable review of *Men Without Art).*

F500 Porteus, Hugh Gordon. "World Without Art," *The Listener,* XII, no. 300 (October) Supplement XI (favorable review of *Men Without Art).*

F501 Spender, Stephen. "One-Way Song," *The Spectator,* CLIII, no. 5547 (October 19) 574-576 (in defense of Virginia Woolf this review finds *Men Without Art* "contradictory and destructive"; see D222).

F502 Grigson, Geoffrey. "The Work of Roger Fry," *The Bookman,* LXXXVII, no. 517 (October) 37 (Lewis was the best "obituarist" of Fry).

F503 Keenan, Peter. "Memories of Vorticism," *The New Hope,* II, no. 6 (October) 5-6, 18-19.

F504 "Mr. Lewis and Mr. Murry," *The Times Literary Supplement,* XXXIII, no. 1712 (November 22) 822 (reviews *Men Without Art* and Rayner Heppenstall's *Middleton Murry: a Study in Excellent Normality.* See D226, D228, F507 and F508).

F505 Chesterton, G. K. "Nothing to Shout About," *The Listener,* XII, no. 307 (November 28) 921 (favorable review of *Men Without Art).*

F506 Dobrée, Bonamy. "Enemy No. 1," *The London Mercury,* XXXI, no. 181 (November) 76-77 (favorable review of *Men With Art* in which Lewis "sustains the position" of Enemy No. 1 with "the careless supremacy of a giant").

F507 The Reviewer. "Mr. Lewis and Mr. Murry," *The Times Literary Supplement,* XXXIII, no. 1714 (December 6) 875 (see F504 and D226).

F508 Murry, John Middleton. "Mr. Lewis and Mr. Murry," *The Times Literary Supplement,* XXXIII, no. 1714 (December 6) 875 (see F504 and D226).

F509 Bridson, D. G. "Sound and Fury," *Poetry,* XLV, no. 3 (December) 165-168 (unfavorable review of *One-Way Song,* "versified pamphleteering").

F510 Collier, John. "Which Book and For Whom?" *The Bookman,* LXXXVII, no. 519 (December) 143-144 (enthusiastic review of *Men Without Art).*

F511 Grigson, Geoffrey. "The Year's Poetry," *The Bookman,* LXXXVII, no. 519 (December) 150-151 (mentions Lewis's answer to the *New Verse* questionnaire).

F512 Grigson, Geoffrey. "The Year's Art," *The Bookman,* LXXXVII, no. 519 (December) 153-154 (Lewis and Henry Moore are among the "deeper and wiser artists").

1935

F513 Cournos, John. *Autobiography.* New York: Putnam's Sons, 268 (brief discussion of *Blast).*

F514 Damon, Forster S. *Amy Lowell: a Chronicle.* Boston: Houghton Mifflin, 229-231 (discussion of Vorticism).

F515 Empson, William. *Some Versions of Pastoral.* London: Chatto and Windus, passim.

F516 Gascoyne, David. *A Short Survey of Surrealism.* London: Cobden-Sanderson, 17 (compares Lewis's comic sense in *The Wild Body* with that of Alfred Jarry).

F517 Goldring, Douglas. *Odd Man Out. The Autobiography of a "Propaganda" Novelist.* London: Chapman and Hall, passim (reminiscences of Ford, *Blast* and Alec Waugh).

F518 Grigson, Geoffrey (editor). "Painting and Sculpture," *The Arts To-Day,* London: John Lane, The Bodley Head, 97-101 (Lewis praised as "the most remarkable artist in England").

F519 Calder-Marshall, Arthur. "Fiction To-Day," *ibid.,* 128-133.

F520 MacNeice, Louis. "Poetry To-Day," *ibid.,* 36-40.

F521 Henderson, Philip. *Literature and a Changing Civilisation.* London: John Lane, The Bodley Head, 136-141 (Lewis is a reactionary).

F522 Read, Herbert and Denis Saurat (editors). *Orage: Selected Essays and Critical Writings.* London: Stanley Nott, 183.

F523 Reade, A. R. *Main Currents in Modern Literature.* London: Nicholson and Watson, passim (compares *The Apes of God* with Aldous Huxley's *Point Counter Point).*

F524 Spender, Stephen. *The Destructive Element.* London: Jonathan Cape, 205-216 (discussion of Lewis's theory of satire).

F525 Swinnerton, Frank. *The Georgian Literary Scene.* London: William Heinemann, 433-459 (discussion concluding that Lewis has "literary genius," but that his subjects are "very nearly worthless").

F526 Bates, Ralph. "Wyndham Lewis," *Time and Tide,* XVI, no. 2 (January 12) 35-37 (the first part of a favorable survey of Lewis's career, regretting Lewis's excessive concern with theory; see F527).

F527 Bates, Ralph. "Wyndham Lewis," *Time and Tide,* XVI, no. 3 (January 19) 90-91 (see F526).

F528 Bridson, D. G. "Men Without Art," *The Criterion,* XIV, no. 55 (January) 335-337 (review of *Men Without Art).*

F529 Wilson, T. C. *The Criterion,* XIV, no. 55 (January) 337 (review of Dobrée's *Modern Prose Style,* see F483).

F530 Königsberg, I. "Wyndham Lewis's Notes on the Way," *Time and Tide,* XVI, no. 10 (March 9) 341 (letter to the editor criticizing Lewis's view of Marxism; see D229).

F531 Thornhill, J. F. P. "Wyndham Lewis's Notes on the Way," *ibid.,* 341 (letter to the editor criticizing Lewis's view of the world of letters and journalism; see D229).

F532 "At the Picture Galleries," *Life and Letters,* XI, no. 63 (March) 755-759 (discussion of Grigson's contribution to *Axis,* in which all British artists but Lewis and Henry Moore are dismissed as unimportant).

F533 Common, Jack. "Martian Opinions," *The Listener,* XIV, no. 339 (July 10) 80 (critical letter concerning Lewis's article "Among the British Islanders"; see D237, D238 and F534).

F534 McKinlay, R. K. S. "Martian Opinions," *ibid.,* 80 (see D237 and D238).

F535 Redwitz, Baron Hans Von. "The Religious Situation in Germany," *The Fascist Quarterly,* I, no. 3 (July) 299-314.

F536 Graham, C. "Wyndham Lewis and the Fanatical Celt," *The Modern Scot,* VI, no. 3 (October) 210-218 (survey of Lewis's career commenting upon the recurrent figure of the extremist Celt in his works).

F537 Tandy, Geoffrey. "Broadcasting Chronicle," *The Criterion,* XIV, no. 57 (July) 627-635 (comment on *Freedom,* see D236).

1936

F538 Barr, Alfred H. *Cubism and Abstract Art.* New York: Museum of Modern Art, passim.

F539 Gorer, Geoffrey. *Nobody Talks Politics. A Satire with an Appendix on our Political Intelligentsia.* London: Michael Joseph, 188-198, passim.

F540 Henderson, Philip. *The Novel To-Day. Studies in Contemporary Attitudes.* London: John Lane, The Bodley Head, 97-102, passim (Lewis and the function of satire).

F541 Hulme, T. E. *Speculations. Essays on Humanism and the Philosophy of Art.* Edited by Herbert Read, with a foreword by Jacob Epstein. London: Kegan Paul, passim.

F542 Sitwell, Edith. "Miss Sitwell on Mr. Grigson," *The Observer* (January 26) 9 (letter to the editor; Grigson is "the very small rabbit that, after years of producing nothing but clouds of bats from under the belfry, Mr. Percy Wyndham Lewis has at length succeeded in producing from under his hat").

F543 Carr, E. H. "The Die-Hard's Dilemma," *The Spectator,* CLVI, no. 5633 (June 12) 1087 (unfavorable review of *Left Wings Over Europe).*

F544 "The Sovereign State," *The Times Literary Supplement,* XXXV, no. 1794 (June 20) 508 (review of *Left Wings Over Europe,* stressing that Lewis "has completely adopted the Nazi outlook").

F545 Howard, Brian, "Seeing *Versus* Believing," *The New Statesman and Nation*, XI, no. 278 (June 20) 991-992 (unfavorable review of *Left Wings Over Europe*, seen as right-wing and self-contradictory, which provoked a reply from Lewis, see D240).

F546 Arns, Karl. "Wyndham Lewis," *Literatur,* XXXVI (June) 85-88 (survey of Lewis's literary production).

F547 Frye, H. Northrop. "Wyndham Lewis: Anti-Spenglerian," *The Canadian Forum,* XVI, no. 185 (June) 21-22.

F548 Muggeridge, Malcolm. "Left Wings Over Europe," *Now and Then,* no. 54 (Summer) 5-6 (review of *Left Wings Over Europe).*

F549 Armitage, Gilbert. "Literary Supplement," *The English Review,* LXIII, no. 1 (July) 83-85 (favorable review of *Left Wings Over Europe).*

F550 "Notes of the Quarter. Left Wings Over Europe," *The Fascist Quarterly,* II, no. 3 (July) (favorable comment on *Left Wings Over Europe).*

F551 T., A. R. [i.e. A. Raven Thompson]. *The Fascist Quarterly,* II, no. 3 (July) 440-443 (review of *Left Wings Over Europe,* considered as "the political book of the year").

F552 Horton, L. M. "The Flights of Wyndham Lewis," *The London Mercury,* XXXIV, no. 201 (July) 277 (favorable review of *Left Wings Over Europe).*

F553 C., J. [i.e. Jack Common]. "Left Wings Over Europe," *The Adelphi,* XII, no. 6 (September) 384 (critical but favorable review).

F554 Höpfl, H. *Literatur,* XXXVIII (September) 597-598 (review of *Left Wings Over Europe).*

F555 Hawkins, A. Desmond. "Books of the Quarter," *The Criterion,* XVI, no. 62 (October) 172-175 (review of *Left Wings Over Europe).*

F556 Stone, Geoffrey. "Left Wings Over Europe. A New Book by Wyndham Lewis," *The American Review,* no. 7 (October) 654-685 (detailed favorable review).

1937

F557 Burke, Kenneth. *Attitudes Towards History, I.* New York: The New Republic, passim (discusses the grotesque, burlesque and satire in Lewis).

F558 Calder-Marshall, Arthur. *The Changing Scene.* London: Chapman and Hall, 115 (Lewis described as a reactionary advocating fascism).

F559 Chamot, Mary. *Modern Painting in England.* London: Country Life, passim (Lewis's pre-war paintings had "far-reaching effects").

F560 Fletcher, John Gould. *Life is My Song.* New York: Farrar and Rinehart, 135-137, passim (recollections of Lewis).

F561 Jepson, Edgar. *Memories of an Edwardian.* London: Richards, 146-149 (about Vorticist social life).

F562 Jerrold, Douglas. *Georgian Adventure.* London: Collins (The "Right" Book Club, 1938) 91-92, passim (mostly about Lewis and T. E. Hulme; for Lewis's review of this book, see D245).

F563 Muller, Herbert J. *Modern Fiction. A Study in Values.* New York: Funk and Wagnalls, 296-297 (Lewis on Joyce).

F564 Nevinson, C. R. W. *Paint and Prejudice.* London: Methuen, passim (numerous recollections of Lewis, described as "the most brilliant theorist" the author had met).

F565 "Select Bibliography," *The British Union Quarterly,* I, no. 1 (January-April) 125 (a selected reading list recommending *Left Wings Over Europe* and *Hitler;* reprinted in later issues with the addition of *Count Your Dead; The Jews, Are They Human?* was advertised in April, 1939 but was dropped afterwards).

F566 Bridson, D. G. "The Old Gang and the New Gang," *The New English Weekly* (March 2) (favorable review of *The Old Gang and the New Gang).*

F567 "A Satirist on the Ideologies," *The Times Literary Supplement,* XXXVI, no. 1840 (May 8) 355 (favorable review of *Count Your Dead,* "decidedly constructive").

F568 "The Revenge for Love," *The Times Literary Supplement,* XXXVI, no. 1842 (May 22) 395.

F569 Reid, Forrest. "Fiction," *The Spectator,* CLVIII, no. 5683 (May 28) 193 (review of *The Revenge for Love).*

F570 Scott-James, R. A. "Two Books by Mr. Wyndham Lewis," *The London Mercury,* XXXVI, no. 212 (June) 201-202 (unfavorable review of *Count Your Dead* with favorable review of *The Revenge for Love).*

F571 Pound, Ezra. "D'Artagnan Twenty Years After," *The Criterion,* XVI, no. 65 (July) 606-617 (Lewis has been "the live writer in England for a quarter of a century").

F572 H., E. D. *The British Union Quarterly,* I, no. 3 (July-September) 99-100 (favorable review of *Count Your Dead).*

F573 "Warfare and Art," *The Times Literary Supplement,* XXXVI, no. 1865 (October 30) 796 (favorable review of *Blasting and Bombardiering).*

F574 Porteus, Hugh Gordon. "Count Your Dead: They Are Alive. The Revenge for Love," *The Criterion,* XVII, no. 66 (October) 133-135 (favorable reviews of *Count Your Dead,* and *The Revenge for Love).*

F575 Smith, James. "Wyndham Lewisite," *The Spectator,* CLXI, no. 812 (November 5) 812 (review of *Blasting and Bombardiering).*

F576 Stonier, George Walter. "Behemoth and Bogyman," *The New Statesman and Nation,* XIV, no. 350 (November 6) 730-732 (favorable review of *Blasting and Bombardiering* combined with a survey of Lewis's books).

F577 "Wyndham Lewis Double Number." Edited by Julian Symons. *Twentieth Century Verse,* nos. 6-7 (November/December) pp. 48 (the first "special issue" devoted to Lewis, see D246 and F578-596).

F578 [Symons, Julian]. "Mr. Wyndham Lewis," *ibid.,* [2] (see F577).

F579 Eliot, T. S. "The Lion and the Fox," *ibid.,* [6-9] (see F577).

F580 Porteus, Hugh Gordon. "Eyes Front (Ideogram)," *ibid.,* [10-15] (Lewis and the philosophy of the Eye, see F577).

F581 Earp, T. W. "The Leicester Galleries Exhibitions," *ibid.,* [15-17] (review of the Leicester Galleries Exhibition, see F577).

F582 Symons, A. J. A. "The Novelist," *ibid.,* [18-21] (evaluates *Tarr, The Childermass* and *The Apes of God,* see F577).

F583 Stonier, G. W. "That Taxi-Driver," *ibid.,* 22-24 (Lewis as literary critic, see F577).

F584 Armitage, Gilbert. "A Note on 'the Wild Body,' " *ibid.,* 24-26 (*The Wild Body* and Lewis's ideological independence, see F577).

F585 Symons, Julian. "A Note on One-Way Song," *ibid.,* 27-29 (*One-Way Song* and Lewis's so-called classicism, see F577).

F586 Lambert, Constant. "An Objective Self Portrait," *ibid.*, 30-32 (*Blasting and Bombardiering*, politics and Lewis's brilliance as both painter and writer, see F577).

F587 Tomlin, E. W. F. "The Philosopher-Politician," *ibid.*, 32-36 (evaluation of Lewis's political and philosophical works, see F577).

F588 Todd, Ruthven. "Comments on a Critic," *ibid.*, 36-38 (Lewis as literary critic, see F577).

F589 Savage, D. S. "Lewis and Lawrence," *ibid.*, 39 (Lewis's polarity to "the one other genius of our time," see F577).

F590 Rhys, Keidrych. "Celtic View," *ibid.*, 40-41 (Lewis's Welsh attitudes, see F577).

F591 Jones, Glyn. "Satiric Eye," *ibid.*, 42 (see F577).

F592 Warner, Rex. "Extract from a Letter," *ibid.*, 43 (see F577).

F593 Ewart, Gawin. "Note," *ibid.*, 43 (brief remarks on a number of books by Lewis, see F577).

F594 Beevers, John. "I Read Lewis," *ibid.*, 44 (seven reasons for reading Lewis, see F577).

F595 Mallalieu, H. B. "Social Force," *ibid.*, 45 (Lewis is more of a social force than the utopists, see F577).

F596 "Checklist," *ibid.*, 45 (announces a Lewis checklist for no. 8, which in fact appeared in no. 9, see F577).

F597 Greene, Graham. "Homage to the Bombardier," *The London Mercury*, XXXVII, no. 218 (December) 219-220 (review of *Blasting and Bombardiering*).

F598 Leavis, F. R. "The Wild Untutored Phoenix," *Scrutiny*, VI, no. 3 (December) 352-358 (review of *Phoenix* with a fresh attack on Lewis. Reprinted in *The Common Pursuit*. London: Harmsworth, 1962).

1938

F599 Connolly, Cyril. *Enemies of Promise*. London: Routledge and Kegan Paul (revised edition, New York: Macmillan, 1949) passim.

F600 Ford, Ford Madox. *Mightier than the Sword. Memories and Criticism.* London: Allen and Unwin, passim (early recollections of Lewis).

F601 Häusermann, H. W. *Studien zur englischen Literarkritik, 1910-1930.* Kölner Anglistische Arbeiten, 34 Band; Bochum-Langendreer, Verlag Heinrich Pöppinghaus, O.H.-G., passim (numerous references to Lewis).

F602 McAlmon, Robert. *Being Geniuses Together. An Autobiography.* London: Martin Secker and Warburg, passim (numerous recollections of Lewis).

F603 Marriott, Charles. *A Key to Modern Painting.* London and Glasgow, Blackie and Son, 88, passim (favorable account of Lewis's artistic activities before the war).

F604 Monroe, Harriet. *A Poet's Life: 70 Years in a Changing World.* New York: Macmillan, 355 (analyzes the *Blast* manifestoes).

F605 Pound, Ezra. *Guide to Kulchur.* Norfolk: New Directions, passim (suggests that disordered minds like Lewis's are of great value in "dead countries" like England).

F606 Roberts, Michael. *T. E. Hulme.* London: Faber and Faber, 20-25, passim (recollections of Lewis including Lewis's reminiscences of T. E. Hulme in *Blasting and Bombardiering*).

F607 Sitwell, Osbert. *Those Were the Days. Panorama with Figures.* London: Macmillan, passim (a reply to *The Apes of God* with a recognizable description of Lewis as "Esor").

F608 Wilson, Arnold. *Wyndham Lewis: Deutschland im Englisch politic Schrifttum.* Kurhess, Erzicher, 82, J. 185.

F609 Yeats, William Butler. *The Autobiography.* London: Macmillan, passim.

F610 Duncan, Ronald. "Blast and About and About," *The Townsman*, I, no. 1 (January) 26-27.

F611 Porteus, Hugh Gordon. "Books of the Quarter," *The Criterion*, XVII, no. 67 (January) 311-314 (favorable review of *Blasting and Bombardiering*, stressing the Irish streak in Lewis).

F612 [*Unsigned review.*] *Apollo,* XXVII, no. 157 (January) 44 (favorable review of the Leicester Galleries exhibition).

F613 [*Unsigned review.*] *The Studio,* LXV, no. 83 (February) 103 (favorable review of *Blasting and Bombardiering).*

F614 Glicksberg, Charles I. "Wyndham Lewis: the Artist in Revolt," *The Calcutta Review,* LXVI (March) 263-279 (on Lewis's political writings).

F615 Hennecke, Hans. "Wyndham Lewis: Vision und Satire," *Europäische Revue,* XIV, no. 3 (March) 205-214.

F616 McGreevy, Thomas. *The Studio,* LXV, no. 84 (March) 154-155 (favorable review of the Leicester Galleries exhibition).

F617 Todd, Ruthven. "Check List of Books and Articles by Wyndham Lewis," *Twentieth Century Verse,* no. 9 (March) 21-27.

F618 "Royal Academy and Mr. Lewis," *The Daily Telegraph and Morning Post* (April 23) 14 (discusses rejected portrait of T. S. Eliot, see following entries and D248; for Lewis's answer, see D249).

F619 "Portrait Rejected by R.A.—Mr. John Resigns," *The Times* (April 26) 3.

F620 Bodkin, Thomas. "The Rejected Portrait," *The Times* (April 27) 19.

F621 Dulac, Edmund. "The Rejected Portrait," *ibid.,* 19.

F622 "The Royal Academy. Retiring R.A.s," *The Times* (April 30) 13.

F623 "The Royal Academy," *ibid.,* 13 (review of the Royal Academy exhibition).

F624 "Variety in Art. Academy Policy. Mr. Churchill on Discipline," *The Times* (May 2) 10 (a report of the Royal Academy Banquet and Winston Churchill's speech in favor of the "disciplinarians"; for Lewis's answer see D252).

F625 Porteus, Hugh Gordon. "Periodicals: English," *The Criterion,* XVII, no. 68 (April) 591-595 (review of the Lewis Number in *Twentieth Century Verse,* see F577).

F626 Lamb, W. R. M. "The Rejected Portrait," *The Times* (May 4) 10 (about Lewis's rejected portrait of T. S. Eliot; for Lewis's answer to this letter, see D253).

F627 "Mortal Blow," *Time,* no. 19 (May 5) 35 (Augustus John on Lewis painting T. S. Eliot).

F628 Nicholson, Sir William. *The Times* (May 5) 17 (for Lewis's answer to this letter, see D253).

F629 Bell, Clive. "The Unacademic Academy," *The New Statesman and Nation,* XV, no. 378 (May 21) 870-872 (expresses complete approval of Lewis's letter to *The Times* (May 2) which described The Royal Academy as "utterly unacademic"; see D251).

F630 Gordon, J. "Split in the Royal Academy," *The Living Age,* no. 354 (June) 362.

F631 March, Richard. "The Apotheosis of Post-Impressionism," *Scrutiny,* VII, no. 1 (June) 21-23 (views Lewis as "tragically attempting the impossible").

F632 Dupee, F. W. "The English Literary Left," *Partisan Review,* V, no. 3 (August-September) 11-21 (England in the 1920's produced modern personalities like Lewis but no modern movement).

F633 Connolly, Cyril. "We English Again," *The New Statesman and Nation,* XVI, no. 407 (December 10) 972-974 (brief review of *The Mysterious Mr. Bull,* "adult and impartial").

F634 "Sleeping John Bull," *The Times Literary Supplement,* XXXVII, no. 1924 (December 17) 795 (review of *The Mysterious Mr. Bull,* "stimulating and mischievous").

1939

F635 Ellis, G. U. *Twilight on Parnassus. A Survey of Post-War Fiction and Prewar Criticism.* London: Michael Joseph, 345-369, passim (many remarks on Lewis's stance as an author).

F636 Ford, Ford Madox. *The March of Literature: from Confucius to Modern Times.* London: Allen and Unwin, 828.

F637 Hone, Joseph. *The Life of Henry Tonks.* London: Heinemann, passim.

F638 Joyce, James. *Finnegans Wake.* London: Faber and Faber (New York: Viking) (contains numerous disguised references to Lewis's personality, philosophy and writings; for critical studies see F784, F942, F1149, F1160, F1173, F1367, F1378 and F1791).

F639 Masterman, Lucy. *C. F. G. Masterman. A Biography.* London, 303-304 (reminiscences of the collection of war paintings).

F640 Pound, Ezra. *Gaudier-Brzeska: a Memoir.* London: Laidlaw, 107 (Lewis and *Timon of Athens).*

F641 Pound, Ezra. *What is Money For?* London: Greater Britain Publications, passim.

F642 Tindall, William York. *D. H. Lawrence and Susan His Cow.* New York: Columbia University Press, passim.

F643 Wilson, Edmund. *The Bit Between my Teeth.* New York, 390 (compares the political attitudes of Lewis, Joyce and Eliot).

F644 T., A. R. [i.e. A. Raven Thomson]. *The British Union Quarterly,* III, no. 1 (January/April) 85-89 (fairly favorable review of *The Mysterious Mr. Bull).*

F645 Pound, Ezra. "René Crevel," *The Criterion,* XVIII, no. 71 (January) 225-235 (reference to Lewis's diatribes).

F646 Symons, Julian. "About Frontiers," *Twentieth Century Verse,* no. 16 (February) 61-63 (favorable review of *The Mysterious Mr. Bull,* seen as "a little brother to *The Art of Being Ruled").*

F647 Rothenstein, John. "Great British Masters—26: Wyndham Lewis," *Picture Post,* II, no. 12 (March 25) 47-50 (general survey accompanied by nine illustrations).

F648 "In Defence of the Jews," *The Times Literary Supplement,* XXXVIII, no. 1938 (March 25) 170 (favorable review of *The Jews, Are They Human?).*

F649 Joad, C. E. M. "Jewish Champion," *The Spectator,* CLXII, no. 5783 (April 28) 718 (favorable review of *The Jews, Are They Human?).*

F650 T., A. R. [i.e. A. Raven Thomson]. *The British Union Quarterly,* III, no. 2 (April/June) 86-89 (review of *The Jews, Are They Human?).*

F651 Spender, Stephen. "The Jews we Deserve." *The New Statesman and Nation,* XVII, no. 428 (May 6) 690-692 (favorable review of *The Jews, Are They Human?*).

F652 "Art and Nature," *The Times Literary Supplement,* XXXVIII, no. 1949 (June 10) 341 (considerations of figurative art inspired by *Wyndham Lewis the Artist, from 'Blast' to Burlington House,* reviewed in the same number, see F653).

F653 "Back to Nature," *ibid.,* 345 ("neutral" analysis of *Wyndham Lewis the Artist, from 'Blast' to Burlington House).*

F654 Kempski, V. S. "Wyndham Lewis: The Enemy—d. Verfassen mysteriösen John Bull," *Adelsblat,* LVII (June) 954.

F655 [*Unsigned review.*] *The Listener,* XXII, no. 550 (July 27) 198-200 (review of *Wyndham Lewis the Artist, from Blast to Burlington House,* which concludes that Lewis is unpopular because he is "so often right").

F656 Pound, Ezra. "Ford Madox (Hueffer) Ford," *The Nineteenth Century and After,* CXXVI, no. 750 (August) 178-181 (reprinted in *Furioso,* Spring 1940, and Ezra Pound's *Selected Prose).*

F657 March, Richard. "The End of the Modern Movement" *Scrutiny,* VIII, no. 2 (September) 209-214 (favorable review of *Wyndham Lewis the Artist, from "Blast" to Burlington House).*

F658 Häusermann, H. W. "Left-Wing Poetry," *English Studies,* XXI, no. 5 (October) 209-212 (Lewis "cannot be called a fascist").

F659 "Smashing the Idol: Mr. Wyndham Lewis on Hitlerism," *The Times Literary Supplement,* XXXVIII, no. 1975 (December 9) 710 (favorable review of *The Hitler Cult).*

1940

F660 Drew, Elizabeth. *Directions in Modern Poetry.* New York: Norton, passim.

F661 Epstein, Jacob. *Let There Be Sculpture. An Autobiography.* New York: Putnam's (reprinted, London, Vista Books, 1963) 59-60, passim.

F662 Graves, Robert and Alan Hodge. *The Long Week-End. A Social History of Great Britain, 1918-1939.* London: Faber and Faber, passim (remarks on Vorticism and Lewis's interest in Fascism).

F663 Muggeridge, Malcolm. *The Thirties: 1930-1940 in Great Britain.* London: Hamish Hamilton, passim (remarks on Lewis and politics).

F664 Pound, Ezra. *Carta da Visita.* Rome: Edizioni di Lettere d'Oggi, passim.

F665 Rutter, Frank. *Modern Masterpieces. An Outline of Modern Art.* London: George Newness, passim (remarks on Lewis's artistic career from the Camden Town Group to the Tyros).

F666 Woolf, Virginia. *Roger Fry. A Biography.* London: Hogarth Press, 192-194 (Omega Workshop).

F667 Wiskemann, Elizabeth. "The Jesuits of To-Day," *The Spectator,* CLXVIII, no. 5880 (January 12) 52 (favorable review of *The Hitler Cult).*

F668 Reckitt, Maurice B. "A Neutral Takes Sides," *The New English Weekly,* XVI, no. 18 (February 22) 265-266 (reviews *The Hitler Cult).*

F669 Kees, Weldon. "Abstract Art Turns Over," *The New Republic,* CII, no. 14 (May 20) (one of the letters occasioned by Lewis's article "The End of Abstract Art," see F670-F673; see also D262 and D263).

F670 Morris, George L. K. *Ibid.*

F671 Reinhardt, Ad. *Ibid.*

F672 Salter, L. J. *Ibid.*

F673 Allen, Cecil. *Ibid.*

F674 "Visiting Englishman," *Time,* no. 10 (September 2) 64 (favorable review of *America, I Presume).*

F675 Dangerfield, John. "What I know About You, Etc," *The Saturday Review of Literature,* XXII (September 7) 14 (reviews *America, I Presume).*

F676 Jenckes, E. N. *The Springfield Republican,* (September 7) 6 (review of *America, I Presume).*

F677 Gannett, Lewis. *The Boston Transcript,* (September 25) 11 (review of *America, I Presume).*

F678 Pruette, Lorine. "Understanding America," *The New York Herald Tribune Weekly Book Review* (September 29) 22 (favorable review of *America, I Presume).*

F679 *The Nation,* CLI, no. 17 (October 26) 400 (review finding *America, I Presume* "amusing but sketchy").

1941

F680 Aldington, Richard. *Life for Life's Sake.* New York: Viking Press, 222 (Lewis and the Sitwells).

F681 Bowen, Stella. *Drawn from Life.* London: Collins, 48-50 (Lewis, Pound and Joyce at the time of *Blast).*

F682 Emmons, Robert. *The Life and Opinions of Walter Richard Sickert.* London: Faber and Faber, 145-148 (Lewis and Sickert at the time of the Camden Group and the London Group).

F683 Levin, Harry. *James Joyce.* Norfolk: New Directions, passim.

F684 Nicholson, Hubert. *Half My Days and Nights.* London: Heinemann, passim (recollections of Lewis).

F685 Pound, Ezra. "Augment of the Novel." Norfolk: *New Directions, VI* (reprinted in the *Agenda* Lewis number; concentrates on *The Apes of God).*

F686 Pevsner, Nicholas. "Ω," *The Architectural Review,* XC, no. 536 (August) 45-48 (references to Lewis and the Omega Workshop).

F687 [*Unsigned review.*] *The Virginia Quarterly,* XVII, no. 1 (Winter) 19 (reviews *America, I Presume).*

F688 Heath, Egon. "New Novels," *Time and Tide,* XXII, no. 51 (December 20) 1130-1132 (review of *The Vulgar Streak,* an "allegory" and a "bomb").

F689 Muir, Edwin. "New Novels," *The Listener,* XXVI, no. 676 (December 24) 862 (review of *The Vulgar Streak* found to be "an unconvincing novel in spite of its brilliant social criticism").

F690 [*Unsigned review.*] *The Observer* (December 28) (a review of *The Vulgar Streak).*

F691 "Cult of Class," *The Times Literary Supplement,* XL, no. 2082 (December 27) 653 (favorable review of *The Vulgar Streak).*

F692 Straus, Ralph. "Novels of the Week," *The Sunday Times* (December 28) 3 (review of *The Vulgar Streak).*

1942

F693 Frierson, William C. *The English Novel in Transition.* Norman: University of Oklahoma Press, 268-269 (Lewis as satirist).

F694 Hone, Joseph. *W. B. Yeats.* London: Macmillan, passim (references to Lewis).

F695 Kunitz, Stanley J. (pen-name: "Dilly Tante") and Howard Haycraft (editors). *Twentieth Century Authors.* New York: H. W. Wilson (biographical note).

F696 J., K. "Notes for the Novel-Reader: Fiction of the Month," *The Illustrated London News* (January 24) 121 (favorable review of *The Vulgar Streak,* "baffling yet tender").

F697 Fane, Vernon. "Wyndham Lewis and the Old School Tie," *The Sphere,* CLXVIII, no. 2193 (January 31) (fairly favorable review of *The Vulgar Streak).*

F698 Hawkins, A. Desmond. "New Novels," *The New Statesman and Nation,* XXIII, no. 574 (February 21) 128-129 (sympathetic but critical appraisal of *The Vulgar Streak).*

1943

F699 Goldring, Douglas. *South Lodge. Reminiscences of Violent Hunt, Ford Madox Ford and the English Review Circle.* London: Constable, 60-71, passim (numerous recollections of Lewis).

1944

F700 Connolly, Cyril. *The Condemned Playground. Essays: 1927-1944.* London: Routledge, 118.

F701 Rothenstein, John. *Augustus John.* London: George Allen and Unwin; New York: Oxford University Press, 9.

F702 Savage, D. S. *The Personal Principle. Studies in Modern Poetry.* London: Routledge, 1-11 (discusses the Lewisian distinction between romanticism and classicism).

F703 McLuhan, H. M. "Wyndham Lewis: Lemuel in Lilliput," *St. Louis Studies in Honour of St. Thomas Aquinas,* II, 58-72.

F704 Rothenstein, John. "Tate Gallery Acquisitions, April 1942-January 1944," *The Studio,* CXXVII, no. 614 (May) 147-151.

1945

F705 Antheil, George. *Bad Boy of Music.* New York: Hurst and Blackett, passim (recollections of Lewis in Paris).

F706 Goldring, Douglas. *The Nineteen Twenties. A General Survey and Some Personal Memories.* London: Nicholson and Watson, passim (many recollections of Lewis).

F707 Ginner, Charles. "The Camden Town Group," *The Studio,* CXXX, no. 632 (November) 129-136.

1946

F708 Ayrton, Michael. *British Drawings.* London: Collins, 45-46 (Lewis is "perhaps the greatest living draughtsman").

F709 Hoffman, Frederick J., Charles Allen and Carolyn F. Ulrich. *The Little Magazine. A History and a Bibliography.* Princeton: Princeton University Press, 23-24, 82-83, passim (discusses *Blast* and *The Enemy).*

F710 Jackson, Holbrook. *The Reading of Books.* London: Faber and Faber, 178-179 (favorable review of *One-Way Song).*

F711 Routh, H. V. *English Literature and Ideas in the Twentieth Century.* London: Methuen, 140 (Lewis and the classical revival).

F712 Orwell, George [i.e. Eric Hugh Blair]. "London Letter," *Partisan Review,* XIII, no. 3 (Summer) 323 (Orwell has been informed that Lewis has become a communist; for Lewis's reaction, see *Rude Assignment,* 78-80).

F713 Sylvester, A. D. B. "Poetry Review," *The Listener,* XXXVI, no. 934 (December 5) 799 (letter to the editor stating that "the Enemy hysteria" ruined Lewis's work).

1947

F714 Hulme, T. E. *The Articles Contributed by T. E. Hulme to "The New Age,"* compiled by Philip J. Leddy Jr. New York: Columbia University Press, passim (numerous references to Lewis).

F715 Grigson, Geoffrey. *The Harp of Aeolus and Other Essays on Art, Literature and Nature.* London: Routledge, 158-159 (on Lewis's attack on *transition* in *The Diabolical Principle).*

F716 Phelps, Gilbert (editor). *Living Writers.* London: The Sylvan Press, passim (includes "Living Writers, 5: Wyndham Lewis," a broadcast talk by Geoffrey Grigson, transmitted by *B.B.C. Third Programme* on November 2, 1946).

F717 Putnam, Samuel. *Paris Was Our Mistress: Memoirs of a Lost and Found Generation.* New York: Viking Press, passim (quotes Gertrude Stein on Lewis).

F718 Sickert, Walter Richard. *A Free House, or the Artist as Craftsman. Being the Writings of Walter Richard Sickert.* Osbert Sitwell, editor. London: Macmillan, passim (Sitwell's recollections of a humiliating dinner for Lewis).

F719 Sitwell, Osbert. *Great Morning.* Boston: Little, Brown and Co. (London: Macmillan, 1948) 229-230 (Lewis's frescoes in the Cabaret Club).

F720 Tindall, William York. *Forces in Modern British Literature.* New York: Alfred A. Knopf, 87-89, passim (even among "right-thinking men Wyndham Lewis seems extravagant").

F721 "Satire in the Twenties," *The Times Literary Supplement,* XLVI, no. 2380 (September 13) 464 (this review of a collected edition of Gerhardi's novels repeatedly mentions *Tarr* to illustrate the influence of Russian fiction in England. For Lewis's response see D279; see also F722).

F722 "Satire in the Twenties," *The Times Literary Supplement,* XLVI, no. 2382 (September 27) 493 (reviewer's answer to Lewis's letter, see F721 and D279; Lewis later admitted his error, see D280).

1948

F723 Ayrton, Michael. "Introduction," *The Unfortunate Traveller, by Thomas Nashe.* London: John Lehmann, 9 (Joyce's and Lewis's debt to Nashe).

F724 Goldring, Douglas. *The Last Pre-Raphaelite. A Record of the Life and Writings of Ford Madox Ford.* London: Macdonald (published under new title, *Trained for Genius.* New York: E. P. Dutton, 1949) passim (many references to the *English Review/Blast* period).

F725 Goldring, Douglas. *Life Interests, with a Preface by Alec Waugh.* London: Macdonald, 193 (Lewis and *The English Review).*

F726 Gorman, Herbert. *James Joyce.* New York: Rinehart, passim.

F727 Hyman, Stanley Edgar. *The Armed Vision. A Study in the Methods of Modern Literary Criticism.* New York: Alfred A. Knopf (reprinted, New York: Vintage Books, 1955) passim (takes a most negative view of Lewis).

F728 Pound, Ezra. *If This Be Treason.* Siena: privately printed for Olga Rudge, 4-6, 29-33, passim (detailed comparison of Joyce, Cummings and Lewis).

F729 Soby, James Thrall. *Contemporary Painters.* New York: Museum of Modern Art, 115-121 (Vorticism as a vital factor in the history of English art).

F730 Porteus, Hugh Gordon. "Resurrection in the Crypt," in *T. S. Eliot. A Symposium.* London: Editions Poetry London, 218-224 (about the impact of the quartet Eliot, Joyce, Pound, Lewis, see also B26).

F731 Mégroz, R. L. "The Pre-Raphaelite Brotherhood," *The Listener,* XXXIX, no. 1005 (April 29) (letter criticizing Lewis for "spreading the current mythology about 'PRB'"; see D282 and D283).

F732 Edwards, Ralph. "Standards in Art Criticism," *The Listener,* XXXIX, no. 1012 (June 17) 975 (letter commenting upon Lewis's article of June 10, see D285, and deploring the lack of common standards among critics; for Lewis's reply, see D286).

F733 Sewter, A C. "Standards in Art Criticism," *The Listener,* XXXIX, no. 1013 (June 24) 1009 (letter describing Lewis as an "average art critic"; for Lewis's reply, see D287).

F734 Stelling, David. "Standards in Art Criticism," *ibid.* (letter supporting a movement to establish "valid standards" of criticism).

F735 Porter, Margery. "Standards in Art Criticism," *The Listener,* XL, no. 1014 (July 1) 22 (a letter criticizing Lewis's idea of critical "standards"; for Lewis's answer, see D288).

F736 Sewter, A. C. "Standards in Art Criticism," *The Listener,* XL, no. 1015 (July 8) 61 (see F733 and D287; for Lewis's answer, see D290).

F737 Sylvester, A. D. B. "Standards in Art Criticism," *ibid.* (letter stressing the personal origin of critical "standards").

F738 Heron, Patrick. "Standards in Art Criticism," *The Listener,* XL, no. 1016 (July 15) 99 (letter on the constant necessary modification of critical standards; for Stelling's answer, see F740).

F739 Edwards, Ralph. "Standards in Art Criticism," *ibid.*, 100 (letter defending critical standards by consensus; for Lewis's answer, see D291).

F740 Stelling, David. "Standards in Art Criticism," *The Listener,* XL, no. 1017 (July 22) 133 (reply to Heron's letter, see F738).

F741 "Salvation from the West," *The Times Literary Supplement,* XLVII, no. 2485 (October 2) 554 (strongly unfavorable review of *America and Cosmic Man;* see D294 and F742).

F742 "America and Cosmic Man," *The Times Literary Supplement,* XLVII, no. 2488 (November 6) 625 (reviewer's answer to Lewis, see F741 and D294).

1949

F743 Gaunt, William. *The March of the Moderns.* London: Jonathan Cape, 146-150, passim (discusses Vorticism).

F744 Hoffman, Frederick J. *The Twenties.* New York: The Viking Press (revised edition, Collier Books Edition, 1962) passim (discusses *Time and Western Man* and *Paleface).*

F745 *James Joyce.* Paris: La Hune, passim (catalogue of the exhibition, October-November; includes reproduction of *The Enemy* with a hostile commentary).

F746 Nash, Paul. *Outline. An Autobiography and Other Writings,* with a preface by Herbert Read. London: Faber and Faber, 166.

F747 Sitwell, Osbert. *Laughter in the Next Room.* London: Macmillan, passim (recollections of Lewis).

F748 Symons, Julian. "The Background of Modern Poetry, no. 9: The Romantic Reaction in Modern Poetry," a broadcast talk, *B.B.C., Third Programme* (January 3) ("Song of Militant Romance" is a brilliant exposition of the extreme romantic attitude).

F749 "Shorter Notices," *The Spectator,* CLXXXII, no. 6290 (January 14) 60-62 (reviews *America and Cosmic Man* as a slapdash effort).

F750 [*Unsigned review.*] *Kirkus,* XVII (March) 12 (review of *America and Cosmic Man).*

F751 Lerner, Max. "On a Certain Conflict in Foreigners," *The New Republic,* CXX, no. 16 (April 18) 16-17 (favorable review of *America and Cosmic Man).*

F752 Ayrton, Michael. "Foreword," *Wyndham Lewis.* London: Redfern Gallery, May 5-8, [3] (preface to the exhibition catalogue; Lewis as an "articulate artist" who is subjected to a "conspiracy of silence").

F753 Heron, Patrick. "Wyndham Lewis," *The New Statesman and Nation,* XXXVII, no. 948 (May 7) 468 (review of the Redfern Gallery exhibition discussing Lewis's art of portraiture).

F754 Melville, Robert. "Portrait of the Artist, no. 7: Wyndham Lewis," *Art News and Review,* I, no. 7 (May 7) 1, 3 (surveys Lewis's career, expressing regret that he wasted his time on polemics).

F755 Newton, Eric. "Emergence of Mr. Lewis," *The Listener,* XLI, no. 1060 (May 19) 852 (reprinted in *In My View.* London: Longmans, Green and Co., 1950).

F756 [*Unsigned review.*] *The New Yorker,* XXV, no. 17 (June 18) 79 (review of *America and Cosmic Man).*

F757 Larabie, Eric. *The New York Times* (June 19) 8 (review of *America and Cosmic Man).*

F758 Bourjaily, Vance. *The San Francisco Chronicle* (June 24) 18 (review of *America and Cosmic Man).*

F759 Nevins, Allan. "Citizens of the World, Unite," *The Saturday Review of Literature,* XXXII (June 25) 14 (reviews *America and Cosmic Man* as a misinformed book but one worth reading).

F760 Perspex. "Current Shows and Comments," *Apollo,* XLIX, no. 292 (June) 140 (favorable review of the Redfern Gallery exhibition).

F761 "The New Look," *Time,* LXIV (July 4) 70-71 (review of *America and Cosmic Man* contrasting Lewis's vision of America with T. S. Eliot's).

F762 Brinton, Crane. "A Mad Hatter's Party," *New York Herald Tribune Weekly Book Review* (July 10) 7 (unfavorable review of *America and Cosmic Man).*

F763 Bazelon, David T. "Rediscovery of America," *Partisan Review,* XVI, no. 8 (August) 861-864 (this review describes *America and Cosmic Man* as "a very rich book").

F764 Kraft, Joseph. "A New Creature," *The Nation,* CLXIX, no. 10 (September 3) 234-235 (*America and Cosmic Man* dismissed as nonsense).

F765 "Wanted: New Goose," *Time,* LIV, no. 13 (September 26) 72 (on Lewis announcing the end of art on the B.B.C.).

F766 Rothenstein, John. "Tate Gallery Acquisitions, 1944-1949," *The Studio,* CXXXVIII, no. 678 (September) 65-71 (includes "The Siege [sic] of Barcelona," Michel P61).

F767 Gordon, Cora J. "London Commentary," *ibid.*, 93-95 (favorable review of the Redfern Gallery Exhibition).

F768 Porteus, Hugh Gordon. "The Great Outsider," *Nine*, I, no. 1 (Autumn) 34-37 (Lewis and the Redfern Gallery exhibition).

F769 Sinclair, Beryl. "Round the London Galleries," *The Listener*, XLII, no. 1086 (November 24) 909 (letter correcting Lewis's description of the Lisle Street Gallery; for Lewis's answer, see D313).

F770 "Pinsent." *Ibid.*, 909 (letter criticizing Lewis for his use of the word "Impressionism"; for Lewis's answer, see D313).

F771 Seaver, Edwin. "My Favorite Forgotten Book," *To-Morrow*, IX, no. 3 (November) 61-62 (*Tarr* is "still a seminal book").

F772 Wrong, Denis H. "America as the Future," *Commentary*, VIII, no. 5 (November) 510-512 (favorable review of *America and Cosmic Man)*.

1950

F773 Allott, Kenneth. *The Penguin Book of Contemporary Verse.* Harmondsworth: Penguin Books, 71-72, passim (bibliographical note accompanied by Lewis's remarks on *One-Way Song*, see B29)

F774 Eliot, T. S. *Selected Essays.* New York: Harcourt Brace, 126-128, passim (discussion of *The Lion and the Fox)*.

F775 Grigson, Geoffrey. *The Crest on the Silver.* London: Cresset Press, passim (recollections of Lewis).

F776 Henn, T. R. *The Lonely Tower (Studies in the Poetry of W. B. Yeats).* London: Methuen, passim.

F777 Herbert-Dell, Mollie. *An Introduction to the Works of P. Wyndham Lewis.* Leeds University (unpublished doctoral thesis, apparently the first one devoted to Lewis).

F778 Johnstone, William. *Creative Art in Britain.* London: Macmillan, 215 (revises the 1936 edition; Lewis created "a new awareness").

F779 Pound, Ezra. *The Letters*, edited by D. D. Paige. New York: Harcourt, Brace and Co., passim (many references to Lewis in the foreword by Paige and in the letters; see F946 and for Lewis's review D336).

F780 Raynal, Maurice [et al]. *Histoire de la Peinture moderne. De Picasso au Surréalisme.* Genève: Albert Skira, 110, passim (discusses Vorticism).

F781 Russell, Peter. "Introduction," *Ezra Pound. A Collection of Essays to be Presented to Ezra Pound on His Sixty-fifth Birthday.* London: Peter Nevill (Vorticism, Lewis and Pound; see also B28).

F782 McLuhan, Herbert Marshall. "Pound's Critical Prose," *ibid.*, 168 (Lewis and others helping Pound before 1922).

F783 Symons, Julian. *A. J. A. Symons, his Life and Speculations.* London: Eyre and Spottiswoode, 123 (about the first Corvine Banquet in December 1929).

F784 Tindall, William York. *James Joyce. His Way of Interpreting the Modern World.* New York: Scribner's, 92 (about Lewis and the fable of The Mookse and the Gripes in *Finnegans Wake*, see F638).

F785 "The Meaning of Nine," *Nine*, II, no. 1 (January) 6 (Chinese characters for "man" and "nine" signifies "the Enemy").

F786 Pryce-Jones, Alan. "Little Reviews and Big Ideas," *The Listener*, XLIII, no. 1099 (February 16) 285-286 (favorable comments on *Blast* and *The Enemy)*.

F787 Russell, Peter. "The Poetry of Roy Campbell," *Nine*, II, no. 3 (Spring) 81-86 (Lewis's "Dumb-Ox" and Campbell's Bull-Fighting).

F788 Symons, Julian. "The Novel of Appearance," *Tribune*, no. 692 (April 14) 16-17 (about *Tarr)*.

F789 Bell, Clive. "How England Met Modern Art," *Art News*, XLIX (October) 24-27, 61.

F790 Lord Brand. "Henry Moore's Head of a Child," *The Listener*, XLIV, no. 1134 (November 23) 595-596 (a letter marking the beginning of the Nature-and-Art controversy, see D326).

F791 Nicholson, Harold. "Discordant Voice," *The Observer* (November 26) 7 (favorable review of *Rude Assignment).*

F792 Russell, Peter. "The Enemy's Defense Measures," *Nine,* III, no. 6 (Winter) 87-88 (review of *Rude Assignment).*

F793 Speed, Harold. "Nature and Art," *The Listener,* XLIV, no. 1136 (December 7) 893 (the Nature-and-Art controversy, see D326 and F790, for Lewis's answer see D329 and D335; also F817).

F794 Allen, Walter. "Writers in Society," *The New Statesman and Nation,* XL, no. 1032 (December 16) 630-632 (very favorable review of both *Rude Assignment* and Geoffrey Grigson's *The Crest of the Silver,* see F775).

F795 Evleigh, J. and H. M. Robson. "Nature and Art," *The Listener,* XLIV, no. 1137 (December 21) (the Nature-and-Art controversy, see D326 and F790, and for Lewis's answer D330).

F796 Lawrence, A. K. "Nature and Art," *The Listener,* XLIV, no. 1138 (December 28) 839 (for Lewis's answer see D331).

1951

F797 Bertram, Anthony. *A Century of British Painting, 1851-1951.* London: The Studio Publications, 90-92, passim (remarks on Lewis's artistic style).

F798 Brooke, Jocelyn. *Ronald Firbank.* London: Arthur Barker Ltd., passim (Lewis belonged to Firbank's circle in 1919).

F799 Calder-Marshall, Arthur. *The Magic of my Youth.* London: Rupert Hart-Davis, passim.

F800 Coffman, Stanley K., Jr. *Imagism. A Chapter for the History of Modern Poetry.* Norman: University of Oklahoma Press, passim (a survey of the period 1910-1915).

F801 Cowley, Malcolm. *Exile's Return.* New York: The Viking Press, 122, passim (Lewis viewed as "a man of amazing intellectual force").

F802 Empson, William. *The Structure of Complex Words.* London: Chatto and Windus, passim (about Lewis on Iago in *The Lion and the Fox).*

F803 Grigson, Geoffrey. *A Master of Our Time. A Study of Wyndham Lewis.* London: Methuen, pp. 32 (for a review of this book, see F825).

F804 Gwynn, F. L. *Sturge Moore and the Life of Art.* Lawrence: University of Kansas Press, passim (*One-Way Song* and Moore).

F805 Handley-Read, Charles. *The Art of Wyndham Lewis. With an Essay on detail in the Artist's style, a Chronological Outline and Notes on the plates by Charles Handley-Read, and a Critical evaluation by Eric Newton.* London: Faber and Faber, pp. 109 (52 plates) (first full-length study of Lewis's art, including reproductions of his work).

F806 Innis, Harold A. *The Bias of Communication.* Toronto: University of Toronto Press, 89-90 (Lewis and "the time-denying mind").

F807 Isaacs, Jakob. *An Assessment of Twentieth Century Literature.* London: Secker and Warburg, passim (remarks on various books by Lewis).

F808 Kenner, Hugh. *The Poetry of Ezra Pound.* London: Faber and Faber (Norfolk: New Directions) passim (on Lewis and Pound).

F809 McLuhan, Herbert Marshall. *The Mechanical Bride: Folklore of Industrial Man.* New York: Vanguard Press, passim (makes use of *Tarr* and *The Art of Being Ruled).*

F810 Moore, Harry T. *The Life and Works of D. H. Lawrence.* New York: Twayne Publishers, 335 (finds *Paleface* "clever").

F811 Neill, S. Diana. *A Short History of the English Novel.* New York: Macmillan (London: Jarrolds) 384-386, passim (focuses on *The Childermass* as the modern *Pilgrim's Progress).*

F812 Scott-James, R. A. *Fifty Years of Literature, 1900-1950*. London: Longmans, Green, 165-166 (Lewis as rebel).

F813 Lord Brand. "Nature and Art," *The Listener*, XLV, no. 1140 (January 4) 22 (for Lewis's response see D332).

F814 "A Cleansing Operation," *The Times Literary Supplement*, L, no. 2553 (January 5) 3 (general assessment of Lewis's career with a favorable review of *Rude Assignment*).

F815 Lawrence, A. K. "Nature and Art," *The Listener*, XLV, no. 1141 (January 11) 64 (for Lewis's response to this letter see D333).

F816 Lord Brand. "Nature and Art," *The Listener*, XLV, no. 1142 (January 18) 110 (for Lewis's response to this letter see D335).

F817 Speed, Harold. "Nature and Art," *The Listener*, XLV, no. 1142 (January 18) 110 (for Lewis's response to this letter see D335).

F818 Miskin, Lionel. "Aspects of Modern British Painting," *Envoy*, IV, no. 16 (March) 33-43 (singles out Lewis as "the greatest" influence in modern English painting).

F819 Fjelde, Rolf. "Time, Space and Wyndham Lewis," *Western Review*, XV, no. 3 (Spring) 201-212 (analyzes Lewis's attack on the neo-romantic time-cult).

F820 Hannah, Marie. "The Enemy," *Britain To-Day*, no. 1180 (April) 42-43 (favorable review of *Rude Assignment* analyzing Lewis's unpopularity).

F821 "British Painting. The Past 25 Years," *The Times* (May 1) 6 (review of the Arts Council exhibition at the New Burlington Galleries).

F822 Scott, J. D. "On Re-Reading Wyndham Lewis," *B.B.C., Third Programme* (June 25) (typescript of a broadcast talk).

F823 Campbell, Roy. "Wyndham Lewis," *Time and Tide*, XXXII, no. 27 (July 7) 650 (review of *Tarr*).

F824 Bridson, D. G. "Outside the City of Heaven," *The Radio Times*, CXI, no. 1440 (June 15) 9 (account of *The Childermass* which was broadcast on Monday (June 18) B.B.C. Third Programme).

F825 "The Price of Singularity," *The Times Literary Supplement*, L, no. 2580 (July 13) 436 (this favorable review of *Tarr* and Grigson's *A Master of Our Time* presents a survey of Lewis's career and an analysis of his isolation, see F803).

F826 Pritchett, V. S. "Books in General," *The New Statesman and Nation*, XLII, no. 1063 (July 21) 73-74 (favorable review of *Tarr* and an analysis of Lewis's style; reprinted in *Books in General* under the title "The Eye-Man," 1953).

F827 Fausset, Hugh P. A. "New Fiction," *Manchester Guardian* (December 7) 4 (favorable review of *Rotting Hill*).

F828 "Political Themes," *The Times Literary Supplement*, L, no. 2601 (December 7) 777 (unfavorable review of *Rotting Hill*).

F829 Lean, Tangye. *The Spectator*, CLXXXVII, no. 6442 (December 14) 832 (unfavorable review of *Rotting Hill*).

1952

F830 Baker, Carlos. *Hemingway: the Writer as Artist*. Princeton: Princeton University Press, passim (about Hemingway as seen in *Men Without Art*).

F831 Bénézit, E. *Dictionnaire Critique et Documentaire des Peintres, Sculpteurs, Dessinateurs et Graveurs*. Paris: Librairie Gründ, 559.

F832 Brooks, Van Wyck. *The Confident Years, 1885-1915*. London: Dent, passim (on Lewis and America).

F833 Brunius, Av Teddy. *Pionjärer och Fullföljare i Modern Engelsk Lyrik ock Kritik*. Stockholm: Natur och Kultur, 1952.

F834 Campbell, Roy. *Light on a Dark Horse. An Autobiography 1901-1935.* Chicago: Regnery, passim (many recollections of Lewis).

F835 Innis, Harold A. *Changing Concepts of Time.* Toronto: University of Toronto Press, 115 (about *The Art of Being Ruled).*

F836 John, Augustus. *Chiaroscuro. Fragments of an Autobiography.* London: Jonathan Cape, passim (many recollections of Lewis).

F837 Leavis, F. R. *The Common Pursuit.* London: Chatto and Windus (reprints "Mr Eliot, Mr Wyndham Lewis and Lawrence," "The Wild Untutored Phœnix," and "Approaches to T. S. Eliot").

F838 Mendilow, A. A. *Time and the Novel.* London: Peter Nevill, passim (on Lewis's vindication of space in *Time and Western Man).*

F839 Scott, Nathan A., Jr. *Rehearsals of Discomposure. Alienation and Reconciliation in Modern Literature: Franz Kafka, Ignazio Silone, D. H. Lawrence, T. S. Eliot.* London: John Lehmann, 119 (about the Romanticism/Classicism controversy).

F840 Read, Herbert. *The Philosophy of Modern Art.* London: Faber and Faber, passim (English artists like Lewis "have suffered from a disastrous form of individualism").

F841 Ross, Margery (editor). *Robert Ross, Friend of Friends.* London: Jonathan Cape, 236 (contains a letter about *The Ideal Giant).*

F842 Sweeney, J. J. "The Literary Artist and the Other Arts," *Spiritual Problems in Contemporary Literature,* edited by Hopper, S. R., The Institute for Religious and Social Studies. New York: Harper and Brothers, passim (discusses *The Caliph's Design).*

F843 Scott, J. D. "New Novels," *The New Statesman and Nation,* XLIII, no. 1087 (January 5) 18 (this review finds *Rotting Hill* both "irritating" and "empty").

F844 Gilling-Smith, Dryden. "The Rotting Hill," *The Social Creditor,* XXVII, no. 19 (January 5) 5-7 (the first part of a detailed favorable study of *Rotting Hill,* see F845).

F845 Gilling-Smith, Dryden. "The Rotting Hill," *The Social Creditor,* XVIII, no. 20 (January 12) 5-7 (see F844).

F846 Heron, Patrick. "Wyndham Lewis the Artist," *The New Statesman and Nation,* XLIII, no. 1088 (January 12) 43-44 (review of Charles Handley-Read's *The Art of Wyndham Lewis,* see F805).

F847 "Satire by Wyndham Lewis," *The Times Literary Supplement,* LI, no. 2607 (January 18) 66 (unfavorable review of *The Apes of God).*

F848 Reade, Brian. "Dragon in a Cage," *The Observer* (January 20) 7 (favorable review of Charles Handley-Read's *The Art of Wyndham Lewis,* see F805).

F849 Nicolson, Benedict. "Wyndham Lewis," *Time and Tide,* XXXIII, no. 7 (February 16) 158 (review of Charles Handley-Read's *The Art of Wyndham Lewis,* see F805).

F850 Richards, I. A. "Talk," *B.B.C.,* Third Programme (March 10) (typescript text of a broadcast, reprinted in the *Agenda* Lewis number).

F851 [*Unsigned review.*] *Kirkus,* XX (March 15) 195 (review of *Rotting Hill).*

F852 Engle, Paul. *Chicago Sunday Tribune* (April 13) 3 (review of *Rotting Hill).*

F853 Sweeney, J. J. *New York Times* (April 13) 5 (review of *Rotting Hill).*

F854 "Raging Briton," *Time Magazine,* LXIX, no. 15 (April 14) 114, 117-118, 120 (detailed favorable review of *Rotting Hill).*

F855 [*Unsigned review.*] *The New Yorker,* XXVIII, no. 9 (April 19) 130 (review of *Rotting Hill).*

F856 [*Unsigned review.*] *The Month,* VII, no. 4 (April) 253-254 (favorable review of *Rotting Hill).*

F857 Curtis, John. *The Studio,* CXLIII, no. 709 (April) 128 (review of Charles Handley-Read's *The Art of Wyndham Lewis* stating that Lewis's lack of popularity is due to his lack of human warmth, see F805).

F858 Webster, Harvey Curtis. "Fiction Notes," *The Saturday Review of Literature,* XXXV, no. 20 (May 17) 40 (rather unfavorable review of *Rotting Hill).*

F859 Munn, L. S. *The Springfield Republican* (May 18) 7 (review of *Rotting Hill).*

F860 Pfafl, William. *The Commonweal,* LVI, no. 7 (May23) 181 (this review of *Rotting Hill* finds it the work of "a tired conservative").

F861 Hughes, Riley. *The Catholic World,* CLXXV, no. 1047 (June) 234 (favorable review of *Rotting Hill).*

F862 "Chronicle of Recent Books," *Nine,* III, no. 4 (Summer/Autumn) 387 (very favorable short reviews of Charles Handley-Read's *The Art of Wyndham Lewis* (see F805) and Lewis's *Rotting Hill, The Writer and the Absolute, Tarr* and *The Revenge for Love).*

F863 Conover, Robert. *The Christian Century,* LXIX, no. 27 (July 2) 782 (review of *Rotting Hill).*

F864 Allen, Walter. "Talking of Books," *B.B.C., Home Service* (typescript of a talk broadcast on July 13).

F865 "Flirting with Politics," *The Times Literary Supplement,* LI, no. 2633 (July 18) (favorable review of *The Writer and the Absolute,* with a comparison of Orwell and Lewis).

F866 [*Unsigned review.*] *Kirkus,* XX (August 1) 473 (review of *The Revenge for Love).*

F867 Pritchett, V. S. "Literary Letter from London," *The New York Times Book Review* (September 28) 43.

F868 Libaire, Beatrice. *The Library Journal,* LXXVII (October 1) 1656 (review of *The Revenge for Love).*

F869 Cohen, J. M. "Wyndham Lewis vs. The Rest," *The Spectator,* CLXXXIX, no. 6476 (October 8) 194 (this review finds Lewis too hard on Mauriac and *The Writer and the Absolute* "wrong-headed").

F870 Howe, Irving. "A Dubious Revival," *The New Republic,* CXXVII, no. 16 (October 20) 27-28 (hostile review of *The Revenge for Love).*

F871 Webster, Harvey Curtis. "Bile and Blisters," *The Saturday Review of Literature,* XXXV, no. 43 (October 25) 22-23 (review of *The Revenge for Love,* "an admirably prejudiced . . . disagreeable and extraordinarily vivid novel").

F872 "Fighters With the Mouth," *Time,* LX, no. 17 (October 27) 60 (review of *The Revenge for Love* which finds it "prophetic").

F873 "Drawings by Two British Artists," *The National Gallery of South Australia Bulletin,* XX, no. 4-5 (October).

F874 Stanford, Derek. *The Month,* VIII, no. 4 (October) 254-255 (reviews *The Writer and the Absolute).*

F875 Dobrée, Bonamy. *Congregation for the Conferment of Honorary Degrees,* University of Leeds, November 12, 10 (a presentation address stressing Lewis's "emotional and intellectual integrity").

F876 Pritchett, V. S. "Everywhere in Chains," *The New Statesman and Nation,* XLIV, no. 1134 (November 29) 656 (favorable review of *The Writer and the Absolute).*

F877 Hilton, James. "Written With Snarling Zest," *New York Herald Tribune Weekly Book Review* (December 28) 4 (favorable review of *The Revenge for Love).*

F878 Rose, William K. *Furioso,* VII, no. 4, 52-55 (finds *Rotting Hill* disappointing in comparison with Lewis's pre-war books).

F879 Hughes, Riley. *The Catholic World,* CLXXVI, no. 1053 (December) 234 (review of *The Revenge for Love).*

1953

F880 Anderson, Sherwood. *Letters* (edited by Howard Mumford Jones) Boston: Little, Brown and Co., 205 (about his contribution to the Western decline according to *Paleface).*

F881 Browse, Lillian (editor). *Sickert,* with an essay on his art by R. H. Wilenski. London: Faber and Faber, passim.

F882 Chamot, Mary. *The Tate Gallery. British School: A Concise Catalogue.* London: The Tate Gallery, 138.

F883 Connolly, Cyril. *Ideas and Places.* London: Weidenfeld and Nicholson, 54 (on Julian Symons and Lewis).

F884 Fraser, G. S. *The Modern Writer and his World.* London: Derek Verschoyle, 102-106, passim (discusses *Tarr* and aspects of Lewis's career; reprinted by Penguin Books, 1964).

F885 Pound, Reginald. *Arnold Bennett.* New York: Harcourt Brace, 289.

F886 Raynal, Maurice. *La Peinture Moderne.* Genève: Albert Skira, passim (references to Lewis).

F887 Rose, William K. *Wyndham Lewis: a Study in Dissent.* Cornell University, February (unpublished doctoral thesis).

F888 Short, Ernest. *A History of British Painting.* London: Eyre and Spottiswoode, 269-273.

F889 Spender, Stephen. *The Creative Element.* London: Hamish Hamilton, 99 (rejects Lewis's vision of sex).

F890 Woolf, Virginia. *A Writer's Diary.* London: Hogarth Press, 228-230, passim (her reactions to *Men Without Art).*

F891 Wykes-Joyce, Max. *Triad of Genius.* London: Peter Owen, passim (how Lewis's reputation suffers from his proficiency in two artistic media).

F892 Bridge, Ursula (editor). *W. B. Yeats to Sturge Moore: their Correspondence, 1901-1937.* London: Routledge and Kegan Paul, passim (references to Lewis).

F893 Ashe, Geoffrey. "War in Spain," *The Commonweal,* LXVII, no. 13 (January 2) 338 (review of *The Revenge for Love).*

F894 Marcus, Stephen. "The Highbrow Know-Nothings," *Commentary,* XV, no. 2 (February) 189-191.

F895 Wagner, Geoffrey. "Wyndham Lewis and Bergson," *The Romantic Review,* XLVI, no. 2 (April 24) 112-124 (incorporated in Wagner's *Wyndham Lewis,* see F1067).

F896 Kenner, Hugh. "The Revenge of the Void," *The Hudson Review,* VI, no. 3 (Autumn) 382-397 (incorporated in Kenner's *Wyndham Lewis,* see F909).

F897 Carter, Thomas H. (editor). *Shenandoah,* IV, nos. 2-3 (Summer-Autumn), (see F898-F904; this "Wyndham Lewis Number" is accompanied by reproductions of five drawings by Lewis; a "Check-List of the Writings of Wyndham Lewis" compiled and with a preface by Geoffrey Wagner is announced by Peter Russell, but was apparently never published; see also Lewis's contribution, D340).

F898 Pound, Ezra. "On Wyndham Lewis," *ibid.,* 17 (quotes from articles in *Fortnightly Review, The Exile, Guide to Kulchur* and a private letter, see F897).

F899 Kenner, Hugh. "The War With Time," *ibid.,* 18-49 (incorporated in Kenner's *Wyndham Lewis,* see F897 and F909).

F900 Kenner, Hugh. "Wyndham Lewis: A List of Writings," *ibid.,* 50-53 (defines Lewis as "one of the three or four most important of modern painters," see F897).

F901 Mudrick, Marvin. "The Double-Artist and the Injured Party," *ibid.,* 54-64 (mechanism and stylization in Lewis's fiction and painting, see F897).

F902 Eliot, T. S. "Wyndham Lewis: Two Views," *ibid.,* 65-71 (reprints articles from *The Egoist* and *Twentieth Century Verse,* see F897).

F903 Russell, Peter. "Wyndham Lewis Today," *ibid.,* 72-73 (brief discussion of *Rotting Hill* and *The Writer and the Absolute,* see F897).

F904 Campbell, Roy. "A Note on Lewis," *ibid.,* 74-76 (Lewis regaining recognition with the decline of the Left, see F897).

F905 McLuhan, Herbert Marshall. "Wyndham Lewis: his Theory of Art and Communication," *ibid.,* 76-78 (*The Lion and the Fox* and the "vortex of power," see F897; reprinted in *The Interior Landscape and the Literary Criticism of Marshall McLuhan.* New York: McGraw-Hill, 1969).

F906 Wagner, Geoffrey. "*The Wild Body:* a Sanguine of The Enemy," *Nine,* IV, no. 1 (Winter) 18-27 (discusses *The Wild Body;* incorporated in Wagner's *Wyndham Lewis,* see F1067).

1954

F907 Allen, Walter. *The English Novel. A Short Critical History.* New York: E. P. Dutton, passim.

F908 Highet, Gilbert. *A Clerk of Oxenford.* New York: Oxford University Press, 170 (on Yeats and Lewis).

F909 Kenner, Hugh. *Wyndham Lewis.* Norfolk: New Directions (incorporates F896 and F899; for reviews of this important study of Lewis's work see F917, F924, F930, F931, F932, F933, F950, F956, F964, F965, F969, F971, F996 and F1026).

F910 McLuhan, Herbert Marshall. *Counterblast.* Toronto: privately printed, passim (revised edition, London: Rapp and Whiting Ltd., 1969).

F911 Pound, Ezra. *Literary Essays of Ezra Pound.* Edited with an introduction by T. S. Eliot. London: Faber and Faber, 423-431.

F912 Read, Herbert. *Anarchy and Order.* London: Faber and Faber, 76.

F913 Scherbacker, Wolfgang. *Der Künstler im modernen englischen Roman.* Tübingen (unpublished doctoral thesis).

F914 Wagner, Geoffrey. *The Writings of P. Wyndham Lewis.* Columbia University (unpublished doctoral thesis; incorporated in F1067).

F915 Yeats, William Butler. *The Letters of W. B. Yeats,* edited by Allan Wade. London: Rupert Hart-Davis (New York: Macmillan, 1955) passim (numerous references to Lewis).

F916 Wagner, Geoffrey. "Wyndham Lewis and Catholic Thought," *The Catholic World,* CLXXVIII, no. 1066 (January) 284-287 (incorporated in Wagner's *Wyndham Lewis,* see F1067)

F917 Howe, Irving. "This Age of Conformity," *Partisan Review,* XXI, no. 1 (January-February) 17 ("a charlatan like Lewis" can only be "revived" by "a Hugh Kenner"; see F909).

F918 Hodgart, Patricia. "New Novels," *Manchester Guardian* (May 4) 4 (favorable review of *Self Condemned).*

F919 Allen, Walter. "The External Approach," *The New Statesman and Nation,* XLVII, no. 1209 (May 8) 604 (enthusiastic review of *Self Condemned).*

F920 [*Unsigned review.*] *The Times Literary Supplement,* LIII, no. 2729 (May 21) 325 (reluctantly favorable review of *Self Condemned).*

F921 Maler, E. Newton. "Der Pionier Wyndham Lewis," *Runscau,* no. 1 (June 4) 6-7.

F922 Strong, L. A. G. "Exile," *The Spectator,* CXCII, no. 6571 (June 4) 694 (favorable review of *Self Condemned).*

F923 Kenner, Hugh. "Inside the Iceberg," *Shenandoah,* V, no. 3 (Summer) 66-71 (review of *Self Condemned;* reprinted in *Nine,* IV, no. 2 (April 1956) 30-34).

F924 Barron, Louis. *The Library Journal* (July) 1307 (unfavorable review of Kenner's *Wyndham Lewis,* see F909; sees Lewis as "perhaps the most neglected figure in the XXth. century").

F925 Gregory, Horace. "An Artist at War With Himself," *New York Times Book Review* (August 22) 4 (reprinted in *The Dying Gladiators and Other Essays,* 1961).

F926 Wagner, Geoffrey. "Wyndham Lewis and the Vorticist Æsthetic," *The Journal of Æsthetics and Art Criticism,* XIII, no. 1 (September) 1-17 (incorporated in *Wyndham Lewis,* see F1067).

F927 Bradley, John L. *Books Abroad,* XXVIII, no. 4 (Autumn) 484 (sees *Self Condemned* as an "implausible novel").

F928 Pryce-Jones, Alan. *The London Magazine,* I, no. 10 (November) 99-102 (review of *Self Condemned).*

F929 Corke, Hilary. "Crime Story," *Encounter,* III, no. 5 (November), 66-68 (considers *Self Condemned* as "in many ways the best book" of "a splendid destroyer").

F930 [*Unsigned review.*] *The Listener,* LII, no. 1345 (December 9) 1031-1033 (favorable review of *The Demon of Progress in the Arts;* Kenner's *Wyndham Lewis* is found "obscure," see F909).

F931 Watson, Francis. "The Necessary Enemy," *The Spectator,* CXCII, no. 6599 (December 17) 791 (favorable review of Kenner's *Wyndham Lewis* (see F909) and *The Demon of Progress in the Arts).*

F932 "Versatile Talent," *The Times Literary Supplement,* LIII, no. 2759 (December 17) 822 (reviews *The Demon of Progress in the Arts* and Kenner's *Wyndham Lewis,* see F909).

F933 Wagner, Geoffrey. "On Kenner's *Wyndham Lewis," The New Mexico Quarterly,* XXIV, no. 4 (Winter) 457-461 (unfavorable review of F909, incorporated in F1067).

1955

F934 Bertram, Anthony. *Paul Nash.* London: Faber and Faber, 116.

F935 Deghy, Guy and Keith Waterhouse. *Café Royal. Ninety Years of Bohemia.* London: Hutchinson, 126-128, passim.

F936 Epstein, Jacob. *Epstein, an Autobiography.* London: Hulton Press, 59-60, passim.

F937 Friedman, Melvin. *Stream of Consciousness in the Modern Novel: a Study in Literary Method.* New Haven: Yale University Press, passim.

F938 Garnett, David. *The Flowers of the Forest.* London: Chatto and Windus, 225 (a recollection of Lewis).

F939 Goldring, Douglas. *Privileged Persons.* London: Richards Press, 129 (discussions with Lewis and Nevinson).

F940 Heron, Patrick. *The Changing Forms of Art.* London: Routledge and Kegan Paul, passim (a number of remarks on Lewis's figurative and non-figurative art).

F941 Hulme, T. E. *Further Speculations by T. E. Hulme,* edited by Sam Hynes. Minneapolis: University of Minnesota Press (reprints Hulme's articles from *The New Age).*

F942 Kenner, Hugh. *Dublin's Joyce.* London: Chatto and Windus (Bloomington: Indiana University Press, 1956) 362-369, passim ("Wyndham Lewis: The Enemy as Alter-Ego," includes remarks on Lewis in *Finnegans Wake,* see F638).

F943 Kunitz, Stanley J. [i.e., "Dilly Tante"]. *Twentieth Century Authors.* New York: H. W. Wilson Co., 579.

F944 Meyerhoff, Hans. *Time in Literature.* Berkeley: University of California Press, passim.

F945 Leavis, F. R. *D. H. Lawrence: Novelist.* London: Chatto and Windus (New York: Alfred A. Knopf, 1956) passim (unfavorable references to Lewis).

F946 Pound, Ezra. *Rockdrill.* Milano: Al'Insegna del Pesce d'Oro (the title is derived from Lewis's review of *The Letters of Ezra Pound,* see F779 and D336).

F947 Rodman, Selden. *The Eye of Man.* New York: Devin-Adair, 143 (Lewis and the "dithyrambic spectator").

F948 Tomlin, E. W. F. *Wyndham Lewis,* Writers and Their Work: no. 64, published for The British Council and the National Book League. London: Longmans, Green and Co, pp. 40 (revised edition, see F1501).

F949 Yeats, W. B. *Autobiographies.* London: Macmillan, 283.

F950 Allen, Walter. "Wyndham Lewis," *The New Statesman and Nation,* XLIX, no. 1244 (January 8) 48-49 (Lewis compared to Matthew Arnold, favorable review of *The Demon of Progress in the Arts;* moderately favorable review of Kenner's *Wyndham Lewis,* see F909).

F951 Leplat, René. *B.B.C., French Service,* January 13 (typescript of a broadcast in French, described in *Lewisletter, no. 5*; favorable review of *The Demon of Progress in the Arts).*

F952 Black, Harvey [i.e. G. D. Gilling-Smith]. "New Books," *The European,* IV, no. 24 (February) 47-48 (favorable review of *The Demon of Progress in the Arts).*

F953 Kenner, Hugh. "Dudley Fitts' Aristophanes," *Poetry,* LXXXV, no. 5 (February) 294-300 (suggests an analogy between Lewis's and Aristophanes' styles).

F954 Shirley, Maria. *Blackfriars,* XXXVI, no. 419 (February) 38-39 (favorable review of *The Demon of Progress in the Arts).*

F955 Daintrey, Adrian. *Punch,* CXXVIII, no. 5975 (March 16) 355 (favorable review of *The Demon of Progress in the Arts).*

F956 Baines, Jocelyn. *London Magazine,* II, no. 4 (April) 82-85 (reviews *The Demon of Progress in the Arts* and Kenner's *Wyndham Lewis,* F909).

F957 Wagner, Geoffrey. "The Politics of the Intellect," *The New Republic,* CXXXII, no. 20 (May 16) 31-33 (incorporated in Wagner's *Wyndham Lewis,* see F1067; an indictment of Lewis's political positions).

F958 Bridson, D. G. "A Modern Divine Comedy," *The Radio Times,* CXXVII, no. 1645 (May 20) 4 (accompanied by a photograph of Lewis and Bridson in the studio, a presentation of Lewis's *The Human Age* trilogy to be broadcast on Tuesday, Thursday and Saturday, May 24, 26 and 28).

F959 Horchler, R. T. "Man Against the Mob," *The Commonweal,* LXII, no. 7 (May 20) 188 (*Self Condemned* "fails ambitiously and intelligently").

F960 "A Tongue That Naked Goes," *Time,* LXV, no. 21 (May 23) 102-104 (favorable review of *Self Condemned* and Lewis's career).

F961 Rienaecker, Victor. *Apollo,* LXI, no. 363 (May) 155 (favorable review of *The Demon of Progress in the Arts).*

F962 Hough, Graham. "The Human Age," *The Listener,* LIII, no. 1370 (June 2) 976-977, 980 (a detailed account of *The Human Age* and a definition of Lewis as "the Shadow").

F963 Salter, William. [i.e. Walter Allen]. "Wyndham Lewis on the Air," *The New Statesman and Nation,* XLIX, no. 1265 (June 4) 783 (enthusiastic review of the B.B.C. adaptations of *Monstre Gai* and *Malign Fiesta,* broadcast the week before with a prefatory talk by T. S. Eliot).

F964 Woodcock, George. "The Intellectual Fury," *The New Yorker,* XXXI, no. 16 (June 4) 104-105, 111-113 (favorable review of *Self Condemned* combined with a survey of Lewis's career and a long analysis of *The Revenge for Love;* Kenner's *Wyndham Lewis* considered valuable but too short, see F909).

F965 Bloom, Edward A. "Artist at War," *The Saturday Review of Literature,* XXXVIII, no. 25 (June 18) 16 (favorable review of Kenner's *Wyndham Lewis,* see F909).

F966 Redman, Ben Ray. "Academic Exile," *The Saturday Review of Literature,* XXXVIII, no. 25 (June 18) 16,42 (favorable review of *Self Condemned).*

F967 Kirk, Russel. "Wyndham Lewis's First Principles," *The Yale Review,* XLIV, no. 4 (Summer) 520-534 (a detailed analysis of Lewis's satirical targets and political attitudes).

F968 Wagner, Geoffrey. "Return of the Enemy," *The Hudson Review,* VIII, no. 2 (Summer) 302-308 (favorable review of *Self Condemned,* with a survey of the critics' reactions; incorporated in Wagner's *Wyndham Lewis,* see F1067).

F969 Williams, Stanley T. *Books Abroad,* XXIX, no. 3 (Summer) 349 (review of Kenner's *Wyndham Lewis,* see F909).

F970 [*Unsigned review.*] *The Booklist,* LI, no. 22 (July 15) 468 (favorable review of *Self Condemned).*

F971 Sharrock, Robert. "Wyndham Lewis," *Essays in Criticism*, V, no. 3 (July) 260-265 (reviews *Self Condemned* and Kenner's *Wyndham Lewis*, see F909).

F972 McLuhan, Herbert Marshall. *Canadian Broadcasting Corporation,* August 21 (radio reviews of *Self Condemned* and *The Demon of Progress in the Arts;* printed text in NIC).

F973 "The Exact Sneer," *The Nation,* CLXXXI, no. 10 (September 3) 209 (unfavorable review of *Self Condemned).*

F974 Tomlin, E. W. F. "Wyndham Lewis: the Philosopher and Social Critic," *Feature Articles Service, Literature,* 10 (1), B.B.C., September, 1-2 (typescript in NIC).

F975 Scott-James, R. A. "Wyndham Lewis: the Novelist," *ibid.,* 10 (2), 1-2 (typescript in NIC).

F976 March, Richard. "Wyndham Lewis: the Literary Critic," *ibid.,* 10 (3) 1-2 (typescript in NIC).

F977 Grigson, Geoffrey. "Wyndham Lewis: the Artist and Art Critic," *ibid.,* 10 (4) 1-2 (typescript in NIC).

F978 [*Unsigned review.*] *The Times Literary Supplement,* LIV, no. 2794 (September 16) 546 (note on Tomlin's *Wyndham Lewis,* see F948).

F979 Ayrton, Michael. "Tarr and Flying Feathers," *Shenandoah,* VII, no. 1 (Autumn) 31-43 (recollections of Lewis, see F994; reprinted in *Golden Sections,* see B32).

F980 Kenner, Hugh. "The Devil and Mr. Lewis," *ibid.,* 15-30 (analysis of *The Human Age).*

F981 Jacobson, O. B. *Books Abroad,* XXIX, no. 4 (Autumn) 420 (*The Demon of Progress in the Arts* reviewed as a "little gem of a book").

F982 Read, Herbert. "The Lost Leader, or the Psychopathology of Reaction in the Arts," *The Sewanee Review,* LXIII, no. 4 (Autumn) 551-566 (reprinted under the title *The Psychopathology of Reaction in the Arts,* The Institute of Contemporary Arts).

F983 [*Unsigned review.*] *The New Yorker,* XXXI, no. 35 (October 15) 175 (favorable review of *The Demon of Progress in the Arts).*

F984 Barry, Edward. *The Chicago Sunday Tribune* (October 16) 9 (reviews *The Demon of Progress in the Arts).*

F985 Barrett, W. *New York Times* (October 30) 43 (review of *The Demon of Progress in the Arts).*

F986 Bergel, Lienhard. "L'Estetica di Cesare Pavese," *Lo spettatore italiano,* VIII, no. 10 (Ottobre) 407-421.

F987 Case, Edward. "Honorable Malice," *Wall Street Journal* (November 11) (favorably reviews *The Demon of Progress in the Arts).*

F988 "Painter in Prose," *The Economist,* CLXXVII (November 12) 6 (favorable review of *The Human Age, Books 2 & 3).*

F989 "The Defeat of Optimism," *The Times Literary Supplement,* LXIV, no. 2807 (November 16) 760 (favorable review of *The Human Age, Books 2 & 3* and of Lewis's prose style).

F990 Wagner, Geoffrey. "Novelty and Development in Painting," *The New Republic,* CXXXIII, no. 21 (November 21) 29 (favorable review of *The Demon of Progress in the Arts;* incorporated in F1067).

F991 Mayne, Richard. "Bloomsbury's Bête Noire," *The New Statesman and Nation,* I, no. 1290 (November 26) 721-722 (favorable review of *The Human Age, Books 2 & 3* with a survey of Lewis's career).

F992 Scott, Nathan A. Jr. "Ex-Heretic," *The Christian Century,* LXXII, no. 48 (November 30) 1400-1401 (denounces the "utter obscurantism" of *The Demon of Progress in the Arts).*

F993 Tomlin, E. W. F. "Wyndham Lewis and the Civilized Intelligence," *Time and Tide,* XXXVI, no. 49 (December 3) 1590-1591 (favorable review of *The Human Age, Books 2 & 3).*

F994 Ayrton, Michael. "Encounters with Wyndham Lewis," *The New Statesman and Nation,* L, no. 1293 (December 17) 826 (extracts from "Tarr and Flying Feathers," see F979; incorporated in B32).

F995 Wagner, Geoffrey. *The Journal of Aesthetics and Art Criticism,* XIV, no. 2 (December) 271-272 (generally favorable review of *The Demon of Progress in the Arts,* incorporated in F1067).

F996 Carter, Thomas H. "Wyndham Lewis: the Metaphysics of Reality," *Accent,* XV, no. 1 (Winter) 69-73 (survey of Lewis's career with a review of *Self Condemned* which has "the inevitability of a glacier," and a review of Kenner's *Wyndham Lewis,* "an incredibly compressed little book," see F909).

F997 Eliot, T. S. "A Note on Monster Gai," *The Hudson Review,* VII, no. 4 (Winter) 522-526 (discusses many aspects of Lewis and defines him as "the greatest prose master of style" of his generation; originally a broadcast talk to accompany *The Human Age, B.B.C. Third Programme,* Wednesday, May 25).

F998 Antonini, G. "Le Insofferenze di Wyndham Lewis," *La Fiera Letteraria,* VI.

1956

F999 Aiken, Conrad. *A Reviewer's ABC.* New York: Meridian Press (reprints F270 and F290; reprinted as *Collected Criticism.* London: Oxford University Press, 1968).

F1000 Aldridge, John W. *In Search of Heresy.* Westport: Greenwood Press, 151-152 (Lewis on the Hemingway hero).

F1001 Hollis, Christopher. *A Study of George Orwell.* London: Hollis and Carter, passim (Lewis seen as one of the best critics of Orwell).

F1002 Kirk, Russell. *Beyond the Dreams of Avarice.* Chicago: Henry Regnery (reprints "Wyndham Lewis's First Principles"; remarks about Lewis in "English Letters in the Age of Boredom").

F1003 Lindsay, Jack. *After the Thirties: The Novel in Britain and its Future.* London: Lawrence and Wishart, passim (remarks on Lewis and the contradictions affecting the thirties).

F1004 Low, David. *Autobiography.* London: Michael Joseph, 266 (Lewis and Colonel Blimp).

F1005 Maisonneuve, André. "Littérature Anglaise," *Encyclopédie de la Pléiade, Histoire des Littératures II,* Paris: N.R.F., passim (*Tarr, Hommes Sans Art* and *L'Ere Humaine* discussed).

F1006 Moore, Marianne. *Predilections.* London. Faber and Faber, passim (*The Tyro* as "a pleasant antidote to jargon").

F1007 *Masters of British Painting, 1880-1950.* New York: Museum of Modern Art, 106-108.

F1008 Nenhaüser, Rudolf. *Eine Studie über Percy Wyndham Lewis. Seine Kritik von erzählenden Werke,* Universität Wien (unpublished doctoral thesis).

F1009 Roberts, William. *The Resurrection of Vorticism and the Apotheosis of Wyndham Lewis at the Tate.* London: Favil Press (included in *The Vortex Pamphlets).*

F1010 Rossiter, Clinton. *Conservatism in America.* New York: Knopf, 311 *(The Art of Being Ruled,* "difficult to classify as conservative").

F1011 Rothenstein, John. *Modern English Painters. Lewis to Moore.* New York: Macmillan, 13-44, passim.

F1012 Bailey, Anthony. "The Limits of Art," *The Commonweal,* LXII, no. 14 (January 6) 356-358 (favorable, detailed analysis of *The Demon of Progress in the Arts).*

F1013 Kenner, Hugh. "A Tongue That Naked Goes," *Poetry,* LXXXVII, no. 4 (January) 247-252 (study of *One-Way Song* and review of *The Demon of Progress in the Arts* and *The Human Age).*

F1014 Carter, Thomas. "Rationalist in Hell," *The Kenyon Review,* XVIII, no. 2 (Spring) 326-336 (a very favorable analysis of the whole of *The Human Age).*

F1015 Mitchison, Naomi. "Sitting for Wyndham Lewis," *Manchester Guardian* (July 9) 5 (recollections of Lewis).

F1016 Rothenstein, John. "Wyndham Lewis and Vorticism," *Wyndham Lewis and Vorticism.* London: The Tate Gallery, 5-7 (foreword to the exhibition catalogue).

F1017 "Wyndham Lewis and Vorticism. Tate Gallery Exhibition," *The Times* (July 6) 11 (favorable review of the Tate Gallery exhibition).

F1018 Bridson, D. G. "A Visual Artist," *The Radio Times,* CXXXII, no. 1705 (July 13) 7 (notes that *Tarr* will be broadcast on Wednesday and Friday, July 18 and 20, *B.B.C. Third Programme).*

F1019 "Wyndham Lewis. Vorticism and After," *The Illustrated London News,* CCXXIX, no. 6111 (July 21) 106 (article with seven reproductions).

F1020 Newton, Eric. "Wyndham Lewis—I," *Time and Tide,* XXXVII, no. 28 (July 14) 845 (favorable review of the Tate Gallery exhibition).

F1021 Newton, Eric. "Wyndham Lewis—II," *Time and Tide,* XXXVII, no. 29 (July 21) 874, 876 (reviews Lewis's portraits).

F1022 Ayrton, Michael. "The Stone Guests," *The New Statesman and Nation,* LII, no. 1329 (July 21) 68 (review of the Tate Gallery exhibition stressing Lewis's importance and defining him as an "ikon" maker; reprinted in *Golden Sections,* see B32, and quoted at length in *The Rudiments of Paradise).*

F1023 "Tate Acquisitions," *The Times* (July 30) 3 (mentions purchase of Lewis's "Bagdad").

F1024 Scott-James, R. A. " 'Twixt Heaven and Hell," *Encounter,* no. 1 (July) 86-88 (reviews *The Human Age* as a "fantastic monstrous but triumphant feat of imagination").

F1025 Roberts, William. *Cometism and Vorticism: A Tate Gallery Catalogue Revised.* [London]: Privately printed, July-August (included in *The Vortex Pamphlets*).

F1026 Mayoux, Jean-Jacques. "Wyndham Lewis, ou J'ai du Génie," *Etudes Anglaises,* IX, no. 3 (Juillet/Septembre) 212-214 (survey of Lewis's literary and artistic career with special reference to *The Demon of Progress in the Arts, Rotting Hill, The Writer and the Absolute* and *Self Condemned;* also Kenner's *Wyndham Lewis,* F909).

F1027 "New Fiction," *The Times* (August 30) 11 (reviews *The Red Priest* as "a difficult, a challenging novel").

F1028 Bell, Quentin. "Reaction in the Arts," *The Listener,* LVI, no. 1429 (August 16) 240 (unfavorable review of *The Demon of Progress in the Arts*).

F1029 "The Climate of Taste," *The Times Literary Supplement,* LV, no. 2842 (August 17) xvi-xxvii (briefly discusses *The Human Age*).

F1030 "New Art Form," *Manchester Evening Chronicle* (August 21) 5 (announces Vorticist exhibition to open in Manchester, September 1).

F1031 Farr, Dennis. "Wyndham Lewis and the Vorticists," *Burlington Magazine,* XCVIII, no. 641 (August) 279-280 (favorable review of the Tate Gallery exhibition).

F1032 Perspex. "Current Shows and Comments. Artists in Search of a Vortex," *Apollo,* LXIV, no. 641 (August) 35-36 (favorable review of Tate Gallery exhibition and discussion of Lewis's attitudes towards abstract art).

F1033 S., N., "Wyndham Lewis and Vorticism," *The Manchester Guardian* (September 2) 5 (review of the exhibition at the Manchester Art Gallery).

F1034 Porteus, Hugh Gordon. "A Winning Card," *Time and Tide,* XXXVII, no. 35 (September 1) 105 (*The Red Priest* reviewed as "the most consistently *readable* book" by Lewis).

F1035 Metcalf, John. "New Fiction," *The Sunday Times* (September 2) 5 (unfavorable review of *The Red Priest*).

F1036 Duchene, Anne. "New Novels," *The Manchester Guardian* (September 4) 4 (*The Red Priest* reviewed as "a very minor" work).

F1037 "Don't Miss Tutsi," *The Manchester Evening Chronicle* (September 4) 5 (review of the "Wyndham Lewis and Voritcism" Exhibition at the Manchester City Art Gallery).

F1038 [*Unsigned review.*] *The Queen,* CCIII, no. 5320 (September 4) 78 (favorable short review of *The Red Priest*).

F1039 "Power Inglorious," *The Times Literary Supplement,* LV, no. 2845 (September 7) 529 (favorable review of *The Red Priest*).

F1040 Wallace, Doreen. "Harvest of Novels," *Eastern Daily Press* (September 9) 7 (mixed review of *The Red Priest,* "a hotch-potch of a book").

F1041 Churchill, R. C. "New Novels," *The Birmingham Post* (September 11) 3 (favorable review of *The Red Priest,* product of "the unorthodox champion of the Right").

F1042 Connell, John. *The Evening Dispatch* (September 14) 17 (reviews *The Red Priest* as "a minor work," "yet powerful and convincing").

F1043 Perspex. "Current Shows and Comments," *Apollo,* LXIV, no. 379 (September) 67-68 (favorably reviews Lewis exhibition at the Tate).

F1044 Singer, Burns. "Another Damned Scotsman," *Twentieth Century* (September) 214-222 (refers to Lewis in connection with the Glasgow School and Colquhoun).

F1045 Sylvester, D. "At the Tate Gallery," *Encounter,* VII, no. 3, (September) 65-68 (review of the Tate Gallery exhibition stressing Lewis's essential romanticism and his debt to Augustus John and Gauguin).

F1046 Bell, Quentin. "Reputations in the Making," *The Listener,* LXVI, no. 1437 (October 11) 569 (review of Rothenstein's *Modern English Painters*).

F1047 Whittet, G. S. "London Commentary," *Studio,* CLII, no. 763 (October) 124 (favorable review of the Tate Gallery exhibition).

F1048 Calder-Marshall, Arthur. "We Can Be Proud of Our Novelists," *Books and Bookmen,* I, no. 12 (September).

F1049 "Exhibitions," *The Architectural Review,* CXX, no. 715 (October) 261 (review of the Tate Gallery exhibition).

F1050 Carter, Thomas H. *Shenandoah,* VIII, no. 1 (Autumn) 56-62 (detailed review of *The Red Priest* seen as a parody of Eliot's *The Cocktail Party).*

F1051 Holloway, John. "Pullman's Progress," *The Spectator,* CXCV, no. 6648 (November 25) 742 (favorable review of *The Human Age).*

F1052 Bone, Stephen. "Word-Men," *The Manchester Guardian* (November 26) 7 (favorable review of *The Demon of Progress in the Arts,* "alarmingly true").

F1053 Cranston, Maurice. "The Red Priest," *Encounter,* VII, no. 5 (November) 82-84 (unfavorable review of *The Red Priest).*

F1054 Aiken, Henry David. "Presumption and Petulance," *The Kenyon Review,* XVIII, no. 1 (Winter) 157-162 (reviews *The Demon of Progress in the Arts).*

F1055 Wagner, Geoffrey. "Wyndham Lewis's Inhuman Tetralogy. An Introduction to the Human Age," *Modern Fiction Studies,* II, no. 4 (Winter) 221-227 (detailed and finally negative review of *The Human Age,* incorporated in F1067).

F1056 Middleton, Michael. "Ett forsök att hetsa den kulturella Britannia—Wyndham Lewis och vorticisterna," *Konstrevy* (Stockholm) XXXII, 180-183.

1957

F1057 Frye, Northrop. *Anatomy of Criticism. Four Essays.* Princeton: Princeton University Press, passim.

F1058 Gilbert, Stuart. *The Letters of James Joyce.* London: Faber and Faber, passim (numerous references to Lewis).

F1059 Grigson, Geoffrey. *Coming to London–7,* edited by John Lehman. London: Phœnix House Ltd., 93 (recollections of Lewis).

F1060 Hutchins, Patricia. *James Joyce's World.* London: Methuen, 129-131, passim (recollections of Lewis).

F1061 McCormick, John. *Catastrophe and Imagination. An Interpretation of the Recent English and American Novel.* London: Longmans, Green and Co, 295-298, passim (Lewis is "the supreme object-lesson on the dangers of allegory").

F1062 Read, Herbert. *The Tenth Muse. Essays in Criticism.* London: Wyman and Sons (New York, Horizon Press, 1958) 261 (Lewis and the Orage circle).

F1063 Roberts, William. *A Reply to My Biographer, Sir John Rothenstein,* September 1956-February 1957. London: privately printed, passim (included in *The Vortex Pamphlets).*

F1064 Roberts, William. *The Resurrection of Vorticism and the Apotheosis of Wyndham Lewis; Cometism and Vorticism; A Press View at the Tate Gallery; A Reply to My Biographer, Sir John Rothenstein.* London: Privately printed for the Author (reprinted as *The Vortex Pamphlets, 1956-1958).*

F1065 Soby, James. *Modern Art and the New Past.* Norman: University of Oklahoma Press, 98.

F1066 Swinnerton, Frank. *Background with Chorus.* New York: Farrar, Straus and Cudahy, passim (remarks on Lewis).

F1067 Wagner, Geoffrey. *Wyndham Lewis. A Portrait of the Artist as the Enemy.* New Haven: Yale University Press (London: Routledge and Kegan Paul), pp. xvi, 363 (full-length study of Lewis's writings and career, which includes an important bibliography of his writings, and a secondary source list).

F1068 Wagner, Geoffrey. "Wyndham Lewis and James Joyce. A Study in Controversy," *The South Atlantic Quarterly,* LXVI, no. 1 (January) 57-66 (incorporated in *Wyndham Lewis,* see F1067).

F1069 MacLaren-Ross, J. *The London Magazine,* IV, no. 1 (January) 66-68 (favorable review of *The Red Priest).*

F1070 "Figures of Allegory," *The Times Literary Supplement,* LXVI, no. 2863 (January 11) 21 (analysis of the differences between *The Childermass* and *The Human Age, Books 2 & 3;* praises Lewis's Carlylean style).

F1071 [*Unsigned obituary notice.*] *The New York Times* (March 9) 19.

F1072 Eliot, T. S. "The Importance of Wyndham Lewis," *Sunday Times,* London (March 10) 10 (obituary tribute).

F1073 Taylor, Basil. "Enemy of the Rose," *The Spectator,* CXCVIII, no. 6716 (March 15) 349-350 (obituary citing Lewis as the most original stylist of his generation and greatest English portraitist in 150 years).

F1074 [*Unsigned obituary notice.*] *Illustrated London News,* CCXXX, no. 6145 (March 16) 433.

F1075 Read, Herbert. "Lone Wolf," *The New Statesman and Nation,* LIII, no. 1357 (March 16) 337 (obituary marked by unfavorable comments about Lewis; for Michael Ayrton's rebuttal see F1082).

F1076 Eliot, T. S. "Homage to Wyndham Lewis 1884-1957," *Spectrum,* I, no. 2 (Spring/Summer) 45 (obituary tribute).

F1077 Ayrton, Michael. "Homage to Wyndham Lewis," *ibid.* 48.

F1078 Bridson, D. G. *Ibid.,* 48.

F1079 [*Unsigned obituary notice.*] *Time,* LXIX, no. 11 (March 18) 48 (obituary describing Lewis as "irascible and erratic").

F1080 [*Unsigned obituary notice.*] *Newsweek,* XLIX, no. 11 (March 18) 36 (obituary describing Lewis as a "life-long warrior against socialism and romantic art").

F1081 Roberts, William. "Wyndham Lewis, the Vorticist," *The Listener,* LVII, no. 1460 (March 21) 470 (early recollections of Lewis).

F1082 Ayrton, Michael. "Wyndham Lewis," *The New Statesman and Nation,* LIII, no. 1359 (March 30) 412 (letter concerning Read's obituary, see F1075).

F1083 Bridson, D. G. [*Letter to the editor*], *The Listener,* LVII, no. 1462 (April 4) 563 (discusses Lewis's radio broadcasts).

F1084 Woodcock, George. "The Retreat of the Twenties," *The Saturday Review of Literature,* XL, no. 16 (April 20) 15-16 (compares Lewis to John Middleton Murry and evaluates Wagner's *Wyndham Lewis,* F1067).

F1085 Rexroth, Kenneth. "An Artist as Thinker," *The New York Herald Tribune Weekly Book Review* (April 21) 9 (largely unfavorable review of Wagner's *Wyndham Lewis,* F1067, judging Lewis as a great painter and poor writer).

F1086 Fraser, G. S. "Wyndham Lewis: an Energy of Mind (an appreciation)," *Twentieth Century,* CLXI, no. 962 (April) 386-392 (detailed survey of Lewis's literary career).

F1087 Stanford, Derek. "Wyndham Lewis," *The Contemporary Review,* CXCI, no. 1096 (April) 209-211 (assessment of Lewis's literary career with particular reference to his political stance of "eternal opposition").

F1088 Cargill, Oscar. "Whose Enemy?" *The Nation,* CLXXXIV (May 4) 398-399 (favorable review of Wagner's *Wyndham Lewis,* see F1067).

F1089 Gregory, Horace. "Displaced Artist," *The Commonweal,* LXVI (May 10) 165-167 (favorable review of Wagner's *Wyndham Lewis,* see F1067).

F1090 Grigson, Geoffrey. "Recollections of Wyndham Lewis," *The Listener,* LVII, no. 1468 (May 16) 785-786 (many vivid recollections; Lewis's painting considered secondary to his writing).

F1091 Pritchett, V. S. *New York Times* (May 19) 22 (review of Wagner's *Wyndham Lewis,* see F1067).

F1092 Henderson, Philip. "Recollections of Wyndham Lewis," *The Listener*, LVII, no. 1469 (May 23) 833 (see F1090).

F1093 Stanford, Derek. "Percy Wyndham Lewis. A Valedictory," *The Month*, XVII, no. 5 (May) 320-324.

F1094 [*Unsigned obituary.*] *The Wilson Library Bulletin*, XXXI (May) 684.

F1095 [*Unsigned review.*] *The New Yorker*, XXXIII, no. 15 (June 1) 106 (review of Wagner's *Wyndham Lewis*, see F1067; Lewis as one of "the moody giants of the twentieth century").

F1096 Bridson, D. G. "The Revenge for Love," *The Radio Times*, CXXXV, no. 1754 (June 21) 7 (defense of *The Revenge for Love* to be broadcast on Sunday and Friday, June 23 and 28, *B.B.C. Third Programme*).

F1097 Muir, Edwin. "The Fortified Eye," *The Observer* (June 23) 13 (critical appraisal of Lewis and favorable review of Wagner's *Wyndham Lewis*, see F1067).

F1098 Townsend, William. "Wyndham Lewis," *The Burlington Magazine*, XCI, no. 651 (June) 202-203 (favorable survey of Lewis's artistic career).

F1099 Allen, Walter. "Wyndham Lewis," *Meanjin*, XVI, no. 2 (June) 189-192 (obituary).

F1100 Ayrton, Michael. "Wyndham Lewis," *ibid.*, 192-195 (obituary, concentrating on Lewis as The Enemy and a "dispassionate" Neo-Classic).

F1101 Eliot, T. S. "Wyndham Lewis," *The Hudson Review*, X, no. 2 (Summer) 167-170 (obituary, recollections of Lewis and an appraisal of his late work).

F1102 Holloway, John. "The Massacre and the Innocents," *ibid.*, 171-188 (detailed thematic survey of Lewis's artistic and literary works).

F1103 Maddocks, Melvin. *The Christian Science Monitor* (July 3) 15 (review of Wagner's *Wyndham Lewis*, see F1067).

F1104 Cranston, Maurice. "The Vorticist," *The Manchester Guardian* (July 9) 4 (review of Wagner's *Wyndham Lewis*, Lewis termed most thoroughly "engagé" of English writers, see F1067).

F1105 Powell, Anthony. "Lewisite," *Punch*, CCXXXIII, no. 6098 (July 10) 52 (review of Wagner's *Wyndham Lewis*, see F1067).

F1106 O'Donnell, Donat [i.e. Conor Cruise O'Brien]. "Thou Art Pierpoint," *The Spectator*, CXCIX, no. 6773 (June 12) 56-58 (particularly hostile view of Lewis with favorable review of Wagner's *Wyndham Lewis*, see F1067; for Symon's reply, see F1108).

F1107 Allen, Walter. "The Blaster," *The New Statesman and Nation*, LIV, no. 1374 (July 13) 63 (review of Wagner's *Wyndham Lewis* as useful but unsatisfactory, see F1067).

F1108 Symons, Julian. "Thou Art Pierpoint," *The Spectator*, CXCIX no. 6774 (July 19) 108 (see F1106 and F1109).

F1109 O'Donnell, Donat [i.e. Conor Cruise O'Brien]. *Ibid.* (reply to Symons's letter, see F1108).

F1110 Porteus, Hugh Gordon. "The Enemy at Bay," *Time and Tide*, XXXVIII, no. 35 (July 27) 941-942 (partly favorable review of Wagner's "inconclusive" *Wyndham Lewis*, see F1067, and a detailed analysis of Lewis's "contradictions").

F1111 "Classic Inhumanism," *The Times Literary Supplement*, LXVI, no. 2892 (August 2) 465-467 (this detailed review of Wagner's *Wyndham Lewis* and account of Lewis's work was to provoke a prolonged controversy).

F1112 Eliot, T. S. "Classic Inhumanism," *The Times Literary Supplement*, LXVI, no. 2893 (August 9) 483 (letter protesting the review of Wagner's *Wyndham Lewis*, see F1111).

F1113 Dukes, Ashley. "Classic Inhumanism," *ibid.* (a letter with the same chronological corrections as made by the previous one, see F1111).

F1114 Your Reviewer. "Classic Inhumanism," *The Times Literary Supplement*, LXVI, no. 2894 (August 16) 495 (see F1111, F1112, F1113).

F1115 Lynch, Bohan. "Boxing in Literature," *The London Mercury*, IV, no. 22 (August 21).

F1116 Eliot, T. S. "Classic Inhumanism," *The Times Literary Supplement*, LXVI, no. 2895 (August 23) 507 (a letter in answer to the reviewer's reply, mostly concerned with the accusation of Fascism and anti-semitism, see F1112 and F1114).

F1117 Wagner, Geoffrey. "Classic Inhumanism," *The Times Literary Supplement*, LXVI, no. 2896 (August 30) 547 (see F1111).

F1118 Kenner, Hugh. "Introduction." *Wyndham Lewis*. Santa Barbara: Santa Barbara Museum of Art, August, [1-2] (introduction to catalogue of an exhibition, August- September, with brief survey of Lewis's visual approaches).

F1119 Kenner, Hugh. "Stele for Hephæstus," *Poetry*, XC, no. 5 (August) 306-310 (obituary, with remarks on *The Trial of Man* and Lewis's "growing interest in the Roman Catholic Church"; reprinted in *Poetry*, October 1972).

F1120 Deleted.

F1121 [*Unsigned review.*] *The Listener*, LVIII, no. 1484 (September 5) 361-362 (review pointing out the "imaginative energy" of Lewis and the limitations of Wagner's *Wyndham Lewis*, see F1067).

F1122 Logue, Christopher. "Classic Inhumanism," *The Times Literary Supplement*, LXVI, no. 2897 (September 6) 533 (see F1111 and F1112).

F1123 Eliot, T. S. "Classic Inhumanism," *The Times Literary Supplement*, LXVI, no. 2898 (September 13) 547 (Eliot's reply to Logue's letter, see F1111 and F1122).

F1124 Mordell, Albert. "Classic Inhumanism," *The Times Literary Supplement*, LXVI, no. 2899 (September 20) 561 (a letter rejecting the reviewer's statement that he had charged Eliot with "Fascism and anti-semitism," see F1111).

F1125 Scott-James, R. A. "Wyndham Lewis' War on the World," *The New Republic*, CXXXVII, no. 14 (September 23) 16-17 (favorable review of Wagner's *Wyndham Lewis;* detailed description of Lewis's personality, see F1067).

F1126 Bergel, Lienhard. "Croce, Wyndham Lewis e il problem dell Arte 'moderna'," *Criterio* (October) 762-777.

F1127 Symons, Julian. "Meeting Wyndham Lewis," *London Magazine*, IV, no. 10 (October) 47-53 (recollections of Lewis).

F1128 "Vorticism and the Politics of Art," *The Times Literary Supplement*, LXVI, no. 2908 (November 22) 700 (review of Roberts's *The Resurrection of Vorticism and the Apotheosis of Wyndham Lewis*, see F1064; see also F1129, F1130 and F1133).

F1129 Rothenstein, John. "Mr. William Roberts and Sir John Rothenstein," *The Times Literary Supplement*, XLVI, no. 2909 (November 29) 728 (letter to the editor accompanying F1130; see F1128).

F1130 Rothenstein, John. *Ibid.* (letter to Roberts; see F1129).

F1131 [*Unsigned review.*] *The Month*, XVIII, no. 3 (November) 314-315 (favorable review of Wagner's *Wyndham Lewis*, see F1067).

F1132 Seymour-Smith, Martin. "Zero and the Impossible," *Encounter*, IX, no. 5 (November) 38-51 (obituary of Campbell, Lewis, Cary and Murry; detailed analysis of various stages in Lewis's exploration of "the essentially dissociative nature of human personality").

F1133 Roberts, William. "Mr. William Roberts and Sir John Rothenstein," *The Times Literary Supplement*, XLVI, no. 2911 (December 13) (see F1129 and F1130).

F1134 Flint, F. Cudworth. *The Journal of Æsthetics and Art Criticism*, XVI, no. 2 (December) 274-275 (fairly favorable review of Wagner's *Wyndham Lewis*, see F1067).

F1135 Frye, Northrop. "Neo-Classical Agony," *The Hudson Review*, X, no. 4 (Winter) 592-598 (favorable review of Wagner's *Wyndham Lewis*, see F1067, with detailed hostile critique of Lewis).

F1136 Edwards, John. *Books Abroad*, XXXII (Winter) 85 (review of Wagner's *Wyndham Lewis*, see F1067).

1958

F1137 Emery, Clark. *Ideas into Action. A Study of Pound's Cantos.* Miami: University of Miami Press, 71-72 (from Imagism to Vorticism).

F1138 Kenner, Hugh. *Gnomon: Essays on Contemporary Literature.* New York: McDowell Obolensky (incorporates "The Devil and Wyndham Lewis," see F1095; includes an analysis of Lewis's projected *Trial of Man).*

F1139 Praz, Mario. *The Flaming Heart.* New York: Doubleday, passim (corrects some of the analyses of *The Lion and the Fox).*

F1140 Roberts, William. *The Vortex Pamphlets, 1956-1958.* London: Canale (includes *The Resurrection of Vorticism and the Apotheosis of Wyndham Lewis at the Tate, Cometism and Vorticism. A Tate Gallery Catalogue Revised, A Press View at the Tate Gallery, A Reply to My Biographer, Sir John Rothenstein,* and *Vorticism and the Politics of Belles-Lettres-ism).*

F1141 Ross, Robert H. *Georgian Poetry, 1911-1922.* Ohio State University (unpublished doctoral thesis).

F1142 Saarinen, Aline B. *The Proud Possessors.* New York: Random House, 223 (John Quinn as art patron of Lewis).

F1143 Ayrton, Michael. "Mr. William Roberts and Sir John Rothenstein," *The Times Literary Supplement,* LVII, no. 2914 (January 3) 7 (letter in defense of Lewis, see F1064).

F1144 Rose, William K. "Pound and Lewis: The Crucial Years," *Southern Review,* IV, no. 1 (January) 72-89 (translated into French in *Ezra Pound II.* Paris: Editions de l'Herne, 1965; reprinted in *Agenda* Lewis number).

F1145 Russell, Peter. "In Memoriam Wyndham Lewis—a Poem," *Poetry,* XCI, no. 4 (January) 255 (Lewis as "the harsh/ Unflattering 3 D mirror of miserable England").

F1146 Roberts, William. *Vorticism and the Politics of Belles-Lettres-Ism.* Privately printed, January (see F1140).

F1147 Carter, Thomas H. "An Universal Prey. A Footnote to *The Lion and the Fox," Shenandoah,* IX, no. 2 (Spring) 25-34 (critical appraisal of *The Lion and the Fox).*

F1148 John, Augustus. "Candid Impressions 2: Elephants with Beards. The Enigma of Wyndham Lewis," *The Sunday Times* (October 5) 19 (many early recollections of Lewis; reprinted as "Elephants With Beards," in *Finishing Touches.* London: Jonathan Cape, 1964).

1959

F1149 Atherton, J. S. *The Books at the Wake.* London: Faber and Faber, 262, passim (numerous remarks on allusions to Lewis in *Finnegans Wake,* see F638).

F1150 Colum, Mary and Padraic. *Our Friend Joyce.* London: Victor Gollancz, 144-146 (recollections of the Lewis-Joyce relationship).

F1151 Ellmann, Richard. *James Joyce.* New York: Oxford University Press, 607-609, passim.

F1152 Fraser, G. S. *Vision and Rhetoric. Studies in Modern Poetry.* London: Faber and Faber, passim (remarks on Lewis, Pound and "modern" critical theory).

F1153 Hassall, Christopher. *Edward Marsh, Patron of the Arts. A Biography.* New York: Harcourt, Brace and Co., passim.

F1154 Kenner, Hugh. *The Invisible Poet: T. S. Eliot.* New York: McDowell Obolensky, passim (Eliot and Vorticism).

F1155 Kenner, Hugh. *The Art of Poetry.* New York: Rinehart, 264-268 (discussion of *One-Way Song).*

F1156 Knoll, Robert E. *Robert McAlmon, Expatriate, Publisher and Writer.* Lincoln: University of Nebraska Press, passim (recollections of Lewis).

F1157 Selver, Paul. *Orage and the New Age Circle. Reminiscences and Reflections.* London: Allen and Unwin, 49 (discusses *Blast).*

F1158 Siciliano, Enzo. "Prefazione," *Tarr.* Milano: Feltrinelli (see E16).

F1159 Snow, C. P. *The Two Cultures and the Scientific Revolution,* The Rede Lecture. Cambridge University Press, passim (Lewis was "not only politically silly but politically wicked").

F1160 Tindall, William York. *A Reader's Guide to James Joyce.* London: Thames and Hudson, passim (remarks on Lewis in *Finnegans Wake,* see F638).

F1161 Wood, Neal. *Communism and British Intellectuals.* London: Victor Gollancz, passim.

F1162 [Lehman, John]. "Foreword," *The London Magazine,* VI, no. 7 (July) 6-9 (mentions *Blast* among the important English magazines).

1960

F1163 Beach, Sylvia. *Shakespeare and Company.* London: Faber and Faber, passim (recollections of Lewis).

F1164 Briggs, Asa (editor). *They Saw It Happen. An Anthology of Eye-Witnesses' Accounts of Events in British History, 1897-1940.* Oxford: Blackwells, 363 (quotes Goldring on Lewis).

F1165 Eliot, T. S. "Foreword," *One-Way Song.* London: Faber and Faber, 7-10 (see A21).

F1166 Fiedler, Leslie. *No! In Thunder. Essays on Myth and Literature.* Boston: Beacon Press (London: Eyre and Spottiswoode, 1963) passim (references to Lewis and *The Revenge for Love).*

F1167 Elliot, Robert C. *The Power of Satire. Magic, Ritual, Art.* Princeton: Princeton University Press, 223-237, passim (magic and satire in Lewis).

F1168 Fraser, G. S. *Ezra Pound.* Edinburgh and London: Oliver and Boyd, passim, 86-93 (Lewis as a critic of Pound).

F1169 Goldman, Arnold. *The Joyce Paradox.* London: Routledge and Kegan Paul, 57-60, passim (on Lewis, time and *Ulysses).*

F1170 Hough, Graham. *Image and Experience. Studies in a Literary Revolution.* London: Duckworth, passim (Lewis's "enormous talent" had "no sense of direction").

F1171 Jones, Alun R. *The Life and Opinions of Thomas Ernest Hulme.* London: Victor Gollancz, 118-124, passim.

F1172 Kavanagh, John. *The John Quinn Letters.* Apandect, passim (pirated collection of excerpts from the Quinn correspondence memorized in New York Library).

F1173 Levin, Harry. *James Joyce. A Critical Introduction.* London: Faber and Faber, 165 (see F638).

F1174 Norman, Charles. *Ezra Pound.* London: Macmillan, 146-162, passim (detailed study of The Great English Vortex).

F1175 Pound, Ezra. *Impact. Essays on Ignorance and the Decline of American Civilization.* Chicago: Henry Regnery, 118.

F1176 Symons, Julian. *The Thirties.* London: Cresset Press, 139-142 (Lewis and Orwell as "terrible memento mori").

F1177 Davis, Frank. "A Page for Collectors," *Illustrated London News,* CCXXXVI, no. 6291 (February 27) 352 (about Lewis's drawing, "Mad James Joyce," see Michel 398).

F1178 Wain, John "The Shadow of an Epic," *The Spectator,* CCIV, no. 6868 (March 11) 360 (review of Pound's *Thrones: Cantos 96-109* stressing the attraction for the Renaissance and tradition in Lewis and others).

F1179 Allen, Walter. "The Enemy in Verse," *The New Statesman,* LIX (April 2) 496 (whether *One-Way Song* "is poetry seems hardly relevant: it is Lewis writing as only Lewis could").

F1180 Wain, John. "Glare and Shadow," *The Spectator,* CCIV, no. 6871 (April 3) 326-328 (unfavorable review of *One-Way Song).*

F1181 "Noisy Briton," *The Times Literary Supplement,* LIX, no. 3033 (April 15) 236 (favorable review of *One-Way Song).*

F1182 Hough, Graham. "One-Way Song," *The Listener,* LXIII, no. 1621 (April 21) 720-722 (*One-Way Song* reviewed as mostly doggerel and lacking central control).

F1183 Deleted.

F1184 Armstrong, Robert. "Poets and Poets," *Poetry Review,* LI, no. 3 (July-September) 172 (*One-Way Song* is "verse" rather than "poetry").

F1185 Edman, John Henry. *Shamanism and Champagne: a Critical Introduction to the Vorticist Theory of Wyndham Lewis.* Syracuse: Syracuse University, August (unpublished doctoral thesis).

F1186 Kahma, David. "Wyndham Lewis and the Archangel Michael," *Spectrum,* IV, no. 3 (Autumn) 176-191.

F1187 Lawrence, Ralph. *English,* XII, no. 75 (Autumn) 112 (favorable review of *One-Way Song).*

F1188 Sitwell, Edith. "Personal Encounters —3: Hazards of Sitting for my Portrait," *The Observer* (November 27) 24 (recollections of Lewis; for Eliot's reply, see F1189).

F1189 Eliot, T. S. "Wyndham Lewis," *The Observer* (December 18) 14 (letter in reply to Sitwell's piece, see F1188).

1961

F1190 Chamot, Mary, Dennis Farr and Martin Butler. *The Modern British Paintings, Drawings and Sculptures, Tate Gallery Catalogues, I.* London: Oldbourne Press, 387-394.

F1191 Dresser, James Allen. *The Apollonian-Dionysian Conflict in the Works of Wyndham Lewis.* University of Washington (unpublished doctoral thesis).

F1192 Goldberg, S. L. *The Classical Temper. A Study of Joyce's Ulysses.* London: Chatto and Windus, 101-103, passim (remarks on Lewis and *Ulysses).*

F1193 Gregory, Horace. "Wyndham Lewis: the Artist at War With Himself," *The Dying Gladiators and Other Essays.* New York: Grove Press (London: Evergreen Books) 21-27 (favorable account of Lewis's career).

F1194 Haftman, W. *Painting in the Twentieth Century.* London: Lund Humphries, 2 vols., 150-155, passim (references to Lewis and the Vorticist period).

F1195 Holloway, John. "The Literary Scene," *The Modern Age,* edited by Boris Ford. Harmondsworth: Penguin Books, 75-76.

F1196 Kenner, Hugh. *Samuel Beckett. A Critical Study.* New York: Grove Press (London: John Calder, 1962) passim (Lewis, Beckett and non-moral satire).

F1197 Laver, James. *Between the Wars.* London: Vista Books, passim.

F1198 Mullins, Eustace. *This Difficult Individual, Ezra Pound.* New York: Fleet Publishing Corporation, 88-92, passim references to Lewis).

F1199 Orpen, William. *The Outline of Art.* London: Newnes, 675-678, passim.

F1200 Phelps, Gilbert. "The Novel To-day," *ibid.*, 475-476, passim.

F1201 Rose, William K. *Wyndham Lewis at Cornell. A Review of the Lewis Papers Presented to the University by William G. Mennen.* Ithaca: Cornell University Library, pp. 18. (for a review of this book, see F1220).

F1202 Snow, C. P. *Recent Thoughts on the Two Cultures. An Oration Delivered at Berbeck College.* London, December 12, passim (Lewis branded as a "reactionary").

F1203 Voorhees, Richard J. *The Paradox of George Orwell.* West Lafayette, Indiana: Purdue University Studies, passim (references to Lewis).

F1204 Wiebe, Dallas Eugene. *Reality and Wyndham Lewis's Theory of Fiction.* University of Michigan (unpublished doctoral thesis).

F1205 H. J. "Retrospect—II. Blast," *Ambit,* no. 8, 18-21 (a description of the two issues).

F1206 MacShane, Frank. "The English Review," *The South Atlantic Quarterly,* LX, no. 3 (Summer) 311-320 (Lewis, "the most spectacular" of the new writers in *The English Review).*

1962

F1207 Cassou, Jean, Emile Langui and Nikolaus Pevsner. *The Sources of Modern Art.* London: Thames and Hudson, 141-143 (places Lewis in the "Apollonian stream").

F1208 Durrell, Lawrence and Henry Miller. *A Private Correspondence,* edited by George Wickes. London: Faber and Faber, passim (remarks on *Time and Western Man).*

F1209 Goldberg, S. L. *Joyce.* Edinburgh and London: Oliver and Boyd, "Writers and Critics," 94 (Lewis on *Ulysses).*

F1210 Grigson, Geoffrey. "Revolutionary Simpletons," *The New Statesman and Nation,* LXIV, no. 1653 (November 16) 713-714 (review of an exhibition at Cardiff, *British Art and the Modern Movement, 1930-1940,* mostly concerned with Lewis).

F1211 Harrison, J. R. *The Social and Political Ideas of W. B. Yeats, Wyndham Lewis, Ezra Pound, T. S. Eliot and D. H. Lawrence.* Sheffield University (unpublished doctoral thesis).

F1212 Harvey, David Dow. *Ford Madox Ford, 1873-1939. A Bibliography.* Princeton: Princeton University Press (references to Lewis).

F1213 Highet, Gilbert. *The Anatomy of Satire.* Princeton: Princeton University Press, 49-50, passim (mostly on *One-Way Song).*

F1214 Knoll, Robert E. (editor). *MacAlmon and the Lost Generation. A Self-Portrait.* Lincoln: University of Nebraska Press, passim (references to Lewis).

F1215 Kumar, Shiv. *Bergson and the Stream-of-Consciousness Novel.* London: Blackie, passim (remarks on Lewis, Bergson, Proust and Joyce).

F1216 McLuhan, Herbert Marshall. *The Gutenberg Galaxy. The Making of Typographic Man.* Toronto: University of Toronto Press, passim (references to Lewis).

F1217 Scott, W. I. D. *Shakespeare's Melancholics.* London: Mills and Boon Ltd., 122-124, passim (in connection with *Timon of Athens* several references to Lewis's "Preface" to Dr. Henry Somerville's *Madness in Shakespearian Tragedy,* B14).

F1218 Speaight, Robert. *William Rothenstein. The Portrait of an Artist in his Time.* London: Eyre and Spottiswoode, passim (references to Lewis).

F1219 Wagner, Geoffrey. "The Fascist Mentality—Wyndham Lewis," *The Wiener Library Bulletin,* no. 22 (Summer) 35-40 (discusses Lewis and Fascism).

F1220 "Americana Bibliographica," *The Times Literary Supplement,* LXI, no. 3156 (August 17) 632 (review of Rose's *Wyndham Lewis at Cornell,* see F1201).

F1221 Rosenthal, T. G. "The Writer as Painter," *The Listener,* LXVIII, no. 1745 (September 6) 349 (Lewis as a genuine "double-artist").

1963

F1222 Callaghan, Morley. *That Summer in Paris. Memories of Tangled Relationships with Hemingway, Fitzgerald and Others.* London: McGibbon and Kee, 103.

F1223 Carrieri, Raffaele. *Futurism.* Milano: Edizioni del Milione, 62.

F1224 Church, Margaret. *Time and Reality.* University of North Carolina Press, 63-64, passim (refers to *Time and Western Man).*

F1225 Connolly, Cyril. *Previous Convictions.* London: Hamilton, passim.

F1226 [Seymour-Smith, Martin]. *The Concise Encyclopædia of Modern World Literature* (Geoffrey Grigson, ed.). London: Hutchinson, 259-262, passim.

F1227 Krzyzanowski, Jerzy R. *Ernest Hemingway.* Warszawa: Wiedza Powszechna, 48 (refers to Lewis's attack of Hemingway in *Men Without Art).*

F1228 Read, Herbert. *The Literary Experience. Recollections.* London: Ebenezer Baylis and Son, 138-140, passim (recollections of Lewis with unfavorable review of *Tarr).*

F1229 Rose, William K. *The Letters of Wyndham Lewis.* London: Methuen (Norfolk: New Directions, 1964) 17-31, passim (a preface and notes; see A42).

F1230 Scheider, H. N. *Ezra Pound's Criticism and the Influence of his Literary Relationships in London, 1908-1920.* Princeton University (unpublished doctoral thesis; Chap. III, "Vorticism and Wyndham Lewis").

F1231 Spender, Stephen. *The Struggle of the Modern.* London: Hamish Hamilton, 217-219 (on modernism and Lewis, "a man belonging to another age").

F1232 Stewart, J. I. M. *Eight Modern Writers.* Oxford: Oxford University Press, passim (Lewis and Joyce).

F1233 Wasserstrom, William. *The Time of the Dial.* Syracuse: Syracuse University Press, passim.

F1234 West, Paul. *The Modern Novel.* London: Hutchinson, passim.

F1235 Whittemore, Reed. *Little Magazines,* Pamphlets on American Writers no. 32. University of Minnesota Press, passim (Lewis's contributions to *The Dial).*

F1236 Michel, Walter. "Vorticism and the Early Wyndham Lewis," *Apollo,* LXXVII, no. 1 (January) 5-9 (analysis of Lewis's Vorticist Period).

F1237 Darracott, Joseph. "Wyndham Lewis. His 'Extraordinary powers of Drawing,' " *The Connoisseur,* CLII, no. 613 (March) 178-182.

F1238 Bone, Gerald. "Artistic Supremacy," *The Oxford Mail* (April 4) (review of *The Letters* expressing "a grudging admiration").

F1239 "When Wyndham Lewis Wrote to Time and Tide," *Time and Tide,* XLIV, no. 14 (April 4-10) 32 (descriptive review of *The Letters).*

F1240 Porteus, Hugh Gordon. *The Listener,* LXIX, no. 1775 (April 4) 603 (favorable review of *The Letters,* accompanied some personal recollections).

F1241 Pryce-Jones, David. "Ego and the Beast," *The Financial Times* (April 4) 26 (review of *The Letters,* analyzing Lewis's career and stressing his "cantankerous" nature and his "Hitler-cult").

F1242 "Two Worthwhile Rebels and Four-letter Words Again," *The Times* (April 4) 16 (review of *The Letters;* reprinted in *The Times Weekly Review* (April 11) 13).

F1243 [Symons, Julian]. "Rebel With a Cause," *The Times Literary Supplement,* LXII, no. 3188 (April 5) 232 (review of *The Letters* and survey of Lewis's career).

F1244 Powell, Anthony. "Too Combative Talent," *The Daily Telegraph* (April 5) 9 (review of *The Letters* acknowledging Lewis's importance in spite of a "superfluity of gifts" and a tendency to "paranoiac" contradiction).

F1245 "Artists in Correspondence," *The Economist,* no. 6241 (April 6) 62 (review of *The Letters* noting Lewis's "persecution mania").

F1246 Heppenstall, Rayner. "Always in a Fight," *The Sunday Telegraph* (April 7) 18 (favorable review of *The Letters).*

F1247 Quennell, Peter. "Wyndham Lewis's iron masks," *The Observer* (April 7) 25 (review of *The Letters).*

F1248 Churchill, R. C. "From An Enemy to His Friends," *The Birmingham Post* (April 9) 4 (favorable review of *The Letters).*

F1249 Kermode, Frank. "Letters from The Enemy," *The Manchester Guardian Weekly* (April 11) 10 (review of *The Letters).*

F1250 "Books in Brief," *The Daily Herald* (April 13) 4 (reviews *The Letters).*

F1251 Graham, Cuthbert. "Tragedy of a Belligerent Genius . . .," *Press and Journal* (April 13) 11 (review of *The Letters*).

F1252 Kiely, Benedict. "The fights and friendships of Wyndham Lewis," *The Irish Press* (April 13) 6 (favorable review of *The Letters*).

F1253 Nye, Robert. "Public Enemy No. 1, 2, 3 & 4," *The Scotsman* (April 13) (review of *The Letters*).

F1254 Puffmore, Henry. "Under Review," *The Bookseller* (April 13) 1594 (short review of *The Letters*).

F1255 Miles, Hamish. "The One-Man Blast Furnace," *The Glasgow Herald* (April 18) 11 (review of *The Letters*).

F1256 Ayrton, Michael. "Too Clever by Half," *The Spectator*, CCX, no. 7034 (April 19) 502 (review of *The Letters*).

F1257 Symons, Julian. "Staggering Along," *ibid.*, 503 (review of "The New Statesman" and "Statesmanship," with a reference to *Tarr*).

F1258 Grigson, Geoffrey. "Wyndham Lewis," *The New Statesman*, LXV, no. 1675 (April 19) 606, 608 (review of *The Letters*, description of Lewis as the last Flaubertian).

F1259 Stone, Geoffrey. "Wyndham Lewis," *The Times Literary Supplement*, LXII, no. 3190 (April 19) 265 (letter to the editor).

F1260 Stone, Peter. "Lovely Sussex Landscapes," *The Jewish Chronicle*, no. 4904 (April 19) 33 (mentions works by Lewis at the Brook Street Gallery).

F1261 Longford, Christine. "The Recent Past," *The Irish Times* (April 20) 8 (favorable review of *The Letters*).

F1262 Rogers, Derek. "Our Man in Cubism," *The Arts Review*, XV, no. 7 (April 20) 24 (review of *The Letters* defining Lewis as a rebel).

F1263 "The Letters of Wyndham Lewis," *The South Wales Argus* (April 22) (favorable review of *The Letters*).

F1264 Mallett, Richard. "The Epistolary Style," *Punch*, CCXLIV, no. 6398 (April 24) 609 (review of *The Letters* with remarks on Lewis's style).

F1265 Callow, Philip. "Lonely Old Volcano," *The Tribune* (April 26) 10 (review of *The Letters*).

F1266 Coffey, Warren. "Wyndham Lewis: Enemy of the Rose," *Ramparts*, II, no. 1 (May) 70-76 (a survey of Lewis's career concluding that Lewis was the greatest writer of his generation).

F1267 Rose, William K. "Wyndham Lewis in his Letters," *ibid.*, 85-89 (revised version of the Preface to *The Letters*).

F1268 Ricks, Christopher. "Blowing the Gaff," *The New Statesman*, LXV, no. 1678 (May 10) 713-714 (review of *The Concise Encyclopædia of Modern World Literature* sharply criticizing the favorable entry for Wyndham Lewis, which led to an exchange of letters, see F1270 and F1271).

F1269 Rose, William K. "Wyndham Lewis," *The New Statesman*, LXV, no. 1678 (May 10) 712 (letter correcting remarks made by Grigson, see F1407).

F1270 Seymour-Smith, Martin. "Wyndham Lewis and Hitler," *The New Statesman*, LXV, no. 1681 (May 31) 830 (letter answering Ricks's article and acknowledging the authorship of the contribution on Lewis, see F1268).

F1271 Ricks, Christopher. "Wyndham Lewis and Hitler," *ibid.* (answer to Seymour-Smith's letter, see F1270).

F1272 Dobree, Bonamy. "A Pride of Lions," *Books of the Month*, LXXVIII, no. 5 (May) 5 (review of *The Letters*).

F1273 Arnold, Bruce. "Blast Bloomsbury—Bless Bloomsbury," *The Dubliner*, II, no. 2 (Summer) 36-44 (review of *The Letters*).

F1274 Woodcock, George. "The Enemy of Man," *Canadian Literature*, no. 17 (Summer) 57-60 (review of *The Letters*).

F1275 [*Unsigned review.*] *The Studio*, CXLVI, no. 843 (July) 44 (favorable review of *The Letters*).

F1276 Fulford, Robert. "An Englishman's Life in a Disgusting Spot Called Toronto," *Maclean's Magazine,* LXXVI, no. 16 (August 24) 45 (favorable review of *The Letters* accompanied by a cartoon of Lewis as "Tyro" sticking Canada into a garbage can).

F1277 Allen, Walter. "Lonely Old Volcano," *Encounter,* XXI, no. 3 (September 3) 63-70 (review of *The Letters).*

F1278 Hammond, Arthur. "The Three Lives of Wyndham Lewis," *The Globe Magazine, The Globe and Mail* (September 28) 15 (finds *The Letters* "a fascinating, entertaining and stimulating book").

F1279 Burns, Howard. *Agenda,* III, no. 1 (August-September) 17-21 (favorable review of *The Letters).*

F1280 Watson, Sheila M. "Wyndham Lewis: a Question of Portraiture," *Tamarack Review,* XXIX (Autumn) 90-98 (review of *The Letters* stressing the "formal structure" of Lewis's work as a whole).

F1281 Rillie, John A. M. *The Library Review,* no. 147 (Autumn) 157 (review of *The Letters).*

F1282 Wiebe, Dallas Eugene. "Wyndham Lewis and the Picaresque Novel," *The South Atlantic Quarterly,* LXII, no. 4 (Autumn) 587-596 (study of Lewis's fiction).

1964

F1284 Allen, Walter. *Tradition and Dream. The English and American Novel from the Twenties to our Time.* London: Phoenix House, 29-33, passim (general survey with analysis of Lewis's "external approach").

F1285 Chamot, Mary, Dennis Farr and Martin Butlin. *Tate Gallery Catalogues. The Modern British Paintings, Drawings and Sculptures,* I. London: Oldbourne Press, 387-394.

F1286 Duncan, Ronald. *All Men are Islands.* London: Hart-Davis, passim (Leavis and Pound about Lewis).

F1287 Gaunt, William. *The Observer's Book of Modern Art from Impressionism to the Present Day.* London: Frederick Warne and Co., passim (references to Lewis).

F1288 Hardy, John Edward. *Man in the Modern World.* Seattle: University of Washington Press, passim (Lewis about Hemingway and Faulkner).

F1289 Hemingway, Ernest. *A Moveable Feast.* New York: Charles Scribner's Sons (London: Jonathan Cape) passim (hostile recollections of Lewis).

F1290 Howarth, Herbert. *Notes on Some Figures Behind T. S. Eliot.* Boston: Houghton Mifflin (London: Chatto and Windus, 1965) passim (remarks on the alliance between Lewis and Eliot).

F1291 Joll, James. *The Anarchists.* London: Eyre and Spottiswoode, 212 (Lewis on Georges Sorel).

F1292 Snow, C. P. *The Two Cultures: and a Second Look.* London: Cambridge University Press, 93 (places Lewis among "the representative" moderns).

F1293 Stead, C. K. *The New Poetic. Keats to Eliot.* London: Hutchinson, passim.

F1294 Stock, Noel. *Poet in Exile: Ezra Pound.* Manchester: Manchester University Press, passim.

F1295 Swinnerton, Frank. *Figures in the Foreground: Literary Reminiscences, 1917-1940.* New York: Doubleday, passim.

F1296 Wees, William C. *Vorticism: the Movement and its Meaning.* Northwestern University (unpublished doctoral dissertation; incorporated in *Vorticism and the English Avant-Garde).*

F1297 Weisstein, Ulrich. "Vorticism: Expressionism English Style," *Year Book of Comparative and General Literature,* XIII, 28-40 (detailed comparison of the styles and objectives of Vorticism and Die Brücke and Der Blaue Reiter).

F1298 Woolf, Leonard. *Beginning Again, 1911-1918.* London: Hogarth Press, 95-96 (analyzes the breach between Fry and Lewis).

F1299 [*Unsigned review.*] *The Yale Review.* LIII, no. 4 (June) 6-8 (favorably reviews *The Letters).*

F1300 Moon, Barbara. "The Man Who Discovered Canadian Painting," *McLean's* (January 4) 16-17, 40, 42-44 (a portrait of Duncan Douglas who is said to have inspired Cedric Furber, one of the characters in *Self Condemned).*

F1301 Thompson, Marjorie. *The Modern Language Review,* LXI, no. 1 (January) 133-134 (a review of *The Letters).*

F1302 [*Unsigned review.*] *The Booklist,* LX, no. 14 (March 15) 732 (review of *The Letters).*

F1303 "Rebel Against the Senses," *Time* (April 3) 108 (favorable review of *The Letters).*

F1304 Read, Herbert. "A Good Artist but a Bad Friend," *The Saturday Review,* XLVII, no. 14 (April 4) 29 and 43 (hostile review of *The Letters* with some personal reminiscences).

F1305 Powell, Anthony. "Holding Out on his Pen Pals," *New York Herald Tribune Weekly Book Review* (April 12) 6 and 16 (review of *The Letters).*

F1306 Clinton, Farley. "Polished and Robust," *National Review,* XVI, no. 18 (May 5) 362-366 (favorable review of *The Letters* ranking Lewis among the "very best masters" of his time).

F1307 Greene, George. "The Wars of Wyndham Lewis," *The Commonweal,* LXXX, no. 7 (May 8) 195-197 (review of *The Letters* and detailed survey of Lewis's career).

F1308 Pritchett, V. S. "Wyndham Lewis," *The New York Review,* II, no. 4 (May 28) 5-6 (review of *The Letters* and appraisal of Lewis's work).

F1309 Bergonzi, Bernard. "Before 1914: Writers and the Threat of War," *The Critical Quarterly,* VI, no. 2 (Summer) 126-134 (remarks on *Blast* and Futurism).

F1310 McLuhan, Marshall. "Explorations," *The Varsity Graduate* (May) 53-57.

F1311 Watson, Sheila. "The Artist as Crowd-Master," *ibid.* (Lewis as precursor in the study of the "corporate image"; reprinted as "Artist-Ape and Crowd-Master").

F1312 W., M. *English,* XV, no. 86 (Summer) 69 (favorable review of *The Letters).*

F1313 [*Unsigned review.*] *The Virginia Quarterly Review,* XL, no. 107 (Summer) 17 (favorable review of *The Letters).*

F1314 Gregory, Horace. "A One-Man Movement to Annihilate Mediocrity," *The New York Times Book Review,* LXIX, no. 32 (August 9) 5 (review of *The Letters* and analysis of Lewis's work stressing its prophetic value).

F1315 [*Unsigned review.*] *The New Yorker,* XL, no. 27 (August 22) 125 (review of *The Letters,* defining Lewis as a "positive, pugnacious man").

F1316 McHugh, V. *The San Francisco Sunday Chronicle* (September 9) 25 (review of *The Letters).*

F1317 Carruth, Hayden. "Pursy Windhum Lucigen," *The Hudson Review,* XVII, no. 3 (Autumn) 465-469 (review of *The Letters* and a particularly hostile analysis of Lewis's "evil," "ugly" personality).

F1318 Bell, Quentin and Stephen Chaplin. "The Ideal Home Rumpus," *Apollo,* LXXX, no. 32 (October) 284-291 (detailed account of the Omega Workshop; reprinted in Rosenbaum's *The Bloomsbury Group).*

F1319 Smith, Grover. "Wyndham Lewis through his Letters," *Shenandoah,* XVI, no. 1 (Autumn) 65-68 (review of *The Letters* seeing Lewis's achievement as "vitiated by an overabundance of spleen").

1965

F1320 Bergonzi, Bernard. *Heroes' Twilight. A Study of the Literature of the Great War.* London: Constable, 28-29, 164-166, passim (comments on *Blast* and *Blasting and Bombardiering).*

F1321 Bianchi, Ruggero. *La Poetica dell' Imagismo.* Milano: U. Mursia & C., passim (references to Lewis).

F1322 Davie, Donald. *Ezra Pound, Poet as Sculptor.* London: Routledge and Kegan Paul, passim (numerous remarks about Lewis).

F1323 George, Margaret. *The Hollowmen (an Examination of British Foreign Policy between the Years 1933 and 1939).* London: Leslie Frewin, passim (Lewis and Douglas Jerrold).

F1324 Hutchins, Patricia. *Ezra Pound's Kensington.* London: Faber and Faber, passim (references to Lewis).

F1325 Kenner, Hugh. "Introduction," *Self Condemned* by Wyndham Lewis. Chicago: Regnery, 7-15 (see A38b).

F1326 *Kindlers Literatur Lexikon.* Zurich: Kindler Verlag, Band I, 769-770; Band III, 2239-2241 (analyses of *The Apes of God* and *The Human Age).*

F1327 MacLaren-Ross, J. *Memoirs of the Forties.* London: Alan Ross, passim (on Lewis, Colquhoun and MacBryde).

F1328 McShane, Frank. *The Life and Works of Ford Madox Ford.* New York: Horizon Press, passim.

F1329 Rothenstein, John. *Summer's Lease. Autobiography 1901-1908.* London: Hamish Hamilton, passim (references to Lewis).

F1330 Stock, Noel (editor). *Ezra Pound Perspectives (Essays in Honor of his Eightieth Birthday).* New York: Regnery, passim (quotes from a letter by Lewis about *Tarr,* December 31, 1915).

F1331 Prichard, William H. "The Real Wyndham Lewis," *The Massachusetts Review,* VI, no. 2 (Winter/Spring) 409-423 (favorable review of *The Letters* and evaluation of Lewis's career).

F1332 Watson, Sheila. *Wyndham Lewis and Expressionism.* Toronto: University of Toronto (unpublished doctoral thesis).

F1333 Wees, William C. "Ezra Pound as a Vorticist," *Contemporary Literature,* VI, no. 1 (Winter-Spring), 56-72 (detailed account of Vorticist movement; incorporated in *Vorticism and the English Avant-Guard).*

F1334 Hamilton, A. "Paperbacks," *Books and Bookmen,* X, no. 6 (March) 10 (favorable review of *The Childermass).*

F1335 Howard, Richard. "Some Poets in their Prose," *Poetry,* CV, no. 6 (March) 397-398 (review stressing "the tedium mortis" of *The Letters).*

F1336 "Wyndham Lewis: his Biting Comments on Canada and Canadians reviewed on CBC TV's 'Other Voices,'" *C.B.C. Times,* April 24-30 (a preview of a CBC-TV program on Lewis, April 27, 10:30 p.m.).

F1337 Lipke, W. C. "Vorticism and the Modern Movement," *Arts Review,* XVII, no. 16 (August 21—September 4) 2 (detailed historical summary of Vorticism).

F1338 Michel, Walter. "Tyros and Portraits: the Early Twenties and Wyndham Lewis," *Apollo,* LXXXII (August) 128-133 (survey of the "second phase" in Lewis's career).

F1339 "Roberts Declares Peace," *London Life* (November 13) [1] (announcing the Roberts exhibition at the Tate Gallery, this article contains many references to the 1956 *Wyndham Lewis and Vorticism* exhibition).

F1340 Lewis, Anne Wyndham. *Arts Review,* XVII, no. 23 (November 27) 22 (letter correcting points in Lipke's article, especially about the Lewis-Bomberg relationship, see F1337 and F1341).

F1341 Lipke, William C. *Ibid.,* 22 (reply to Mrs. Lewis's letter; see F1340).

1966

F1342 Butter, P. H. *Edwin Muir, Man and Poet.* Edinburgh: Oliver and Boyd, 108 (about the Schiffs and the Muirs in *The Apes of God).*

F1343 Connolly, Cyril. *The Modern Movement. (One Hundred Key-Books from England, France and the United States).* New York: Atheneum, 34-35, passim (*Tarr* one of the selected books).

F1344 Ellmann, Richard. *Letters of James Joyce.* New York: The Viking Press, (3 vols.), passim (numerous references to Lewis).

F1345 Farmer, Albert J. *Les Ecrivains Anglais d'Aujourd'hui,* Paris: Que Sais-Je? P.U.F., 22-23 (defines Lewis as the anti-D. H. Lawrence).

F1346 Goodwin, K. L. *The Influence of Ezra Pound.* London: London University Press, 28-31, passim (numerous references to Lewis).

F1347 Grant, Joy. *Harold Monro and the Poetry Book Shop.* Berkeley: University of California Press, passim (Lewis and *The Chapbook).*

F1348 Greenbaum, Leonard. *The Hound and Horn. The History of a Literary Quarterly*. The Hague: Mouton, 31-32 (favorably discusses *The Enemy*).

F1349 Harrison, John R. *The Reactionaries, W. B. Yeats, Wyndham Lewis, Ezra Pound, T. S. Eliot, D. H. Lawrence.* London: Victor Gollancz (New York, Schoken Books, 1967) passim.

F1350 Empson, William. "Preface," *ibid.*, 9-12.

F1351 Kenner, Hugh. "The Trial of Man," *Malign Fiesta* by Wyndham Lewis. London: Calder (afterword discussing synopsis of projected fourth book of *The Human Age)*.

F1352 Kermode, Frank. *The Sense of an Ending. Studies in the Theory of Fiction.* Oxford: Oxford University Press, passim (analyzes the apocalyptic element in *The Human Age)*.

F1353 Levin, Harry. *Refractions. Essays in Comparative Literature.* New York: Oxford University Press, passim (Lewis and modernism).

F1354 Lipke, William C. *A History and Analysis of Vorticism.* University of Wisconsin (unpublished doctoral thesis).

F1355 Meisel, James H. *The Genesis of Georges Sorel.* London: The Athena Publishing Company, 255-259 (analyzes Lewis's view of Sorel).

F1356 Rosenthal, Raymond. "Introduction," *A Soldier of Humor and Selected Writings*. New York: The New American Library, 9-18.

F1357 Rothenstein, John. *Brave Day, Hideous Night. Autobiography 1939-1965.* London: Hamish Hamilton, passim (numerous recollections of Lewis).

F1358 Stansky, Peter and William Abrahams. *Journey to the Frontier. Julian Bell and John Cornford: their lives and 1930s.* London: Constable, passim.

F1359 Young, Philip. *Ernest Hemingway, a Reconsideration.* University Park: The Pennsylvania State University Press, passim (opposes Lewis's view of the Hemingway hero).

F1360 Bell, Quentin and Stephen Chaplin. "Rumpus Revived," *Apollo*, LXXXIII, no. 47 (January) 75 (in answer to Michel's article, a letter defending Fry's reputation, see F1338 and F1361; reprinted in *The Bloomsbury Group)*.

F1361 Michel, Walter. "Author's Reply," *ibid.* (answer to the preceding letter, see F1360; reprinted in *The Bloomsbury Group)*.

F1362 Muir, Edwin. "Some Letters of Edwin Muir," *Encounter*, XXVI, no. 1 (January) 3-10 (discussion of *Tarr, The Enemy* and *The Lion and the Fox)*.

F1363 Lafourcade, Bernard. "Wyndham Lewis au Purgatoire," *Etudes Anglaises*, XIX, no. 1 (Janvier-Mars) 37-44 (review of *The Letters* and analysis of Lewis's personality).

F1364 Quinn, R. M. *The Arizona Quarterly*, XXII, no. 1 (Spring) 92 (a review of Kenner's *Wyndham Lewis* and *The Letters*, opposing the view that Lewis is "a truly significant" artist).

F1365 Read, Herbert. "T. S. Eliot: A Memoir," *The Sewaneee Review*, LXXIV, no. 1 (January-March) 31-58 (reviews Lewis's attack in *The Demon of Progress in the Arts* and Herbert Read's reply in "The Lost Leader," see F982).

F1366 Bergel, Lienhard. "Lewis and Dostoievsky," *Elsinore*, Rome, April.

F1367 Burgess, Anthony. "Lewis as Spaceman," *The Spectator*, CCXVI, no. 7195 (May 20) 640-641 (unfavorable assessment of *The Apes of God* based on the assumption that a great painter cannot be a great writer, with references to *Finnegans Wake*, F638; reprinted in *Urgent Copy*. London: Jonathan Cape, 1968; 96-99).

F1368 Bellow, Saul. "Speaking of Books: Cloister Culture," *The New York Times Book Review* (July 10) 2.

F1369 Cox, C. B. "Shakespeare as Executioner: The Lion and the Fox," *The Spectator*, CCXVII, no. 7203 (July 15) 85 (review of *The Lion and the Fox)*.

F1370 Lipke, William C. and Bernard W. Rozran. "Ezra Pound and Vorticism: a Polite Blast," *Contemporary Literature*, VII, no. 2 (Summer) 201-210 (article meant to complete William Wees's analysis of Vorticism, see F1296 and F1333).

F1371 Kermode, Frank. "The New Apocalyptists," *Partisan Review,* XXXIII, no. 3 (Summer) 339-361.

F1372 Wees, William C. "Pound's Vorticism: Some New Evidence and Further Comments," *Contemporary Literature,* VII, no. 2 (Summer) 210-216 (Wees's rejoinder to Lipke/Rozran's article, see F1370; includes a letter by Pound with numerous references to Lewis and Vorticism).

F1373 Rees, David. "The View from Rot-Hill," *The Spectator,* CCXVII no. 7208 (August 19) 227 (reflections on Pound, Lewis and Notting Hill).

F1374 Toynbee, Philip. "Poetry and Fascism," *The Observer Weekend Review* (August 28) (unfavorable review of Harrison's *The Reactionaries,* see F1349).

F1375 Bannon, B. A. *Publisher's Weekly,* no. 190 (August 29) 348 (favorable review of Rosenthal's anthology, *A Soldier of Humor,* see F1356).

F1376 "Politics and Poetry," *The Economist,* CCXX, no. 6419 (September 3) 923 (hostile review of Harrison's *The Reactionaries,* see F1349).

F1377 "Art and Autocracy," *The Times Literary Supplement,* LXV, no. 3368 (September 15) 855 (critical review of Harrison's *The Reactionaries,* see F1349).

F1378 Klawitter, Robert. "Henri Bergson and James Joyces's Fictional World," *Comparative Literature Studies,* III, no. 4 429-437 (remarks about Lewis and *Finnegans Wake,* see F638).

F1379 Enright, D. J. "No Cheer for Democracy," *The New Statesman,* LXVII, no. 1854 (September 23) 443-444 (review of Harrison's *The Reactionaries,* defining Lewis as a "political" writer, see F1349; reprinted in *Man is an Onion.* London: Chatto and Windus, 1972; 166-168).

F1380 Langman, F. H. "Coriolanus: The Poetry and the Critics," *The Critical Review* (Melbourne), no. 9, 92-105 (employs *The Lion and the Fox).*

F1381 Bergonzi, Bernard. *The London Magazine,* VI, no. 8 (November) 88-94 (unfavorable review of Harrison's *The Reactionaries,* considered to be insufficiently documented on Lewis, see F1349).

F1382 Seymour, William Kean. "Creation and Criticism," *The Contemporary Review,* CCIX, no. 1210 (November) 276 (favorable review of *The Lion and the Fox,* "highly idiosyncratic" work).

1967

F1383 Benson, Frederick R. *Writers in Arms. The Literary Impact of the Spanish Civil War.* New York: New York University Press, passim.

F1384 Burgess, Anthony. *The Novel Now.* London: Faber and Faber, passim ("Lewis is too massive a writer to be ignored by posterity").

F1385 Cooper, Douglas. *The Work of Graham Sutherland.* London: Lund Humphries, passim.

F1386 Easton, Malcolm. *Art in Britain, 1890-1940.* University of Hull (an exhibition catalogue).

F1387 Ellmann, Richard. *Eminent Domain.* Oxford: Oxford University Press, 83 (Lewis in Pound's *Cantos).*

F1388 French, Warren. *The Thirties: Fiction, Poetry, Drama.* Everett Edwards, passim.

F1389 Halliday, F. E. *An Illustrated Cultural History of England.* London: Thames and Hudson, 279-280, passim (views Lewis as "essentially a manipulator").

F1390 Hamilton, G. H. *The Pelican History of Art.* Harmondsworth: Pelican Books, passim (a number of interesting references to Lewis).

F1391 Hillegas, Mark Robert. *The Future as Nightmare: H. G. Wells and the Anti-Utopians.* New York: Oxford University Press, passim.

F1392 Holroyd, Michael. *Lytton Strachey. A Critical Biography.* London: William Heinemann, (2 vols.), passim (number of references to Lewis whose character Matthew Plunket in *The Apes of God* was modelled on Strachey).

F1393 Lewis, Anne Wyndham. "Preface to the New Edition," *Blasting and Bombardiering.* London: Calder and Boyars (see A26).

F1394 Lipke, William C. *Bomberg*. London: Evelyn, Adams and Mackay Ltd., passim (numerous references to Lewis).

F1395 Martin, Wallace. *The New Age Under Orage*. Manchester: Manchester University Press, passim (many references to Lewis).

F1396 Praz, Mario. *James Joyce. Thomas Stearns Eliot. Due Maestri dei Moderni*. Torino: Eri, Edizioni Rai Radiotelevisione Italiana, passim (Lewis on Joyce).

F1397 Rabinovitz, Rubin. *The Reaction Against Experiment in the English Novel*. New York: Columbia University Press, 99-100 (C. P. Snow's paradoxical reaction to Lewis).

F1398 Reck, Michael. *Ezra Pound. A Close-up*. New York: McGraw-Hill, passim (number of references to Lewis and obituary poem by Omar Pound).

F1399 Ross, R. H. *The Georgian Revolt. Rise and Fall of a Poetic Ideal*. Carbondale: Southern Illinois Press (London: Faber and Faber), passim (numerous references to Lewis).

F1400 Salter, Elizabeth. *The Last Years of a Rebel. A Memoir of Edith Sitwell*. Boston: Houghton Mifflin (London: The Bodley Head), 61-62, passim (account of the feud between Lewis and the Sitwells).

F1401 Stevenson, Lionel. *The English Novel. A Panorama*. London: Constable, 481-483, passim (Lewis's novels "rank among the major books of his generation").

F1402 Stevenson, Lionel. *Yesterday and After* (Vol. XI, *The History of the English Novel*, Ernest Baker). New York: Barnes and Noble, 168-183 (substantial survey of Lewis's fiction).

F1403 Stewart, Allegra. *Gertrude Stein and the Present*. Cambridge: Harvard University Press, 10-13, passim.

F1404 McCooey, Mereel. "Blast," *The Sunday Times Magazine* (January 8) 18-21.

F1405 [*Unsigned review.*] *The Catholic Library World*, XXXVIII (March) 492 (review of *The Lion and the Fox*).

F1406 Cixous, Hélène. "Survivances d'un Mythe: le Gentleman," *Le Monde* (April 5) 7 (analysis of Lewis's style and *The Human Age*).

F1407 Bergonzi, Bernard. "Roy Campbell: Outsider on the Right," *The Journal of Contemporary History*, II, no. 2 (April) 149-158 (account of Lewis's influence on Campbell and his changing political attitudes; reprinted in Bergonzi's *The Turn of a Century*).

F1408 Tarratt, Margaret. "Puce Monster," *Studio International*, CLXXIII, no. 888 (April) 168-170 (survey of the two issues of *Blast* and their effect).

F1409 Rozran, B. W. "A Vorticist Poetry with Visual Implications. The 'Forgotten' experiment of Ezra Pound," *ibid.*, 170-172.

F1410 Lipke, William C. "Futurism and the Development of Vorticism," *ibid.*, 173-178.

F1411 Harrison, Charles. "Abstract Painting in Britain in the early 1930s," *ibid.*, 180-191 (references to Lewis).

F1412 Benski, Lawrence M. *The New York Times* (May 17) 49 (review of Harrison's *The Reactionaries*, see F1349).

F1413 Curley, Arthur. *The Library Journal*, XCII (June 1) (review of Harrison's *The Reactionaries*, F1349).

F1414 Paul, Sherman. "The Politics of Art," *The Nation*, CCIV, no. 25 (June 19) 792 (favorable review of Harrison's *The Reactionaries*).

F1415 Symons, Julian. "The Blaster," *The London Magazine*, VII, no. 3 (June) 90-95 (review of *Blasting and Bombardiering*, with recollections of Lewis and an analysis of his personality).

F1416 Spender, Stephen. "Writers and Politics," *The Partisan Review*, XXXIV, no. 3 (Summer) 360-381 (review of Harrison's *The Reactionaries*, F1349, including discussion of Lewis's political attitudes).

F1417 Burgess, Anthony. "Gun and Pen," *The Spectator*, CCXIX, no. 7254 (July 7) 15-16 (review finding *Blasting and Bombardiering* dated and dull).

F1418 Toynbee, Philip. "The Ho-ho-ness of Things," *The Observer* (July 16) 21 (favorable review of *Blasting and Bombardiering* with some personal recollections).

F1419 Hart, Jeffrey. "Literature and Politics," *The National Review,* XIX, no. 29 (July 25) 809-811 (unfavorable review of Harrison's *The Reactionaries,* F1349).

F1420 Deleted.

F1421 Pritchett, V. S. "Public Eye," *The New Statesman,* LXXIV, no. 1898 (July 28) 119-120 (review of *Blasting and Bombardiering).*

F1422 [*Unsigned review.*] *Time,* XC, no. 4 (July 28) 86-88 (descriptive review of *Blasting and Bombardiering).*

F1423 Martin, Kingsley. "And Those Before Cried 'Back!'," *Punch,* CCLII, no. 6621 (August 2) 181 (review of *Blasting and Bombardiering).*

F1424 Kermode, Frank. "Bungling," *The Listener,* LXXVIII, no. 2001 (August 3) 150-151 (review describing *Blasting and Bombardiering* as a "minor classic" and listing deletions and errors in the editing).

F1425 "Painter under Arms," *The Times* (August 17) (favorable review of *Blasting and Bombardiering* complaining about careless editing).

F1426 Donoghue, Denis. "Literary Fascism," *Commentary,* XLIV, no. 44 (August) 82-86 (unfavorable review of Harrison's *The Reactionaries,* see F1349).

F1427 Howe, Irving. "Beliefs of the Masters," *The New Republic,* CLVII, no. 12 (September 16) 19-26 (review of Harrison's *The Reactionaries,* see F1349).

F1428 Macaulay, Robie. *The New York Times Book Review* (September 17) 26 (review of Harrison's *The Reactionaries,* see F1349).

F1429 Mott, Michael. *The Kenyon Review,* XXIX, no. 4 (September 29) 574-578 (review of *Blasting and Bombardiering).*

F1430 Egbert, Donald D. "Art Critics and Modern Social Radicalism," *The Journal of Æsthetics and Art Criticism,* XXVI, no. 1 (Fall) 34.

F1431 Schwartz, Michael. "The Treachery of Literature," *The New Leader* (October 23) 23-24 (unfavorable review of Harrison's *The Reactionaries,* see F1349).

F1432 Jones, D. A. N. *The New York Review of Books,* IX, no. 7 (October 26) 20 (apart from the fiction included, this review finds *Blasting and Bombardiering* "profoundly stupid and narcissistic"; see F1433).

F1433 Rosenthal, Raymond. *The New York Review of Books,* IX, no. 8 (November 2) (a letter answering Jones's review, see F1432).

F1434 Watson, Sheila. "The Great War: Wyndham Lewis and the Underground Press," *Arts Canada,* XXIV (November) 1-17 (survey of Lewis's artistic career, accompanied with 34 reproductions and a 45 rpm record of Lewis reading from *One-Way Song* and Marshall McLuhan recalling Lewis).

F1435 Paliwall, B. B. "T. E. Hulme's Poetics," *The Literary Criterion,* VIII, no. 1 (Winter) 33-38 (Richards and Lewis supplement Hulme's æsthetics).

F1436 Panichas, George A. "Politics and Literature," *The Modern Age,* XII, no. 1 (Winter 1967-1968) 84-89 (this review sees Harrison's *The Reactionaries* as "alarmingly" superficial and dogmatic, see F1349).

1968

F1437 Bell, Quentin. *Bloomsbury.* London: Weidenfeld and Nicholson, 56, passim.

F1438 Bergonzi, Bernard. "Thoughts on the Personality Explosion," *Innovations. Essays on Art and Ideas,* edited by Bernard Bergonzi. London: Macmillan, 188-189, passim.

F1439 Kermode, Frank. "Modernisms," *ibid.,* passim.

F1440 Burgess, Anthony. [J. A. B. Wilson] "Introduction," *Titus Groan* by Mervyn Peake. Harmondsworth: Penguin Books, 10.

F1441 Clark, Ronald W. *The Huxleys.* London: Heinemann, 223.

F1442 Fauchereau, Serge. *Lecture de la Poésie Américaine.* Paris: Les Editions de Minuit, passim.

F1443 Ford, Hugh. "Foreword," *Nancy Cunard: Brave Poet, Indomitable Rebel, 1896-1965,* edited by Hugh Ford. Philadelphia: Chilton Book Co. (Ontario, Thomas Nelson and Sons), 9 (Lewis's portrait).

F1444 Lye, Len. "Introductory," *ibid.,* 36-37 (October 1922 in Venice).

F1445 Cunard, Nancy. "Visits from James Joyce," *ibid.,* 81-82 ("I knew Lewis rather well").

F1446 Flanner, Janet. "Nancy Cunard," *ibid.,* 87-90 (Cunard, "a member of London's Blast Group").

F1447 Cunard, Nancy. "London at War," *ibid.,* 206-222 (The Blitz: a Lewis drawing "under a tree").

F1448 Strachan, W. J. "Nancy Cunard," *ibid.,* 271-274 (Lewis's drawing).

F1449 Rose, William K. "Remembering Nancy," *ibid.,* 316-319 (Venice 1922 and Nancy Cunard as the probable heroine of *The Roaring Queen).*

F1450 Benkowitz, Mirian J. "A memoir: Nancy Cunard," *ibid.,* 320-323 (the "intimacies of the twenties").

F1451 Fraser, G. S. *Lawrence Durrell.* London: Faber and Faber, 152-153, passim (Lewis's influence on Durrell).

F1452 Joost, Nicholas. *Ernest Hemingway and the Little Magazines. The Paris Years.* Barre, Massachusetts: Barre Publishers, passim (references to Lewis).

F1453 Kenner, Hugh. *The Counterfeiters.* Bloomington: Indiana University Press, 164-167 (discusses *The Revenge for Love* and *The Vulgar Streak).*

F1454 Lafourcade, Bernard. "Introduction," *Cantleman's Spring Mate, The Code of a Herdsman.* Paris: Minard (Passeport no. 21, Lettres Modernes) 3-21.

F1455 Lehman, John. *A Nest of Tigers.* London: Macmillan, 124-131, passim.

F1456 Levy, William Turner and Victor Scherle. *Affectionately, T. S. Eliot.* Philadelphia: J. B. Lippincott, 82 (about the Cambridge portrait of Eliot).

F1457 Materer, Timothy. *Wyndham Lewis and the Era of Violence.* Stanford University (unpublished doctoral thesis; incorporated in *Wyndham Lewis the Novelist,* see F1838).

F1458 Mosley, Oswald. *My Life.* London: Nelson, passim.

F1459 Poggioli, Renato. *The Theory of the Avant-Garde.* Cambridge: Harvard University Press, 73-74, passim (on Vorticist "nihilism").

F1460 Pontus Hulten, K. G. *The Machine.* New York: Museum of Modern Art, 66 (discusses "The Crowd" (Michel P17) as a constructivist painting).

F1461 Pritchard, William H. *Wyndham Lewis.* New York: Twayne Publishers, pp. 180 (discusses Lewis "as a novelist and critic of modern culture").

F1462 Reck, Michael. *Ezra Pound. A Close-up.* London: Rupert Hart-Davis, passim (references to Lewis).

F1463 Reid, B. L. *The Man from New York. John Quinn and his Friends.* New York: Oxford University Press, passim (references to Lewis).

F1464 Temple, Ruth Z. and Martin Tucker. *Twentieth Century British Literature. A Reference Guide and Bibliography.* New York: Frederick Ungar Publishing Co., passim.

F1465 Schneidau, Herbert N. "Vorticism and the Career of Ezra Pound," *Modern Philology,* LXV, no. 3 (February) 214-227 (survey and analysis of Vorticism).

F1466 Pritchard, William H. "On Wyndham Lewis," *Partisan Review,* XXXV, no. 2 (Spring) 253-267.

F1467 Woolf, Geoffrey. "Writers and Politics," *The American Scholar,* XXXVII, no. 2 (Spring) 356-362 (review of Harrison's *The Reactionaries,* Lewis supported "directly . . . the fascist cause").

F1468 Grigson, Geoffrey. "Recollections of 'New Verse,' " *The Times Literary Supplement,* LXVII, no. 3452 (April 25) 410-411 (recollections of Lewis).

F1469 Bradbury, Malcolm. " 'Rhythm' and 'The Blue Review,' " *ibid.,* 423-424.

F1470 " 'The Enemy,' " *ibid.*, 428.

F1471 " 'The Little Review,' " *ibid.*, 435.

F1472 " 'The New Age,' " *ibid.*, 436.

F1473 Kenner, Hugh. "The Last European," *Canadian Literature*, no. 36 (Summer) 5-13 (reprinted in *Wyndham Lewis in Canada*, see F1481 and F1604).

F1474 Clutton-Brock, A. "Fifty-Year Rule," *The Times Literary Supplement*, LXVII, no. 3463 (July 11) 735 (reprints the 1918 review of *Tarr*, see F107).

F1475 "Inside Out," *The Times Literary Supplement*, LXVII, no. 3469 (August 22) 889 (review of *Tarr*).

F1476 [*Unsigned review.*] *The New York Times* (August 22) 889 (review of *Tarr*).

F1477 Thomson, T. R. "Tarr," *The Times Literary Supplement*, LXVII, no. 3471 (September 5) 945 (letter suggesting the name Tarr might be derived from C. V. Tarbox, see F1478).

F1478 Your Reviewer. *The Times Literary Supplement*, LXVII, no. 3473 (September 19) 1051 (letter objecting that C. V. Tarbox first played in 1921, see F1477).

F1479 [*Unsigned review.*] *The Yale Review*, LVIII (December) 24-26 (favorable review of Pritchard's *Wyndham Lewis* stressing Lewis's importance, see F1461).

F1480 [*Unsigned review.*] *The Carleton Miscellany*, IX no. 1 (Winter) 114 (review of *Blasting and Bombardiering*).

F1481 Wyndham Lewis in Canada. Edited by George Woodcock, *Canadian Literature*, no. 35 (Winter) (augmented, this special Lewis issue was reprinted in book form in 1971, see B33; for critical studies see F1482–F1486; for articles by Lewis included see D353–D356).

F1482 [Woodcock, George (unsigned editorial)]. "Momaco Revisited," *ibid.*, 3-8 (survey of Lewis's Canadian experience).

F1483 Lewis, Anne Wyndham. "The Hotel," *ibid.*, 26-28 (recollections of the Tudor Hotel in Toronto).

F1484 Fox, C. J. "The Wild Land. A Celebration of Globalism," *ibid.*, 29-36 (impact of Lewis's American experience on his universalism).

F1485 Watson, Sheila. "Canada and Wyndham Lewis the Artist," *ibid.*, 44-61 (detailed survey of Lewis's artistic career in Canada starting with his service with Canadian War Records, 1917-1918).

F1486 Pierce, Lorne. "A Recollection of Wyndham Lewis," *ibid.*, 62-63 (records sitting for Lewis and the genesis of *Anglosaxony: A League that Works*, see A33).

1969

F1487 Benkowitz, Miriam J. *Ronald Firbank. A Biography*. New York: Weidenfeld and Nicolson, 222-223, passim (Firbank sitting for Lewis).

F1488 Grigson, Geoffrey. *Poems and Poets*. London: Macmillan, 206, passim (discusses *Men Without Art*).

F1489 Gross, John. *The Rise and Fall of the Man of Letters. English Literary Life since 1800*. London: Weidenfeld and Nicolson (Pelican Books, 1973) passim (references to Lewis).

F1490 Hamburger, Michael. *The Truth of Poetry. Tensions in Modern Poetry from Baudelaire to the 1960s*. London: Weidenfeld and Nicolson, passim (Lewis's debt to modern German movement).

F1491 Hodgart, Matthew. *Satire*. London: Weidenfeld and Nicolson, 216.

F1492 Deleted.

F1493 Hoskins, Katherine Bail. *Today the Struggle. Literature and Politics in England during the Spanish Civil War*. University of Texas Press, 67-77 (an analysis of *The Revenge for Love*).

F1494 McLuhan, Herbert Marshall and Harley Parker. *Through the Vanishing Point. Space in Poetry and Painting*. New York: Harper and Row, passim.

F1495 Mayoux, Jean-Jacques. *La Peinture Anglaise*. Paris: Armand Colin, 266-268 (sees "Surrender of Barcelona" (Michel P61) as possibly Lewis's masterpiece).

F1496 Michel, Walter and C. J. Fox (editors). "Introductions and Notes," *Wyndham Lewis on Art. Collected Writings, 1913-1956,* New York: Funk and Wagnalls (London: Thames and Hudson, 1971). See A45.

F1497 Press, John. *A Map of Modern English Verse.* London: Oxford University Press, passim.

F1498 Read, Forrest (editor). *Pound/Joyce. The Letters of Ezra Pound to James Joyce with Pound's Essays on Joyce.* London: Faber and Faber, passim.

F1499 Schneidau, Herbert N. *Ezra Pound. The Image and the Real.* Baton Rouge: Louisiana State University Press, passim.

F1500 Tomlin, E. W. F. "Introduction," *Wyndham Lewis. An Anthology of his Prose,* edited by E. W. F. Tomlin. London: Methuen, 1-20 (general introduction including reminiscences of Lewis, see A44).

F1501 Tomlin, E. W. F. *Wyndham Lewis.* Writers and their Works no. 64, The British Council. London: Longmans, Green and Co. (revises the 1955 edition, see F948).

F1502 Zable, Arnold. "Wyndham Lewis, Fascist? A Case Study," *The Melbourne Journal of Politics,* II, 36-49.

F1503 Zéraffa, Michel. *Personne et Personnage. Le Romanesque des Années 1920 aux Années 1950.* Paris: Klincksieck, 390-391, passim (analysis of *Self Condemned* compared to Kafka's *Der Prozess).*

F1504 Bridson, D. G. "Wyndham Lewis and Vorticism," *The Listener,* LXXXI, no. 2079 (January 30) 138-139.

F1505 Hall, D. "Wyndham Lewis's Portrait of Edwin Evans (Scottish National Gallery of Modern Art)," *Burlington Magazine,* CXI, no. 790 (January) 32.

F1506 "Moral Thriller," *The Times Literary Supplement,* LXVIII, no. 3496 (February 27) 203 (favorable review of Pritchard's *Wyndham Lewis* as "the most reasoned and sensible" study of Lewis yet published, see F1461).

F1507 Grigson, Geoffrey. "The Great Crystalliser," *The Guardian* (March 27) 8 (unfavorable review of Tomlin's *Wyndham Lewis,* see F1500).

F1508 Seymour-Smith, Martin. "Enemy in our Midst," *The Spectator,* CCXXII, no. 7344 (March 28) 403-404.

F1509 Nye, Robert. "Pugilist of the Intellect," *The Times* (March 29) 22 (review of Tomlin's *Wyndham Lewis* viewing Lewis as "the only real artist of his generation who made an art of being unpopular"; see F1500).

F1510 Connolly, Cyril. "At War With the Philistines," *The Sunday Times* (March 30) 61 (critical review of Tomlin's *Wyndham Lewis,* F1500, finding much of Lewis's thought "mere shadow-boxing").

F1511 Toynbee, Philip. "The Worst of Wyndham Lewis," *The Observer* (March 30) 30 (this review of Tomlin's *Wyndham Lewis* regrets the resurrection of "Lewis the Prophet," F1500).

F1512 Ayrton, Michael. "A Brain in Armour," *The New Statesman,* LXXVII, no. 1987 (April 4) 523 (review of Tomlin's *Wyndham Lewis,* which stresses that it was found easier to dismiss Lewis than to dismiss his arguments; see F1500).

F1513 "Bent upon Being True," *The Times Literary Supplement,* LXVIII, no. 3509 (May 29) 580 (favorable review of Tomlin's *Wyndham Lewis,* see F1500).

F1514 Pritchard, William H. "Rare Performances," *The London Magazine,* IX, no. 4-5 (July-August) 512-518 (favorable review of Tomlin's *Wyndham Lewis,* see F1500).

F1515 Bergonzi, Bernard. "Black Cartesian," *The Hudson Review,* XXII, no. 3 (Autumn) 508-512 (favorable review of Pritchard's *Wyndham Lewis,* see F1461; reprinted in Bergonzi's *The Turn of a Century).*

F1516 D'Offay, Anthony. "Introduction," *Abstract Art in England 1913-1915,* 11 November–5 December. London: d'Offay Couper Gallery (preface to the exhibition catalogue).

F1517 Burr, James. "The Torments of Delirium," *Apollo,* XC, no. 93 (November) 436 (review of the exhibition "Abstract Art in Britain").

F1518 McLuhan, Marshall. "Wyndham Lewis," *The Atlantic,* CCXXIV, no. 6 (December) 93-98 (recollections of Lewis).

F1519 Reid, John. "Journey out of Anguish," *Canadian Literature,* no. 39 (Winter) 20-26 (recollections of Lewis; reprinted in *Wyndham Lewis in Canada).*

F1520 [Cookson, William.] "A Note by the Editor," *Agenda* (Wyndham Lewis Special Issue. Edited by William Cookson) VII, no. 3–VIII, no. 1 (3 issues), (Autumn-Winter) 7 (for critical studies, see F1521–F1546; for pieces by Lewis, see D357–D361).

F1521 Seymour-Smith, Martin. "Wyndham Lewis as Imaginative Writer," *ibid.,* 9-15 (Lewis as "tragic writer").

F1522 Adams, John J. "To W. L. on his 'Human Age,' spoken printed and bound," *ibid.,* 15 (a poem, not mentioned in the contents).

F1523 Richards, I. A. "A Talk on 'The Childermass,' " *ibid.,* 16-21.

F1524 Palmer, Penelope. "The Human Age," *ibid.,* 22-30 (detailed study stressing the difference in vision between *The Childermass* and *The Human Age).*

F1525 Dale, Peter. "Self Condemned," *ibid.,* 31-36 (finds *Self Condemned* partly "disoriented" by the unconvincing presentation of Harding).

F1526 Symons, Julian. "The Thirties Novels," *ibid.,* 37-48 (provides information about sales and sums received by Lewis for these novels which "are the work of a man fascinated by the violence he condemns").

F1527 Pound, Ezra. "Augment of the Novel," *ibid.,* 49-56 (see F685).

F1528 Materer, Timothy. "The Great English Vortex," *ibid.,* 57-65 (analyzes the stylistic violence of *The Apes of God;* incorporated in *Wyndham Lewis the Novelist,* F1838).

F1529 West, Rebecca. "Tarr," *ibid.,* 67-69 (see F113).

F1530 Dale, Peter. "The Revenge for Love," *ibid.,* 71-77 (Lewis's "objective" mirror is "a broken one").

F1531 Michel, Walter. "Wyndham Lewis the Painter," *ibid.,* 78-87 (Lewis's artistic career).

F1532 Pound, Ezra. "The War Paintings of Wyndham Lewis," *ibid.,* 85-87.

F1533 Gray, Edmund. "Wyndham Lewis and the Modern Crisis of Painting," *ibid.,* 88-92 (laudatory survey of Lewis's artistic career).

F1534 Porteus, Hugh Gordon. "Random Samples," *ibid.,* 93-96 (review of *A Soldier of Humor and Selected Writings, An Anthology of his Prose,* and Pritchard's *Wyndham Lewis).*

F1535 Tomlin, E. W. F. "Reflections on 'Time and Western Man,' " *ibid.,* 97-108 (describes *Time and Western Man* as "one of the major works of the century" and "the key to his entire *œuvre").*

F1536 Sisson, C. H. "The Politics of Wyndham Lewis," *ibid.,* 109-116 (survey and vindication of Lewis's political pronouncements).

F1537 Rose, William K. "Pound and Lewis: The Crucial Years," *ibid.,* 117-133.

F1538 Cox, Kenneth. "Dualism and Les Autres," *ibid.,* 134-139.

F1539 Pritchard, William H. "Lawrence and Lewis," *ibid.,* 141-147.

F1540 Bold, Alan. "One-Way Song," *ibid.,* 148-155 (*One-Way Song* reviewed as Lewis's greatest work and clearest philosophical statement).

F1541 Sala, Annamaria. "Some Notes on Vorticism and Futurism," *ibid.,* 156-162.

F1542 Bridson, D. G. "The Making of 'The Human Age,'" *ibid.,* 163-171 (recollections of the B.B.C. broadcast of *The Human Age;* incorporated in Bridson's *Prospero and Ariel).*

F1543 Porteus, Hugh Gordon. "A Man Apart. A Few Recollections of Wyndham Lewis," *ibid.,* 172-179 (includes recollections of G. B. Shaw and T. S. Eliot; Lewis is said to have been "all his life a keen socialist").

F1544 Kenner, Hugh. "Excerpts from 'The Man of the World,' " *ibid.,* 181-182.

F1545 Kenner, Hugh. "Hoodopip," *ibid.,* 183 (note including excerpts from *The Man of the World).*

F1546 Kenner, Hugh. "Note on 'Joint,' " *ibid.*, 197 (introduction to excerpts from *The Man of the World).*

F1547 Rumney, Ralph. "Kill John Bull With Art! What Went Wrong?" *Studio International,* CLXXVIII, no. 917 (December) 216-221 (a review of "Abstract Art in England, 1913-1915" seeing the show as dominated by Lewis).

F1548 Stewart, David H. *College English,* XXXI, no. 3 (December) 330-334 (review of Harrison's *The Reactionaries,* see F1349).

1970

F1549 Bateson, F. W. "The Poetry of Learning," *Eliot in Perspective,* edited by Graham Martin. London: Macmillan, passim (Lewis on Shakespeare).

F1550 Brooks, Harold F. "Four Quartets: the Structure in Relation to the Themes," *ibid.,* passim (Lewisian rejection of time-philosophers).

F1551 Peter, John. "Eliot and The Criterion," *ibid.,* passim.

F1552 Bennett, Arnold. *Letters of Arnold Bennett* (edited by James Hepburn) III. London: Oxford University Press, 121-122 (recollections of a dinner at Osbert Sitwell's).

F1553 Bergonzi, Bernard. "The Advent of Modernism," *The Sphere History of Literature in the English Language, The Twentieth Century,* VII, edited by Bernard Bergonzi. London: Barrie and Jenkins, Sphere Books, passim.

F1554 Bradbury, Malcolm. "The Novel in the 1920's," *ibid.,* 210-213, passim (Lewis's "immense" contribution to comedy and satire).

F1555 Bliss, Arthur. *As I Remember.* London: Faber and Faber, passim.

F1556 Butler, Christopher. *Number Symbolism.* London: Routledge and Kegan Paul, 162.

F1557 Cooper, Douglas. *The Cubist Epoch.* Oxford: Phaidon, 181-182 (survey of Vorticist movement).

F1558 Lafourcade, Bernard. "Introduction," *Tarr.* Paris: Christian Bourgois, 7-10.

F1559 Durrell, Lawrence. "A Propos de Tarr," *ibid.,* 567-568 (an afterword to Lafourcade's French translation of *Tarr,* acknowledging Lewis's influence).

F1560 Gillis, Willard Leon. *The Poetics of Reaction: A Study of Wyndham Lewis.* New York University (unpublished doctoral thesis).

F1561 Lidderdale, Jane and Mary Nicholson. *Dear Miss Weaver.* London: Faber and Faber, passim (numerous references to Lewis, publication information for Egoist editions of Lewis's writings).

F1562 Moore, Harry T. "Preface," *Richard Aldington. Selected Critical Writings, 1928-1960.* Carbondale: Southern Illinois University Press, 7-14.

F1563 Sitwell, Edith. *Selected Letters,* edited by John Lehmann and Dereck Parker. London: Macmillan, passim.

F1564 Skelton, Robin. *Herbert Read. A Memorial Symposium.* London: Methuen, 255 (ten holograph and typed letters from Lewis in the McPherson Library, University of Victoria, British Columbia).

F1565 Spears, Monroe K. *Dionysus and the City: Modernism in Twentieth Century Poetry.* New York: Oxford University Press, passim.

F1566 Stock, Noel. *The Life of Ezra Pound.* London: Routledge and Kegan Paul, passim.

F1567 Treese, Williams. *The Library Journal Book Review, 1970.* New York: R. R. Bowker (favorable review of *Wyndham Lewis on Art).*

F1568 Trevor-Roper, Patrick. *The World Through Blunted Sight. An Inquiry into the Influence of Defective Vision on Art and Character.* London: Thames and Hudson, 130, passim (the history of Lewis's tumour and a comparison with Milton).

F1569 Bertram, Anthony. "Enigma Variations," *The Tablet,* CCXXIV, no. 6767 (February 7) 130-131 (review of the *Agenda* Lewis issue by an "Ex-Fan"; see F1521).

F1570 Fauchereau, Serge. "Revues Etrangères," *La Quinzaine Littéraire*, no. 89 (Février 15-28) 14 (review of the *Agenda* Lewis issue presenting Lewis as an antipathetic man of genius, see F1521).

F1571 Lafourcade, Bernard. "Wyndham Lewis," *ibid.*, no. 91 (25 Février–4 Mars) 6 (letter correcting errors in Fauchereau's article, see F1570 and F1575).

F1572 "A Neglected Phase of British Art," *Apollo*, XCI, no. 97 (March) 182, passim.

F1573 Lipke, William C. "The Omega Workshop and Vorticism," *Apollo*, XCI, no. 97 (March) 224-231.

F1574 Levy, David, "Wyndham Lewis Reconsidered," *Monday World* (Spring) 19-20 (review of the *Agenda* Lewis issue and Tomlin's *Wyndham Lewis* stressing Lewis's Europeanism, see F1500 and F1521).

F1575 Fauchereau, Serge. "Wyndham Lewis," *La Quinzaine Littéraire*, no. 92 (1-15 Avril) 27 (letter answering Lafourcade's, see F1571).

F1576 Tomlin, E. W. F. "Wyndham Lewis Reconsidered," *Eigo Seinen*, no. 116, 202-203.

F1578 Dale, Peter. "A Brush With Words," *Art and Artists*, V, no. 2 (May) 25-27.

F1579 Fraser, Nicks H. *Arts*, XLIV (May) 14 (review of *Wyndham Lewis on Art*).

F1580 Grigson, Geoffrey. "A Conversation With Geoffrey Grigson," *The Review*, no. 22 (June) 15-16 (interview with remarks on Lewis).

F1581 Thatcher, David S. "Richard Aldington's Letters to Herbert Read," *Malahat Review*, no. 15 (July) 5-44, passim.

F1582 Kenner, Hugh. "The Standpoint of Genius," *The National Review*, XXII, no. 31 (August 11) 846-847 (review of *Wyndham Lewis on Art*).

F1583 Chapman, Robert T. "Lawrence, Lewis and the Comedy of Literary Reputation," *Studies in the Twentieth Century*, no. 6 (Fall) 85-95.

F1584 Materer, Timothy. "The Short Stories of Wyndham Lewis," *Studies in Short Fiction*, VII, no. 3 (Fall) 615-624 (reviews *The Wild Body;* incorporated in *Wyndham Lewis the Novelist*).

F1585 Spanos, William V. "Modern Literary Criticism and the Spatialization of Time: An Existential Critique," *The Journal of Æsthetics and Art Criticism*, XXIX, no. 1 (Fall) 87-104.

F1586 Durrell, Lawrence. "Wyndham Lewis," *Le Figaro Littéraire* (30 Novembre-6 Décembre) 23.

1971

F1587 Ayrton, Michael. *The Rudiments of Paradise*. London: Secker and Warburg, 257-267, passim (incorporates F994 and F1022).

F1588 Bradbury, Malcolm. *The Social Context of Modern Literature*. London: Blackwell, passim (Lewis and "the modern tradition").

F1589 Bridson, D. G. *Prospero and Ariel: the Rise and Fall of the Radio. A Personal Recollection*. London: Victor Gollancz (recollections of Lewis and the B.B.C.; incorporates F1542).

F1590 Cunard, Nancy. *Thoughts About Ronald Firbank*. New York: Albondocani Press, 11.

F1591 Fiedler, Leslie. *Collected Essays*. New York: Stein and Day, passim.

F1592 Groth, Peter. *Der Vortizismus in Literatur, Kunst and Wissenschaft. Studien zur Bewegung der "Men of 1914" Ezra Pound, Wyndham Lewis, Gaudier-Brzeska, T. S. Eliot v.o.* Hamburg: Helmut Buske Verlag (Hamburger Philologische Studien, no. 18; photographic edition of a doctoral thesis).

F1593 Hamilton, Alastair. *The Appeal of Fascism, 1919-1945*. London: Anthony Blond, 281-285, passim (sees Lewis as "trying to achieve an intellectual integrity untarnished by politics").

F1594 Lilly, Marjorie. *Sickert. The Painter and his Circle*. London: Elek, 121.

F1595 Michel, Walter. *Wyndham Lewis. Paintings and Drawings*. London: Thames and Hudson (Berkeley: University of California Press) pp. 456 (contains "Preface," pp. 7-8, "Chapters I-VII," pp. 43-158 and a section of extensive notes about Lewis's art works, pp. 331-455, see B33 and F1596).

F1596 Kenner, Hugh. "The Visual World of Wyndham Lewis," *ibid.*, 11-40 (see F1595).

F1597 Kirk, Russell. *Eliot and his Age.* New York: Random House, passim.

F1598 Pound, Reginald. *Arnold Bennett. A Biography.* Bath: Cedric Chivers Ltd., 289 (letter from Bennett about Lewis).

F1599 Press, John. *The Lengthening Shadows. Observation on Poetry and its Enemies.* London: Oxford University Press, passim.

F1600 Rosenthal, T. G. "Introduction," *Word and Image I & II, Wyndham Lewis 1882-1957, Michael Ayrton b. 1921.* London: The National Book League, 5-9 (introduction to the catalogue of the exhibition held in London, 7 Albemarle Street, November).

F1601 de Sencourt, Robert. *T. S. Eliot. A Memoir,* edited by Donald Adamson. London: Garnstone Press, passim.

F1602 Sisson, C. H. *English Poetry, 1900-1950. An Assessment.* London: Rupert Hart-Davis, 222-231, passim (analysis of "Grignolles" and *One-Way Song).*

F1603 Thrall, Donald F. *The Medium is the Rear View Mirror.* Montreal: McGill-Queen's University Press, passim.

F1604 Woodcock, George (editor). *Wyndham Lewis in Canada.* Canadian Literature Series, with an introduction by Julian Symons. Vancouver: University of British Columbia Publications Centre (a revised and expanded reprint of the 1968 special issue of "Canadian Literature" (F1481); see F1605 and F1606). "Introduction," by Julian Symons, 1-6 (assessment of Lewis's "sad" years spent in Canada).

F1605 Kenner, Hugh. "The Last European," *ibid.,* 12-20 (see F1473)

F1606 Reid, John. "Journey out of Anguish," *ibid.,* 97-103 (see F1520).

F1607 Watts, Emily Stipes. *Ernest Hemingway and the Arts.* Urbana: University of Illinois Press, 182-183 (Hemingway's reaction to *Men Without Art).*

F1608 Denmar, Della. "Katé Lechmere. Recollections of Vorticism," *Apollo,* XCIII, no. 107 (January) 52-53 (recollections of Lewis and the Rebel Art Centre).

F1609 D., P. "Note de Lecture," *Les Lettres Françaises* (February 24) (review stressing the documentary interest of *Tarr,* to illustrate the ideological hesitations of the avant-garde).

F1610 Stolowicki, Ch. "Tarr de Wyndham Lewis," *Combat* (March 18).

F1611 Spender, Stephen. "Blasting the Bloomsberries," *The Observer* (March 28) 33 (review of *Wyndham Lewis on Art* and Michel's *Wyndham Lewis. Paintings and Drawings).*

F1612 Fauchereau, Serge. "Wyndham Lewis," *La Quinzaine Littéraire* (15-31 Mars) 7 (favorable review of *Tarr).*

F1613 Chapman, Robert T. "Satire, Apes and Æsthetics: A Study of the Apes of God," *Contemporary Literature,* XII, no. 2 (Spring) 133-145 (sees Lewis's satire as "a paradigm for the state of art in the modern world").

F1614 Pritchard, William H. "Wyndham Lewis and Lawrence," *Iowa Review,* II, no. 2 (Spring) 91-96 (criticizes Leavis's view of Lewis and Lawrence).

F1615 Smith, Rowland. "The Spanish Civil War and the British Literary Right," *Dalhousie Review,* LI, no. 1 (Spring) 60-76 (discusses Lewis's attitude towards Franco).

F1616 Melville, Robert. "The Great Tyro," *The New Statesman,* LXXXI, no. 2089 (April 2) 463-464 (review of Michel's *Wyndham Lewis. Paintings and Drawings* and *Wyndham Lewis on Art).*

F1617 Bridson, D. G. "Art Without Shadows," *The Listener,* LXXXV, no. 2193 (April 8) 455-456 (favorable review of *Wyndham Lewis on Art* and Michel's *Wyndham Lewis. Paintings and Drawings;* Lewis compared to Blake).

F1618 Piper, David. "Euclid in the Flesh," *The Guardian Weekly* (April 8) 9 (favorable review of *Wyndham Lewis on Art* and Michel's *Wyndham Lewis. Paintings and Drawings* finding Lewis's "most enduring achievement . . . to be his portraiture of the late twenties and thirties").

F1619 Read, Piers Paul. "Treacherous Streak," *New Society* (April 8) 598 (favorable review of Hamilton's *The Appeal of Fascism,* see F1593).

F1620 Ford, Michael. *Arts Review,* XIII, no. 7 (April 10) 218 (review of Michel's *Wyndham Lewis. Paintings and Drawings).*

F1621 Causey, Andrew. "Wyndham Lewis Revalued," *The Illustrated London News* (April 17) 26-27 (favorable review of *Wyndham Lewis on Art* and Michel's *Wyndham Lewis. Paintings and Drawings).*

F1622 Ayrton, Michael. "Galvanic Giant," *The Sunday Times,* no. 7715 (April 18) 27 (review of Michel's *Wyndham Lewis. Paintings and Drawings* and *Wyndham Lewis on Art,* concluding that Lewis was both a "luminous" art-critic and a "draughtsman of the first rank and the pre-eminent portraitist of his time").

F1623 Sutton, Denys. "Wyndham Lewis," *The Financial Times* (April 20) 3 (favorable review of *Wyndham Lewis on Art* and Michel's *Wyndham Lewis. Paintings and Drawings).*

F1624 Fletcher, John. "Vorticism's Villain-Hero," *Essays in Criticism,* XXI, no. 2 (April) 204-210 (unfavorable review of Pritchard's *Wyndham Lewis,* see F1461).

F1625 Barkman, John. "Blind British Artist Finally Wins Renown," *The Saturday Review of Literature,* LIV, no. 18 (May 5) (reviews Michel's *Wyndham Lewis. Paintings and Drawings;* published also in the *Ohio Vindicator,* May 9; *The New York Times-Union,* Albany, May 9; *The San Francisco Sunday Examiner and Chronicle,* June 21).

F1626 Laws, Frederick. "Pre-Echoing Blast," *The Daily Telegraph* (May 6) 6 (favorable review of *Wyndham Lewis on Art* and Michel's *Wyndham Lewis. Paintings and Drawings).*

F1627 Skipwitch, Peyton. "Foreword," *The Art of War 1914-1918.* London: The Morley Gallery, 4 (catalogue of the exhibition held between May 18 and June 12; for reviews see F1628, F1629 and F1631).

F1628 Cork, Richard. "The Message from the First War Trenches," *Evening Standard* (May 20) 8 (review of the Morley Gallery exhibition, see F1627).

F1629 Neve, Christopher. "The Eye of the Storm. Four Official War Artists," *Country Life,* 149 (May 20) 1210-1211 (see F1627).

F1630 Cork, Richard. "Introduction," *David Bomberg and Lilian Holt.* London: Reading Museum and Art Gallery (catalogue of the exhibition held between June 4 and July 17).

F1631 Vaizey, Marina. *The Connoisseur,* CLXXVII, no. 712 (June) 162 (review of "The Art of War," an exhibition held at Morley College Gallery, 18 May-12 June; see F1627).

F1632 Woodcock, George. "Editorial: Criticism and Other Arts," *Canadian Literature,* no. 49 (Summer) 9 (reviews Michel's *Wyndham Lewis. Paintings and Drawings* and *Wyndham Lewis on Art* with evaluation of Lewis's "ambiguous Canadian links").

F1633 MacSween, R. J. *The Antigonish Review,* II, no. 2 (Summer) 95-96 (review of *Wyndham Lewis on Art,* stressing "the extraordinary power and range" of Lewis's art-criticism).

F1634 Paniker, K. Ayyappa. "Myth and Machine in Hart Crane," *The Literary Criterion,* IX, no. 4 (Summer) 27-41.

F1635 Woodcock, George. "Making it Up to a Snubbed Artist," *Daily Times,* Victoria (July 17).

F1636 Davenport, Guy. "Unsung Man for All Media," *Life,* LXXI, no. 5 (July 30) 14 (favorable review of Michel's *Wyndham Lewis. Paintings and Drawings,* comparing Lewis and Van Gogh).

F1637 Halpern, Henry. *The Library Journal* (July) (review of Michel's *Wyndham Lewis. Paintings and Drawings,* stressing Lewis's "enormous" contribution to the "artistic revolution").

F1638 Cork, Richard. "What Went Wrong," *Studio International,* CLXXII, no. 935 (July-August) 41 (review of Michel's *Wyndham Lewis. Paintings and Drawings,* attributing the deterioration of Vorticism to Lewis's "bias towards the literary").

F1639 S., R. [i.e. Robert Skelton]. "The Arts," *Malahat Review,* no. 19 (July) 121-122 (favorable review of Michel's *Wyndham Lewis. Paintings and Drawings).*

F1640 Montgomery, Max [i.e. Guy Davenport]. "Obscured Genius," *National Review* (August 10) 876-878 (review of Michel's *Wyndham Lewis. Paintings and Drawings,* stating that Lewis may be "the most original painter of the twentieth century").

F1641 [*Unsigned review.*] *British Book News* (August) 646-647 (favorable review of *Wyndham Lewis on Art).*

F1642 Powell, Anthony. "The Art of the Enemy," *Apollo,* XCIV, no. 115 (September) 241-243 (review of Michel's *Wyndham Lewis. Paintings and Drawings* and *Wyndham Lewis on Art;* discusses Lewis's career).

F1643 Parsons, D. S. J. "Roy Campbell and Wyndham Lewis," *Papers on Language and Literature,* VII, no. 4 (Fall) 406-421 (detailed study of Lewis's influence on Campbell).

F1644 Fox, C. J. "David Jones and the New Cosmopolis," *The Antigonish Review,* no. 7 (Autumn) 25-33.

F1645 Wise, Julia. *The Journal of Æsthetics and Art Criticism,* XXX, no. 1 (Fall) 142 (notice of *Wyndham Lewis on Art).*

F1646 *Virginia Quarterly Review,* XLVII, no. 4 (Autumn) CLXXXV (favorable review of Michel's *Wyndham Lewis. Paintings and Drawings).*

F1647 Kenedy, R. C. "London Letter," *Art International,* XV, no. 8 (October 20) 66.

F1648 Holloway, John. "Modernity," *The Listener,* LXXXVI, no. 2222 (October 28) 564, 566 (review of Bradbury's *The Social Context of Modern Literature,* with reference to Lewis and his interest in Egyptian sculpture).

F1649 McLuhan, Marshall. "Letters," *ibid.,* 575.

F1650 Glasheen, Adeline. "Rough Notes on Joyce and Wyndham Lewis," *A Wake Newsletter,* VIII, no. 5 (October) 67-75 (*Ulysses* in *Time and Western Man, Work in Progress* in *The Childermass,* and *Tarr* in *Finnegan's Wake,* all suggest a paradoxical collaboration).

F1651 Darracott, Joseph. "A Note of Intensity," *Arts Review,* XIII, no. 10 (November) 308.

F1652 Kenedy, R. C. "Wyndham Lewis or the Stand Against Aphrodite's Sunset-Struck Star," *Art International,* XV, no. 9 (November 20) 71-77, 80.

F1653 Downes, Rackstraw. "More Words and Pictures," *New York Times Book Review* (December 5) 7, 76 (unfavorable review of Michel's *Wyndham Lewis. Paintings and Drawings).*

F1654 Holloway, John. "From Between the Dragon's Teeth," *The Critical Quarterly,* XIII, no. 4 (Winter) 367-376 (review of *Wyndham Lewis on Art).*

F1655 Sale, Richard B. "An Interview in New York with Walter Allen," *Studies in the Novel,* III, no. 4 (Winter) 405-409 (Lewis and "comic tradition in English fiction").

1972

F1656 Bergonzi, Bernard. *T. S. Eliot.* London: Macmillan, passim.

F1657 Bridgewater, Patrick. *Nietzsche in Anglosaxony.* Leicester: Leicester University Press, 132-135, passim.

F1658 Bridson, D. G. *The Filibuster. A Study of the Political Ideas of Wyndham Lewis.* London: Cassell and Co., pp. xiv, 306 (full-length study of Lewis's political philosophy).

F1659 Daniels, Mary F. "Introduction [*and compilation of Lewis's manuscript materials*]," *Wyndham Lewis: A Descriptive Catalogue of the Manuscript Material in the Department of Rare Books Cornell University Library.* Ithaca: Cornell University Library, pp. 171 (important descriptive checklist of holdings at Cornell University Library of Lewis manuscript materials; includes facsimiles of previously unpublished fragments of Lewis manuscripts, see B35).

F1660 Ferguson, John. *War and the Creative Arts.* London: Macmillan and the Open University Press, 177-178 (*Blast* and Lewis's war paintings).

F1661 James, Philip. *Vision and Satire in the Art and Fiction of Wyndham Lewis.* University of Toronto (unpublished doctoral thesis).

F1662 Kenner, Hugh. *The Pound Era.* Berkeley: University of California Press (London: Faber and Faber) passim (numerous references to Lewis, including a chapter primarily about Lewis, "Vortex Lewis," pp. 232-247).

F1663 Margolis, John D. *T. S. Eliot's Intellectual Development, 1922-1929.* Chicago: University of Chicago Press, passim, 76-83 (analysis of the evolution of Lewis's and Eliot's classicism).

F1664 McLuhan, Herbert Marshall. "Challenge and Collapse: the Nemesis of Creativity," *The Discontinuous Universe* (edited by Sallie Sears and Georgianna W. Lord). New York: Basic Books, 267.

F1665 Pritchard, William. *Wyndham Lewis.* Profiles in Literature. London: Routledge and Kegan Paul, pp. 102 (full-length study of Lewis's work).

F1666 Rosenberg, Harold. *The De-definition of Art. Action Art to Pop to Earthworks.* New York: Horizon Press, 235 (makes use of Lewis's notion of "revolutionary simpleton").

F1667 Rothenstein, John. *British Art Since 1900.* London: Phaidon Press, passim.

F1668 Salt, J. *The Electric Desert: a Study of the Myths of New Technology in the Works of Wyndham Lewis, with particular reference to The Apes of God and The Childermass.* Montreal: McGill University (unpublished doctoral thesis).

F1669 Smith, Rowland. *Lyrics and Polemics. The Literary Personality of Roy Campbell.* Montreal: McGill-Queen's University Press, passim.

F1670 Sutton, Denys (editor). *Letters of Roger Fry* (2 vols.). London: Chatto and Windus, passim.

F1671 Wees, W. C. *Vorticism and the English Avant-Garde.* Manchester: Manchester University Press, passim.

F1672 Woodcock, George. *Herbert Read: The Stream and the Source.* London: Faber and Faber, passim.

F1673 Woodeson, John. *Mark Gertler.* London: Sidgwick and Jackson, passim.

F1674 Fox, C. J. "Sorel," *The Times Literary Supplement,* LXXI, no. 3645 (January 7) 14 (mentioning *The Art of Being Ruled,* this letter completes Isaiah Berlin's piece on the influence of Sorel, see F1675).

F1675 Berlin, Isaiah. "Sorel," *The Times Literary Supplement,* LXXI, no. 3646 (January 14) (response to Fox's letter, see F1674).

F1676 Raine, Kathleen. "The Mask of the Enemy," *The Sewanee Review,* 80, no. 1 (January-March) 196-200 (favorable review of Michel's *Wyndham Lewis. Paintings and Drawings* defining Lewis as the "Ishmael of his generation" and comparing his use of masks with Yeats's).

F1677 Farmer, A. J. *Les Livres,* no. 181 (Février) 51 (favorable review of *Tarr).*

F1678 Mayne, Richard. "Wyndham Lewis," *Encounter,* XXXVIII, no. 2 (February) 42-51 (survey of Lewis's career and personality; argues that Lypiatt in Huxley's *Antic Hay* was based on Lewis).

F1679 Rosenthal, Michael. *New York Times Book Review* (March 26) 7, 34-35 (review of Kenner's *The Pound Era).*

F1680 Korg, Jacob. "Language Change and Experimental Magazines, 1910-1930," *Contemporary Literature,* XIII, no. 2 (Spring) 144-161 (Lewis as "leader in the revolt of the magazines").

F1681 Payne, Robert T. "On the Prose of T. E. Lawrence," *Prose,* no. 4 (Spring) 91-108 (Lawrence's mature style was influenced by Malory, Doughty and Lewis).

F1682 Regnery, Henry. "Eliot, Pound and Lewis: a creative friendship," *The Modern Age,* XVI, no. 2 (Spring) 146-160.

F1683 "The Creator of Vorticism," *The Times Literary Supplement,* LXXI, no. 3658 (April 7) 386 (critical reviews of Michel's *Wyndham Lewis. Paintings and Drawings, Wyndham Lewis on Art* and Pritchard's *Wyndham Lewis).*

F1684 Michel, Walter. "Wyndham Lewis," *The Times Literary Supplement,* LXXI, no. 3660 (April 28) 495-496 (letter to the editor, see F1685).

F1685 The Reviewer. "Wyndham Lewis," *ibid.* (answer to Michel's letter, see F1684).

F1686 Heymann, C. David. *The Saturday Review,* LV, no. 20 (May 13) 71, 76 (favorable review of Kenner's *The Pound Era).*

F1687 Chapman, Robert. "The 'Enemy' versus Bloomsbury," *Adam*, XXXVII, nos. 364-366 (Summer) 81-84.

F1688 Mahon, C. Michael. *The Western Humanities Review*, XXVI, no. 3 (Summer) 275-279 (favorable review of *The Pound Era*).

F1689 Smith, Rowland. "Wyndham Lewis and the Sanctimonious Ice-Box," *The Dalhousie Review*, LII, no. 2 (Summer) 302-308 (favorable review of *Wyndham Lewis in Canada*).

F1690 Pritchard, William H. "Paradise Lost," *The Hudson Review*, XXV, no. 2 (Summer) 316-322 (review of Kenner's *The Pound Era*, with many references to Lewis as a critic of Pound).

F1691 Holroyd, Michael. "Damning and Blasting: the Volcanic Friendship Between Wyndham Lewis and Augustus John," *The Listener*, LXXXVIII, no. 2258 (July 6) 8-11 (reprinted as "Damn and Blast: the Friendship of Wyndham Lewis and Augustus John," in *Unreceived Opinions*. London: Heinemann, 1973, and in *Essays by Divers Hands: Being the Transactions of the Royal Society of Literature* (edited by John Guest), Vol. XXXVIII. London: Oxford University Press, 1974).

F1692 Dodsworth, Martin. "The Marshall Plan," *The New Statesman*, LXXXIV, no. 2158 (July 28) 129 (favorable review of *The Pound Era* with references to Lewis and McLuhan).

F1693 "The Last of the Galaxy," *The Economist*, CCXXIX, no. 6727 (July 29) 47-48 (favorable review of *The Pound Era*).

F1694 Hardy, Barbara. "Barbara Hardy on a New Monument to Ezra Pound," *The Spectator*, CCXXIX, no. 7522 (August 26) 319-320 (critical study of *The Pound Era*).

F1695 Ruthven, K. K. "On the So-Called Fascism of Some Modernist Writers," *The Southern Review*, V, no. 3 (September) 225-230 (review article comparing *The Appeal of Fascism* to *The Reactionaries*).

F1696 Kerr, D. C. "Energy in the Vortex," *Tribune* (October 6) 9 (favorable review of Kenner's *The Pound Era*).

F1697 Chapman, Robert T. "Parties . . . Parties . . . Parties . . . : Some of the Images of the Gay Twenties," *English*, XXI, no. 3 (Autumn) 93-97 (*The Apes of God* exposes the stupidity of the social gatherings of the gay 20's).

F1698 Dooley, D. J. "The Satirist and the Contemporary Nonentity," *Satire Newsletter*, X, no. 1 (Fall) 1-9 (Nigel Dennis's affinity with Lewis).

F1699 Materer, Timothy. "Wyndham Lewis: Satirist of the Machine Age," *ibid.*, 9-18 (identifies with Lewis with Huxley's Lypiatt in *Antic Hay;* incorporated in F1838).

F1700 Allen, Walter. "Crusty Old Tory-Bolshevik," *The Daily Telegraph*, (October 12) (favorable review of *The Filibuster*).

F1701 Skipwirth, Peyton. "A Synthesis of War. The Paintings of C. R. W. Nevinson, 1914-1916," *The Connoisseur*, CLXXXI, no. 728 (October) 100-103 (references to Lewis).

F1702 Gelpi, Albert. *American Literature*, XLIV, no. 3 (November) 502-504 (review of Kenner's *The Pound Era*).

F1703 "In the Service of the Intelligence," *The Times Literary Supplement*, LXXI, no. 3693 (September 15) 1535 (favorable review of Daniels' *A Descriptive Catalogue*, see F1659, and Bridson's *The Filibuster*, contrasts what is best in Lewis's political writings to what is "stupid").

F1704 Lomas, Herbert. "Going off the Motorway," *The London Magazine*, XII, no. 5 (December 1972/January 1973) 152-155 (favorable review of Bridson's *The Filibuster*).

F1705 Appenzel, Anthony. "The Migrant," *Canadian Literature*, no. 51 (Winter) 100-101 (favorable review of *Wyndham Lewis on Art*).

F1706 Coldwell, Joan. "The Mind of the Exile," *ibid.*, 88-90 (review of *Wyndham Lewis in Canada* drawing a parallel between *Self Condemned* and *Under the Volcano*).

F1707 Davie, Donald. "The Universe of Ezra Pound," *Paideuma*, I, no. 2 (Winter) 263-269 (review of Kenner's *The Pound Era*, attributing Lewis's "failure" to his milieu).

1973

F1708 Allen, Walter. "Introduction," *The Roaring Queen,* by Wyndham Lewis. London: Secker and Warburg, 5-23 (see A47).

F1709 Baron, Wendy. *Sickert.* London: Phaidon, 119-120 (the Camden Town Group).

F1710 Bergonzi, Bernard. *The Turn of a Century. Essays on Victorian and Modern English Literature.* London: Macmillan, 177-182, passim.

F1711 Bradbury, Malcolm. *Possibilities. Essays on the State of the Novel.* London: Oxford University Press, 144-150, passim.

F1712 Brophy, Brigid. *Prancing Novelist (In Praise of Ronald Firbank).* London: Macmillan, passim.

F1713 Chapman, Robert T. *Wyndham Lewis: Fictions and Satires.* London: Vision Press (full-length study of Lewis's satiric writings).

F1714 Eates, Margot. *Paul Nash, the Master of the Image, 1889-1946.* London: John Murray, passim (Lewis's quarrels with Nash).

F1715 Grayson, Rupert. *Stand Fast the Holy Ghost.* London: Tom Stacey Ltd, 129-134 (recollections of Lewis).

F1716 Pound, Ezra. *Selected Prose, 1909-1965,* edited by William Cookson. London: Faber and Faber, passim.

F1717 Fiedler, Leslie. *The Stranger in Shakespeare.* London: Croom Helm, 74-75 (agrees with Lewis on Shakespeare as "a shamanized man").

F1718 Fox, C. J. and Robert T. Chapman. "Introduction," *Unlucky for Pringle. Unpublished and Other Stories,* by Wyndham Lewis. London: Vision, 7-17 (see A46).

F1719 Frank, Armin Paul. *Die Sehnsucht nach dem unkilbaren Sein. Motive und Motivation in der Literaturkritik T. S. Eliots.* Munchen: Wilhelm Fink Verlag, passim.

F1720 Holroyd, Michael. *Unreceived Opinions.* London: Heinemann, passim, 244-255 (references to Lewis).

F1721 Kramer, Hilton. *The Age of the Avant-Garde. An Art-Chronicle of 1956-1972.* New York: Farrar, Straus and Giroux, 166.

F1722 Lafourcade, Bernard. "Wyndham Lewis," *Ecrivains Anglais et Irlandais,* recueil I, edited by Bernard Cassen, 109-112 (one of 64 leaflets with an introductory essay supplemented by biographical and bibliographical sections).

F1723 Matthews, T. S. *Great Tom. Notes Towards the Definition of T. S. Eliot.* London: Weidenfeld and Nicholson, passim.

F1724 Spender, Stephen. "D. H. Lawrence, England and the War," *D. H. Lawrence, Novelist, Poet, Prophet* (edited by Stephen Spender). London: Weidenfeld and Nicolson, 75 (compares Lawrence's *Aaron's Rod* and *The Apes of God).*

F1725 Donoghue, Denis. " 'Till the fight is finished': D. H. Lawrence in his Letters," *ibid.,* 197.

F1726 Lucie-Smith, Edward. "The Poetry of D. H. Lawrence with a Glance at Shelley," *ibid.,* 225 (influence of Vorticism on Eliot's poetry).

F1727 Thody, Philip. *Aldous Huxley.* London: Studio Vista, passim (Lewis as "Lypiatt" in *Antic Hay).*

F1728 Williams, George G. *Guide to Literary London.* London: B. T. Batsford Ltd., passim (mentions a number of Lewis's haunts).

F1729 Reid, David and Mark Turner. "A Conversation with Hugh Kenner," *Occident,* VII, no. 1, 18-48 (anecdotes about Lewis and Voriticism).

F1730 Lipsius, Frank. "Wyndham Lewis on Politics," *Books and Bookmen,* XVIII, no. 6 (March) 59-60 (favorable review of Bridson's *The Filibuster* stating that Lewis's politics is "a dead issue but that the world has finally caught up with him).

F1731 Rosenthal, M. J. *The Connoisseur,* CLXXXII, no. 734 (April) 300 (review of an exhibition at Crane Kelman Gallery with "Red Portrait" (Michel P76) defined as "one of the great portraits of this century").

F1732 Lafourcade, Bernard. "Wyndham Lewis. Du Purgatoire au Panorama," *Etudes Anglaises,* XXVI, no. 2 (Avril-Juin) 195-211 (survey of recent criticism).

F1733 Nye, Robert. "The Blasting of Gunner Lewis," *The Scotsman* (May 26) (review of *Unlucky for Pringle* and *Fictions and Satires).*

F1734 Ackroyd, Peter. "He Who Blasts Last," *The Spectator,* CCXL, no. 7563 (June 9) 717-718 (favorable review of *Fictions and Satires* and *Unlucky for Pringle,* stressing Lewis's evolution towards "moralism without a morality").

F1735 Grigson, Geoffrey. "Wyndham Lewis," *The Spectator,* CCXL, no. 7565 (June 23) 773 (letter correcting points in Ackroyd's article, see F1734).

F1736 Hungiville, Maurice. "Ezra Pound's Letter to Olivet," *The Texas Quarterly,* XVI, no. 2 (Summer) 77-87 (includes a 1939 letter in which Pound asks the President of Olivet College to recruit Lewis).

F1737 Jameson, Fredric. "Wyndham Lewis as Futurist," *The Hudson Review,* XXVI, no. 2 (Summer) 295-329 (detailed analysis of Lewis's "immensely energetic" style and narrative art).

F1738 Powell, Anthony. "One Man's Bookworld," *The Spectator,* CCXL, no. 7565 (June 23) (review of Seymour-Smyth's *Guide to Modern Literature* with references to Lewis).

F1739 Wolfe, Peter. *Modern Fiction Studies,* XIX, no. 2 (Summer) 256-261 (review of Pritchard's *Wyndham Lewis,* seeing Lewis as "sour," "nasty" and "destructive").

F1740 Nye, Robert. "Neglected Modern," *The Times* (July 12) 12 (review of Chapman's *Wyndham Lewis* and *Unlucky for Pringle).*

F1741 Connolly, Cyril. "Chronicle of Creative Hatred," *The Sunday Times* (July 29) 36 (review of *The Roaring Queen* mostly concerned with the identification of the characters).

F1742 Toynbee, Philip. "With Malice Towards All," *The Observer* (July 29) 32 (very unfavorable review of *The Roaring Queen, Unlucky for Pringle* and Chapman's *Fictions and Satires,* describing Lewis as "a rotten satirist").

F1743 Hern, Anthony. *The Evening Standard* (July 31) 23 (review of *The Roaring Queen).*

F1744 Wordsworth, Christopher. "Melting Point for Wax," *The Guardian* (August 2) 7 (reviews *The Roaring Queen,* defining Lewis as a "maligning and blustering solipsist").

F1745 Powell, Anthony. "A Period Squib on Literary London," *The Daily Telegraph* (August 2) 8 (moderately favorable review of *The Roaring Queen).*

F1746 [Symons, Julian]. "Shodbutt is Staggered," *The Times Literary Supplement,* LXXII, no. 3726 (August 3) 893 (favorable review of *The Roaring Queen, Satires and Fictions* and *Unlucky for Pringle* which notices "a decline of the prose in the later stories").

F1747 Ackroyd, Peter. "Queen of Trades," *The Spectator,* CCXL, no. 7571 (August 4) (favorable review of *The Roaring Queen).*

F1748 Fuller, Roy. "Lewis's Libel," *The Listener,* XC, no. 2315 (August 9) 192 (review of *The Roaring Queen* as a pot-boiler).

F1749 Seymour-Smith, Martin. "Lampooning the Literati," *The Financial Times* (August 9) (favorable review of *The Roaring Queen,* criticizing Wordsworth's definition of Lewis "as a solipsist," and analyzing Lewis's treatment of Arnold Bennett).

F1750 Cassidy, Victor M. "Roaring Queen," *The Times Literary Supplement,* LXXII, no. 3727 (August 10) 931 (letter to the editor asserting that *The Roaring Queen* was already written in 1930).

F1751 King, Francis. "Blast from the Past," *The Sunday Telegraph* (August 12) (unfavorable review of *The Roaring Queen* with remarks about the identification of the characters).

F1752 Allen, Walter. "The Roaring Queen," *Encounter,* XL, no. 41 (August) 41-67.

F1753 Roberts, Cecil. "Memories of Arnold Bennett," *Books and Bookmen,* XVIII, no. 12 (September) 32-35 (review of *The Roaring Queen* seen as "the most idiotic book of the year," with recollections of Lewis as a swashbuckler).

F1754 Lipsius, Frank. "Favourite Enemy," *ibid.,* 55 (favorable reviews of *Unlucky for Pringle* and *Fictions and Satires).*

F1755 Weintraub, Stanley. "A Literary Minefield," *The New Republic,* CLXIX, no. 15 (October 13) 28 (favorable review of *The Roaring Queen* seen as "a Jonsonian extravaganza").

F1756 Cushman, Keith. *The Library Journal,* (October 15) (review of *Fictions and Satires).*

F1757 Hesse, Eva. "Notes and Queries," *Paideuma,* II, no. 2 (Fall) 333-339 (*re* Henry Swabey, see *The Letters,* p. 509).

F1758 Materer, Timothy. "A Reading from Canto CXV," *ibid.,* 205-207.

1974

F1759 Brian, John. *Supreme Fictions.* Montreal: McGill-Queen's University Press, 252 (considers Lewis's attack on Lawrence as "hysterical" and misplaced").

F1760 Butter, P. H. (editor). *Selected Letters of Edwin Muir.* London: The Hogarth Press, passim.

F1761 Cantillon, Watt J. *The Æsthete in the Novels of Ronald Firbank, Wyndham Lewis and James Joyce.* Urbana: University of Illinois (unpublished doctoral thesis).

F1762 Currie, Robert. *Genius. An Ideology in Literature,* London: Chatto and Windus, 116-143 (detailed analysis of Lewis's philosophy).

F1763 Drabble, Margaret. *Arnold Bennett. A Bibliography.* London: Weidenfeld and Nicholson, 290-291, passim (contains a short analysis of *The Roaring Queen).*

F1764 Holroyd, Michael. *Augustus John: a Biography,* (2 vols.). London: Heinemann, passim (incorporates F1691).

F1765 Kennedy, Alan. *The Protean Self. Dramatic Action in Contemporary Fiction.* London: Macmillan, 54-55.

F1766 Kinninmont, T. H. *The Novels of Wyndham Lewis.* Glasgow: University of Glasgow (unpublished doctoral thesis).

F1767 Lucas, John. *Arnold Bennett. A Study of his Fiction.* London: Methuen, passim (hostile view of *The Roaring Queen).*

F1768 Martin, Wallace (editor). *Orage as Critic.* London: Routledge and Kegan Paul, passim.

F1769 Mylett, Andrew (editor). "Introduction," *The Evening Standard Years. Arnold Bennett.* London: Chatto and Windus, passim.

F1770 Overy, Paul. "Vorticism," *Concepts of Modern Art* (edited by Tony Richardson and Nikos Stangos). Harmondsworth: Penguin Books, 105-108.

F1771 Roberts, William. *Memoirs of the War to End War, 1914-1918.* London: Privately printed by Lund Humphries, 32 (recollections of the Eiffel Tower Restaurant).

F1772 Sandler, Linda. *The Revenge for Love by Wyndham Lewis: Editorial, Genetic and Interpretive Studies.* Toronto: University of Toronto (unpublished doctoral thesis reconstructing the text of the novel from the manuscript at Lockwood Memorial Library, Buffalo).

F1773 Watson, Sheila. "A Collection," *Open Letter,* Third Series (reprints "Wyndham Lewis: A Question of Portraiture," "The Great War: Wyndham Lewis and the Underground Press," "Canada and Wyndham Lewis the Artist," "Artist Ape as Crowd-Master," "Myth and Countermyth"; includes also "Unaccomodated Man" mostly concerned with *The Lion and the Fox).*

F1774 Young, Alan (editor). *Edgell Rickword. Essays and Opinions, 1921-1931.* Cheadle, Cheshire: Carcanet Press Publication, passim.

F1775 [*Unsigned review.*] *Choice,* X (February) 1867 (review of *The Roaring Queen).*

F1776 Wilson, Colin. "Wyndham Lewis: A Refracted Talent?" *Books and Bookmen,* XIX, no. 5 (February) 44-48 (the first part of a study, see F1777 and F1778; Lewis as a critical genius who knows more than Eliot or Lawrence but who lacks self-control).

F1777 Wilson, Colin. "Wyndham Lewis: Divided by Art," *Books and Bookmen,* XIX, no. 6 (March) 51-52 (discusses *The Enemy of the Stars* and the making of the Enemy, see F1776).

F1778 Wilson, Colin. "Wyndham Lewis: Self-Expression Versus Reality," *Books and Bookmen,* XIX, no. 7 (April) 39-42 (Lewis's failure as an artist when he could have been a great foreign correspondent, see F1776).

F1779 Materer, Timothy. "Wyndham Lewis's Portraits of T. S. Eliot," *T. S. Eliot Newsletter,* I, no. 1 (Spring) 4 (the history of the 1938 and 1949 portraits of Eliot).

F1780 Neve, Christopher. "Pull of the Vortex: Italian Influence on a British Revolution," *Country Life,* 155 (April 25) 980-981.

F1781 Woodeson, John. "Spencer Gore," *The Connoisseur,* CLXXXV, no. 745 (March) 175-180 (references to Lewis).

F1782 Spender, Stephen. "An Emigrant from Heaven," *The Times Literary Supplement,* LXXIII, no. 3772 (June 21) 666-667.

F1783 Renzio, Toni del. "London," *Art and Artists,* IX, 3, no. 99 (June) 38-39 (review of the "Vorticism and its Allies" exhibition, expressing contempt for Lewis's "fascism, bitter cantankerousness, over-weening presumption, frustration, chauvinism . . . ").

F1784 "Hayward Gallery," *ibid.,* 39.

F1785 Munton, Alan. "Muir and Lewis," *The Times Literary Supplement,* LXXIII, no. 3774 (July 5) 728 (letter to the editor correcting Spender's review, and showing that Muir's attitude to Lewis changed, see F1782).

F1786 Cowan, Robert. "Wyndham Lewis," *The Times Literary Supplement,* LXXIII, no. 3775 (July 12) 749 (letter announcing a Lewis symposium).

F1787 Materer, Timothy. "English Vortex: Modern Literature and the 'Pattern of Hope,' " *The Journal of Modern Literature,* III, no. 5 (July) 1123-1139 (survey of Vorticism).

F1788 Clark, Kenneth. "A Peer Gynt from the Slade," *The Times Literary Supplement,* LXXIII, no. 3789 (October 18) 1149-1150 (review of Holroyd's *Augustus John).*

F1789 Armato, Philip M. *Studies in Short Fiction,* XI, no. 4 (Fall) 437-438 (favorable review of Chapman's *Wyndham Lewis).*

F1790 Chapman, Robert T. "Edited by Wyndham Lewis," *Durham University Journal,* LXVII, no. 1 (December) 13-24 (a survey of the three journals edited by Lewis).

F1791 Dohmen, William F. "Chilly Spaces: Wyndham Lewis as Ondt," *James Joyce Quarterly,* XI, 241-246 (see F638).

F1792 Kinninmont, Tom. "Wyndham Lewis and the Cornell University Library," *Lewisletter.* Edited by Robert Cowan. The Wyndham Lewis Society (Glasgow), I (December) 1-3 (survey of the Lewis collection at Cornell; this is the first number of the only journal entirely devoted to Lewis criticism, see F1793, F1794 and F1795 for other articles in this number; for subsequent issues see F1813, F1821, F1857, F1879, F1905 and F1916).

F1793 Kinninmont, Tom. "The Vulgar Streak," *ibid.,* 3-4.

F1794 "Merlyn Evans," *ibid.,* 4 (explores the relationship between the two painters, Evans and Lewis).

F1795 Kinninmont, Tom. "Max Stirner and the Enemy of the Stars," *ibid.,* 5-6 (on the influence of *The Ego and his Own* on *Enemy of the Stars).*

1975

F1796 Abse, Joan. *The Art Galleries of Britain and Ireland. A Guide to their Collections.* London: Sidgwick and Jackson, passim.

F1797 Boulton, Marjorie. *The Anatomy of the Novel.* London: Routledge and Kegan Paul, 78-79, passim.

F1798 Coker, Joseph. *Journey to the Trenches. The Life of Isaac Rosenberg.* London: Robson Books, passim.

F1799 Ford, Hugh. *Published in Paris. American and British Writers in Paris, 1920-1939.* London: Garnstone Press, passim.

F1800 Fox, C. J. (editor). "Introduction," *Enemy Salvoes. Selected Literary Criticism by Wyndham Lewis.* London: Vision Press (discussion of Lewis's critical writings).

F1801 Sisson, C. H. "General Introduction," *ibid.*, 7-18 (survey and evaluation of Lewis's criticism).

F1802 Gowrie, Grey. "The Twentieth Century," *The Genius of British Painting* (edited by David Piper). London: Weidenfeld and Nicholson,304-309, passim.

F1803 Harmer, J. B. *Victory in Limbo. Imagism, 1908-1917.* London: Secker and Warburg, passim.

F1804 Gurewitch, Morton. *Comedy. The Irrational Vision.* Ithaca: Cornell University Press, 44-45 (Lewis and satire).

F1805 Hobhouse, Janet. *Everybody who was Anybody. A Biography of Gertrude Stein.* London: Weidenfeld and Nicholson, passim, 125-126.

F1806 Lago, Mary M. and Karl Beckson (editors). *Max and Will. Max Beerbohm and William Rothenstein: their Friendship and Letters.* London: John Murray, passim, 155-156.

F1807 Laws, Frederick. "Introduction," *Merlyn Evans Memorial Exhibition,* Welsh Art Council, Cardiff (Evan's "overstated debt to Wyndham Lewis").

F1808 McMillan, Dougald. *transition. The History of a literary Era, 1927-1938.* London: Calder and Boyars, passim.

F1809 Piper, David (editor). *The Genius of British Painting.* London: Weidenfeld and Nicholson, 304-309, passim.

F1810 Rosenbaum, S. P. (editor). *The Bloomsbury Group. A Collection of Memoirs, Commentary and Criticism.* London: Croom Helm (reprints "The Ideal Home Rumpus," and letters from Michel, Bell and Chaplin see F1318, F1360 and F1361).

F1811 Schneider, Elizabeth. *T. S. Eliot. The Pattern in the Carpet.* Berkeley: University of California Press (Eliot and Lewis on Shakespeare).

F1812 Simpson, Louis. *Three on the Tower. The Lives and Works of Ezra Pound, T. S. Eliot and William Carlos Williams.* New York: William Morrow and Co., passim.

F1813 Munton, Alan. "Music Ho! Lewis and Music Criticism," *Lewisletter.* Edited by Robert Cowan. The Wyndham Lewis Society, no. 2 (March) 1-3 (a re-evaluation of Lewis's attitude towards music; for Ayrton's corrections, see F1822).

F1814 Kinninmont, Tom. "The Wyndham Lewis Collection at Buffalo," *ibid.*, 3-4 (a survey of the Buffalo Collection).

F1815 Kinninmont, Tom. "The Revenge for Love," *ibid.*, 4-5 (remarks on the manuscript of *The Revenge for Love* in Buffalo).

F1816 Kinninmont, Tom. "The Missing Lewis Art Book," *ibid.*, 5-6 (on the Buffalo version of *The Role of Line in Art).*

F1817 "Blast Area," *The Times Literary Supplement,* LXXIV, no. 3816 (April 25) 454 (announces the Lewis symposium of April 26 and reviews the first numbers of *Lewisletter,* see F1792).

F1818 Cowan, Robert. "Wyndham Lewis," *ibid.*, LXXIV, no. 3819 (May 16) 539 (letter to the editor about *The Role of Line in Art* and *Snooty Baronet).*

F1819 McCorquodale, Charles. "London," *Art International,* XIX, no. 6 (June 15) 60-65.

F1820 Kermode, Frank. "Not Much More than a Name," *Daily Telegraph,* (September 27) 9.

F1821 "The Wyndham Lewis Symposium," *Lewisletter.* Edited by Robert Cowan. The Wyndham Lewis Society no. 3 (September) 1 (a record of the first Symposium held in the Tate Gallery, April 26, 1975, mentioning talks by Christopher Mullen, John Hart, Alan Munton, Geoffrey Bridson, Paul Edwards, Tom Kinninmont; see F1822, F1823, F1824, F1825 and F1826).

F1822 Ayrton, Michael. "Lewis and Music Criticism," *ibid.*, 1-2 (a letter correcting some of Munton's assertions, see F1813, and for Munton's reply, F1823).

F1823 Munton, Alan. *Ibid.*, 2 (a reply to Ayrton's letter, see F1822).

F1824 Edwards, Paul and Steve Walker. "Lewis's Critique of Relativity in One-Way Song," *ibid.*, 3-6 (stresses Lewis's knowledge of the theory of relativity).

F1825 Kinninmont, Tom. "A Note on One-Way Song," *ibid.*, 6-8 (studies the deleted passages, all refering to the Hitler book, in the second edition of *One-Way Song).*

F1826 Kinninmont, Tom. "Review: *Unrequited Loves* by Elliot Baker," *ibid.* (analyzes a story depicting Lewis in Buffalo).

F1827 Pritchard, William H. "Novel Sex and Violence," *The Hudson Review,* XXVIII, no. 1 (Spring) 147-160 (favorable note on reprints of *Tarr* and *The Vulgar Streak).*

F1828 Kermode, Frank. "Fiction Written With the Eye," *The Daily Telegraph* (October 11) 9 (study of style of *Tarr* with its "great many bizarre and comic moments").

F1829 Kermode, Frank. "Genius Who Lacked Talent," *The Daily Telegraph* (October 25) 11 (a discussion of Lewis's career).

1976

F1830 Ackroyd, Peter. *Notes for a New Culture. An Essay on Modernism.* London: Vision Press, 36-38 (discussion about Vorticism).

F1831 Bradbury, Malcolm. "London 1890-1920," *Modernism* (edited by Malcolm Bradbury and James McFarlane). Harmondsworth: Penguin Books, passim.

F1832 Bush, Ronald. *The Genesis of Ezra Pound's Cantos.* Princeton: Princeton University Press, passim.

F1833 Cork, Richard. *Vorticism and Abstract Art in the First Machine Age. Volume I: Origins and Developments. Volume II: Synthesis and Decline.* London: Gordon Fraser (Berkeley: University of California Press), passim (includes study of Lewis's early art and the Vorticist movement of which he was co-founder).

F1834 Durman, Michael. *The Painter as Satirist: A Study of the Art of Wyndham Lewis (1898-1912).* Nottingham: University of Nottingham (unpublished doctoral thesis).

F1835 Hamilton, Ian. *The Little Magazines. A Study of Six Editors.* London: Weidenfeld and Nicholson, passim.

F1836 Heymann, C. David. *Ezra Pound. The Last Rower.* London: Faber and Faber, passim.

F1837 Jarroch, Sandra Dobson. *Ottoline. The Life of Lady Ottoline Morrell.* London: Chatto and Windus, 125.

F1838 Materer, Timothy. *Wyndham Lewis the Novelist.* Detroit: Wayne University Press (study of Lewis's fiction).

F1839 Munton, Alan. *Wyndham Lewis: the relation between the theory and the fiction, from his earliest writings to 1941.* Cambridge: University of Cambridge (unpublished doctoral thesis).

F1840 Rogers, E. H., David Mellor and Andrew Crozier. "Introduction," *Wyndham Lewis,* University of Sussex (an exhibition catalogue).

F1841 Rosenblum, Robert. *Cubism and Twentieth Century Art.* New York: Harry N. Abrams, passim.

F1842 Seymour-Smith, Martin. *Who's Who in Twentieth Century Literature.* London: Weidenfeld and Nicholson, 210-212.

F1843 Shone, Richard. *Bloomsbury Portraits. Vanessa Bell, Duncan Grant and their Circle.* London: Phaidon, passim.

F1844 Woolf, Virginia. *The Question of Things Happening. The Letters of Virginia Woolf, 1912-1922,* II (edited by Nigel Nicolson). London: Hogarth Press, passim.

F1845 de Vere White, Terence. "The Art of Spotting Winners," *The Irish Times* (January 17) 8 (favorable review of *Enemy Salvoes).*

F1846 Luckett, Richard. "Blast," *The Spectator,* CCXXV, no. 7701 (January 31) 14-15 (reviews *Enemy Salvoes).*

F1847 Hodgart, Matthew. "In Battle Order," *The Times Literary Supplement,* LXXV, no. 3856 (February 6) 128 (review of *Enemy Salvoes).*

F1848 "A Blast of Lewis," *ibid.,* 138 (review of "The World of Wyndham Lewis," an exhibition held at the University Library, University of Sussex).

F1849 Grigson, Geoffrey. "Wyndham Lewis," *The Times Literary Supplement,* LXXV, no. 3857 (February 13) 168 (letter correcting Hodgart, see F1847).

F1850 Nye, Robert. "A Pretty Kettle of Critics," *The Scotsman* (February 14) 2 (review of *Enemy Salvoes* which sees Lewis as an unorthodox cult-figure standing "at another extreme from the creeping critical stance of T. S. Eliot").

F1851 Dennis, Nigel. "When Lewis Laid About Him," *The Sunday Telegraph* (February 1) 20 (favorable review of *Enemy Salvoes).*

F1852 Grigson, Geoffrey. "Fighting Terms," *The New Statesman,* XCI, no. 2344 (February 20) 234-235 (favorable review of *Enemy Salvoes* which sees Lewis as "a great affirmer").

F1853 Marshall, Kenneth. "Customers and Friends: Memoirs of a Bookseller," *The London Magazine,* XV, no. 6 (February-March) 79-90 (recollections of Lewis and identification of some of his characters).

F1854 Cushman, Keith. *The Library Journal,* CI (April 1) 901 (reviews *Enemy Salvoes,* finding Lewis more "iconoclastic than persuasive").

F1855 Sandler, Linda. "Critic's Essays Attest to Artistry of an Extinct Bird," *Toronto Star* (April 17) (review of *Enemy Salvoes* with description of Lewis's career and his influence on Canada).

F1856 Sykes, Christopher. "Paradoxical Writer," *Books and Bookmen,* XII, no. 7 (April) 36-37 (review of *Enemy Salvoes* emphasizing Lewis's inconsistency).

F1857 "Vorticist Film," *Lewisletter.* Edited by Frank Fitzpatrick. The Wyndham Lewis Society, no. 4 (April) 1 (about a short film entitled *Blast,* made by Viz Ltd. of Edinburgh, for the Arts Council of Great Britain and released December 1975; see F1858–F1866).

F1858 Bridson, D. G. "In Memoriam Michael Ayrton (1921-1975)," *ibid.,* 2 (includes a survey of the relationship between Lewis and Ayrton).

F1859 Barker, Jonathan. "Lewis Painting in London," *ibid.,* 2 (a letter about some paintings by Lewis in the Arts Council collection).

F1860 Chaney, Edward. "Some Thoughts on Wyndham Lewis," *ibid.,* 4 (a satirical poem involving some of Lewis's detractors).

F1861 Lafourcade, Bernard. "The Role of Line in Art," *ibid.,* 4 (a letter identifying another copy of *The Rôle of Line in Art).*

F1862 Kinninmont, Tom. "The Role of Line in Art," *ibid.,* 4 (a letter corroborating the preceding entry and comparing the Buffalo and Cornell copies of the missing art-book).

F1863 "Lewis Gossip," *ibid.,* 4 (a commentary on "Customers and Friends," F1853).

F1864 "Enemy Salvoes: Critical Volleys," *ibid.,* 4-5 (a survey of reviews of *Enemy Salvoes).*

F1865 "Bibliography," *ibid.,* 6 (describes three articles by Lewis omitted from Wagner's checklist).

F1866 "The Second Wyndham Lewis Symposium," *ibid.,* 6 (an announcement of the symposium to be held in The Victoria and Albert Museum on May 8).

F1867 Tisdall, Caroline. "Offensive Art," *The Guardian Weekly* (May 2) (review of Cork's *Vorticism).*

F1868 Cushman, Keith. *The Library Journal,* CI (May 15) 1213 (favorable review of Materer's *Wyndham Lewis the Novelist).*

F1869 [*Unsigned review.*] *Choice,* XIII (June) (favorable review of *Enemy Salvoes).*

F1870 Shone, Richard. "In a Whirl," *New Statesman,* XCI, no. 2361 (June 18) 818-819 (review of Cork's *Vorticism).*

F1871 Munton, Alan. "The Politics of Wyndham Lewis," *PN Review,* IV, no. 1, 34-39 (detailed study seeing Lewis's politics as "potentially revolutionary").

F1872 Young, Alan. "Wyndham Lewis as a Critic," *ibid.*, 58-59 (favorable review of *Enemy Salvoes* and Materer's *Wyndham Lewis the Novelist* which considers Lewis "a major force in twentieth century literary criticism")

F1873 Smith, P. "Wyndham Lewis's America and Cosmic Man," *Journal of Religion*, LVI (July) 255-262.

F1874 [*Unsigned review.*] *Choice*, XIII (July-August) 665 (favorable review of Materer's *Wyndham Lewis the Novelist*).

F1875 Adams, Robert M. "Apples, Basketballs and Hardboiled Eggs," *The Times Literary Supplement*, LXXV, no. 3881 (August 6) 974 (favorable review of Materer's *Wyndham Lewis the Novelist*).

F1876 Blow, Simon. "The Dilettante Myth," *The Guardian* (August 25) 10 (an interview in which Sacheverell Sitwell reflects that *The Apes of God* as "a time-bomb failed to go off, because it bored everybody").

F1877 Compton, S. P. "Malevich's Suprematism," *Burlington Magazine*, CXVIII, no. 881 (August) 582 (contains a comparison between Lewis and Malevich based on the publication of "Portrait of an Englishwoman" in *The Archer* (Strelets), Petrograd).

F1878 [*Unsigned review.*] *Choice*, XIII (October) 807 (a favorable review of Cork's *Vorticism*).

F1879 "The Second Wyndham Lewis Symposium," *Lewisletter*. Edited by Frank Fitzpatrick. The Wyndham Lewis Society, no. 5 (October) 1-2 (a record mentioning talks by C. J. Fox, E. W. F. Tomlin, David Mellor and C. H. Sisson; see F1880–F1889).

F1880 "Posters," *ibid.*, 2 (a description of the posters used to publicise the second symposium).

F1881 Kinninmont, Tom. "Wyndham Lewis the Novelist," *ibid.*, 2-3 (a discussion of *Wyndham Lewis the Novelist*).

F1882 Fox, C. J. "Two Pioneer Broadcasts," *ibid.*, 4 (describes a broadcast in French by René Leplat on *The Demon of Progress in the Arts*, January 13, 1955 and the televised discussion of June, 1939).

F1883 Fox, C. J. "Lewis Lairs," *ibid.*, 5-6 (completes and corrects *Guide to Literary London*).

F1884 Lafourcade, Bernard. "Wyndham Lewis: An Additional Checklist," *ibid.*, 6-10, 12.

F1885 McLuhan, Marshall. "The Global Lewis," *ibid.*, 11 (excerpts from a letter with anecdotes of Lewis).

F1886 "Information Please," *ibid.*, 11 (about *Snooty Baronet*).

F1887 "Lewis Paintings," *ibid.*, 11 (about the exhibition *British Art 1910-1916* organised by the University of East Anglia; see F 1909).

F1888 "Lewis Exhibition," *ibid.*, 12 (about a Lewis exhibition planned by Manchester Art Galleries for the autumn of 1978).

F1889 "Blasting Off," *ibid.*, 12 (comments on Snow's review of *Enemy Salvoes*).

F1890 Sandler, Linda. "Sheila Watson as Lewisite Critic," *Canadian Literature*, no. 70 (Autumn) 91-93.

1977

F1891 Fauchereau, Serge (editor). *Paris-New York. Echanges Littéraires au Vingtième Siècle*. Paris: Centre National d'Art et de Culture Georges Pompidou, passim (one of the catalogues of the exhibition, June 1-September 9).

F1892 Hulten, Pontus (Commissaire Général). *Paris-New York*. Paris: Centre National d'Art et de Culture Georges Pompidou, passim (general catalogue of the exhibition, June 1-September 19).

F1893 Ellmann, Richard. *The Consciousness of Joyce*. London: Faber and Faber, passim (Lewis on Joyce's middle-class mentality).

F1894 Humphreys, Richard. *A Reading of "The Inca and the Birds" by Wyndham Lewis*. London: Courtauld Institute of Art (unpublished doctoral dissertation).

F1895 Lyndall, Gordon. *Eliot's Early Years*. London: Oxford University Press, passim.

F1896 Pritchard, William H. *Seeing Through Everything. English Writers 1918-1940.* London: Faber and Faber, 44-50, 200-208, passim.

F1897 Stanford, Derek. *Inside the Forties: Literary Memoirs 1937-1957.* London: Sidgwick and Jackson, passim.

F1898 Watson, George. *Politics and Literature in Modern Britain.* London: Macmillan, passim.

F1899 Wilson, Edmund. *Letters on Literature and Politics, 1912-1972.* London: Routledge and Kegan Paul, passim (recollections of Lewis).

F1900 Woolf, Virginia. *A Change of Perspective. The Letters of Virginia Woolf, 1923-1928* (edited by Nigel Nicolson) III, passim.

F1901 Sisson, C. H. "Editorial," *P N Review,* no. 3 (Spring) 1-2 (refers to *The Art of Being Ruled).*

F1902 Russell, John. "British Drawings at the Modern—One More Symptom of Anglomania," *The New York Times* (April 3) 27 (review of the show of British drawings at the Museum of Modern Art with emphasis on Vorticism, Lewis and Bomberg).

F1903 Kramer, Hilton. "The Unfulfilled Promises of Vorticism," *The New York Times* (April 17) 25, 33 (review of Cork's *Vorticism* and of a Vorticist exhibition at the Davis and Long Company; negative view of Lewis and Vorticism).

F1904 Young, Vernon. "The Late Lamenting Wyndham Lewis," *The Hudson Review* (Spring) 464-470 (highly critical article occasioned by *Enemy Salvoes).*

F1905 [Fitzpatrick, Frank.] "Editorial," *Lewisletter,* Edited by Frank Fitzpatrick. The Wyndham Lewis Society, no. 6 (June) 2 (announces the forthcoming publication of letters from Lewis to T. Sturge Moore).

F1906 Fox, C. J. "Lewisnews," *ibid.,* 3-4 (some remarks on a proof copy of *The Wild Body,* and a survey of recent criticism).

F1907 Lafourcade, Bernard. "Obituary," *ibid.,* 4 (about Dominique de Roux's interest in Lewis).

F1908 "Academic Courtesy," *ibid.,* 4-5 (on the influence of Max Stirner on Lewis, see F1795).

F1909 "Lewis Exhibition in Manchester," *ibid.,* 5 (The Lewis exhibition postponed until 1979, see F1887).

F1910 "Lewis Bibliography," *ibid.,* 5 (about two Lewis bibliographies in preparation).

F1911 "Lewis Anniversary," *ibid.,* 5 (records a commemoration of the twentieth anniversary of Lewis's death, marked by a lecture by C. J. Fox).

F1912 "New Book on Lewis," *ibid.,* 10 (announces an edition of Lewis's poems and plays).

F1913 "A New Source for Tarr?" *ibid.,* 10 (an examination of Currie's *Genius: An Ideology in Literature,* see F1762).

F1914 Faulkner, Peter. *Modernism.* London: Methuen, passim.

F1915 Sypher, Wylie. "A Mechanical Operation of the Spriit," *Arts and Letters,* LXXXV, no. 3 (Summer) 512-519 (reviews Cork's *Vorticism,* terming Lewis "our modern Ruskin").

F1916 Fox, C. J. "Lewis News," *Lewisletter.* Edited by Tom Kinninmont. The Wyndham Lewis Society, no. 7 (October) 4-7 (surveys new books and articles about Lewis; this issue includes A49 and A50 loosely inserted).

F1917 Cassidy, Victor. "Letters to Thomas Sturge Moore," *ibid.,* 8-23 (introduction and notes to fifteen previously unpublished letters from Lewis to Moore, see D363).

F1918 Lafourcade, Bernard. "The Purloined Letter," *ibid.,* 24-25 (a note on the composition of *The Code of a Herdsman* and *Imaginary Letters).*

F1919 Kinninmont, Tom. "Tarr: a Detective Story," *ibid.,* 26-28 (discusses variant textual versions of *Tarr).*

F1920 Thomas, Denis. "Wyndham Lewis: into a dark room," *The Listener,* XCVIII, no. 2540 (December 22 and 29) 829-831 (Lewis's association with *The Listener).*

1978

F1921 Seymour-Smith, Martin. "An Atmosphere of Warm Indifference," *Bananas* (Emma Tennant, editor).London: Quartet Books, 84-101.

G. Miscellanea

G1 WHEELS, FIFTH CYCLE 1920

Lewis is listed on the title page as being among the contributors to this book, along with Aldous Huxley, John Adams, Sherard Vines, McTavish Cohen, Geoffrey Cookson, Alan Porter, W. Kean Seymour, Osbert Sitwell, Sacheverell Sitwell and Edith Sitwell. However, no contribution by Lewis is present in the text. London: Leonard Parsons, 1920. Published in November, 1920 at 6s. See Richard Fifoot, *A Bibliography of Edith, Osbert and Sacheverell Sitwell* (London: Rupert Hart-Davis, [1971]) EB7, for futher bibliographic details.

G2 A TIP FROM THE AUGEAN STABLE [1932]

A Tip from the Augean Stable was announced for publication by Desmond Harmsworth, who published three other titles by Lewis between May 1932 and January 1933—*The Enemy of the Stars* (A17), *Thirty Personalities and a Self-Portrait* (A19) and *The Old Gang and the New Gang* (A20)—but was in fact never separately published.

Although no proof copy or galley sheets have been discovered, it is evident that production of the book may have advanced to this stage before the project was abandoned by Harmsworth. The first published announcement for the title is included in an advertisement pamphlet, *More from the Enemy* (B16), published in late April, 1932. This eight-page pamphlet includes "A Tip from the Augean Stable. Description" (pp. 6-7) written by Lewis himself, describing *A Tip* as a discussion which "deals with the urgent contemporary problem of the decay of literary standards in face of . . . Big-Business [publishing] methods . . ." This summary is followed by detailed specifications of the book's format (crown 8vo), length (50 pp.), appearance (with a "portrait jacket by the author"), price (3/6) and publication date ("Ready June 14th"). The same information is printed later on the back inner flap of the dustjacket for *The Enemy of the Stars* (May 31, 1932) and for *The Old Gang and the New Gang* (January, 1933).

Why the book was never published is unclear. It is possible, however, that delays in publishing *The Enemy of the Stars, Thirty Personalities* and *The Old Gang and the New Gang* caused by numerous and time-consuming corrections made by Lewis on the proofs of the first and last books contributed to the final abandonment of the project (this theory was suggested in a letter from Desmond Harmsworth to Morrow, April 1977).

The essay was published in two parts, in *Time and Tide,* March 19 and March 26, 1932. See D178 and D179.

G3 THE RÔLE OF LINE IN ART [1941]

THE RÔLE OF LINE | IN ART WITH | SEVEN DRAWINGS | TO ILLUSTRATE | THE ARGUMENT BY | WYNDHAM LEWIS

The Rôle of Line in Art was to be published in Autumn, 1941 by George Viscount Carlow's Corvinus Press, in an edition of 120 copies, signed by Lewis, printed on white hand-made paper. Lewis and Lord Carlow (1907-1944) became friends during the 1930's, through the influence of mutual friends at Cassell and Co., A. J. A. Symons and Desmond Flower. Carlow purchased numerous manuscripts, first editions, drawings and corrected proof copies from Lewis throughout this period, and had much of it bound or slipcased by Sangorski and Sutcliffe. Sometime in 1938-1939 Lewis and Carlow agreed to publish Lewis's brief essay concerning the history and importance of "linear expression" and the "enfeeblement of the appetite for the linear in the present century," *The Rôle of Line in Art.*

In a letter from Carlow to Lewis dated August 11, 1939 (NIC) it is apparent that production of the book was already underway, mentioning that the illustrations to the text will be colored. By April 26, 1941 the printing was sufficiently advanced so that Carlow wired Lewis, in Canada, advising him that the book was not yet published as Lewis still had several pages to correct and the colophon pages to sign. On June 16, [1941] Carlow sent Lewis another letter from Helsingfors, Holland (NIC), mentioning again the "two or three pages which need correcting" and the unsigned colophon pages. In this letter Carlow also discusses the fact that another book being published by Corvinus Press, "of which 350 pages has already been printed," had been destroyed by a bomb which had reduced his warehouse to "a pile of bricks and rubble." He expresses his apprehension that the illustrations for *The Rôle of Line in Art* were also destroyed in the blitz: " . . . If this is so, it will mean printing those pictures again, which will be a long job."

Eventually news reached Carlow that the sheets for the entire book had been destroyed in the bombing, and in a letter to Lewis sent from London on March 9, 1942 Carlow informed him of the unfortunate event, mentioning that "the only copy which remains whole was the special copy on yellow paper." Carlow suggests that the book be printed again sometime in the future, but his death two years later in an airplane crash prevented them from completing the project.

The single surviving copy is apparently in the possession of Carlow's son, George Lionel Yuill Seymour Dawson-Damer, 7th Earl of Portarlington, a xerox copy of which is in the Carlow Lewis collection at the Lockwood Memorial Library, State University of New York at Buffalo. Cornell possesses proof sheets of pp. *1-12,* which bear several corrections in Lewis's hand, and which were probably in Lewis's possession in Canada at the time of the bombing of the Corvinus offices in 1941.

The Rôle of Line in Art consists of 24 pp.: *1-17* text; *18-23* plates; *24* colophon. Although the title indicates that the text is accompanied with "Seven Drawings to Illustrate the Argument," in fact only six drawings are included, as follows:

18 "Drawing of James Joyce" (Michel 396)
19 "Portrait of the Artist's Wife" (Michel 865)
20 "Study of a Young Woman" (Michel 875)
21 "Tut" (Michel 730)
22 "Girl Sewing" (Michel 461)
23 drawing of seated woman, not in Michel catalogue.

For convenience in identification of other examples of this text which may exist, the leading words for each page are given herebelow:

1 "Here are a group . . ."
2 "Drawing (it was Ingres . . ."
3 "It might be true . . ."
4 "drawing. And that applies . . ."
5 "The Impressionist Movement . . ."
6 "impression. And let it not . . ."
7 "expand, as well as . . ."
8 "My central theme . . ."
9 "for their works . . ."
10 "It has not been my wish . . ."
11 "then one of your first cares . . ."
12 "that for us, or we think . . ."
13 "TAILPIECE . . ."
14 "Seventy per cent . . ."
15 "William Llewyln . . ."
16 "no longer Impressionist . . ."
17 "by the great impression . . ."

The colophon page, printed especially for inclusion in the Carlow "yellow paper" copy, reads as follows: This book exists in one copy only, printed on a | yellow "Lineweave" paper. It was originally | intended to print an edition of 120 copies on a | white hand-made paper, but these were all des- | troyed when a bomb was dropped on the offices of Messrs. Yuills, Ltd., where the pages had | been sent for safety. | [signed] Carlow |.

The argument set forth in *The Rôle of Line in Art* essentially contrasts the use of strong, controlled lines in the work of the Old Masters with the absence of "linear content" in Impressionist compositions. Lewis equates "line" and "form" and consequently determines that French Impressionism was, finally, "antagonistic to form." The second half of the essay, under the subtitle "Tailpiece," constitutes an attack on the impressionist tendencies of the Royal Academy and Bloomsbury artists.

INDEX

All references in this index are to entry numbers in the bibliography. The titles of books and articles by Lewis are capitalized. Periodicals and other books listed are italicized. Initial definite and indefinite articles are disregarded in alphabetization. Section F is indexed selectively to include only books entirely devoted to Lewis and special Lewis issues of periodicals.

ADDENDA

ADDENDA

ADDENDA

ADDENDA

ADDENDA

Bradford Morrow, formerly a Danforth Fellow in English Literature at Yale University, has lived and worked in Italy, France, England and the United States. He graduated summa cum laude from the University of Colorado in English and comparative literature and has published a number of critical articles about Ezra Pound, Italian lyric poetry, Vorticism and other topics. Mr. Morrow is a specialist and dealer in rare books and manuscripts, presently residing in Santa Barbara, California.

Bernard Lafourcade teaches English literature at the University of Savoy in Chambéry, France, after spending several years teaching at the University of Tunis, Tunisia. Professor Lafourcade has published translations of *Cantleman's Spring-Mate* and *Tarr* in French and is at present at work on "Wyndham Lewis, Space and the Absurd."

Hugh Kenner teaches English literature at John Hopkins University in Baltimore, Maryland. Dr. Kenner is an internationally recognized authority on modern literature and has published numerous books and articles including *The Poetry of Ezra Pound, Wyndham Lewis, The Counterfeiters: An Historical Comedy* and *The Pound Era.*

Printed September 1978 in Santa Barbara & Ann Arbor for the Black Sparrow Press by Mackintosh and Young & Edwards Brothers Inc. Design by Barbara Martin. 200 special copies of this edition have been bound in two volumes & slipcased by Earle Gray with a previously unpublished story by Wyndham Lewis & are numbered & signed by the authors.